BIOGRAPHICAL ENCYCLOPEDIA of MATHEMATICIANS

BIOGRAPHICAL ENCYCLOPEDIA of MATHEMATICIANS

Volume 2
Janovskaja – Zermelo
Indexes

Editor

DONALD R. FRANCESCHETTI

Marshall Cavendish
New York • London • Toronto

Project Editor: Tracy Irons-Georges
Research Supervisor: Jeffry Jensen
Research Assistant: Jun Ohnuki
Acquisitions Editor: Mark Rehn
Photograph Editor: Karrie Hyatt
Production Editor: Cynthia Breslin Beres
Layout: William Zimmerman

Published By
Marshall Cavendish Corporation
99 White Plains Road
Tarrytown, New York 10591-9001
United States of America

Library of Congress Cataloging-in-Publication Data

Biographical encyclopedia of mathematicians / editor Donald R. Franceschetti.
    p.   cm.
  Complete in 2 v.
  Includes bibliographical references and index.
  1. Mathematicians—Biography—Encyclopedias.   I. Franceschetti, Donald R.,
1947-   .
ISBN 0-7614-7069-7 (set)
ISBN 0-7614-7071-9 (vol. 2)
QA28.B544   1999
510'.92'2
[B]—dc21   98-25846
                                                                           CIP

First Printing

Contents

As an aid to users of the *Biographical Encyclopedia of Mathematicians*, guides to pronunciation for profiled mathematicians with foreign names have been provided with the first mention of the name in each entry. These guides are rendered in an easy-to-use phonetic manner. Stressed syllables are indicated by capital letters.

Letters of the English language, particularly vowels, are pronounced in different ways depending on the context. Below are letters and combinations of letters used in the phonetic guides to represent various sounds, along with examples of words in which those sounds appear and corresponding guides for their pronunciation.

Symbols	*Pronounced As In*	*Spelled Phonetically*
a	answer, laugh	AN-sihr, laf
ah	father, hospital	FAH-thur, HAHS-pih-tul
aw	awful, caught	AW-ful, kawt
ay	blaze, fade, waiter	blayz, fayd, WAYT-ur
ch	beach, chimp	beech, chihmp
eh	bed, head, said	behd, hehd, sehd
ee	believe, leader	bee-LEEV, LEED-ur
ew	boot, loose	bewt, lews
g	beg, disguise, get	behg, dihs-GIZ, geht
i	buy, height, surprise	bi, hit, sur-PRIZ
ih	bitter, pill	bih-TUR, pihl
j	digit, edge, jet	DIH-jiht, ehj, jeht
k	cat, kitten, hex	kat, KIH-tehn, hehks
o	cotton, hot	CO-tuhn, hot
oh	below, coat, note	bee-LOH, coht, noht
oo	good, look	good, look
ow	couch, how	kowch, how
oy	boy, coin	boy, koyn
s	cellar, save, scent	SEL-ur, sayv, sehnt
sh	issue, shop	IH-shew, shop
uh	about, enough	uh-BOWT, ee-NUHF
ur	earth, letter	urth, LEH-tur
y	useful, young	YEWS-ful, yuhng
z	business, zest	BIHZ-ness, zest
zh	vision	VIH-zhuhn

BIOGRAPHICAL
ENCYCLOPEDIA
of
MATHEMATICIANS

Sof'ja Aleksandrovna Janovskaja

Area of Achievement: Mathematical logic
Contribution: Janovskaja developed a materialist philosophy of mathematics that included mathematical logic as an important component.

Jan. 31, 1896	Born in Pruzhany, Poland (now in Belarus)
1915	Enters the Higher School for Women
1918-1923	Works for the Russian Communist Party, serving as a political commissar in the Red Army, editing the Communist newspaper *Kommunist*, and being active in the Odessa Regional Communist Party
1924-1929	Studies at the Institute of Red Professors
1925	Begins directing seminars in mathematics at Moscow State University
1926	Joins the faculty at Moscow State University
1930	Publishes her first important paper, on the philosophy of mathematics
1931	Promoted to professor
1932	Edits a collection of the mathematical works of Karl Marx
1935	Earns a doctorate
1941-1943	Teaches at Perm University
1943	Returns to Moscow State University
1951	Awarded the Order of Lenin
1959	Appointed head of the department of mathematical logic at Moscow State University
Oct. 24, 1966	Dies in Moscow, Soviet Union

Early Life

Sof'ja Aleksandrovna Janovskaja (pronounced "yaw-nuhv-SKUH-yuh"), née Neimark, was born on January 31, 1896, in Pruzhany, a town in a region of eastern Poland that became part of the Soviet Union in 1939 and part of the new nation of Belarus in 1991. At an early age, she moved with her family to Odessa, a large city on the shore of the Black Sea in southwestern Russia. This region became part of the newly formed Soviet Union in 1922 and part of the new nation of Ukraine in 1991.

Janovskaja studied Greek and Roman classics and mathematics at the Odessa Gymnasium, a primary school designed to prepare students for a university education. Her teachers included Ivan Jure'vich Timchenko, a noted historian of mathematics. In 1915, she entered the Higher School for Women in Odessa, where she studied logic under S. O. Shatunovskii.

Revolution and Civil War

Janovskaja's education was interrupted by the outbreak of the Russian Revolution in 1917. After the abdication of Tsar Nicholas II in February, a struggle between the Mensheviks (socialists) and the Bolsheviks (Communists) ended when the Bolsheviks seized power in October. Janovskaja joined the Bolsheviks in November of 1918.

From 1918 to 1921, a civil war raged between the Communist "Reds" and the anti-Communist "Whites." Janovskaja served as a political commissar (Communist Party official) in the Red Army in 1919. She also served as the editor of the Communist newspaper *Kommunist* in Odessa and was active in the Odessa Regional Communist Party. The victorious Communists formed the Soviet Union in 1922. Janovskaja returned to her studies in 1923.

From Odessa to Moscow to Perm

In 1924, Janovskaja moved several hundred miles north from Odessa to Moscow, the capital and largest city in the new Soviet Union. She studied mathematics at the Institute of Red Professors in Moscow from 1924 to 1929. At the same time, she attended seminars in mathematics at Moscow State University and began directing seminars in 1925. She became an official faculty member at Moscow State Univer-

The Materialist Philosophy of Mathematics

Janovskaja developed a philosophy of mathematics that shared the materialist philosophy of communism and made mathematical logic an important part of that philosophy.

The study of the philosophy of mathematics deals with the basic nature, the underlying assumptions, and the scope of mathematical knowledge. A wide variety of philosophies of mathematics have been developed since the time of the ancient Greeks. Modern philosophies began to emerge in the late nineteenth century. Their development was closely linked to the development of mathematical logic in the twentieth century.

As an active member of the Communist Party and a loyal citizen of the Soviet Union, Janovskaja worked to create a philosophy of mathematics that agreed with the materialist philosophy of communism. In the materialist philosophy of mathematics, all mathematical concepts are ultimately derived from physical reality. The basic concepts of geometry, for example, are taken from observations of the shapes of physical objects. A mathematical statement is "true" only if it can be applied to the real world.

Materialism is directly opposed to idealism, in which mathematical concepts exist without reference to physical reality. In this philosophy, the concepts of geometry are abstract ideas that are manipulated by arbitrary rules. A mathematical statement is "true" if it is consistent with previously defined rules.

Janovskaja was particularly interested in defending mathematical logic as a part of the materialist philosophy. Some materialist philosophers saw the rules of mathematical logic as arbitrary. From this viewpoint, mathematical logic was inherently a part of the idealist philosophy and therefore unacceptable. Janovskaja argued that the rules of mathematical logic were derived from human experiences in the physical world and were therefore a necessary part of the materialist philosophy.

Although her ideas were sometimes controversial, Janovskaja was eventually successful in having mathematical logic accepted as an important part of the philosophy of mathematics in the Soviet Union. As a result of her efforts, Soviet philosophers were often more familiar with mathematical logic than were philosophers from other nations. Her work also encouraged the development of mathematical logic in the Soviet Union.

Bibliography

Introduction to the Philosophy of Mathematics. Hugh Lehman. Totowa, N.J.: Rowman & Littlefield, 1979.
Mathematics: A Concise History and Philosophy. W. S. Anglin. New York: Springer-Verlag, 1994.
The Philosophy of Mathematics. Kaarlo Jaakko Juhani Hintikka, ed. London: Oxford University Press, 1969.

sity in 1926 and was promoted to professor in 1931. She earned a doctorate from Moscow State University in 1935.

Janovskaja published her first important paper in 1930. It dealt with the philosophy of mathematics, which was to be Janovskaja's main interest during her entire career. In 1932, she edited a collection of the mathematical works of Karl Marx, the founder of communism. During the 1930's, she also wrote encyclopedia articles intended to educate the general public on such topics as mathematical paradoxes, mathematical logic, and the philosophy of mathematics.

World War II interrupted Janovskaja's career when Nazi Germany invaded the Soviet Union on June 22, 1941. Janovskaja was evacuated from Moscow to Perm, a large city several hundred miles to the east. From 1941 to 1943, she taught at Perm University. In 1943, after Moscow was no longer in danger of being captured by the Germans, she returned to Moscow State University, where she served as the director of the seminar on mathematical logic.

After the War

In 1946, Janovskaja began teaching mathematical logic to philosophy students as a faculty member of the department of philosophy at Moscow State University. In 1951, she received the Order of Lenin, the highest civilian honor awarded by the Soviet Union. In 1959, she became the first head of the newly created department of mathematical logic at Moscow State University.

Janovskaja's work after World War II largely involved mathematical logic and the creation of a philosophy of mathematics that was compatible with the philosophy of communism. As a result of her efforts, mathematical logic was accepted as an important part of the philosophy of mathematics in the Soviet Union.

Janovskaja was also a noted historian of mathematics. She wrote on topics ranging from ancient Egyptian mathematics to the nineteenth century Russian mathematician Nikolay Ivanovich Lobachevsky. She was particularly interested in the history of mathematical logic in the Soviet Union. Janovskaja died on October 24, 1966.

Bibliography

By Janovskaja
"Idealizm v sovremennoy filosofii matematiki" (idealism in the modern philosophy of mathematics), *Estestvoznanie i Marksizm* 2-3, 1930

Matematicheskie rukopisi Marksa, 1932 (as editor; *The Mathematical Manuscripts of Karl Marx*, 1968)

"Osnovaniya matematiki i matematicheskaya logika" (foundations of mathematics and mathematical logic), *Matematika v SSSR za 30 Let*, 1948

"Matematicheskaya logika i osnovaniya matematiki" (mathematical logic and foundations of mathematics), *Matematika v SSSR za 40 Let (1917-1957)* 1, 1959

Metodologicheskie problemy nanki, 1972 (methodological problems of science)

About Janovskaja
"S. A. Janovskaja." Josef M. Bochenski. *Studies in Soviet Thought* 13 (1973).

"Sof'ja Aleksandrovna Janovskaja (1896-1966)." Irving H. Anellis. In *Women of Mathematics: A Biobibliographic Sourcebook*, edited by Louise S. Grinstein and Paul J. Campbell. New York: Greenwood Press, 1987.

"Sof'ya Aleksandrovna Yanovskaya." I. G. Bashmakova. *Russian Mathematical Surveys* 21, no. 3 (May/June, 1966).

(Rose Secrest)

Camille Jordan

Area of Achievement: Topology
Contribution: Jordan formalized the principles of group theory and developed the framework for the study of surfaces.

Jan. 5, 1838	Born in Lyon, France
1855	Enters the École Polytechnique
1862	Marries Isabelle Munet
1866	Introduces topological concepts
1870	Publishes *Traité des substitutions et des équations algébriques* (treatise on substitutions and algebraic equations)
1873	Begins to teach simultaneously at the École Polytechnique and the Collège de France
1881	Elected a member of the Académie des Sciences
1882-1887	Publishes the three-volume work *Cours d'analyse de l'École Polytechnique*
1912	Retires from teaching
1919	Becomes a foreign member of the Royal Society of London
Jan. 20 or 21, 1922	Dies, probably in Paris, France, but possibly in Milan, Italy

Early Life

Marie-Ennemond-Camille Jordan (pronounced "zhawr-DAHN") was raised in the Croix-Rousse, the richest quarters of Lyon, France. His family was wealthy and distinguished. His grand uncle, for whom he was named, was a well-known political figure. Camille Jordan's father, Esprit-Alexandre Jordan, was an engineer; his mother, Josephine Puvis de Chavannes, was the daughter of the chief engineer of the mines at Lyon and the sister of a famous painter. Jordan had one sister.

The Jordan family was characterized by their strong morals and Protestant beliefs. Although they were rich and well respected, they were firm believers in kindness and generosity. They were well educated and knowledgeable about the famous lecturers and classic literature of the time. Members of the Jordan family were also political attachés. Although they were conservatives, they were innovators, driven by their openness to progress.

Camille Jordan had a happy and peaceful childhood in a close-knit, comfortable, and educated home. He spent his winters in the village and his summers in the little village of Bressous, on property bought by his father for the purpose of being near his wife's parents.

Jordan's grandfather obtained admission for his son, Camille's uncle Pierre, to attend the École Polytechnique. When Pierre fell ill, his mathematical studies were interrupted, and he subsequently took up painting. This was a great scandal in the family that resulted in Camille being encouraged to enroll in a special mathematical class at the Lycée de Lyons, a high school.

Life as a Student

Camille Jordan continued his education at the school of Oullins, where he found mathematics to be his strength. He would pore over math books that he found in his teachers' desk drawers and read them secretly. Because he was Protestant, his studies at Oullins ended when the school passed into the hands of Dominican monks.

In 1855, at the age of seventeen, Jordan entered the École Polytechnique and attained the rank of first in his class. The committee that decided rank was composed of five mathematicians. One of them, who had a reputation of being extremely difficult and rigorous, gave Jordan a score of 19.8 out of a possible 20.0.

When Jordan was graduated from the École Polytechnique, he was rated in second place because of his lack of ability in graphical mathematics. Although he was qualified as an engineer, mathematics was still what he loved to do most. He retained the title of engineer but continued to conduct mathematical research. Most of the 120 papers that he wrote were completed before his retirement as an engineer in 1885.

Life at the University

In 1873, Jordan began teaching simultaneously at the École Polytechnique and at the Collège de France. As a teacher, he was considered by his students to have a firm kindness that was altogether unique. He was held in high esteem by his students and was known to have a fine sense of humor. While it is unclear if Jordan was similarly appreciated by the college administration at the École Polytechnique, his starting salary was 7,500 francs, a more-than-ample amount for the time.

One unique characteristic of Jordan was that he always had a glass of sweetened water at his desk when he lectured. He would drink two or three glasses per lecture, continually stirring them with a spoon. It was a habit that his students never forgot: At the École Polytechnique, Jordan was forever thought of as the professor with a glass of water.

Another memorable aspect of Jordan's classes was that a cloud hung about the professor when he lectured. It was never determined if the cloud resulted from his smoking habit, the dust from his reputed furious use of chalk, or both. Whatever the cause, it also left an impression on his students.

Mathematical Work

Jordan was considered an algebraist. His mathematical career started with a study of the little-known works of Évariste Galois. Jordan was the first to develop a systematic theory of finite groups based on that work. He was also the first to develop the concept of a composition series and the structure of both the general linear groups and the classical groups over a finite field. He used these concepts to determine the structure of the Galois group of equations, which have as roots the parameters of some common geometric configurations.

Jordan devoted much time to the study of solvable finite groups. The result of his exhaustive study was the development of new concepts in group theory. The publication of *Traité des substitutions et des équations algébriques* (1870) represented all of his work during the previous ten years. This text became the primal source of information for successive generations of mathematicians studying group theory.

Jordan's book aroused much interest, and students flocked to Lyon to attend his lectures. Two of his students, Felix Klein and Sophus Lie, went on to develop theories on discontinuous and continuous groups, respectively.

Jordan developed his "fitness" theorems in the years following the publication of *Traité des substitutions et des équations algébriques*. These theorems included those for subgroups of symmetric groups, the determination of all finite subgroups of a general linear group, and the vector space of all homogeneous polynomials.

In topology, Jordan developed new approaches to combinatorial topology by examining a polyhedron. He also formulated a proof for the "decomposition" of a plane by demonstrating that a closed curve divides a plane into exactly two regions. Jordan's later work involved functions, and the bounded curve to which he applied his theorems is called the Jordan curve.

Later Life
In 1862, Jordan married Isabelle Munet, a member of one of the better Lyon families. They had eight children; one became a professor of history at the Sorbonne and another became an influential minister. As adults, two of Jordan's sons, Édouard and Camille, both moved into Jordan's former office that was located next to the family residence.

Jordan lived simply, and his only luxurious indulgence was a large, plush armchair. He would seat his visitors in the chair, where they endured the strong odor of tobacco. Jordan was known as an incorrigible smoker.

Jordan died without suffering at the age of eighty-four, probably in the early morning

Group Theory

Jordan conducted the first major investigation of infinite groups and introduced the term "group."

Évariste Galois demonstrated that for each equation, there exists a corresponding set of substitutions that are related to its solution. These substitutions are reflective of the general characteristic properties of the equation. Knowing one of these characteristics makes the deduction of the others possible. The result is a determination of which polynomial equations are solvable by radicals.

Using these ideas as a beginning, Jordan embarked on a systematic development of the theory of finite groups. Until this point, no one had attempted to define a general curve. Jordan began with the most elemental curve, the straight line, which was not previously considered to be a curve. Extending the ideas of groups to other curves resulted in the classification that led to all solvable groups of order *n*. If a curve can be so classified into a group, then the solvability of the equation can be so determined based on the properties of that group.

Topology is the study of the properties of geometric figures not normally affected by changes in size or shape. Jordan investigated symmetries in polyhedrons using properties of similar shapes to classify them and to determine if their equations are solvable. He is best known for laying the groundwork for homological or combinatorial topology.

Jordan set the standard for a rigorous proof and demonstrated that a simply closed curve divides a plane into exactly two regions. His work, which forms the basis for many modern theories in topology and matrices, provided the criteria for the convergence of Fourier series and led to the development of theories of continuous and discontinuous groups. Jordan's contributions extended into almost every area of mathematics, including abstract algebra, matrices, determinates, and functions, as well as group theory.

Bibliography
A Concise History of Mathematics. Dirk J. Struik. 3d. rev. ed. New York: Dover, 1967.

A History of Algebraic and Differential Topology, 1900-1960. Jean Dieudonné. Boston: Birkhäuser, 1989.

A History of Mathematics: An Introduction. Victor J. Katz. New York: HarperCollins College Publishers, 1993.

hours of January 21, 1922. This was almost exactly one year after the death of his closest friend and colleague, Georges Humbert.

Bibliography
By Jordan
Traité des substitutions et des équations algébriques, 1870 (treatise on substitutions and algebraic equations)

Cours d'analyse de l'École Polytechnique, 1883-1893 (course in analysis of the École Polytechnique)

Œuvres de Camille Jordan, 1961-1964 (René Garnier and Jean Dieudonné, eds.)

About Jordan
"Camille Jordan." Jean Dieudonné. In *Dictionary of Scientific Biography*, edited by Charles Coulston Gillispie. New York: Charles Scribner's Sons, 1991.

"Camille Jordan." *Proceedings of the London Mathematical Society*, 2d ser., 21 (1923): 43-45.

"Marie Ennemond Camille Jordan." In *The Biographical Dictionary of Scientists: Mathematicians*, edited by David Abbott. London: Blond Educational, 1985.

(William M. Casolara and Corinne G. Casolara)

Johannes Kepler

Areas of Achievement: Applied math and geometry

Contribution: Kepler greatly expanded the knowledge of tiling of the plane by regular polygons (equal-sided, equal-angled plane figures) and of the classification of regular polyhedrons (equal-sided, equal-faced solids).

Dec. 27, 1571	Born in Weil, Swabia (now Weil der Stadt, Württemberg, Germany)
1588	Passes his baccalaureat examination in Tübingen
1596	Publishes *Mysterium cosmographicum* (*Mysterium Cosmographicum*, 1981)
1600	Works with Tycho Brahe in Prague
1601	Named Imperial Mathematician to Holy Roman Emperor Rudolf II
1609	Publishes *Astronomia nova* (*New Astronomy*, 1992), which contains his first and second laws of planetary motion
1610	Defends Galileo in *Dissertatio cum Nuncio sidereo* (*Kepler's Conversation with Galileo's Sidereal Messenger*, 1965)
1611	Publishes *Dioptrice*, which contains a theory of the telescope
1617	Rushes to defend his mother, who is tried for witchcraft
1619	Publishes *Harmonices mundi* (*The Harmony of the World*, 1997), which contains his third law of planetary motion
1627	Travels to Ulm and publishes *Tabulae Rudolphinae*
Nov. 15, 1630	Dies in Ratisbon, Bavaria (now Regensburg, Bavaria, Germany)

Early Life

When Johannes Kepler was three years old, his parents left him for two years because his father became a mercenary. Johannes was taken in by grandparents, who treated him badly. After his parents returned, he was impressed when they took him out, at ages seven and ten, to see a comet and a lunar eclipse.

Although Kepler was unhappy and sickly as a youth, he was recognized as bright enough to pursue an intellectual career. At thirteen, he entered a theological seminary and later attended a university. At the seminary, young Kepler was very serious about religion, and he came to disagree with both Protestants and Catholics over doctrine. This position led to dangers and difficulties during the violent religious wars that continued throughout his life.

The Regular Solids

At the university, Kepler learned mathematical astronomy from a professor who taught the new, sun-centered system of Nicolaus Copernicus. When he became an instructor himself, Kepler discussed the five regular or Platonic solids known to the ancient Greeks. These solids have all sides, angles, and faces equal, such as the cube.

It occurred to Kepler that the distances of the orbits of the planets from the sun could be represented by the regular solids nested inside one another. Kepler was in ecstasy over his supposed discovery, which linked pure mathematics to the physical structure of the universe. He published it in *Mysterium cosmographicum* (1596; *Mysterium Cosmographicum: The Secret of the Universe*, 1981). Although the theory was wrong, it showed that he was concerned with explaining something, the precise distances of the planetary orbits, that previous astronomers had not attempted to explain.

Kepler also found the first new regular solid since the time of the Greeks. The equal-edged solids were an object of fascination to him. While writing about the packing of shapes in space in his text *Strena seu De nive Hexangula* (1611; *The Six-Cornered Snowflake*, 1966), Kepler discovered a rhombic solid in a study of close-packing of spheres. Later in his life, in the book *Harmonices mundi* (1619; *The Harmony of the World*, 1997), he attempted to correct and save

his original theory of the planetary orbits in terms of regular solids. During these investigations, Kepler discovered another regular solid, the seventh one.

Tycho Brahe and the Conquest of Mars

Kepler became assistant to the astronomer Tycho Brahe. Tycho, a nobleman who had lost his nose in a duel and replaced it with a gold one, was opposite in personality to Kepler. Tycho was outgoing and boisterous, and he entertained nightly. Shy and irritable, Kepler found the atmosphere distracting from his work. Kepler and Tycho knew, however, that they needed each other. Tycho had the best observational data available, and Kepler had the mathematical skill that Tycho lacked.

A year after Kepler joined him, Tycho died during a banquet from a ruptured bladder. Kepler replaced him as the Imperial Astronomer in the court of Holy Roman Emperor Rudolf II in Prague. Rudolf was a distrustful and neurotic man who surrounded himself with scientists but also with magicians and charlatans of all sorts. As part of his duties, Kepler had to

(Library of Congress)

Constructing and Classifying Equal-Sided Figures

Kepler investigated the capacity of polygons in repetitive patterns to fill two-dimensional space (tiling) and of polyhedrons and spheres to fill three-dimensional space (close-packing). In doing so, he discovered four new polyhedrons, including two new regular solids.

Kepler organized and expanded knowledge of equal-sided figures in two dimensions (polygons) and three dimensions (polyhedrons). The ancient Greeks had found five regular solids, the Platonic solids, with all sides, faces, and angles equal. Until Kepler, it was thought there were only five: the tetrahedron (four sides), the cube (six sides), the octahedron (eight sides), the dodecahedron (twelve sides), and the icosahedron (twenty sides). Kepler discovered two more, called stellated or starred polyhedrons.

They are constructed by adding a pentagonal pyramid to each face of the dodecahedron (the stellated dodecahedron) and a tetrahedron to each side of the icosahedron (the stellated icosahedron). Many mathematicians overlooked Kepler's discovery. Louis Poinsot rediscovered Kepler's stellated polyhedrons in the nineteenth century (see A and B in the accompanying figure).

In ancient times, Archimedes had discovered thirteen "Archimedean" solids, which have equal polyhedral angles, but with several kinds of faces, each of which is a regular polygon. Kepler proved that no others were possible. Kepler also discovered two rhombic solids (those with diamond or parallelogram sides), the rhombic dodecahedron and the rhombic triacontahedron (see C and D in the figure). He discovered the first one during studies of the close-packing of spheres—that is, how to pack the most spheres into a given volume.

Kepler was also the first to investigate the general problem of the kinds of polygons that can tile, or completely cover without gaps, a two-dimensional surface. He was the first to solve rigorously a problem of tilings, or tessellations. He showed that there are eleven tessellations by regular polygons with all vertices of the same type; this is called Kepler's theorem (see E in the figure). About 350 years later, mathematicians such as Branko Grünbaum were still mining unexploited ideas in Kepler's work.

Bibliography

An Adventure in Multidimensional Space: The Art and Geometry of Polygons, Polyhedra, and Polytopes. Koji Miyazaki. New York: John Wiley & Sons, 1986.

Introduction to Geometry. H. S. M. Coxeter. 2d ed. New York: John Wiley & Sons, 1969.

Polyhedra: A Visual Approach. Anthony Pugh. Berkeley: University of California Press, 1976.

Polyhedron Models. Magnus J. Wenninger. Cambridge, England: Cambridge University Press, 1971.

Shapes, Space, and Symmetry. Alan Holden. New York: Columbia University Press, 1971.

Tilings and Patterns. Branko Grünbaum and G. C. Shephard. New York: W. H. Freeman, 1987.

A. Stellated Dodecahedron

B. Stellated Icosadedron

C. Rhombic Dodecahedron

D. Rhombic Triacontahedron

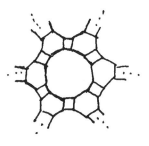

E. Tesselation

draw up astrological charts, although he rejected the standard astrology based on an earth-centered universe.

Kepler had begun calculating the orbit of Mars. He thought that it would take him eight days, but it took him nearly eight years. He first calculated a circular orbit but found it slightly inaccurate. Kepler then tried other orbits, including an egg-shaped one. At one point, he used an ellipse as approximation for his egg. Finally, he exclaimed "How ridiculous I've been!" and embraced the elliptical orbit. This idea overthrew the two-thousand-year-old "rule" that planets move in combinations of perfect circles. Kepler formulated his first two laws of planetary motion: that planets move in an ellipse with the sun at one focus and that they sweep out equal areas in equal times. Unfortunately, the publication of his book *Astronomia nova* (1609; *New Astronomy*, 1992) was delayed by Tycho's heirs, who demanded personal credit and objected to Kepler's modifications of Tycho's theory.

Shortly after Kepler developed his laws, Galileo's telescopic observations became a center of controversy, as they suggested that the moon, Venus, and Jupiter were like the earth, not made of some special celestial matter. After Kepler asked Galileo to lend him a telescope and Galileo did not reply, Kepler obtained one from a nobleman, made observations, and wrote a defense of Galileo, the *Dissertatio cum Nuncio sidereo* (1610; *Kepler's Conversation with Galileo's Sidereal Messenger*, 1965). In his book *Dioptrice* (1611) Kepler developed a theory of the optics of the telescope to justify its accuracy, which Galileo had not done.

Later Travels and Tragedies

While Kepler was printing the *Epitome astronomiae Copernicanae* (1618-1621; *Epitome of Copernican Astronomy*, 1939), his mother was accused of witchcraft. Kepler rushed home to defend her. She sold healing potions and often battled with her neighbors. Kepler himself portrayed her as a witch in his science-fiction tale *Somnium* (1634; *Kepler's Dream*, 1965), in which he travels to the moon. Trial proceedings dragged on for years. She was jailed, tortured, and died a year after being released.

During this period, during which his wife and child also died from disease, Kepler escaped from the horrors around him and into the mathematical vision of *Harmonices mundi* (1619; *The Harmony of the World*, 1997). In this work, Kepler claimed to show that the ancient Pythagorean notion of the harmony of the spheres, the musical chord supposedly made by the planetary motions, could be given geometrical meaning.

He calculated the fastest and slowest velocities of the planets and used their ratios to construct geometrical and musical ratios. In this work, among the musical scales and strange speculations, is Kepler's third law of planetary motion: The square of the planetary period (year) is proportional to the cube of the longer axis of the orbit. For Kepler, this law was simply an aid to performing his other calculations concerning polygons and music. Afterward, along with the first two laws, it became central to astronomy.

Kepler was sustained through the bloody religious wars, his mother's persecution, and the death of family members by the beauty of geometry and the belief that God had made the universe in the most mathematically harmonious fashion. Kepler died in 1630.

Bibliography

By Kepler

Mysterium cosmographicum, 1596 (*Mysterium Cosmographicum: The Secret of the Universe*, 1981)

Astronomia nova, 1609 (*New Astronomy*, 1992)

Dissertatio cum Nuncio sidereo, 1610 (*Kepler's Conversation with Galileo's Sidereal Messenger*, 1965)

Strena seu De nive Hexangula, 1611 (*The Six-Cornered Snowflake*, 1966)

Dioptrice, 1611

Epitome astronomiae Copernicanae, 1618-1621 (3 parts; *Epitome of Copernican Astronomy*, 1939)

Harmonices mundi, 1619 (partial trans. as *Harmonies of the World* in *Great Books of the Western World*, 1952; also as *The Harmony of the World*, 1997)

Tabulae Rudolphinae, 1627

Somnium, seu opus posthumum de astronomia lunari, 1634 (*Kepler's Dream*, 1965; also as *Kepler's Somnium: The Dream, or Posthumous Work on Lunar Astronomy*, 1967)

About Kepler

The Discovery of Kepler's Laws: The Interaction of Science, Philosophy, and Religion. Job Kozhamthadam. Notre Dame, Ind.: University of Notre Dame Press, 1994.

The Eye of Heaven: Ptolemy, Copernicus, Kepler. Owen Gingerich. New York: American Institute of Physics, 1993.

Kepler. Max Caspar. Translated and edited by C. Doris Hellman. 1959. Reprint. New York: Dover, 1993.

Kepler's Geometrical Cosmology. J. V. Field. Chicago: University of Chicago Press, 1988.

The Watershed: A Biography of Johannes Kepler. Arthur Koestler. Garden City, N.Y.: Doubleday, 1960.

(Val Dusek)

al-Khwarizmi

Areas of Achievement: Algebra, applied math, and arithmetic

Contribution: Al-Khwarizmi was the first Muslim mathematician to write books on algebra and arithmetic, building on Hindu and Greek sources and providing the basis for the development of mathematics in medieval Europe.

c. 780	Born in Khwarizm (now in Uzbekistan) or in Qutrubbull, near Baghdad (now in Iraq)
c. 813	Becomes a faculty member of the "House of Wisdom" at Baghdad
c. 815	Accompanies a mission to Afghanistan, with a possible return through India
c. 818	Writes a treatise on geography
c. 820	Composes a set of astronomical tables
c. 821	Writes the first Arabic treatise on algebra
c. 822	Writes the first Arabic treatise on the use of Hindu-Arabic numerals
c. 824	Writes a treatise on the Jewish calendar
c. 825	Composes books on the use of the astrolabe and sundial
c. 827	Writes a chronicle of history
c. 847	Agrees with a false prediction that Caliph al-Wathiq will live another fifty years
c. 850	Dies, possibly in Baghdad

Early Life

Muhammad ibn-Musa al-Khwarizmi (pronounced "ahl-KWAWR-ihz-mee") was the first important Muslim mathematician. Little is known about the details of his life except for brief comments by Islamic bibliographers, geographers, and historians. The name "al-Khwarizmi" would usually indicate that he was from Khwarizm, corresponding to the region around modern Khiva, Uzbekistan, in central Asia south of the Aral Sea.

The Muslim historian Abu Ja'far Muhammad ibn-Jarir at-Tabari, however, adds the designation "al-Qutrubbulli" to his name, indicating that he came from the region of Qutrubbull between the Tigris and Euphrates Rivers near Baghdad. It is most likely that his ancestors came from Khwarizm. At-Tabari also includes the designation "al-Majusi," indicating that his family background might have been in the Persian Zoroastrian religion, but a pious preface to al-Khwarizmi's book on algebra identifies him as an orthodox Muslim.

Career Highlights

Al-Khwarizmi served under the Caliph al-Ma'mun, who reigned from 813 to 833. The seventh and greatest of the Abbasid caliphs, he encouraged scientific studies. During this time, the caliph's "House of Wisdom" (Dar al-Hikma) at Baghdad, with its own library and observatory, became the premiere center of learning in the first golden age of Islamic science. According to some accounts, al-Khwarizmi was librarian for the House of Wisdom.

In about 815, al-Khwarizmi accompanied a mission to Afghanistan, possibly returning through India. This may have been the source of his knowledge of Hindu mathematics, including the works of the Indian mathematician Brahmagupta. According to at-Tabari, in the year 847, al-Khwarizmi was one of a group of astronomers who were summoned to the Caliph al-Wathiq's sickbed and who predicted from the caliph's horoscope that he would live another fifty years. They were puzzled by his death ten days later.

Works and Influence

Al-Khwarizmi was the most important mathematician of his time, initiating many of the themes in Islamic mathematics and astronomy. His book on algebra, based on Babylonian, Greek, and Hindu sources, was the first written in Arabic as Kitab al-jabr w'al-muqabala (c. 821;

book of restoration and simplification). It was translated into Latin by Robert of Chester in 1145 as Liber algebrae et almucabala, giving the word "algebra" from the Arabic word al-jabr in the title of al-Khwarizmi's book. This text, often called the Algebra, was the chief influence on European algebra. An English translation by Frederic Rosen entitled The Algebra of Mohammed ben Musa appeared in 1831. A treatise on Hindu-Arabic numerals, written after the Algebra and referring to it, is preserved only in an anonymous Latin translation entitled Algoritmi de numero indorum (c. 822; al-Khwarizmi on Hindu numerals), giving the term "algorithm" as a corruption of al-Khwarizmi's name. It introduced Europeans to the decimal place-value number system with Arabic numerals, including zero.

In addition to his mathematical works, al-Khwarizmi published a book on geography entitled Kitab surat al-ard (c. 818; book of the form of the earth), listing longitudes and latitudes of cities and localities more accurately than Claudius Ptolemy's Geography (c. 160). He also compiled the first known Arabic astronomical tables, entitled Zij al-sindhind (c. 820; astronomical tables). They were based largely on the Sanskrit work Brahmasphutasidd'hanta (628) of Brahmagupta and translated into Latin by Adelard of Bath in 1126. The only other surviving work by al-Khwarizmi is a short treatise on the Jewish calendar. His historical work Kitab al-ta'rikh (c. 827; chronicle) is known only from quotations by Islamic historians. He is also known to have written works on the astrolabe and the sundial.

Bibliography

By al-Khwarizmi

Kitab surat al-ard, c. 818 (book of the form of the earth)

Zij al-sindhind, c. 820 (astronomical tables)

Kitab al-jabr w'al-muqabala, c. 821 (The Algebra of Mohammed ben Musa, 1831)

Algoritmi de numero indorum, c. 822 (al-Khwarizmi on Hindu numerals)

Istikhraj ta'rikh al-yahud, c. 824 (extraction of the Jewish era)

Kitab al-amal bi'l-asturlab, c. 825 (book of the operation of the astrolabe)

Kitab al-ta'rikh, c. 827 (chronicle)

Algebra and Arithmetic

Al-Khwarizmi wrote the first books in Arabic on algebra and arithmetic. His texts later introduced Europeans to these subjects, including the use of Hindu-Arabic numerals.

The works of al-Khwarizmi are the basis for the development of Arabic and medieval European algebra and arithmetic. Although his algebra is based on the work of Brahmagupta and shows signs of influence from Diophantus of Alexandria, it goes beyond both works by providing a systematic exposition of the solutions of equations of the first and second degree. It is on a more elementary level, however, than that of the Diophantine problems and is completely rhetorical, with numbers written out in words rather than as symbols. The unknown quantity in equations is called "the thing" or "the root," and the square of the unknown is called "the power."

The Latin version of al-Khwarizmi's *Kitab al-jabr w'al-muqabala* (c. 821) known as the *Algebra*, opens with a brief introduction to the Hindu decimal place-value system that came to be known as Arabic numerals, including the number zero. The positional system is further elaborated in his short work on arithmetic, with a discussion of fractions and of the basic operations of addition, subtraction, multiplication, division, and the extraction of square roots.

The *Algebra* is divided into five parts, beginning with solutions of linear and quadratic equations. The rules for solving equations are applied to six standard forms (modern notation in parentheses, where *a*, *b*, and *c* are positive integers): squares equal to roots ($ax^2 = bx$), squares equal to numbers ($ax^2 = b$), roots equal to numbers ($ax = b$), squares and roots equal to numbers ($ax^2 + bx = c$), squares and numbers equal to roots ($ax^2 + c = bx$), and squares equal to roots and numbers ($ax^2 = bx + c$). What appear as redundant cases are needed, since al-Khwarizmi does not recognize negative numbers or zero as a coefficient.

In the second part of *Algebra*, al-Khwarizmi gives geometrical proofs of these rules (see the accompanying figure). In the third part, he de-

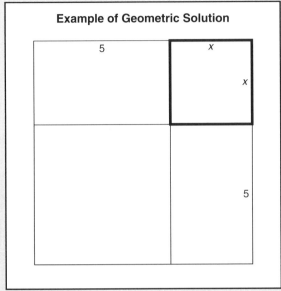

Example of Geometric Solution

In the equation "$x^2 + 10x = 39$," a square of side x has an area of x^2. Two rectangles placed on the sides, each $^{10}/_2 = 5$ units long, have an area of $10x$. The square formed by the long sides has an area of $5 \times 5 = 25$ units. The large square has a total area of $x^2 + 10x + 25 = 64$ and side $x + 5 = (64)^{1/2} = 8$, so $x = 3$.

scribes the products of $(x \pm a)$ and $(x \pm b)$. In the fourth part, he states rules for the addition and subtraction of expressions involving the unknown, its square, or its square root, as well as rules for working with different forms of square roots. In the last part, he gives examples of various kinds of problems. Although al-Khwarizmi only considers real and positive roots, he surpasses the Greeks in recognizing the existence of two roots.

Bibliography

Classics of Mathematics. Ronald Calinger, ed. Englewood Cliffs, N.J.: Prentice Hall, 1995.

Robert of Chester's Latin Translation of the Algebra of al-Khowarizmi. Louis Charles Karpinski, trans. and ed. New York: Macmillan, 1915.

A Short Account of the History of Mathematics. W. W. Rouse Ball. Reprint. New York: Dover, 1960.

About al-Khwarizmi

"Al-Khwarizmi." A. B. Arndt. *The Mathematics Teacher* 76, no. 9 (December, 1983).

"Al-Khwarizmi on the Jewish Calendar." E. S. Kennedy. *Scripta Mathematica* 27, no. 1 (June, 1964).

The Astronomical Tables of al-Khwarizmi. Otto Neugebauer. Copenhagen: I kommission hos Munksgaard, 1962.

A History of Mathematics. Carl B. Boyer and Uta C. Merzbach. 2d. rev. ed. New York: John Wiley & Sons, 1989.

(Joseph L. Spradley)

Felix Klein

Areas of Achievement: Algebra, calculus, and geometry

Contribution: Klein showed how the essential properties of a given geometry could be represented by the group of transformations that preserve those properties.

Apr. 25, 1849	Born in Düsseldorf, Prussia (now Germany)
1865	Becomes a student at Bonn University, where he studies mathematics
1868	Receives a Ph.D. in mathematics from Bonn
1869	Meets Sophus Lie in Berlin
1872-1875	Appointed a professor at the University of Erlangen
1880-1886	Serves as a professor of geometry at Leipzig University
1882	Publishes the booklet *Über Riemann's Theorie der algebraischen Functionen*
1884	Publishes his lectures on the icosahedron
1885	Elected a member of the Royal Society of London
1886-1913	Heads the department of mathematics at Göttingen University
1887	Elected president of the German Mathematical Society
1912	Receives the Copley Medal of the Royal Society of London
June 22, 1925	Dies in Göttingen, Germany

Early Life

Educated at a Prussian Gymnasium (high school) in Düsseldorf, Christian Felix Klein attended Bonn University between 1865 and

(Library of Congress)

In 1872, Klein was offered his first professorial position, at the University of Erlangen. His inaugural talk, known as the Erlanger programm, would profoundly influence mathematical development for the next half century. Klein proposed to use the group concept to classify and unify the diverse and seemingly unrelated geometries that had developed since the beginning of the nineteenth century.

In 1880, he was appointed a professor of geometry at Leipzig University. His lectures there yielded *Vorlesungen über das Ikosaeder und die Auflösung der Gleichungen vom fünften Grade* (1884; *Lectures on the Icosahedron and the Solution of Equations of the Fifth Degree*, 1913). In it, he synthesized all the results of his predecessors (including his own) relative to the solutions of equations of fifth degree in terms of the rotation group of a regular icosahedron around its axes of symmetry.

His interest then switched to Bernhard Riemann's ideas on geometric function theory. The result of this work was Klein's theory of automorphic functions. It was an exhausting work; in the midst of his research, he became aware that French mathematician Henri Poincaré was concentrating his efforts in the same direction. Klein drove himself to reach the goal before his competitor. The aftermath was a nervous breakdown.

The Göttingen Years
In 1886, Klein was offered a position in the United States, at The Johns Hopkins University, in Baltimore. He refused it and accepted an appointment as chair at the University of Göttingen. Founded in 1737, Göttingen was at that time one of the most renowned places of culture in Europe. Under Klein's leadership, the university—with its tradition of such renowned mathematicians as Carl Friedrich Gauss, Peter Gustav Lejeune Dirichlet, and Riemann—became a world center of mathematical research.

Klein's reputation drew students to Göttingen from all over the world, particularly from the United States. His lectures were prepared to the finest detail; nothing put on the blackboard during the lecture ever had to be erased. His theory, however, was that students should work the proofs on their own, following the

1868, where he received a broad education not only in mathematics but also in the natural sciences. There, he met his first mentor, Julius Plücker. Plücker was a professor of mathematics and physics, with original contributions in both fields. As a mathematician, he produced major works in the area of analytical geometry and the study of algebraic curves.

Klein received his doctoral degree in 1868. The German education system required, however, that he had to deliver another piece of original research, known as *Habilitation*, before he was allowed to lecture. If this was acceptable to the faculty, he would obtain the title of privatdozent, which carried the privilege of delivering lectures without pay under the sponsorship of the university.

The Creative Years
Klein spent 1869 and 1870 studying in Berlin and Paris. It was at this time that lie met Sophus Lie, a Norwegian mathematician with whom he had a close friendship and collaboration.

general guidelines. The result was that a student had to spend at least four hours in individual study for each hour spent in class in order to master the material.

As a leader, Klein proved to have exceptional organizational skills. He established a reading room, the Lesezimmer, that was like no other mathematical library existing at that time. Books were available on open shelves,

and the students could go directly to them.

In 1893, Klein, as the official representative of the German government, participated in the international mathematical congress held by Midwestern mathematicians in conjunction with the Chicago World's Fair. It was his first and only visit to the United States. During his stay, he delivered a series of lectures at Northwestern University, in Evanston, Illinois,

The Erlanger Programm

Klein used the group concept to classify and unify the principal geometries then existing. He defined geometry as the study of those properties that are preserved under a certain group of transformations.

A set of elements together with an operation is a group if four conditions are satisfied: The set is closed under the operation, the set contains an identity element with respect to the operation, each element has an inverse with respect to the operation, and the operation is associative. The elements can be numbers (as in arithmetic), points (as in geometry), or transformations (as in algebra or geometry). The operation can be arithmetic (addition or multiplication), geometric (rotation or translation), or any other rule for combining two elements in a set to form a third element in the same set.

If the set under consideration is the set of all points in the plane and the transformations are the translations and rotations, the resulting geometry is the plane Euclidean geometry. The properties of planar figures that remain invariant under these transformations are length, area, congruence, parallelism, collinearity of points, perpendicularity, and concurrency of lines. If the group of transformations is enlarged to include the homothety—in which a point P is carried into a point P' such that $AP = k \times AP'$, where A is a fixed point, k is a fixed constant and A, P, and P' are collinear—such properties as length, area, and congruencies no longer remain invariant. Parallelism, collinearity of points, perpendicularity, and concurrency of lines, however, are still invariant.

If (x,y) denotes the Cartesian coordinates of P and (x',y') denotes the coordinates of P', then one

such transformation can be described analytically by the following equations:

$$\begin{cases} x' = ax + by + c \\ y' = dx + ey + f \end{cases}$$

where $ae - bd$ does not equal 0. These transformations characterize the affine geometry. With the restriction $ae - bd = 1$, one recovers the translations and rotations in the plane, so that Euclidean geometry is only a special case of affine geometry. Affine geometry, in its turn, is a special case of a more general geometry called projective geometry. Of the above-mentioned properties, only collinearity of points and concurrency of lines are invariant under projective transformations.

In all of the above geometries, the transformations act on a set of points. If the set of elements is defined to be the lines in the plane or circles on a sphere, then other geometries are obtained. In this way, the construction of a new geometry becomes evident.

Bibliography

"The Erlanger Programm of Felix Klein: Reflections on Its Place in the History of Mathematics." Thomas Hawkins. *Historia Mathematica* 11, no. 4 (November, 1984): 442-470.

Foundation of Euclidean and Non-Euclidean Geometries According to F. Klein. Lazlo Rédei. New York: Pergamon Press, 1968.

Projective and Euclidean Geometry. William Thompson Fishback. New York: John Wiley & Sons, 1969.

known as the Evanston Colloquium.

After 1900, Klein became increasingly involved in the reform of mathematics education. He attempted to improve the scientific education offered in the German middle schools in order to prepare the students for the technical and mathematical training at the university level. Klein died on June 22, 1925, at the age of seventy-six.

Bibliography

By Klein

Vergleichende Betrachtungen fiber neuere geometrische Forschungen, 1872 (commonly known as the Erlanger programm)

Über Riemann's Theorie der algebraischen Functionen und ihrer Integrale, 1882 (*On Riemann's Theory of Algebraic Functions and Their Integrals*, 1893)

Vorlesungen über das Ikosaeder und die Auflösung der Gleichungen vom fünften Grade, 1884 (*Lectures on the Icosahedron and the Solution of Equations of the Fifth Degree*, 1913)

The Evanston Colloquium: Lectures on Mathematics . . ., 1893

Vorlesungen über die Theorie der automorphen Functionen, 1897-1912 (2 vols.; with Robert Fricke)

Vorlesungen über die Entwicklung der Mathematik im 19 Jahrhundert, 1926 (*Development of Mathematics in the Nineteenth Century*, 1979)

About Klein

Felix Klein and Sophus Lie: Evolution of the Idea of Symmetry in the Nineteenth Century. Isaak Moiseevich Iaglom. Boston: Birkhäuser, 1988.

Hilbert. Constance Reid. New York: Springer-Verlag, 1970.

"Pure and Applied Mathematics in Divergent Institutional Settings in Germany: The Role and Impact of Felix Klein." Gert Schubring. In *The History of Modern Mathematics*, edited by David E. Rowe and John McCleary. Boston: Academic Press, 1989.

(Anda Gadidov)

Andrey Nikolayevich Kolmogorov

Areas of Achievement: Algebra, applied math, calculus, geometry, mathematical logic, probability, set theory, statistics, topology, and trigonometry

Contribution: Kolmogorov, the most honored Russian mathematician of the twentieth century, is best known for establishing the axiomatic basis for probability theory. His wide-ranging mind produced seminal contributions to almost all areas of modern mathematics.

Apr. 25, 1903	Born in Tambov, Russia
1920	Enters Moscow University
1925	Receives a doctorate from Moscow University
1929	Obtains a junior faculty position at the Institute of Mathematics and Mechanics at Moscow University
1931	Promoted to professor
1933	Publishes *Grundbegriffe der Wahrscheinlichkeitsrechnung*
1937	Appointed to the chair in probability theory at Moscow University
1938	Writes the mathematics article for the first edition of the *Bol'shaya Sovyetskaya Entsiklopediya* (great Soviet encyclopedia)
1939	Elected to the Soviet Academy of Sciences
1940	Criticizes Lysenkoist genetics
1942	Marries Anna Dmitriyevna Egorov
1954	Applies his methods for random processes to planetary motion
Oct. 20, 1987	Dies in Moscow, Soviet Union

Early Life

On April 25, 1903, Andrey Nikolayevich Kolmogorov (pronounced "kul-muh-GAW-ruf") was born in Tambov, Russia. His mother, an aristocratic woman named Mariya Yakovlevna Kolmogorova, died giving birth to him. Little is known of his father. He was raised by his mother's sister, Vera Yakovlevna Kolmogorova, on the family estates until the Russian Revolution of 1917.

After the revolution, Kolmogorov worked for a while as a railway conductor before entering Moscow University in 1920; he would remain there in various capacities for the rest of his life. This was a time of hardship at the university. Scholarships consisted of rations of bread and fat, and the lecture halls went unheated through the Russian winter. Kolmogorov supplemented his income by teaching in an experimental school. He persisted and advanced rapidly in his studies, taking an interest in Russian history and poetry as well as mathematics.

Foundations of Probability

After completing his doctorate in 1925, Kolmogorov was permitted to remain at the university for four more years as a research student. In 1929, Pavel Sergeevich Aleksandrov obtained a permanent position for him at the Institute for Mathematics and Mechanics at Moscow University, and, in 1931, Kolmogorov was promoted to full professor. Aleksandrov and Kolmogorov became close friends and remained so until Aleksandrov's death in 1982.

Much of Kolmogorov's early work concerned mathematical logic—he developed a theory called intuitionistic logic—and probability. Although methods had long existed for calculating some specific probabilities, no general axiomatic theory of probability existed before Kolmogorov's 1929 paper on a general theory of measure and the calculus of probabilities. He continued this line of research with papers on random processes and summarized his work in 1933 with a monograph *Grundbegriffe der Wahrscheinlichkeitsrechnung* (*Foundations of the Theory of Probability*, 1950).

Rise to Prominence

Following this triumph, Kolmogorov rose swiftly to become the preeminent figure in So-

viet mathematics. Over the course of his career, he accumulated every honor and title that the Soviet Union could bestow on a mathematician, including the Order of Lenin (seven awards), the Order of the October Revolution, and Hero of Socialist Labor. His work was internationally recognized by election to more than twenty scientific societies, including the Royal Society of London in 1964 and the Paris Académie des Sciences in 1968. He received honorary doctorates from many universities and in 1963 won the international Bolzano Prize.

In 1937, Kolmogorov received the chair in probability theory at Moscow University. In 1938, he was permitted to write the lengthy article "Matematika" for the *Bol'shaya Sovyetskaya Entsiklopediya* (great Soviet encyclopedia). He was elected to the Soviet Academy of Sciences in 1939.

His prominence, as well as his long-established loyalty to the Soviet Union, permitted him to survive publishing a paper in 1940 critical of the statistics used by some Lysenkoist geneticists. During Joseph Stalin's rule, Trofim D. Lysenko dominated Soviet biology with a crackpot genetic theory that gave politically correct (from a communist point of view) but scientifically ludicrous predictions. Lysenko became a favorite of Stalin and was able to have his opponents ruined, exiled, or even murdered. Kolmogorov's paper was an act of defiance on behalf of scientific integrity, but it did nothing to check the rise of Lysenko.

In 1942, Kolmogorov married Anna Dmitriyevna Egorov. The marriage produced no children, and Kolmogorov left no descendants. Throughout his career, he took an active interest in primary and secondary education, especially in mathematics.

Varied Work

By the end of the 1930's, Kolmogorov had begun to take an interest in physical problems. In 1941, he published two important papers on turbulent flows. He did important work on stationary time series during World War II. Following the war, he pursued various interests in mechanics, function theory, information theory, and the theory of algorithms. In 1954, he wrote a paper about perturbations in planetary motion that helped open the way to modern

Axiomatic Probability

Using the tools of set theory and measure theory, Kolmogorov created a simple axiomatic framework for the study of probability. Under this framework, the assumptions inherent in modeling a physical system become explicit and purely mathematical methods can be used to establish relationships among random quantities.

Axiomatic probability begins with the abstraction of an experiment as having a set E of outcomes called elementary events. If the experiment is drawing one card from a standard deck of fifty-two cards, an example of an elementary event might be "the four of diamonds is drawn." In axiomatic probability, a field F of subsets of elementary events is constructed, according to the following axioms:

1. F is a field of sets. This means that for all pairs of sets in F, their union (all elements in either set), intersection (all elements in both sets), and difference (all elements in one set but not the other) must also be in F. Sets in F are called events.

2. F contains E.

3. To each set A in F is assigned a nonnegative number P(A) called the probability of the event A.

4. P(E) equals 1.

5. If events A and B have no elements in common, then the probability of their union (the probability that one event or the other occurs) equals the sum of their probabilities.

For the card drawing experiment described above, the elementary events are the individual cards that might be drawn, so E is the fifty-two possible cards. For F, all possible combinations of cards can be used. This will satisfy the first two axioms. Events would be such events as "a deuce is drawn," "a club is drawn," or "a face card is drawn." In order to calculate probabilities, it is necessary to define the probability function described in the third axiom. This is where modeling of the physical system occurs. Questions can be asked, such as "Was the deck fairly shuffled?" Explicit assumptions must be made at this point and must be consistent with the last three axioms.

Once the modeling is complete, however, Kolmogorov's axiomatic system reduces everything else to simple computation. It is easy to compute probabilities for all possible events and to compute relationships among events, such as the probability that the drawn card is the queen of hearts given that a red face card is drawn. These methods also facilitate the definition and use of random variables and random processes.

Bibliography

Foundations of the Theory of Probability. Andrey Nikolayevich Kolmogorov. Translated by Nathan Morrison. New York: Chelsea, 1950.

Modern Probability Theory and Its Applications. Emanuel Parzen. New York: John Wiley & Sons, 1960.

Probability, Random Variables, and Stochastic Processes. Athanasios Papoulis. New York: McGraw-Hill, 1965.

chaos theory. His work on automata, algorithms, and information theory contributed to the development of computer science, creating a new field called algorithmic information theory or Kolmogorov complexity theory. His last paper, published in 1987, was on this topic.

Kolmogorov died in Moscow on October 20, 1987, at the age of eighty-four. During his career, he had published more than three hundred research papers, textbooks, and monographs; supervised more than sixty students to their doctorates; and held at one time or an-

other virtually every office of prominence in the Soviet mathematical community.

Bibliography

By Kolmogorov
"Zur Deutung der intuitionistischen Logik," *Mathematische Zeitschrift* 35, 1932

Grundbegriffe der Wahrscheinlichkeitsrechnung, 1933 (*Foundations of the Theory of Probability*, 1950)

"Zur Theorie der Markoffschen Ketten," *Mathematische Annalen* 112, 1935

"Matematika" in *Bol'shaya Sovyetskaya Entsiklopediya*, 1938

"Dissipation of Energy in the Locally Isotropic Turbulence," *Comptes Rendus (Doklady) de l'Académie des Sciences de l'URSS* 32, 1941

Elementy teorii funktsii i funktsional'nogo analiza, 1954 (with Sergei Vasil'evich Fomin; translated as *Elements of the Theory of Functions and Functional Analysis*, 1957-1961, and as *Introductory Real Analysis*, 1970)

Matematika i mekhanika, 1985 (*Mathematics and Mechanics*, 1991)

Teoriia informatsii i teoriia algoritmov, 1987 (*Information Theory and the Theory of Algorithms*, 1993)

About Kolmogorov

"Andrei Nikolaevich Kolmogorov." P. M. B. Vitányi. *CWI Quarterly* 1 (1988).

"Andreii Nikolaevich Kolmogorov (April 25, 1903-October 20, 1987)." T. Berger, L. A. Bassalygo, R. L. Dobrushin, and M. S. Pinsker. *IEEE Transactions on Information Theory* 34, no. 2 (1988).

"The Life and Work of Andrei Nikolaevich Kolmogorov." V. M. Tikhomirov. *Russian Mathematical Surveys* 43, no. 6 (November/December, 1988).

"On A. N. Kolmogorov." V. I. Arnol'd. In *Golden Years of Moscow Mathematics*, edited by Smilka Zdravkovska and Peter L. Duren. Providence, R.I.: American Mathematical Society, 1993.

(Firman D. King)

Sofya Kovalevskaya

Area of Achievement: Applied math
Contribution: Kovalevskaya was one of the first women to receive a Ph.D. in mathematics. She was also the most widely known Russian mathematician of the late nineteenth century.

Jan. 15, 1850	Born in Moscow, Russia
Sept., 1868	Marries Vladimir Kovalevsky
1871	Begins studies with Karl Weierstrass
1874	Receives a Ph.D. from the University of Göttingen, Germany, and takes some time off from mathematics
1878	Gives birth to her only child
1880	Returns to her work in mathematics
1881	Elected to membership in the Moscow Mathematical Society
1883	Her husband commits suicide
1883	Appointed lecturer at University of Stockholm, Sweden
1888	Receives the Prix Bordin from the French Académie des Sciences
1888	Falls in love with the historian Maxim Kovalevsky
1889	Appointed Professor for Life at Stockholm University
Feb. 10, 1891	Dies in Stockholm, Sweden

Early Life

Sofya Kovalevskaya (pronounced "kuh-vul-YAYF-skuh-yuh")—known in the West as Sonya Kovalevsky (pronounced "koh-vuh-LEHF-skee")—was born Sofya Vasilyevna Korvin-Krukovskaya in Moscow on January 15, 1850. Her family had an aristocratic background. Her father was a Russian artillery general. Being the middle of three children, Sofya often felt neglected. For much of her childhood, she was raised by a strict governess. As a result, she became nervous and withdrawn.

Sofya's father refused to let her pursue mathematics, so she studied secretly. Because of a wallpaper shortage, the nursery had been papered with her father's old calculus notes. Sofya studied these notes. She also studied a physics book that she had obtained from a family friend, Professor Tyrtov. At fourteen, she taught herself trigonometry so that she could understand the physics book. Tyrtov was so impressed that he persuaded her father to let her study mathematics. Sofya went to St. Petersburg to study.

The Struggle for a Ph.D.
After her secondary schooling, Sofya wished to attend a university. The closest university open to women was in Germany. Since single women were not permitted to travel alone, she married Vladimir Kovalevsky in September, 1868. Their marriage was solely one of convenience. They moved to Heidelberg, Germany.

Sofya Kovalevskaya studied at the University of Heidelberg. In 1871, she moved to the University of Berlin to study with Karl Weierstrass. Women were not allowed to attend university lectures, but he tutored her privately for four years. Without ever attending a university lecture, she was awarded a Ph.D. from the University of Göttingen, Germany, in 1874. While working on her doctorate, Kovalevskaya had done original research on various topics and had produced four papers.

Years Away from Mathematics
Despite her reputation, Kovalevskaya was unable to find a university appointment. In 1874, Sofya and Vladimir returned to Russia. Shortly after her return, her father died unexpectedly. It was during this time that Sofya and Vladimir seem to have fallen in love. Their only child, a daughter, was born in 1878.

From 1874 until 1880, Kovalevskaya ignored mathematics and developed her literary skills. She wrote fiction, theater reviews, and science

Research on Rotations

Kovalevskaya received the prestigious Prix Bordin in 1888 from the French Académie des Sciences for her paper about the rotation of a solid body about a fixed point.

Kovalevskaya's paper "Sur le problème de la rotation d'un corps solide autour d'un point fixe" won for her the coveted Prix Bordin from the Académie des Sciences in 1888. The title translates as "on the rotation of a solid body about a fixed point." The paper was so highly regarded that the prize money was increased from 3,000 to 5,000 francs.

The paper involved both complex analysis and nonelementary integrals. Previously, Leonhard Euler, Siméon-Denis Poisson, and Joseph-Louis Lagrange had all considered simpler cases of rotations of solid bodies about a fixed point. The only complete solutions to the differential equations involved in the motion of a rigid body about a fixed point had been developed for the two cases where the body is symmetric.

Kovalevskaya's paper generalized this work.

In her paper, Kovalevskaya developed a theory for an unsymmetrical rigid body. She considered the case in which the center of its mass is not on an axis of the body. Kovalevskaya had found a totally new case in which the complete solution was thoroughly worked out. Her solution depended on some ideas from her studies with Karl Weierstrass. The solution also depended on ultraelliptic integrals.

Her solution was so general that no new case of rotatory motion about a fixed point has been researched. Kovalevskaya's further research in this area earned for her a prize from the Swedish Academy of Sciences in 1889.

Bibliography
The Mathematics of Sonya Kovalevskaya. Roger Cooke. New York: Springer-Verlag, 1984.
"Modern Dynamics and Classical Analysis." Michael Tabor. *Nature* 310 (July 26, 1984): 277-282.

articles for newspapers. She became a respected novelist. Kovalevskaya wrote several novels, along with some autobiographical sketches. Her works reflect Russian life and her childhood.

Return to Mathematics

Kovalevskaya returned to mathematics in 1880. She went to France and Germany, often leaving her husband and daughter in Russia. She presented a paper at a conference and was well received. Still unable to find mathematical work, Kovalevskaya returned to Berlin to study with Weierstrass. In 1883, while in Berlin, she received news of her husband's suicide following business failures. Kovalevskaya was overcome with guilt and tried to starve herself.

Weierstrass persuaded Gosta Mittag-Leffler to offer Kovalevskaya a lectureship at Stockholm University. There, she was later appointed professor of higher mathematics. During this time, Kovalevskaya still worked on her literary pursuits. She cowrote a play with Anna Leffler.

In 1888, Kovalevskaya received the Prix Bordin from the French Académie des Sciences for a paper entitled "Sur le problème de la rotation d'un corps solide autour d'un point fixe" (on the rotation of a solid body about a fixed point). The paper was so highly received that the prize money was increased from 3,000 to 5,000 francs. Kovalevskaya became the first female member of the Russian Imperial Academy of Science. Since she was a woman, however, she was not allowed to attend its meetings.

Her Last Years

In 1888, Kovalevskaya fell in love with Maxim Kovelevsky, a historian. He proposed marriage on the condition that she give up her work. Kovalevskaya declined the proposal and fell into a depression. She then turned to her writing and finished a memoir of her childhood.

Kovalevskaya contracted pneumonia and died in Stockholm on February 10, 1891. She was the most widely known Russian mathematician of the nineteenth century. Through her struggle to obtain the best possible education, she had opened doors at universities for women. During her career, she published ten

(Library of Congress)

papers in mathematics and mathematical physics. She also produced several literary works.

Bibliography

By Kovalevskaya

"Zur Theorie der partiellen Differentialgleichungen," *Journal für die reine und angewandte Mathematik 80,* 1875

"Sur le problème de la rotation d'un corps solide autour d'un point fixe" (on the rotation of a solid body about a fixed point), *Acta Mathematica* 12, 1889

Ur ryska lifvet: Systrarna Rajevski, 1889 (trans. into Swedish; pub. in Russian as "Vospominaniia detstva," *Vestnik Evropy* 7, 1890; trans. into English as *Sonya Kovalevsky: Her Recollections of Childhood,* 1895, and as *A Russian Childhood,* 1978)

About Kovalevskaya

A Convergence of Lives: Sofia Kovalevskaia, Scientist, Writer, Revolutionary. Ann Hibner Koblitz. Rev. ed. New Brunswick, N.J.: Rutgers University Press, 1993.

The Mathematics of Sonya Kovalevskaya. Roger Cooke. New York: Springer-Verlag, 1984.

"Sonya Kovalevskaya." Teri Perl. *Math Equals: Biographies of Women Mathematicians and Related Activities.* Menlo Park, Calif.: Addison-Wesley, 1978.

"Why Were So Few Mathematicians Female?" Loretta Kelley. *The Mathematics Teacher* 89, no. 7 (October, 1996).

Women in Science: Antiquity Through the Nineteenth Century. Marilyn Bailey Ogilvie. Cambridge, Mass.: MIT Press, 1986.

(Rena Denise Taunton)

Leopold Kronecker

Areas of Achievement: Algebra and number theory

Contribution: Kronecker advocated the philosophy of intuitionism, in which all mathematics is based on the natural numbers.

Dec. 7, 1823	Born in Liegnitz, Prussia (now Legnica, Poland)
1845	Receives a Ph.D. from the University of Berlin
1861	Gains membership in the Academy of Sciences in Berlin
1861-1883	Gives lectures at the University of Berlin
1870	Gives his first proof of a basic theorem in algebra
1882	Leads a study dealing with an arithmetic theory of algebraic quantitites
1883	Appointed to a professorship at the University of Berlin, succeeding Ernst Kummer
1887	Publishes the essay "Über den Zahlbegriff" (on number concepts)
1891	His wife dies in an accident
Dec. 29, 1891	Dies in Berlin, Germany

Early Life

Leopold Kronecker (pronounced "KROH-nehk-ur") was the son of wealthy and prosperous Jewish parents. During his youth, he was under the influence of his father and Ernst Kummer, a mathematician. Kronecker attended the Gymnasium (secondary school) and then went on to attend the University of Breslau. Kummer was his teacher at both institutions. Kronecker finished his education at the University of Berlin, obtaining a doctoral degree in 1845.

Despite Kummer's presence, Kronecker chose to handle the family's financial interests, particularly after the death of his parents. He focused his mathematical interest in the form of a hobby during this period, volunteering to teach at the University of Berlin and conducting mathematical research.

Infinity and Natural Numbers

During the late nineteenth century, mathematicians who were investigating the calculus concentrated on the idea of the infinite. The concept of infinite series and infinitesimally small quantities dominated most studies. Because of the philosophical influence of his father and of Kummer, Kronecker developed a very conservative view of mathematics. He believed that all quantities and entities in mathematics could be explained through a set number of steps that had an ending and that gave a natural number. As a result, he doubted the concept of infinity. This view alienated him from many noted mathematicians, particularly Karl Weierstrass. At this time, Weierstrass was developing a theory of real numbers (including irrational numbers) using infinite series.

It was a major conflict for Kronecker, who only accepted the counting numbers. This had been the view of the early Greeks, including

---

Describing Intuitionism

Kronecker strongly urged the mathematical community to accept the intuitionist philosophy that all mathematics should be based on natural numbers.

Kronecker established four reasons that mathematics should be based on the philosophy of intuitionism. First, the set of natural numbers and the operations of addition are intuitive to human thinking. Second, all definitions of concepts and proofs of theorems should be obtained in a set number of steps. Showing that a concept exists implies that it can be constructed. Proofs by contradiction and indirect proofs are not accepted. Third, significant differences exist between logic and mathematics. A proof of a theorem in logic that is valid in logic might not be valid in mathematics. Fourth, infinity cannot be considered as complete infinity but potential infinity. One may consider at any given point in time what is occurring with the operations, but one can never consider this to be the last step.

After Kronecker, these views of mathematics became part of a silent movement that did not resurface until L. E. J. Brouwer completed his doctoral dissertation in 1907. The intuitionist movement stagnated again before being revived in 1968 by Erret Bishop and Douglass Bridges. Kronecker was unaware of the impact that intuitionism would have on the evolution of mathematics. His concerns were making mathematics more rigorous and eliminating the paradoxes that began to surface in the nineteenth century. Kronecker wanted to strengthen mathematics.

In the field of algebra, he applied intuitionism by giving a definition of a group. In order to do so, he described what properties an element of a group must have. These properties include basic operations, the closure property, the associative and commutative properties, and the existence of a unique inverse for each element in a group. Using these properties, Kronecker proved several theorems. One theorem states that when one element from the group is raised to a power, the results must be equal to 1.

Proof of a basic theorem in algebra was a major victory for Kronecker. It demonstrated the actual construction of elements in a group. In summary, his proof stated that each element in a collection of elements can be represented once as a product of elements in the group.

Bibliography

A History of Mathematics. Carl B. Boyer and Uta C. Merzbach. 2d ed. New York: John Wiley & Sons, 1991.

Mathematical Thought from Ancient to Modern Times. Morris Kline. 3 vols. New York: Oxford University Press, 1972.

Pie in the Sky: Counting, Thinking, and Being. John D. Barrow. New York: Oxford University Press, 1992.

Aristotle, and the idea continued for centuries; it was supported in the seventeenth century by Isaac Barrow, the teacher of Sir Isaac Newton. This idea, which several mathematicians believed explained how mathematics had evolved, came to be known as intuitionism; it is one of the foundational philosophies of mathematics. Kronecker became well known for his statement, "God made the integers, all the rest is the work of man."

Kronecker made several contributions to different areas of mathematics, such as algebra, geometry, the calculus, and number theory. He wanted to establish the foundation or basis of the calculus and algebra by using the arithmetic of natural numbers.

Throughout his career, Kronecker was concerned with the state of mathematics. The battle between the practical and theoretical mathematicians separated many of the greatest thinkers in the field. Kronecker summed up this battle in a letter to Hermann von Helmholtz, a physiologist turned mathematician: "The wealth of your practical experience with sane and interesting problems will give to mathematics a new direction and a new impetus. . . . One sided and introspective mathe-matical speculation leads into sterile fields." In algebra, Kronecker was one of the first mathematicians to solve the quintic equation $(x^5 - A = 0)$.

War with Cantor

Kronecker became influential during his tenure at the University of Berlin. One of his students, Georg Cantor, publicly took the counter position of intuitionism. Cantor wrote papers that used nonconstructive methods and infinities. This deeply angered Kronecker, creating an adversarial relationship between teacher and student.

Cantor continued to work in the new field that he was developing called set theory while pursuing a position at the University of Berlin. He blamed Kronecker for his inability to reach this goal. When Cantor attempted to publish papers on set theory, he encountered either editors influenced by Kronecker or Kronecker himself, who was also an editor. Kronecker's power in the mathematical community in Germany was so strong that Cantor gradually became paranoid and suffered several nervous breakdowns.

Kronecker's philosophical views were channeled through lectures. He did little publishing of his own work despite the fact that he was an editor of a scholarly journal. Kronecker and Cantor had an opportunity to resolve their differences at a convention in 1891. Kronecker's wife was in a fatal accident, however, and he was unable to attend the convention. Later the same year, Kronecker died in Berlin.

Bibliography
By Kronecker
"Grundzüge einer arithmetischen Theorie der algebraischen Grössen" (elements of an arithmetic theory of algebraic quantities), *Journal für die reine und angewandte Mathematik* 92, 1882
"Über den Zahlbegriff" (on number concepts), *Journal für die reine und angewandte Mathematik* 101, 1887
Leopold Kronecker's Werke, 1895-1931 (Kurt Hensel, ed.)

About Kronecker
"An Appreciation of Kronecker." H. M. Ed-

wards. *The Mathematical Intelligencer* 9 (1987): 28-35.

Dictionary of Scientific Biography. Charles Coulston Gillispie, ed. New York: Charles Scribner's Sons, 1970-1990.

"Kronecker's Place in History." H. M. Edwards. In *History and Philosophy of Modern Mathematics*, edited by William Aspray and Philip Kitcher. Minneapolis: University of Minnesota Press, 1988.

(*Barbara Ann Lawrence*)

Joseph-Louis Lagrange

Areas of Achievement: Algebra, applied math, calculus, and number theory

Contribution: A key member of a group of eighteenth century French mathematicians, Lagrange contributed to myriad fields of mathematics. During the French Revolution, he gained further influence as a teacher and an author of textbooks.

Jan. 25, 1736	Born in Turin, Sardinia (now Italy)
1755	Named a mathematics professor at the Royal Artillery School, Turin
1756	Elected an associate foreign member of the Berlin Academy of Sciences
1764	Awarded the first of five prizes by the French Académie des Sciences
1766	Named director of the mathematics section, the Berlin academy
1767	Marries Vittoria Conti
1772	Elected a foreign associate member of the French academy
1783	Elected honorary president of the Academy of Turin
1787	Becomes a pensionnaire at the French academy
1788	Publishes *Mécanique analytique* (*Analytical Mechanics*, 1997)
1792	Marries his second wife, Renée-Françoise-Adélaïde Le Monnier
1794	Begins teaching at the École Polytechnique
1795	Elected chair of the mathematics section, the Institut National
Apr. 10, 1813	Dies in Paris, France

(Library of Congress)

Early Life

Joseph-Louis Lagrange (pronounced "law-GRAHNZH") was born and raised in Italy, although his family came from the French aristocracy. His father served as a public official but was not wealthy. He hoped that his son would become a lawyer, but Lagrange became devoted to mathematics early in his studies. By the age of seventeen, he was studying analysis. In 1754, he began to correspond with Leonhard Euler and the geometer Giulio da Fagnano. These men helped make others aware of Lagrange's talents.

In 1755, a royal decree named Lagrange a professor at the Royal Artillery School in Turin. He taught classes on mechanics and analysis. During this time, he researched the calculus of variations, which deals with maximizing and minimizing the areas of planar figures. In addition, Lagrange advanced the technique of integration by parts. He developed the principle of virtual velocities and applied it to planetary movement in several prize-winning papers. He also helped found the Royal Academy of Sciences of Turin and was later elected to the Berlin Academy of Sciences.

To the Berlin Academy

In 1766, Lagrange was offered more money and better scientific facilities to work at the Berlin Academy of Sciences. He became director of the mathematics section, a position that Euler had vacated. Lagrange wrote sixty-three papers during his twenty-one years in Berlin. He also married his cousin, Vittoria Conti. Both Lagrange and his wife suffered from poor health throughout their lives. She passed away in 1783 after a long illness. The couple had no children.

Lagrange continued to study celestial mechanics, writing a prize-winning essay on the theory of the moon and another on the effect of the attraction of celestial bodies on the moon. He spent much time considering the perturbations of the planets, finally ascertaining that the plane of any given planet oscillates around an average value of inclination. Lagrange's astronomical research culminated with his 1788 book *Mécanique analytique* (*Analytical Mechanics*, 1997). This work was one of the greatest Enlightenment achievements in the analytic method of the calculus and mechanics.

Lagrange made numerous other mathematical discoveries before leaving Berlin. In 1770, he proved that every integer could be expressed as the sum of no more than four squares. He foreshadowed tools of linear algebra, such as determinants and matrices, in a 1775 paper. He gave the first solution to Fermat's equation "$x^2 - ay^2 = 1$." He established the basis for all future work on solutions of algebraic equations. He even found time to compose a few memoirs on probability theory. Finally, Lagrange published many papers on ordinary and partial differential equations.

A Teacher in Paris

Lagrange accepted a position at the French Académie des Sciences in 1787. Two years later, the French Revolution disrupted all aspects of French life. Lagrange was able to make himself useful to every ruling party. Under the Jacobins, he was the chair of the Commission on Weights and Measures and a founding member of the Bureau of Longitudes. He was named a count by Napoleon. Still, Lagrange was horrified by the violent deaths of colleagues such as Antoine-Laurent Lavoisier, and he devoted himself to bettering university education as one way of restoring peace. Lagrange created no original mathematics during the revolutionary period, but he authored influential textbooks and became a respected teacher.

In 1795, Lagrange taught elementary mathematics at the short-lived École Normale. He taught analysis at the École Polytechnique from its creation in 1794 until 1799. He served in the Institut National, which replaced the French academy. During these years, Lagrange repaid the mentoring that he had received from Euler and Jean Le Rond d'Alembert by assisting younger mathematicians. For example, he influenced Augustin-Louis Cauchy to take up pure mathematics and found him positions at the École Polytechnique and the Collège de France. Lagrange also supported Sophie Germain's study of mathematics after she read the lecture notes from his École Polytechnique courses.

Lagrange remarried in 1792. His years with the daughter of astronomer Pierre Charles Le Monnier were happy. Ceremonies were held across France and Italy after Lagrange's death

An Algebraic Calculus

The necessity of giving mathematical rigor to calculus was a concern for some eighteenth century mathematicians. Lagrange hoped to establish the algebra of power series as the foundation for analysis.

Lagrange did so much mathematical work—some successful, some not—that it is impossible to list every contribution here. One of his most well-known projects was his attempt to base the calculus on power series. He worked on this problem throughout his career, publishing his vision in *Théorie des fonctions analytiques* (1797).

Lagrange believed that infinitesimals and limits lacked proper mathematical definitions. For his justification of the calculus, he turned to reduction of the calculus to algebra. This technique, it seemed to him, would be rigorous in the manner of ancient Greek mathematicians. Thus, Lagrange replaced every function with a power series expansion ($f(x + h) = f(x) + ph + qh^2 + rh^3 + sh^4 + \ldots$). He used these expansions to derive the rules of the calculus. For example, he defined the derivative as the coefficient $p(x)$ of the linear term h in the above general expansion.

A number of problems arise with founding the calculus on power series, beginning with the fact that Lagrange's approach was too restrictive. He ignored infinite derivatives and functions containing radicals. In addition, even though he claimed to have escaped the use of the limit concept, Lagrange actually used limits in his most central proof, that of the fundamental theorem of calculus. He also did not deal with the notions of convergence and divergence, both of which depend on limits. Most serious is that he did not realize that not every function can be expressed as a series.

Yet, Lagrange's effort did influence later mathematicians who were successful in making the calculus rigorous. His work led the mathematicians who founded modern analysis to use algebra rather than geometry in their arguments. Lagrange's writings were popularized by the Analytical Society of Cambridge University, while his protégé, Augustin-Louis Cauchy, developed the modern definitions of derivatives and limits. Lagrange's use of power series was also adopted for certain aspects of twentieth century analysis.

Bibliography

"Changing Attitudes Toward Mathematical Rigor: Lagrange and Analysis in the Eighteenth and Nineteenth Centuries." Judith V. Grabiner. In *Epistemological and Social Problems of the Sciences in the Early Nineteenth Century*, edited by Hans Wiels Jahnke and Michael Otte. Dordrecht, the Netherlands: D. Reidel, 1981.

Handbook of Analysis and Its Foundations. Eric Schechter. San Diego: Academic Press, 1997.

"Joseph Louis Lagrange's Algebraic Vision of the Calculus." Craig G. Fraser. *Historia Mathematica* 14 (1987): 38-53.

A Source Book in Classical Analysis. Garrett Birkhoff, ed. Cambridge, Mass.: Harvard University Press, 1973.

Reductionism

Reduction of the physical sciences to mathematics or of one branch of mathematics to another was a goal of Enlightenment mathematicians. Lagrange's 1788 text Mécanique analytique *is an outstanding example of this effort.*

Mathematicians and scientists in the eighteenth century placed the sciences into a hierarchy from natural history to physiology to electricity to mechanics. Sciences at the end closest to mechanics were considered the most fundamental and mathematical. Much of Enlightenment science was directed toward the explanation of less basic sciences in the language of more advanced ones. In other words, the goal was reduction of one science to another. At the same time, many French mathematicians tried to establish algebra as the basic language for all of mathematics. These two aspects of the reductionist program came together in Lagrange's work.

In *Mécanique analytique* (*Analytical Mechanics*, 1997), Lagrange gave a purely analytical treatment of classical mechanics, reducing all of mechanics to the calculus. Further, in an additional reduction within mathematics, he eliminated all appeals to geometrical arguments and all geometrical diagrams. Instead, he filled the pages of *Mécanique analytique* with a system for describing motion that was comprised solely of ordinary and partial differential equations. Other examples of Lagrange's reductionism are his text *Théorie des fonctions analytiques* (1797), which was an attempt to reduce the calculus to algebraic power series, and his research in reducing higher-degree equations into simpler forms. The following is an example of Lagrange's mathematical reduction. In *Philosophiae Naturalis Principia Mathematica* (1687), Sir Isaac Newton provided a geometrical proof of Kepler's law that planets sweep out equal areas in equal times. The equations with which Lagrange replaced Newton's diagram, from *Mécanique analytique*, are found in the accompanying box.

$$\Xi = d\,\frac{\delta T}{\delta\,d\xi} - \frac{\delta T}{\delta\xi} + \frac{\delta V}{\delta\xi}$$

$$\Psi = d\,\frac{\delta T}{\delta\,d\psi} - \frac{\delta T}{\delta\psi} + \frac{\delta V}{\delta\psi}$$

$$\Phi = d\,\frac{\delta T}{\delta\,d\varphi} - \frac{\delta T}{\delta\varphi} + \frac{\delta V}{\delta\varphi}$$

Mécanique analytique was seen as a model for mathematical physics into the nineteenth century, but its importance in this respect faded along with the reductionist program. Wholescale unification ceased to be a goal of mathematicians and scientists. The abstract structures of mathematics became the focus of mathematicians, as they reinterpreted the nature of mathematics after the 1830's. Meanwhile, physicists and chemists found specific theories to be more successful than a single, general language for explaining the specialized disciplines that were rapidly developing. Finally, new philosophical approaches to science, such as empiricism and positivism, replaced reductionism.

Bibliography

Cartesian Method and the Problem of Reduction. Emily R. Grosholz. Oxford, England: Clarendon Press, 1991.

Concepts of Reduction in Physical Science. Marshall Spector. Philadelphia: Temple University Press, 1978.

Mechanics, Analysis, and Geometry: 200 Years After Lagrange. Mauro Francaviglia. New York: Elsevier Scientific, 1991.

The Problem of Reductionism in Science. Evandro Agazzi, ed. Dordrecht, the Netherlands: Kluwer Academic, 1991.

in 1813 following a long illness. Much of his work was rendered obsolete by nineteenth century developments, yet his papers on algebra also inspired modern abstract mathematics.

Bibliography
By Lagrange
Mécanique analytique, 1788; 2d ed., 1811-1815 (*Analytical Mechanics*, 1997)

Théorie des fonctions analytiques, 1797

De la résolution des équations numériques de tous les degrés, 1798

"Leçons sur le calcul des fonctions," *Journal de l'École Polytechnique*, 1801

Œuvres de Lagrange, 1867-1892 (14 vols.; Joseph-Alfred Serret, ed.)

Correspondance de Leonhard Euler avec A. C. Clairaut, J. d'Alembert, et J. L. Lagrange, 1980

About Lagrange

"Lagrange Analytical Mathematics: Its Cartesian Origins and Reception in Comte Positive Philosophy." Craig G. Fraser. *Studies in the History and Philosophy of Science* 21 (1990): 243-256.

"Lagrange's Early Contributions to the Theory of First-Order Partial Differential Equations." Steven B. Engelsman. *Historia Mathematica* 7 (1980): 7-23.

"The Theory of Equations in the Eighteenth Century: The Work of Joseph Lagrange." Robin Rider Hamburg. *Archive for History of Exact Sciences* 16 (1976): 17-36.

(Amy Ackerberg-Hastings)

Johann Heinrich Lambert

Area of Achievement: Number theory

Contribution: Lambert proved pi to be an irrational quantity and introduced hyperbolic functions into trigonometry.

Aug. 26, 1728	Born in Mülhausen, Alsace, France
1740	Quits school to work in his father's tailor business
1744	Determines geometric theorems for studying the paths of comets
1759	Publishes *Die freye Perspective*, regarding descriptive geometry
1761	Publishes *Cosmologische Briefe über die Einrichtung des Weltbaues* (*Cosmological Letters on the Arrangement of the World-Edifice*, 1976)
1764	Publishes *Neues Organon*
1765	Joins the Prussian Academy of Sciences in Berlin
1766	Writes *Die Theorie der Parallellinien*
1767	Proves that pi is an irrational number
Sept. 25, 1777	Dies in Berlin, Prussia (now Germany)

Early Life

Johann Heinrich Lambert (pronounced "LAWM-bert") was born and raised in Mülhausen, Alsace, France, a long-disputed region west of the middle Rhine between France and Germany. Before he was born, Lambert's family had moved to Mülhausen from Lorraine to escape persecution for practicing the Calvinist faith.

Lambert was the son of Lukas Lambert and the former Elisabeth Schmerber. Lambert's father was a tailor who provided meagerly for Lambert and his four brothers and two sisters. When he was only twelve, Lambert had to quit school so he could help his father in the tailoring business. He relied on the little education he had as a basis to teach himself at night when the work in his father's shop was done for the day. This is how he acquired most of his scientific knowledge.

At seventeen, Lambert became the secretary to Johann Iselin, the editor of the *Basler Zeitung* and a law professor at Basel University in Switzerland. While working for Iselin, Lambert continued his self-education in the fields of humanities and the sciences and was made a member of the Swiss Scientific Society at Basel. Three years later, he became a tutor in Chur, Switzerland, for the children of Reichsgraf Peter von Salis. Lambert tutored the von Salis children for ten years, taking advantage of this noble family's extensive library and the spare time to use it.

Travel Years

Lambert traveled extensively throughout Europe during the next several years, continuing to teach himself as he went. While in Göttingen, Germany, he met the astronomer Johann Tobias Mayer and the renowned physicist Pieter van Musschenbroek, and this city was where his first book on the path of light was published in 1758. Lambert met French mathematician Jean Le Rond d'Alembert in Paris. In Augsburg, Germany, he met the famous instrument-maker Georg Friedrich Brander.

Pi: An Irrational Number

In 1767, Lambert became the first to prove that pi is an irrational number.

Pi (π) is the ratio between the diameter and the circumference of any circle. It is a number that cannot be shown completely or exactly in any finite form; it is approximately equal to 3.1416 and has an infinite number of digits.

Since Archimedes discovered π in approximately 200 B.C.E., mathematicians have been fascinated by its unique properties. One of the most significant characteristics is that it is irrational. An irrational number is one that cannot be a fraction—or be written as the ratio of two numbers. Unlike rational numbers, irrational numbers do not have decimal expansions that either terminate or have a repeating pattern. For example, .75 is a rational number because it has a finite number of digits after the decimal point. The decimal equivalent of $\frac{1}{7}$ is also a rational number because the digits 142857 repeat themselves infinitely. Lambert proved that π does not possess either of these characteristics.

Lambert was working on natural logarithms when he happened onto the proof of π as an irrational number. He used Leonhard Euler's results on continued fraction representation of a series to determine that the base of the natural logarithm, e, is irrational. From that result, Lambert proved that the tangent of any rational number is irrational. The corollary is that if the tangent is rational, then the number is irrational.

It was well-known at the time that the tangent of $\frac{\pi}{4}$ is equal to the rational number 1. Lambert proved that $\frac{\pi}{4}$ must be irrational; therefore, π is irrational. Until Lambert's discovery, mathematicians were calculating π to many decimal places, hoping to find a repeated or terminal digit, looking for the rules of rational behavior. Although Lambert did not plan to prove π irrational, his discovery permanently altered the understanding and subsequent work related to π.

Mathematicians continue to study π. Computer programs exist simply to calculate this number out to any desired place. In addition to its use in geometry problems, π occurs in hundreds of equations in many sciences, including those describing the DNA double helix, a rainbow, the pupil of the eye, and ripples spreading from where a raindrop falls into water.

Bibliography

A History of π. Petr Beckmann. 5th ed. Boulder, Colo.: Golem Press, 1982.

"Is π Normal?" Stan Wagon. *The Mathematical Intelligencer* 7, no. 3 (1985): 65-67.

Journey Through Genius: The Great Theorems of Mathematics. William Dunham. New York: John Wiley & Sons, 1990.

Lambert finally settled in Berlin in 1764 when he was offered a position at the Academy of Sciences. Frederick the Great delayed this appointment for a year because of Lambert's perceived odd behavior—probably owing to his devotion to Calvinist simplicity—and because he doubted Lambert's abilities. Later, however, Frederick recognized Lambert for his immeasurable insight and granted the appointment.

At the Academy of Sciences, Lambert worked with mathematicians Leonhard Euler and Joseph-Louis Lagrange. During the last ten years of his life, mostly at the academy, Lambert devoted his interests to mathematical inquiry.

Contributions to Math and Other Areas

Lambert may be known most significantly for proving that pi (π) is an irrational number. His interest in number theory helped him create a method of determining the prime factors of a given number. Lambert also developed hyperbolic functions used in trigonometry. His monumental work with quadrangles set the course for the future discovery of non-Euclidean geometry.

In addition to his mathematical work, Lambert contributed much to the fields of astronomy, cartography, and the study of light.

Because of the appearance of a comet when Lambert was only sixteen, he became fascinated by paths of comets and studied the properties of these paths. This was the beginning of Lambert's fascination with astronomy. He later created a formula to determine whether the distance between the earth and the sun is greater than the distance from the earth to a given comet. He speculated that the stars surrounding the sun constituted a connected system and that groups of such systems made up what is now known as the Milky Way galaxy.

Lambert also made contributions to mapmaking through his method of parallel projections. This method allowed him to determine the true distance between two places on a map. He was the first to come up with methods for measuring light intensities accurately; consequently, the unit of brightness is named "lambert" in his honor. He died in 1777 at the age of only forty-nine.

Bibliography

By Lambert

Die freye Perspective, 1759

Cosmologische Briefe über die Einrichtung des Weltbaues, 1761 (*Cosmological Letters on the Arrangement of the World-Edifice*, 1976)

Neues Organon, 1764

Die Theorie der Parallellinien, 1766

Opera Mathematica, 1946-1948 (2 vols.; Andreas Speiser, ed.)

About Lambert

Bibliographia Lambertiana. Max Steck. Berlin: Hildesheim, 1943.

"J. H. Lambert's Work on Probability." O. B. Sheynin. *Archive for History of Exact Sciences* 7, no. 3 (1971).

"Johann Heinrich Lambert, Mathematician and Scientist, 1728-1777." J. J. Gray and Laura Tilling. *Historia Mathematica* 5, no. 1 (February, 1978): 13-41.

(Karen Elting Brock)

Pierre-Simon Laplace

Areas of Achievement: Algebra, applied math, calculus, and probability
Contribution: Laplace made outstanding contributions to celestial mechanics and probability theory and to the uses of differential equations and their solutions.

Mar. 23, 1749	Born in Beaumont-en-Auge, Normandy, France
1766	Enters the University of Caen
1768	Moves to Paris to study under Jean Le Rond d'Alembert
1768	Appointed to the chair of mathematics at the École Militaire in Paris
1773	Becomes a member of the Paris Académie des Sciences
May 15, 1788	Marries Marie-Charlotte de Courty de Romanges
1795	Becomes a member of the French Institute
1796	Presents his nebular hypothesis of the origin of the solar system
1799-1825	Publishes his treatise on celestial mechanics in five volumes
1805	Awarded the Legion of Honor
1806	Becomes Count of the Empire
1812	Publishes *Théorie analytique des probabilités*
1817	Named a marquis
Mar. 5, 1827	Dies in Paris, France

(AIP Niels Bohr Library)

Early Life

Pierre-Simon Laplace (pronounced "lah-PLAHS") was born in Beaumont-en-Auge in Normandy on March 23, 1979. His father, Pierre, was a business agent for the parish and was also in the cider business. His mother, Marie-Anne Sochen, came from a prosperous farm family. Laplace attended a local Benedictine school from the age of seven to sixteen and then enrolled at the University of Caen. Following his father's wishes, Laplace began studying for a career with the church, but his interests eventually took him into mathematics.

At age nineteen, he left for Paris with a letter of recommendation to Jean Le Rond d'Alembert, one of the foremost mathematicians of the day. According to tradition, d'Alembert presented Laplace with a mathematical problem and told him to come back in a week. Instead, Laplace returned with the solution the next day. D'Alembert presented him with a second problem, and the results were the same. D'Alembert not only became Laplace's mentor but also secured an appointment for him as a professor of mathematics at the École Militaire in Paris.

Election to the Academy

After only five years in Paris, Laplace won election to the Académie des Sciences. The academy's secretary wrote that never had it received so many important papers on such varied and difficult topics in such short time from so young a candidate. Laplace had submitted thirteen papers on such diverse topics as adapting integral calculus to the solution of difference equations, the mathematics of chance and games, and problems of mathematical astronomy.

Believing there to be attractive forces between particles of matter just as between planets, Laplace explored the phenomenon of capillary action. As he did so, he was gradually drawn into collaboration with the scientific leader of the academy, Antoine-Laurent Lavoisier. Their measurements of thermal properties of materials helped lay the foundation for thermodynamics.

In 1784, Laplace was appointed examiner of cadets for the Royal Artillery; the following year, he examined and passed the sixteen-year-old Napoleon Bonaparte. At age thirty-nine, Laplace married the nineteen-year-old Marie-Charlotte de Courty de Romanges. They had two children. A son, Charles-Émile, was born in 1789, and a daughter, Sophie-Suzanne, soon followed.

Public Office

It is unclear exactly what Laplace's political convictions were, since he enthusiastically supported whoever was in power, but this was a practical policy during the turbulent years of the French Revolution. In the early 1790's, La-

Gravity

Dealing fully with the law of gravity requires sophisticated mathematics.

Isaac Newton gave the universal law of gravitation as

$$F = \frac{GM_1M_2}{R^2}$$

where F is the gravitational force between a body of mass M_1 and a body of mass M_2 located a distance R apart. G has the value of 6.673×10^{-11} N $\times$ m^2/kg^2 and is called the universal gravitational constant.

Both Newton and Laplace developed proofs to show that the law held not only between point masses but also between uniform spherical bodies. A rotating body such as the earth, however, is not a sphere; it is an ellipsoid, fatter at the equator than from pole to pole. Laplace found enough interesting problems in applying the law of gravitation that he published a five-volume masterwork, *Traité de mécanique céleste* (1799-1825; *Celestial Mechanics*, 1829-1839), in which he compiled his solutions along with various mathematical techniques. This text earned for him the title of "the French Isaac Newton."

As written, the law of gravitation implies that one body can exert a force on another body some distance away. Newton found the idea of "action at a distance" absurd, but he saw no way around it. Laplace suggested that the problem could be restated in terms of a potential function. He sup-

posed that the sun, for example, changed space by establishing a gravitational field and showed how this field could be determined at each point in space from the potential function.

In this view, a second body such as the earth does not interact directly with the sun, which is distant, but with the sun's field at the location of the earth. Furthermore, one could account for the effect of other bodies on the earth by adding in their potential functions. It was later determined that changes in the potential function travel outward at the speed of light.

Laplace attacked the problem of the stability of the solar system. For example, every time that Jupiter passes Saturn as they orbit the sun, Jupiter and Saturn give each other gravitational tugs. Could these tugs accumulate to change Saturn's orbit so that it might come crashing inward toward the sun? Laplace convinced himself that the effect of such tugs would average out nearly to zero over time.

Bibliography

The Birth of a New Physics. I. Bernard Cohen. Rev. ed. New York: W. W. Norton, 1985.

Gravity. Chuji Tsuboi. Boston: George Allen & Unwin, 1983.

Newton's Clock-Chaos in the Solar System. Ivars Peterson. New York: W. H. Freeman, 1993.

The Story of Astronomy. Lloyd Motz and Jefferson Hane Weaver. New York: Plenum Press, 1995.

Probability

According to Laplace, the mathematics of probability follow simply from applying common sense to events.

Laplace was one of the founders of the mathematical study of probability. Besides his technical works, he also wrote a book on probability for the novice. In this work, he explains that if all the outcomes of an event are equally possible, then probability may be defined as the ratio of the number of favorable outcomes to the total number of possible outcomes. For example, what is the probability of throwing a coin into the air twice and having it land heads up at least once? The possible outcomes are heads the first time and heads the second time, heads and then tails, tails and then heads, or tails both times. Three of the four possible cases are favorable, so the probability is $\frac{3}{4}$.

On the other hand, it could be said that there are only three cases: heads on the first throw (therefore, the second throw is immaterial), tails and then heads, and tails on both throws. Thus, it seems that the probability is $\frac{2}{3}$, since two of the three cases are favorable. This is wrong, however, since the outcomes are not equally likely. The chance of heads on the first throw is $\frac{1}{2}$. The chance of tails on the first throw followed by heads on the second throw is $\frac{1}{4}$ $(= \frac{1}{2} \times \frac{1}{2})$, so the correct probability is again $\frac{3}{4}$ $(= \frac{1}{2} + \frac{1}{4})$.

Another common mistake is to assume that past events influence the future in cases where there is no connection. Suppose that it is discovered through a large number of trials that a certain coin lands heads up more often than tails up (the coin is not sufficiently symmetric). The chances are that it will be more likely to land heads up on the next throw. Now consider a different coin that is symmetric. Suppose that it has landed tails up twelve times in a row (possible, but unlikely). The probability that it will land heads up on the next throw is still only $\frac{1}{2}$. Here, each throw is an independent event and is not related to previous throws.

Bibliography

An Introduction to Sets, Probability, and Hypothesis Testing. Howard F. Fehr, Lucas N. H. Bunt, and George Grossman. Lexington, Mass.: D. C. Heath, 1964.

A Philosophical Essay on Probabilities. Pierre-Simon Laplace. New York: John Wiley & Sons, 1902.

Principles of Statistics and Probability. Robert A. Crovelli. Boston: Prindle, Weber & Schmidt, 1973.

place served on a committee to establish a new system of weights and measures. The result of the committee's work was the metric system.

Consistent with the spirit of the times, the system was to be based on natural physical quantities instead of on such things as the length of the king's arm. An expert on measuring the exact shape of the earth, Laplace supported the proposition that the unit length be one ten-millionth (.0000001) of the quadrant measured along the meridian through Paris. It was Laplace who proposed the now-familiar names "meter," "centimeter," and "millimeter."

At Laplace's request, Napoleon (now emperor) appointed him minister of the interior in 1799, but he was so unsuited for the post that he was dismissed after six weeks. To retain his support, Laplace was elevated to the senate and in 1806 named a count of the empire. When Napoleon fell, Laplace switched his allegiance to the monarchy and was named a marquis in 1817 after the Bourbons returned to power.

Laplace Mellows

With some justification, Laplace regarded himself as the greatest mathematician in France. He was widely recognized as a mathematical genius, but he was also seen as petty. He freely incorporated the works of others into his own writings without giving them sufficient credit. He was quick to ridicule the mistakes of others. Being very widely read and having a phenomenal memory, he arrogantly believed that he had to give his opinion on every matter that came up.

Toward the end of his life, however, Laplace became more generous, especially with his pupils. In at least one case, he suppressed his own work so that his pupil might receive sole credit for it. Laplace died in Paris on March 5, 1827, a few weeks before his seventy-eighth birthday.

Bibliography
By Laplace
Théorie du mouvement et de la figure elliptique des planètes, 1784

Exposition du système du monde, 1796 (*The System of the World*, 1830)

Traité de mécanique céleste, 1799-1825 (5 vols.; *Celestial Mechanics*, 1829-1839)

Théorie analytique des probabilités, 1812

Essai philosophique sur les probabilités, 1814 (*A Philosophical Essay on Probabilities*, 1902)

About Laplace
"Laplace, Pierre-Simon, Marquis de." I. Grattan-Guinness. In *Dictionary of Scientific Biography*, edited by Charles Coulston Gillispie, ed. Vol. 15. New York: Charles Scribner's Sons, 1978.

Pierre-Simon Laplace, 1749-1827: A Life in Exact Science. Charles Coulston Gillispie. Princeton, N.J.: Princeton University Press, 1997.

The World of Mathematics. James Roy Newman, ed. Vol. 2. New York: Simon & Schuster, 1956.

(*Charles W. Rogers*)

Henri-Léon Lebesgue

Area of Achievement: Calculus

Contribution: Lebesgue developed a theory of integration that greatly extended the number and type of problems that could be solved by integral calculus.

June 28, 1875	Born in Beauvais, France
1894-1897	Studies at the École Normale Supérieure
1899-1902	Serves on the faculty of the Lycée Central, Nancy
1902	Receives a Ph.D. from the Sorbonne, Paris
1902-1906	Teaches at the University of Rennes
1906-1910	Moves to the faculty of the University of Poitiers
1910-1920	Serves as a faculty member at the Sorbonne
1912	Awarded the Prix Houllevique
1914	Awarded the Prix Poncelet
1917	Awarded the Prix Saintour
1919	Awarded the Prix Petit d'Ormay
1921	Joins the faculty of the Collège de France, Paris
1922	Elected to the Académie des Sciences
1934	Appointed a Fellow of the Royal Society of London
July 26, 1941	Dies in Paris, France

Early Life
Henri-Léon Lebesgue (pronounced "luh-BEHG") was born in Beauvais, France, in 1875. His father was a printer, and his mother an elementary school teacher. He enrolled in the École Normale Supérieure in 1894 and was graduated four years later. In college, he displayed a great talent for mathematics and, for

two years following graduation, remained at the college to improve his mathematical skills further.

In 1899, Lebesgue accepted a teaching position at the Lycée Central in Nancy, France. While there, he studied for his doctoral degree and in 1902 received a Ph.D. from the Sorbonne, in Paris. Upon completion of his degree, he accepted a position at the University of Rennes. He later taught at the University of Poitiers before joining the faculty at the Sorbonne in 1910.

The Lebesgue Integral

During the two years after his graduation from the École Normale Supérieure, Lebesgue familiarized himself with the current concepts of mathematics. He was particularly interested in computations using the calculus, especially those dealing with integration.

The concept of integration was introduced by Bernhard Riemann, a German mathematician, in 1854. In the years that followed its introduction, various theorems of integration were developed and applied to more diverse

Lebesgue Integration

The Lebesgue integral developed in the early twentieth century was able to solve a greater number of mathematical problems than prior integration methods.

Lebesgue himself stated in his 1902 doctoral dissertation that with the application of his integration procedure, he hoped to define more generally the integral as a viable mathematical function, to calculate more properly the length of a curve, and to evaluate the area bounded by a curved surface. In its simplest form, the Lebesgue integral

$$\int_L^U f(x)dx$$

represents the integration of the function $f(x)$ between an upper maximum limit, U, and a lower minimum limit, L. The interval between U and L is divided into a series of subsets represented by e_i—that is, subsets $e_1, e_2, e_3 \ldots e_i \ldots e_n$. Each subset has an upper and lower limit represented by u_i and l_i, respectively. Solution of the function $f(x)$ within any subset results in a value for that subset $m_i(e_i)$. The Lebesgue integral is defined as the limit of the sum, Σ, of all the values of $m_i(e_i)$:

$$\sum_l^n u_i m(e_i)$$

as any differences in these values approaches zero.

The definition of the Lebesgue integral, requiring as it does that certain rules be met before it can be applied, gives rise to various terms, both for the integration procedure and for the values associated with the integration results. These terms have also become associated with Lebes-

gue and include the Lebesgue criterion, the Lebesgue decomposition, the Lebesgue exterior and interior measure, the Lebesgue function, the Lebesgue number, the Lebesgue space, and the Lebesgue transform.

The Lebesgue integral, when considered as a solution for some unanswered questions that prevailed in the early twentieth century, was successful in providing answers that had not been previously possible. Other mathematicians have built on and continue to build on the interest created by Lebesgue. His approach finds even wider application now than in his own time.

The Lebesgue integral does not apply to all integration problems, but for those meeting the criteria implicit in the definitions of the integral, it is a most successful mathematical approach.

Bibliography

Lebesgue's Theory of Integration: Its Origins and Development. Thomas Hawkins. Madison: University of Wisconsin Press, 1970.

McGraw-Hill Dictionary of Scientific and Technical Terms. Sybil P. Parker, ed. 5th ed. New York, McGraw-Hill, 1994.

Mathematics Dictionary. Glenn James and Robert Clarke James. 5th ed. New York: D. Van Nostrand, 1992.

The Penguin Dictionary of Mathematics. John Daintith and R. David Nelson, eds. London: Penguin Books, 1989.

The Structure of Lebesgue Integration Theory. George Frederick James Temple. Oxford, England: Clarendon Press, 1971.

problem types. By the late nineteenth century, it was evident that Riemann's integral approach would not solve all problem types to which it was applied. Lebesgue, and others, recognized this and sought to expand, modify, or replace the Riemann integral with a more general approach.

Lebesgue formulated a more general idea of integration. His ideas took shape during the time that he taught at the Lycée Central and were summarized in a report that he submitted to the Sorbonne as his doctoral dissertation. Later mathematicians would refer to his dissertation as one of the most important papers dealing with integration theory. The integration procedure that he introduced and the formula that he presented for the integral equation could be more generally applied than could the Riemann integral. The Lebesgue integral method solved a greater variety of mathematical problems.

Lebesgue spent the next few years improving upon and expanding the concepts contained in the Lebesgue integral approach. Other mathematicians, as his theory became familiar to them, also recognized its significance and adopted it as a means to solving the mathematical equations in which they were interested.

One important problem for which the Lebesgue integral method proved successful was to support a concept put forth by Joseph Fourier, a French mathematician and physicist. He proposed that a bounded mathematical relation—that is, one valid between a fixed upper and a fixed lower limit—could be represented by a series of trigonometric terms and that for an infinite number of trigonometric terms in the bounded relation, integration term-by-term was possible. Lebesgue was able to confirm Fourier's theories for terms to which the Lebesgue integral applied.

During the 1902-1903 and 1903-1904 academic years, Lebesgue was invited to present lectures in Paris at the Collège de France. It was there that his ideas regarding his new integration theory became widely known. Paris was a center of scholarly activity, and many famous mathematicians and scholars of the day heard him speak. He later published his lectures in book form. They were widely read throughout the academic world.

The Productive Years

Lebesgue continued to expand upon his integration theory, applying it to various area of mathematics including unbounded relations, monotonic functions, and measure theory. He also studied sets of values, curve rectification, the calculus of variations, and theories of surface area. He published numerous papers in mathematical journals detailing aspects of his various interests.

In 1910, Lebesgue joined the faculty of the highly prestigious Sorbonne and later, in 1921, the faculty of the Collège de France. He was elected to the French Académie des Sciences in 1922 and to the Royal Society of London in 1934.

The last twenty years of Lebesgue's life were spent studying the history of mathematics and improving the teaching of mathematics. He died in Paris on July 26, 1941, at the age of sixty-six.

Bibliography

By Lebesgue

Leçons sur l'intégration et la recherche des fonctions primitives, 1904

Leçons sur les séries trigonométriques, 1906

Notice sur les travaux scientifiques de M. Henri Lebesgue, 1922

About Lebesgue

The Biographical Dictionary of Scientists: Mathematicians. David Abbott. New York: Peter Bedrick Books, 1986.

"Henri Lebesgue, 1875-1941, French Mathematician." Robert Messer and Tom Chen. In *Notable Twentieth-Century Scientists*, edited by Emily J. McMurray. Vol. 3. New York: Gale Research, 1995.

"Henri Léon Lebesgue." Thomas Hawkins. In *Dictionary of Scientific Biography*, edited by Charles Coulston Gillispie. Vol. 8. New York: Charles Scribner's Sons, 1973.

A History of Mathematics. Carl B. Boyer and Uta C. Merzbach. 2d ed. New York: John Wiley & Sons, 1991.

Measure and the Integral. Henri-Leon Lebesgue. Edited by Kenneth O. May. San Francisco: Holden-Day, 1966.

(Gordon A. Parker)

Solomon Lefschetz

Areas of Achievement: Geometry and topology
Contribution: Lefschetz originated many of the basic ideas of algebraic topology.

Sept. 3, 1884	Born in Moscow, Russia
1884	Moves with his family to Paris
1902	Enters the École Centrale des Arts et Manufactures
1905	Graduated as a mechanical engineer
Jan., 1907	Becomes an engineering apprentice at Westinghouse Electric and Manufacturing Company in Pittsburgh
Nov., 1907	Loses both hands in a testing accident
1910	Leaves Westinghouse and enters Clark University, in Worcester, Massachusetts, as a graduate student
1911	Earns a Ph.D. summa cum laude
1911	Works as an assistant at the University of Nebraska
1913	Marries Alice Berg Hayes
1913	Moves to the University of Kansas
1919	Awarded the Bordin Prize
1924	Joins Princeton University
1943	Turns his interest to ordinary differential equations and control theory
1944	Joins the Instituto de Matematicas of the National University of Mexico
1953	Named emeritus professor at Princeton
Oct. 5, 1972	Dies in Princeton, New Jersey

Early Life

Solomon Lefschetz was born in Moscow as the son of an importer, Alexander Lefschetz, and his wife Vera, Turkish citizens. Soon afterward, his parents moved to Paris, where he grew up with five brothers and a sister.

From the age of thirteen, Lefschetz was "mathematics mad." Not being a French citizen, however, he saw no hope of a career in pure mathematics. As a second best, he studied engineering. From 1902 to 1905, he attended the École Centrale des Arts et Manufactures, graduating as a mechanical engineer.

A Terrible Accident

Lefschetz decided to go to the United States to observe American engineering. In January, 1907, he became an engineering apprentice in the transformer testing section of the Westinghouse Company in Pittsburgh. In November, he lost both hands in an accident there.

For his remaining sixty-five years, Lefschetz wore false hands. Over each hand, he wore a black glove. They looked like loosely clenched hands, but they did not move. He could not turn a doorknob. He would write enormous letters on the blackboard, like a child learning to write. Albert Tucker, his friend and successor as chair of the Princeton math department, wrote,

> He would never say "You'll have to do that for me." Instead he made a simple polite request. "Please cut my meat" or "Please open that door." The courage that he had—he would go into New York by himself and ask strangers in the subway to take a token out of his pocket and put it in the turnstile.

Lefschetz never spoke of his disability. In "Reminiscences of a Mathematical Immigrant," he simply wrote, "I graduated from the École Centrale in 1905 and for six years worked as an engineer. I soon realized that my true path was not engineering but mathematics."

A Return to Mathematics

After some months of convalescence, Lefschetz went back to Westinghouse, but he found the work routine. As a hobby, he returned to the mathematics that he had neglected for five years. He left Westinghouse to become a graduate student at Clark University, where he attacked a problem suggested by Professor William Edward Story: How many cusps can a plane curve of given degree have? Lefschetz made a contribution to this problem and earned his Ph.D. summa cum laude in 1911.

At Clark, he became close to another mathematics student, Alice Berg Hays; they married on July 3, 1913. She was a pillar of strength for Lefschetz all his life, helping him rise above his disability and encouraging his work. After leaving Clark, Lefschetz taught at the Universities of Nebraska and Kansas for twelve years. Those years were happy and fruitful, even though they were almost totally isolated mathematically.

Another major American topologist in the 1920's was James Alexander at Princeton University. Alexander was reputedly a "left-winger"—he was opposed to racism and anti-Semitism. He proposed bringing Lefschetz to Princeton. His proposal was bitterly resisted, but he had enough financial and social clout to win the day. In 1925, Solomon Lefschetz became the first Jewish mathematics professor at Princeton University.

From 1945 to 1953, Lefschetz chaired the Princeton math department. His sagacity is credited with keeping Princeton in its leading research position. According to biographer Stephen G. Krantz,

(Archive Photos)

> Lefschetz was famous for his aggressive self-confidence. He could terrorize most other mathematicians easily. At committee meetings he would pound his fist on the table with terrifying effect.

Differential Equations and Stability Theory

In 1943, Lefschetz switched from geometry and topology to differential equations, devoting his last twenty-five years to this new field. He wrote more than forty papers, articles, and books on the topic and created a vigorous and distinguished school, guiding students and young mathematicians to work on significant problems. He opened up the rich field of optimal control theory, previously ignored outside the Soviet Union.

Lefschetz established a research center on differential equations at Martin Aircraft Company in Baltimore. This group later became a major component of the applied mathematics department at Brown University. Lefschetz worked with that group until 1970.

From 1944 to 1966, he belonged to the Instituto de Matematicas of the National University of Mexico. He found capable young mathematicians there and sent several to Princeton for advanced training.

It is thought-provoking that along with his brilliant achievements in mathematics, Lefschetz was notoriously unreliable. As Tucker wrote,

> He was very quick and very imaginative. But he had great difficulty giving a rigorous argument . . . I've heard it said that any proof Lefschetz would give would be wrong. But any result he would announce would be right. He had a tremendously sound intuition, but he was just so restless and impatient that he wouldn't take time to make rigorous arguments.

Lefschetz wrote seven books. Among his many awards were the Bordin Prize, the Bocher

The Lefschetz Fixed Point Theorems

Topology is the study of those geometric properties not affected by stretching, shrinking, or bending but that may change after gluing or cutting—that is, properties preserved under continuous mappings. Lefschetz is credited with introducing the term "topology."

One important topological property is the fixed point property. Given a space S and a transformation T mapping S into S, a point x in S is called a fixed point of T if $Tx = x$. In brief, x is mapped onto itself by T. For example, rotating a disc about its center leaves exactly one fixed point—the center. On the other hand, shifting a horizontal line to the right leaves no fixed point—every point is mapped onto a point to the right.

Fixed points are relevant to algebra as well as geometry. An algebraic relation, such as "$y = 5x^2 + 3x + 2$," can be thought of as a transformation, mapping each number x onto another number y.

If one wants to solve "$5x^2 + 3x + 2 = 0$," one can rewrite the equation as "$5x^2 + 4x + 2 = x$." Then, the solution x is a fixed point of the transformation "$5x^2 + 4x + 2$." Thus, any equation can be reformulated as finding fixed points of a related transformation.

A fixed point theorem gives conditions on the space S and the transformation T to guarantee that there is at least one solution, a fixed point x. In one dimension, the problem is easy to visualize. A mapping from an x-axis to a y-axis is pictured by the usual graph in the x-y plane. The identity mapping is $y = x$; it takes every number to itself. Its graph is a line bisecting the angle between the two positive axes. Some other equation, such as the quadratic one above, has its own graph, a curve in the x-y plane. The fixed points of the quadratic transformation are simply the values of x where that graph intersects the line $y = x$.

Most of Lefschetz's topology arose from efforts to prove fixed point theorems. He discovered a "magic number" $N(T)$ such that if and only if $N(T)$ is different from zero, then at least one fixed point exists. In the one-dimensional example, $N(t)$ is the difference between the number of times the graph crosses the line $y = x$ from the right and the left.

Lefschetz's general result includes many previous special cases, notably the famous fixed point theorems discovered by L. E. J. Brouwer. To establish this $N(t)$ property in full generality, Lefschetz created his intersection theory, which is at the root of much modern algebraic topology.

Bibliography

Algebraic Topology. Solomon Lefschetz. New York: American Mathematical Society, 1942.

"A Page of Mathematical Autobiography." Solomon Lefschetz. *Bulletin of the American Mathematical Society* 74 (September, 1968): 854-879.

"Solomon Lefschetz, September 3, 1884-October 5, 1972." Phillip Griffiths, Donald Spencer, and George Whitehead. In *Biographical Memoirs of the National Academy of Sciences.* Vol. 61. Washington, D.C.: National Academy Press, 1992.

Topology. Solomon Lefschetz. Princeton, N.J.: Princeton University Press, 1930.

Prize, and the Feltrinelli prize. He died in 1972 at the age of eighty-eight.

Bibliography

By Lefschetz
Topology, 1930
Algebraic Topology, 1942
Introduction to Topology, 1949
Algebraic Geometry, 1953
Differential Equations: Geometric Theory, 1957
Stability by Liapounov's Direct Method, 1961 (with Joseph P. Lasalle)

Stability of Nonlinear Control Systems, 1965
"A Page of Mathematical Autobiography," *Bulletin of the American Mathematical Society* 74, 1968
"Reminiscences of a Mathematical Immigrant in the United States," *American Mathematical Monthly* 77, 1970

About Lefschetz
Indiscrete Thoughts. Gian-Carlo Rota. Boston: Birkhäuser, 1997.
"Mathematical Anecdotes." Stephen G. Krantz.

The Mathematical Intelligencer 12, no. 4 (Fall, 1990).

"Solomon Lefschetz: A Reminiscence." Albert W. Tucker. In *Mathematical People: Profiles and Interviews*. Boston: Birkhäuser, 1985.

(Reuben Hersh)

Adrien-Marie Legendre

Areas of Achievement: Applied math, calculus, geometry, and number theory

Contribution: Legendre was active in many areas of concern to mathematicians in the eighteenth and nineteenth centuries. He also founded or kept alive other fields until additional mathematicians became interested in those subjects.

Sept. 18, 1752	Born in Paris, France
1775	Begins to teach mathematics at École Militaire
1782	Receives a prize from the Berlin Academy of Sciences
1783	Elected to the French Académie des Sciences as adjunct member
1784	Publishes his work on Legendre polynomials
1785	Promoted to associate member of the Académie des Sciences
1787	Elected to the Royal Society of London
1794	Becomes a professor of pure mathematics at the Institut de Marat
1795	Elected to the Institut National
1799	Appointed an examiner in mathematics at the École Polytechnique
Jan. 10, 1833	Dies in Paris, France

Early Life

Adrien-Marie Legendre (pronounced "luh-ZHAWN-druh") grew up in a wealthy family. He received an advanced education in science and mathematics at the Collège Mazarin under the well-known mathematician Abbé Joseph-François Marie. After defending his theses in mathematics and physics at the college in 1770,

Legendre used his family's money to spend all of his time on research.

Even though he did not need employment, Legendre accepted a position teaching mathematics at the École Militaire, which he held from 1775 to 1780.

Legendre worked to establish himself in the European mathematical community during this time. He won a prize of the Berlin Academy of Sciences in 1782 for an essay on ballistics, which caught the attention of the mathematician Joseph-Louis Lagrange. Legendre also became acquainted with Pierre-Simon Laplace, who assisted Legendre in becoming a member of the French Académie des Sciences, an important step toward scientific legitimacy in France.

A Name in Mathematics

Legendre's name has become attached to work in analysis that he did in the 1780's: the Legendre function, Legendre polynomials, and Legendre conditions. For example, Legendre polynomials first appeared in a paper that he

(Library of Congress)

read to the French academy in 1784. These functions can be used in a variety of applications in mathematical physics, such as to determine heat flow on a spherical surface.

Legendre remained busy during the French Revolution. Although the academy was closed by the Jacobins and Legendre lost his modest fortune during the upheaval, his abilities were respected by the revolutionaries. He was asked to serve on the committee that reformed weights and measures in 1791. He then became professor of pure mathematics at the Institut de Marat in 1794 before heading the National Executive Commission of Public Instruction.

During the revolution, Legendre was married to a nineteen-year-old woman. Little is known of their life together, except that they had no children and that she worshiped her husband's memory until her death in 1856.

In 1794, Legendre published the work for which he is best known in the United States, the *Éléments de géométrie*. He was concerned that French educators had departed from the logical structure of Euclid considered so useful in teaching, but he also wanted to improve upon problems with Euclid's work, such as the arrangement of the propositions. Legendre's textbook went through nearly forty editions in France. It was introduced in the United States in 1819 as *Elements of Geometry*, serving as the model for elementary geometry textbooks well into the twentieth century. Throughout his life, Legendre also made several attempts to prove Euclid's fifth, or parallel, postulate.

Legendre's Best Work

Despite the success of *Éléments de géométrie*, no one considered Legendre a geometer. Rather, Legendre himself was most proud of his work on elliptic integrals and number theory. For forty years, he was the only mathematician to study elliptic integrals. He systematized the study of these integrals, which could be represented by the arc of an ellipse or hyperbola. Legendre also discovered many of the basic principles of elliptic integrals.

Legendre was not the most influential number theorist of his lifetime, but he was an active contributor. In fact, his book *Essai sur la théorie* (1797-1798) was the first treatise that dealt exclusively with the theory of numbers.

Least Squares

Legendre developed a mathematical tool for fitting a set of observations to a line, which became indispensable to statistics.

Another of Legendre's many contributions to mathematics was the technique of least squares, also discovered independently by Carl Friedrich Gauss. Legendre did substantial research in geodesy, the branch of mathematics concerned with determining the shape of the earth. In this work, he needed to take observations of the earth's surface and ascertain the mathematical relationship between those observations. He developed approximate equations, but he quickly found that he had more approximate equations than he had variables. In other words, he had an overdetermined system of linear equations.

Legendre began to use the methods of the calculus to solve the system of equations for the "best" values of the variables. He tried to minimize the deviations of the observations from the mean of the observations. He ultimately found a technique for manipulating the sum of the squares of the deviations. This gave the minimum that he needed and enabled him to reduce the overdetermined system of equations to two equations. When solved simultaneously, those equations gave the arbitrary constants in the equation that best described the original observations. The general form of the overdetermined system of linear equations and the least squares equations used to solve that system are shown in the accompanying box.

Legendre was the first to publish the tool of least squares, in *Nouvelles méthodes pour la déter-*

$$a_i x + b_i y + c = 0, \; i = 1, 2, \ldots, n$$

$$\left(\sum a_i^2\right)x + \left(\sum a_i b_i\right)y + \sum a_i c_i = 0$$

$$\left(\sum b_i a_i\right)x + \left(\sum b_i^2\right)y + \sum b_i c_i = 0$$

mination des orbites des comètes (1806). The technique was the most important method in statistics in the nineteenth century, as that discipline grew into maturity. In the twentieth century, its use continued to expand until it was employed in all fields of statistical data analysis. Social scientists, physical scientists, surveyors, and computer scientists are among those who use least squares to fit data to a curve. Their work has been eased by the development of computer programs that carry out the least squares computations.

Bibliography

"An Attack on Gauss, Published by Legendre in 1820." Stephen M. Stigler. *Historia Mathematica* 4 (1977): 31-35.

Linear Least Squares Computations. R. W. Farebrother. New York: Marcel Dekker, 1988.

Practical Handbook of Curve-Fitting. Sandra Lach Arlinghaus, ed. Boca Raton, Fla.: CRC Press, 1994.

Statistics the Easy Way. Douglas Downing and Jeff Clark. 2d ed. New York: Barron's Educational Series, 1989.

In 1794, Legendre proved that π^2 is irrational. He also believed that π could not be expressed as the root of an algebraic coefficient with rational coefficients. This suggestion led to the discovery of different types of irrational numbers.

Legendre also worked on Fermat's last theorem. In 1823, he proved there are no integer solutions to the equation "$x^5 + y^5 = z^5$." Legendre supported the work of Sophie Germain, who authored a theorem which was an impor-

tant step toward the proof of Fermat's last theorem.

Legendre managed to adapt himself to every political system under which he lived, making peace with both Napoleon Bonaparte and then the restored monarchy. Legendre served as examiner in mathematics at the recently founded École Polytechnique from 1799 to 1815. He was elected, in its first year of existence, to the Institut National, which filled the function of the French Académie des Sciences. He reviewed the work of younger institute members and continued to update his own research until his death in 1833.

Bibliography

By Legendre

Theses mathematicae ex analysi, geometria, mecanica exerptae, ex collegio Mazarinaeo, 1770

Recherches sur la trajectoire des projectiles dans les milieux résistants, 1782

Mémoire sur les transcendantes elliptiques, 1793

Éléments de géométrie, avec des notes, 1794 (*Elements of Geometry with Notes,* 1819)

Essai sur la théorie, 1797-1798

Méthodes analytiques pour la détermination d'un arc de méridien, par Delambre et Legendre, 1799

Nouvelles méthodes pour la détermination des orbites des comètes, 1806

Exercices de calcul intégral, 1811-1817 (3 vols.)

Traité des fonctions elliptiques et des intégrales eulériennes, avec des tables pour en faciliter le calcul numérique, 1825-1828 (3 vols.)

About Legendre

"Historical Elegy of Adrien-Marie Legendre." Élie de Beaumont. *Annual Reports of the Smithsonian* (1874): 131-157.

"Legendre's Work." Jeremy Gray. In *Ideas of Space: Euclidean, Non-Euclidean, and Relativistic.* 2d ed. Oxford, England: Clarendon Press, 1989.

Number Theory: An Approach Through History from Hammurapi to Legendre. André Weil. Boston: Birkhäuser, 1984.

(Amy Ackerberg-Hastings)

Gottfried Wilhelm Leibniz

Areas of Achievement: Calculus and mathematical logic

Contribution: Leibniz discovered the calculus and devised notation for it that made its use popular. He also conceived the need for a mathematical logic.

July 1, 1646	Born in Leipzig, Saxony (now Germany)
1661	Enrolls at the University of Leipzig
1663	Graduated with a baccalaureate degree in moral philosophy
1664	Receives a master's degree in law
1667	Earns a doctoral degree in law from University of Altdorf and moves to Nuremburg
1668	Accepts a position in the court of Archbishop Johann Philipp, elector of Mainz
1672-1676	Undertakes a diplomatic mission from Mainz to Paris and studies under Christiaan Huygens
1675	Introduces modern symbols for integration and differentiation and realizes their inverse nature
1676	Becomes the librarian to the court of Duke Johann Friedrich of Hanover
1682	Cofounds *Acta Eruditorum,* a journal to publish ideas in mathematics and natural philosophy
1700	Founds the Berlin Academy of Sciences
Nov. 14, 1716	Dies in Hanover (now Germany)

Early Life

Gottfried Wilhelm Leibniz (pronounced "LIP-nihtz") was the son of Frederick Leibniz, a notary, jurist, and professor of moral philosophy at the University of Leipzig, and his third wife, the former Katherina Schmuck, daughter of a law professor. Gottfried's early childhood was marred by the death of his father in 1652 when the boy was six years old; thereafter, he was raised by his mother. At the age of eight, he was permitted access to his father's library and taught himself Latin by reading many of the classical books contained in it.

In 1661, Leibniz became a student at the University of Leipzig, where the rhetorician and historian Jacob Thomasius supervised his baccalaureate dissertation in moral philosophy in 1663. After graduation, a lengthy visit with a maternal uncle at the University of Jena afforded Leibniz the opportunity to learn the rudiments of geometry from Erhard Weigel.

Leibniz returned to Leipzig from Jena in the fall and received his master's degree in law in 1664. Perhaps owing to his age and inexperience, the faculty at this university denied his admission to candidacy for the Doctor of Law degree in 1666. This rejection and the death of his mother in 1664 ended his ties to Leipzig. Instead, he went to the University of Altdorf, where he defended his dissertation *Disputatio de casibus perplexis* (on difficult problems in the law) and received his doctorate in 1667.

The time of Leibniz's birth was a turbulent one in Germany. The Thirty Years' War (1618-1648) ended two years after his birth; during this conflict, approximately one-third of the population of his homeland was killed. This situation and his youthful reading convinced Leibniz that he wanted a career that would influence policy and politics in government; he did not want to become an academic. Therefore, he turned down an invitation to become a professor at Jena in favor of moving to Nuremburg in the hope of finding a position as a courtier and counselor to a nobleman.

Mainz and Paris

A treatise on law dedicated to the elector of Mainz, Archbishop Johann Philipp, secured for Leibniz a position in his court. There, he accepted the task of recodifying Roman law to

(Library of Congress)

replace Saxon (German) law. Anticipating that France would soon go to war against the Netherlands, the archbishop sent Leibniz and a delegation to Paris in 1672 to dissuade Louis XIV from also attacking Germany.

From Paris in 1673, Leibniz was sent to England on a diplomatic mission. He met Henry Oldenburg, secretary of the Royal Society of London, who arranged for Leibniz to demonstrate a wooden calculating machine that he had made as an improvement on one constructed earlier by Blaise Pascal. Leibniz was elected a Fellow of the society as a result. Discussions with English mathematicians during this visit taught him how ignorant he was of contemporary mathematics. At Leibniz's request, Oldenburg wrote a letter to introduce him to Christiaan Huygens, a dominant figure in the Paris Académie des Sciences. Huygens agreed to tutor Leibniz in mathematics and science; he quickly progressed through the mathematical works of his predecessors.

Notes he wrote in 1675 show that Leibniz had developed the d-notation for the derivative and the integral sign $\int$ for antidifferentiation and that he recognized these to be inverse operations; this is the fundamental theorem of the calculus. Based on these and other achievements, he sought an appointment as a paid member of the Paris academy, but his petition was denied because he was Lutheran rather than Catholic.

The Hanover Period

The death of the elector of Mainz left Leibniz with only a small pension on which to live, so, in 1676, he agreed to become librarian to the court of Duke Johann Friedrich of Hanover. In this position, he was allowed time for research and scholarship; he also provided respected diplomatic and legal advice to the duke. Over the years, however, Leibniz's influence and status in the court deteriorated with each succeeding duke. Nevertheless, he was successful in petitioning on behalf of Hanover for the court to become an elector of the Holy Roman Empire in 1692, and he later argued for George Louis to become King George I of England.

From the beginning, Leibniz had corresponded in writing with other mathematicians and scientists, so when Otto Mencke approached him with the idea of founding a scholarly journal, Leibniz readily agreed. In 1682, they cofounded *Acta Eruditorum* to publish papers on topics in mathematics and sci-

Discovery of the Calculus

Leibniz discovered the calculus and developed a notation for it that enabled other mathematicians to use it effectively.

A calculus is a set of rules or procedures for the calculation or computation of something. The calculus is describable as two sets of such rules or procedures, called differential calculus and integral calculus. The fundamental theorem of calculus shows that one set of these rules is the reverse of the other. Leibniz discovered and named differential calculus, demonstrated the fundamental theorem of calculus, and created an easy-to-use notation for both differential and integral calculus.

Essentially, differential calculus is concerned with finding the instantaneous rate of change of one variable with respect to another; this result is called the derivative of the first variable with respect to the second. One use of the derivative is to determine the tangent line to a plane curve at a specified point. Mathematicians before Leibniz had developed procedures for finding tangents, but no one had produced an effective notation to do so. In an article published in 1684, he did precisely this; so simple and elegant was his notation that it is still widely used today.

In this article, Leibniz used differentials such as *dy* and *dx* and stated all the basic rules for calculating derivatives of simple and more complicated functions. For example, the rule for dif-

ferentiating the product of two functions is stated as "*d(xv) = xdv + vdx*." After stating the rules, Leibniz explained how to use derivatives to find tangents and maximum, minimum, and inflection points for a plane curve. He concluded his paper by introducing the integral sign to represent the reverse of differentiation; the context of its use was the solution of what he called differential equations. For example, he wrote

$$\int x dx = \tfrac{1}{2} xx$$

where *xx* means x^2.

Historically, the second set of rules, integral calculus, arose from finding the area of plane figures bounded by curves. In an article published in 1693, Leibniz states the fundamental theorem of calculus and shows how finding the area under a plane curve is equivalent to finding the tangent line of a curve that can be determined from this area.

Bibliography
Calculus: An Historical Approach. William McGowen Priestley. New York: Springer-Verlag, 1979.

A History of Mathematics. Carl B. Boyer and Uta C. Merzbach. 2d ed. New York: John Wiley & Sons, 1989.

Makers of Mathematics. Stuart Hollingdale. New York: Penguin Books, 1989.

ence. Leibniz contributed many papers to this journal during the rest of his life, and in its pages, in 1684, is found the first published account of the differential calculus. His remarkable paper clearly states all the usual rules for differentiating integer and fractional exponents, along with the product and quotient rules; the notation that he used can be understood by anyone who has studied a modern calculus book.

Leibniz also developed a calculus (or set of rules) for logic in the hope of eliminating difficulties in logical arguments. From this calculus, he successfully proved a number of fundamental theorems. His publication of these ideas, however, was not as well received as that of his mathematical calculus, and two hundred years would pass before his vision for logic would be achieved.

Scientific Societies and Controversy

In 1698, with the death of Ernst August, the first elector of Hanover, Leibniz found himself working for his son George Louis, who described him as a walking encyclopedia. The only use that George Louis wished to make of Leibniz's talents was that of court historian, and for the remainder of his life, this was his official position.

Nevertheless, Leibniz was still given diplomatic assignments, and, during such a visit to Brandenburg-Prussia in 1700, he helped Frederick III found a Brandenburg Science Society. This society later became the Berlin Academy of Sciences. Leibniz was appointed its first member and president for life. In this position, he was able to draw up a charter for what later became the St. Petersburg Academy of Sciences in Russia.

In this same time period, articles began to appear in England accusing Leibniz of having plagiarized Sir Isaac Newton in developing the calculus. It did not seem to matter to the authors of these polemics that Leibniz had published his ideas well before those of Newton were made public in 1705. Ultimately, an investigation by a commission of the Royal Society of London as to who deserved credit for developing the calculus concluded that the discovery was Newton's; it should be noted that Newton authored this report.

Leibniz's final years were spent corresponding with European scientists and writing on the history of the House of Hanover. When Leibniz died in 1716, the only person to attend his funeral was his secretary.

Bibliography
By Leibniz
Nova Methodus pro Maximus et Minimis, itemque Tangentibus, quae nec Irrationales Quantitates Moratur, et Singulare pro illis Calculi Genus in *Acta Eruditorum* 2, 1684 (*A New Method for Maxima and Minima as Well as Tangents, Which Is Neither Impeded by Fractional nor Irrational Quantities, and a Remarkable Calculus for Them* in *Classics of Mathematics*, 1995, Ronald Calinger, ed.)

Supplementum Geometriae Dimensoriae, seu Generalissima Omnium Tetragonismorum Effectio per motumi Similiterque Multiplex Constructio Lineae ex Data tangentium Conditione in *Acta Eruditorum* 12, 1693

Ad Specimen Calculi Universalis Addenda in *Opuscules et fragments inédits de Leibniz*, 1903 (Louis Couturat, ed.)

About Leibniz
Equivalence and Priority: Newton Versus Leibniz. Domenico Bertoloni Meli. New York: Oxford University Press, 1993.

Gottfried Wilhelm Leibniz. Ronald Calinger. Troy, N.Y.: Edwin B. Allen Mathematics Memorial, Rensselaer Polytechnic Institute, 1976.

Leibniz: A Biography. E. J. Aiton. Boston: Adam Hilger, 1985.

(David K. Urion)

Leonardo of Pisa (Leonardo Fibonacci)

Areas of Achievement: Algebra, applied math, arithmetic, and number theory

Contribution: Leonardo of Pisa introduced the use of Arabic numerals into Western culture to replace the awkward Roman numeral system. He taught mathematics and wrote several books with problems in algebra and arithmetic.

c. 1170	Born in Pisa, Italy
c. 1192	Moves to Algeria and learns the Arabic numeral system
c. 1190's	Travels to Egypt, Syria, Greece, and France
c. 1200 to the 1230's	Teaches mathematics in Pisa
c. 1202	Publishes a treatise on numerical computations and algebra
c. 1202	Develops the Fibonacci series to solve the "rabbit problem"
the 1220's	Competes with John of Palermo in mathematical puzzles
c. 1225	Meets Emperor Frederick II of Sicily
c. 1225	Solves a cubic equation by numerical methods
c. 1240	Receives a plaque and honorarium from the Pisa city council
c. 1240	Dies in Pisa, Italy

Early Life

Leonardo Fibonacci (pronounced "fee-boh-NAWT-chee") was born in Pisa, northern Italy; he is often called Leonardo of Pisa or Leonardo Pisano, although his mathematical discoveries bear the name "Fibonacci." The son of a well-to-do government official, he received a traditional education in the seven liberal arts: grammar, rhetoric (speech), logic, arithmetic, geometry, astronomy, and music. He learned to read and write Latin, the language of the intellectual class.

Pisa was a leading commercial center in the twelfth century, with custom houses to collect duty on imports. Scribes kept handwritten records of goods received or shipped out. Much of the trade was with Arabic merchants from Syria, North Africa, and Spain.

In the early 1190's, Leonardo's father moved to Algeria as a representative for the merchants of Pisa. Leonardo learned to speak and read Arabic there. While on business trips to Damascus, Baghdad, and elsewhere, he learned about Arab culture, which had advanced well beyond Western Europe during its Dark Ages.

From Roman to Arabic Numerals

In Leonardo's time, Roman numerals had been used for more than a thousand years. They worked well for recording the number of items received and for adding or subtracting from the total. Multiplication and division, however, were quite impractical.

Suppose that a merchant received twelve barrels of oil, each one worth 75 denarii, and the customs officer was to collect an 8 percent import duty. An abacus (sliding beads on a wire frame) was used to calculate 12 times 75 and then take 8 percent. None of the figuring was written down, only the result. The only way to check for accuracy was to repeat the calculation.

In his travels through the Arab world, Leonardo became aware of their number system, using digits from zero to 9. A number such as three hundred eighty-seven could be represented by only three digits, 387. Writing it in Roman numerals, CCCLXXXVII, required ten symbols. In his book *Liber Abaci* (1202; book of computation), Leonardo promoted the advantages of Arabic numerals and showed how the basic operations of addition, subtraction, multiplication, and division could be applied to practical problems.

Algebra and Number Theory

Leonardo also broke new ground in algebra and number theory. He showed how to solve two equations in two unknowns. He was able

The Fibonacci Series

The Fibonacci series is a sequence of numbers in which each one is the sum of the preceding two numbers: 1, 2, 3, 5, 8, 13, 21, 34 . . . . This series has remarkable applications in architecture, geometry, and biology.

In his book *Liber Abaci* (1202), Leonardo of Pisa presents a puzzle for the reader: How many pairs of rabbits can be produced in a year starting with a single pair? Assume that every month, each pair begets a new pair, which becomes productive from the second month on.

At the start, there is one pair. After one month, a new pair is born, making two pairs. After two months, one additional pair is produced by the original rabbits, giving three pairs. After another month, the original pair and the first month's offspring each produce a new pair, giving a total of five. Continuing this series for twelve steps, one obtains 377 rabbit pairs after twelve months.

In the seventeenth century, mathematicians began to study the properties of number sequences. The Fibonacci series was found to have an interesting result if one forms ratios of successive terms. The ratios $\frac{1}{2}$, $\frac{2}{3}$, $\frac{3}{5}$, $\frac{5}{8}$, $\frac{8}{13}$, $\frac{13}{21}$, $\frac{21}{34}$ . . . gradually approach a fixed value of 0.618. . . . This number is equal to the "divine proportion" of Greek antiquity. In the design of the Parthenon and other temples, the ratio of height to width was chosen to be 0.618 . . . because it formed a pleasing proportion.

An interesting geometric puzzle is to determine the height and width of a rectangle ABCD, such that when a square is subtracted, the remaining area will have the same relative dimensions as the original rectangle. The original rectangle must have a height to width ratio of 0.618 . . . , exactly equal to the divine proportion.

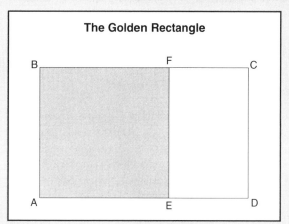

The Golden Rectangle

If the ratio of height to width in the rectangle ABCD is exactly 0.618, and if a square is subtracted, the remaining rectangle CDEF has the same height-to-width ratio.

Some surprising examples of Fibonacci numbers have been found in spiral patterns of plant growth. For example, the skin of an ordinary pineapple has intersecting swirls of eight and thirteen rows. The seeds in a large sunflower head form intersecting spirals with fifty-five and eighty-nine rows, respectively.

In 1963, a group of mathematicians formed the Fibonacci Society, which publishes a quarterly research journal. The Fibonacci series continues to be a fertile source of interesting mathematical patterns.

Bibliography

Fascinating Fibonaccis: Mystery and Magic in Numbers. Trudi Hammel Garland. Palo Alto, Calif.: Dale Seymour, 1987.
The Main Stream of Mathematics. Edna E. Kramer. New York: Oxford University Press, 1955.
Mathematics. David Bergamini and the editors of *Life.* New York: Time, 1963.

to solve quadratic equations by the method of completing the square, as it is taught to students today. He noted that successive integers squared (1, 4, 9, 16, 25, . . .) differ by the sequence of odd numbers (3, 5, 7, 9 . . .).

In Leonardo's time, the use of x and y for unknown quantities was not established yet. Algebraic equations had to be written out in words. Also, symbols for arithmetic operations did not come into use until two hundred years later. In spite of these handicaps, Leonardo was able to solve challenging problems.

A sample problem from *Liber Abaci* is the following:

A king sent thirty men into his orchard to plant trees. If they set out 1,000 trees in nine days, how many days would it take thirty-six men to plant 4,400 trees? (The answer is thirty-three.)

Other examples are given in the book *Leonard of Pisa and the New Mathematics of the Middle Ages* (1969), by Joseph and Frances Gies.

An Imperial Mathematics Competition

Emperor Frederick II of Sicily was known for his interest in the arts and other intellectual pursuits. In 1225, he traveled to northern Italy with his retinue of scholars, entertainers, and exotic animals. Leonardo was introduced at court, where he was given three problems by the chief mathematician, John of Palermo.

One of the problems was to solve a cubic equation. In modern notation, it would be written as "$x^3 + 2x^2 + 10x = 20$." Leonardo showed that x had to be between 1 and 2: If $x = 1$, then "$x^3 + 2x^2 + 10x$" would be less than 20; if $x = 2$, then it would be more than 20. By continued trial and error, he narrowed down his answer correct to six decimal places.

Leonardo was a man of outstanding intellectual ability and curiosity. He was a contemporary of St. Francis of Assisi. Through their respective contributions to mathematics and religious faith, they helped to bring Europe out of the Dark Ages.

Bibliography

By Leonardo of Pisa

Liber Abaci, 1202; rev. ed. 1228 (book of computation)
Practica geometriae, 1220 (practice of geometry)
Flos, 1225 (flower)
Liber quadratorum, 1225 (*The Book of Squares*, 1987)

About Leonardo of Pisa

"Fibonacci, Leonardo, or Leonardo of Pisa." Kurt Vogel. In *Dictionary of Scientific Biography*, edited by Charles Coulston Gillispie. New York: Charles Scribner's Sons, 1981.
History of Mathematics. David Eugene Smith. Boston: Ginn, 1923.
Leonard of Pisa and the New Mathematics of the Middle Ages. Joseph Gies and Frances Gies. New York: Thomas Y. Crowell, 1969.

(Hans G. Graetzer)

Joseph Liouville

Areas of Achievement: Algebra, calculus, and number theory
Contribution: Liouville discovered transcendental numbers, started a major French mathematical journal, and studied differential and integral equations.

Mar. 24, 1809	Born in Saint-Omer, Pas-de-Calais, France
1825	Admitted to the École Polytechnique
1827	Transferred to the École des Ponts et Chaussées
1830	Graduated with an engineering degree
1831	Accepts a faculty position at the École Polytechnique
1831	Marries Marie-Louise Balland
1836	Receives a doctorate
1836	Founds the *Journal de Mathématiques Pures et Appliquées*
1839	Elected a member of the Académie des Sciences
1844	Presents his work on transendental numbers
1848	Elected as a representative to the Constituent Assembly
1849	Loses a reelection bid to the Constituent Assembly
1851	Accepts a faculty position at the Collège de France
1874	Resigns as editor of the *Journal de Mathématiques Pures et Appliquées*
Sept. 8, 1882	Dies in Paris, France

Early Life

Joseph Liouville (pronounced "lyoo-VEEL") was born the second son to Claude-Joseph

Liouville, a French army officer, and Thérèse Balland. He attended school in Commercy and then in Toul. In 1825, Liouville was admitted to the École Polytechnique. He transferred to the École des Ponts et Chaussées to pursue an intended career in engineering, but he soon began original research in mathematics. He found his mathematics research more interesting than the applied mathematics of engineering. He received his doctorate in 1836.

Liouville continued his work in mathematics with only a one-year interruption, from April, 1848, to May, 1849, when he served as an elected representative to the Constituent Assembly. After his defeat in the election of 1849, he never returned to politics.

Liouville's Journal
In the 1830's, there were no French-language journals in which mathematicians might publish their works. Although French mathematicians might publish in German or English journals, Liouville believed that it would be preferable if a French-language journal were available.

Liouville's Theorem

Liouville's theorem states that a function which is bounded and analytic throughout the complex plane must be a constant.

Most students of complex analysis are familiar with Liouville's theorem, the proof of which is frequently assigned as a homework problem. Complex numbers are those numbers that contain both real and imaginary parts. Imaginary numbers are those which are multiples of i, where i is the square root of −1.

Analytic functions are those for which a derivative exists. Bounded functions are functions whose absolute values are less than the constant

$$|f(z)| < M$$

Thus, a bounded function cannot approach infinity anywhere.

A proof of Liouville's theorem can be made by using Cauchy's inequality for a single derivative, proposed by Augustin-Louis Cauchy:

$$|f'(z)| \leq \frac{M}{r}$$

For a function analytic at all points in the complex plane, a derivative exists everywhere. Taking the limit as the magnitude of the complex number goes to infinity, the magnitude of the derivative goes to zero. Since only a constant has a derivative equal to zero everywhere, then the function $f(z)$ must be a constant.

One application of Liouville's theorem is its use to prove the fundamental theorem of algebra, which states that every polynomial of at least order one has a root. In other words,

$$P(z) = a_0 + a_1 z + a_2 z^2 + \ldots + a_n z^n = 0$$

where n is greater than or equal to 1 and a_n is not equal to zero.

To prove the fundamental theorem of algebra using Liouville's theorem, one first postulates the antithesis of the fundamental theorem—that is, one assumes that a polynomial does not have a root. In this case, then, a function given by the equation "$f(z) = 1/P(z)$" is analytic and bounded for all values of z. In this case, the function $f(z)$ must be a constant by Liouville's theorem. If $f(z)$ is constant, then the polynomial must also be a constant. This is clearly a contradiction for a polynomial with nonzero coefficients. Therefore, the assumption that the polynomial has no roots must be false, thus proving the fundamental theorem of algebra.

In addition to its use in a new proof of the fundamental theorem of algebra, Liouville's theorem is used in several aspects of physics, notably in the computation of potentials.

Bibliography
Advanced Calculus. Wilfred Kaplan. 3d ed. Reading, Mass.: Addison-Wesley, 1984.

Advanced Engineering Mathematics. Erwin Kreyszig. 4th ed. New York: John Wiley & Sons, 1979.

Schaum's Outline of Theory and Problems of Complex Variables. Murray R. Spiegel. New York: McGraw-Hill, 1964.

Following his receipt of his doctorate, Liouville founded a new French mathematical journal, the *Journal de Mathématiques Pures et Appliquées*, in 1836. Soon known as the *Journal de Liouville*, it quickly became a major source for mathematical publications. The *Journal de Mathématiques Pures et Appliquées* was open to studies in both pure and applied mathematics. Many of the great names in nineteenth century mathematics published papers in the journal. Liouville remained its editor until his retirement in 1874.

Teaching
After his graduation from the École des Ponts et Chaussées in 1830, Liouville turned down an offer for a job as an engineer in order to pursue a teaching career. In 1831, he accepted a position at the École Polytechnique. From 1833 to 1838, Liouville also taught mathematics and mechanics at the École Centrale des Arts et Manufactures.

In 1851, Liouville accepted a faculty position at the Collège de France. This post had no set duties, so Liouville was free to teach mathematical topics of personal interest. He retired from this position in 1879.

During the last ten years of his career, Liouville became less productive in mathematical research. Soon after his retirement from the Collège de France, he ceased to be a factor in the French mathematical community. He died in 1882 at the age of seventy-three.

Mathematical Investigations
One of Liouville's more memorable contributions to mathematics was in the area of transcendental numbers. Transcendental numbers are numbers that cannot be roots of polynomials having rational coefficients. Liouville showed that entire classes of transcendental numbers exist. In particular, he showed that both the numbers e and e^2 cannot be solutions of any linear or quadratic equation. (The expression e is the exponential function.) Later mathematicians expanded upon Liouville's discovery of transcendental numbers, including Charles Hermite, who showed in 1873 that all expressions containing e are transcendental.

In 1840, Liouville offered a proof of the fundamental theorem of algebra. This theorem asserts that any polynomial with nonzero rational coefficients has at least one root.

With the Swiss mathematician Jacques-Charles-François Sturm, Liouville investigated the properties and solutions of differential equations. This work led to the recognition of a set of boundary value problems, called Sturm-Liouville problems, that are important in mathematical physics.

Liouville also worked with integral equations. In particular, he studied expressions containing complex numbers. Complex numbers are those containing i, the square root of -1. His work in complex numbers led to Liouville's theorem. It states that if a function of a complex number is bounded and analytic for all complex numbers, then that function must be a constant.

Bibliography
By Liouville
Sur le développement des fonctions ou parties des fonctions en séries de sinus et de cosinus, dont on

fait usage dans un grand nombre de questions de mécanique et de physique, 1836
Journal de Mathématiques Pures et Appliquées, 1836-1874 (as editor)
Résumé des leçons de trigonométrie, 1838
Résumé des leçons d'analyse données à l'École Polytechnique, by Claude-Louis-Marie-Henri Navier, 1840 (as editor)
Application de l'analyse à la géométrie, by Gaspard Monge, 1850 (5th ed.; as editor)

About Liouville

Asimov's Biographical Encyclopedia of Science and Technology. Isaac Asimov. 2d rev. ed. Garden City, N.Y.: Doubleday, 1982.
A History of Mathematics. Carl B. Boyer. New York: John Wiley & Sons, 1968.
A History of Mathematics. Florian Cajori. 3d ed. New York: Chelsea House, 1980.
"Joseph Liouville." G. Chrystal. *Proceedings of the Royal Society of Edinburgh* 14 (1888): 83-91.

(Raymond D. Benge, Jr.)

Nikolay Ivanovich Lobachevsky

Area of Achievement: Geometry
Contribution: Lobachevsky established that there could be consistent systems of geometry based on postulates other than those of Euclid. He thus discovered and developed non-Euclidean geometry.

Dec. 1, 1792	Born in Nizhny Novgorod, Russia
1807	Enters Kazan University
1811	Earns a master's degree in physics and mathematics from Kazan
1812	Becomes assistant professor in physical and mathematical sciences at Kazan
1822	Appointed Ordinary Professor and begins his administrative career at Kazan
1820-1821, 1823-1825	Serves as dean of the department of physics and mathematics at Kazan
1827-1846	Serves as rector (president) of Kazan University
1829-1830	Publishes his first work on a non-Euclidean system of geometry
1832	Marries Lady Varvara Aleksivna Moisieva
1837	Raised to hereditary nobility in recognition of his mathematical work
1846	Dismissed from his professorial appointment at Kazan
1855	Publishes an account of his "pan-geometry" with the Kazan University Press
Feb. 24, 1856	Dies in Kazan, Russia

(Library of Congress)

Early Life

Nikolay Ivanovich Lobachevsky (pronounced "loh-buh-CHEHF-skee") was the son of Ivan Maksimovich Lobachevsky, a government clerk and a peasant of Polish descent, and Praskovia Aleksandrovna Lobachevskaya. When Nikolay was six, his father died. Without an income, his mother moved to Kazan, Russia, in 1800. She enrolled her sons in the local grammar school, which awarded public scholarships.

Lobachevsky spent the rest of his life in Kazan, a city located in the remote Asiatic hinterland. The Russian government offered educational support and money to Kazan because it wanted to aid in the spread of Russian influence in this area of Islamic culture. Thus, universal public education, and the public scholarship that allowed Lobachevsky to attend school, were government policy.

As a student, Lobachevsky was independent-minded, stubborn, and relentless. He was often disciplined by school officials. His teachers, however, saw his potential in mathematics and helped him to graduate. In 1807, Lobachevsky entered the University of Kazan, where he spent the next forty years of his life as student, professor, and president.

Developing Non-Euclidean Geometry

Although Lobachevsky lived in a remote area and never studied in or traveled to the West, he made a conceptual leap that had eluded geometers for centuries. At Kazan, there were not enough Russian teachers, so they were brought from Western Europe. Lobachevsky's main teacher was the German Johann Martin Christian Bartels, who was a part of the European mathematical community. Bartels provided Lobachevsky with the basic stance of early nineteenth century mathematics, which was to examine fundamental beliefs critically.

In 1811, Lobachevsky received a master's degree from Kazan, and he was appointed assistant professor there in 1812. For centuries, geometry had been based on Euclid's work, but no one had effectively proved Euclid's fifth, or parallel, postulate. Between 1813 and 1817, Lobachevsky tried to work some proofs of this postulate into his lectures and a textbook that he was writing. Work on the textbook, however, convinced him that the attempts were futile. He went from trying to perfect and prove the Euclidean system of geometry to building a new one.

By 1826, Lobachevsky had developed a non-Euclidean alternative geometry and presented a paper on the subject to the department of physics and mathematics at Kazan. He called his new system "imaginary geometry," meaning simply that it was distinct from another system. In Lobachevsky's geometry, Euclid's parallel postulate was false, which went against centuries of accepted fact in mathematics.

Administrative and Educational Work

During his lifetime, Lobachevsky was praised in Russia for his educational and administrative work, not his mathematical work. In 1825, he became university librarian at Kazan and curator of the university museum. In both cases, he cleaned up chaotic messes.

In the 1820's, a conservative backlash in Russia threatened Kazan University. Several faculty members were dismissed. Lobachevsky kept his faculty position, probably because he was working in mathematics, an area that the politicians did not understand and thought of as nonpolitical. In Russia, mathematics was often a sanctuary from political oppression.

By 1827, Lobachevsky had become rector, or president, of Kazan University, and the university thrived. In 1830, he led an effective fight against cholera by implementing sanitary regulations at the university. In 1842, he fought to keep the university open after a great fire on campus; it was rebuilt within two years.

Lack of Recognition

Lobachevsky's mathematical work was little recognized during his lifetime. Even mathematicians at the Russian Academy of Science did not understand his achievement and reviewed his work badly. His work was only published in Russia in 1829-1830 in a journal at the University of Kazan.

Eventually, politics caught up with Lobachevsky, and he was dismissed from his position at the university in 1846. He was blind for approximately the last ten years of his life. Mathematics remained his sanctuary and refuge. In his final years, he dictated his final work, on "pan-geometry," to an assistant. It was published by Kazan University in 1855-1856. Lobachevsky died without having received one word of public approval from any of the leading mathematicians of his time.

Bibliography

By Lobachevsky
"O nachalakh geometrii" (on the foundations of geometry), *Kazanski viestnik*, 1829-1830

A New Geometry

Lobachevsky was the first mathematician to publish a description of a non-Euclidean system of geometry.

Lobachevsky's new geometry made him "Copernicus of geometry": It shattered self-evident truths that had reigned in mathematics for centuries by proving that there could be consistent systems of geometry based on postulates other than those of Euclid. János Bolyai and Carl Friedrich Gauss also developed non-Euclidean geometries in the nineteenth century, but they were reluctant to publish and develop their work because it was such a strong break with the mathematical tradition in Europe.

For centuries, geometers had been concerned with Euclid's fifth postulate: Through a point external to a line, one and only one parallel can be drawn. In other words, given a line and a point not on it, one can draw through the point one and only one coplanar line not intersecting the given line. Lobachevsky, Gauss, and Bolyai made different assumptions about the number of possible parallels to a given line, and they developed different, but universal and rigorous, geometries.

Lobachevskian geometry accepts all of Euclid's postulates except the fifth one. Lobachevskian geometry assumes that through a point external to a given line, an infinite number of parallels can be drawn. Euclidean geometry holds if one assumes that the earth is flat, or on a plane. (For small areas, this works fine.) Lobachevskian geometry works on a curved surface, or sphere, with two lines always meeting in one direction and diverging in the other. In this case, there is not one but two parallels through a fixed point to a given straight line. Neither of them meets the line to which both are parallel, nor does any straight line drawn through the fixed point and lying within the angle formed by the two parallels.

Lobachevsky's work was only widely accepted after the work of physicist Albert Einstein, whose general theory of relativity showed that the geometry of space-time is non-Euclidean. For most uses, the differences between Euclid's geometry and Lobachevsky's are minuscule. Euclidean geometry is used as a special case for everyday purposes. Although Earth is a sphere, a small section of its surface can be studied effectively with Euclidean geometry even if it is assumed to be flat.

Bibliography

An Introduction to Non-Euclidean Geometry. David Gans. New York: Academic Press, 1973.
Non-Euclidean Geometry. Roberto Bonola. La Salle, Ill.: Open Court, 1955.
Non-Euclidean Geometry. Lillian R. Lieber. 2d ed. Lancaster, Pa.: Science Press Printing, 1940.

"Algebra ili ischislenie konechnykh," 1834 (algebra, or calculus of finites)

"Voobrazhaemaya geometriya" (imaginary geometry), *Uchenye zapiski*, 1835

"Primenenie voobrazhaemoi geometrii k nekotorym integralam" (application of imaginary geometry to certain integrals), *Uchenye zapiski*, 1836

Geometrische Untersuchungen zur Theorie der Parallellinien, 1840 (*Geometrical Researches on the Theory of Parallels*, 1891)

Pangéométrie, 1855-1856 (pan-geometry)

About Lobachevsky

Men of Mathematics. E. T. Bell. New York: Simon & Schuster, 1937.

N. Lobachevsky and His Contribution to Science. V. F. Kagan. Moscow: Foreign Languages, 1957.

"Nikolai Ivanovich Lobachevskii: The Man Behind the First Non-Euclidean Geometry." Alexander Vucinich. *Isis* 53, part 4, no. 174 (December, 1962): 465-481.

Science in Russia and the Soviet Union: A Short History. Loren R. Graham. Cambridge, England: Cambridge University Press, 1993.

(*Linda Eikmeier Endersby*)

Augusta Ada Lovelace

Area of Achievement: Mathematical logic

Contribution: Lovelace linked Charles Babbage's Analytical Engine to its potential use for sound and graphics and provided what has come to be termed the first "computer program."

Dec. 10, 1815	Born in Piccadilly Terrace, Middlesex (now in London), England
1832	Meets Mary Fairfax Somerville
1833	Meets Charles Babbage
1834	Marries William Lord King, who will become the earl of Lovelace
1843	Translates L. F. Menabrea's paper describing Babbage's Analytical Engine
Nov. 27, 1852	Dies in London, England

Early Years

Augusta Ada Byron was born to the famous poet Lord Byron (George Gordon) and Anna Isabella Millbanke Byron, on December 10, 1815, in London. Her parents' marriage was over when Ada was only five weeks old. Lady Byron asked for a formal separation and sole custody of her child. Lord Byron never saw his daughter again. The story of the love triangle between Byron, his wife, and his half-sister, Augusta, has become a legend. Augusta, for whom Ada was named, was Lord Byron's mistress before and during his marriage. As a parting shot, he wrote, "When shall we three meet again?" Infuriated, Ada's mother made Augusta's life a nightmare with her relentless vindictiveness.

Ada Byron had her father's good looks and poetic mind. Her mathematics was often laced with imagination and described metaphorically. Lady Byron, terrified that Ada might become a poet, focused on her daughter's mathematical skills, which soon exceeded her mother's mathematical abilities. Her mother, a domineering hypochondriac, was detested by the entire household staff for her fits of rage and harsh treatment of her daughter. As Ada outgrew the need for a governess, her love of learning prompted her to further her education through self-study. Augustus De Morgan, a professor at the University of London, helped Ada in her advanced studies, writing that he had never had a student who mastered a concept so quickly yet so completely.

From Teenager to Wife to Mother

At the age of seventeen, Ada Byron met another female mathematician, Mary Fairfax Somerville, who became a friend, encourager, and mentor. Somerville endeavored to put mathematics and technology in an appropriate context for Byron. It was Somerville's son who introduced Byron to her future husband, Lord William King, who was eleven years her senior. After their marriage, he became the earl of Lovelace, thus elevating her to the title of Lady Lovelace.

The earl was very proud of his wife's abilities and accomplishments, recognizing her intellectual superiority. Unlike the marriage of Ada's parents, theirs was one of love and caring. They had three children, two sons and a daughter. Ada allowed others to take the responsibility for the rearing of her children, as her mother had done with her. Although she had felt abandonment as a child, she was careful to never let her children experience those feelings.

Collaboration with Babbage

At a dinner party in the home of Somerville, in November, 1834, Ada Lovelace heard Charles Babbage's ideas of a new concept for a calculating engine, which he called the Analytical Engine. It was his conjecture that this engine could foresee and then act on what it foresaw. Although hardly anyone else was impressed, Lovelace was intrigued by the unlimited possibilities of Babbage's ideas. Their common interest in mathematics and her eagerness to continue her studies of the subject developed into a friendship that flourished through the mail.

Lovelace, even more than Babbage, clearly understood the limitations of the machine. In her final letter to Babbage concerning her

(Archive Photos)

translation of L. F. Menabrea's paper on the Analytical Engine, she wrote that the engine had no possibility for originating anything on its own and could do only what a human knows how to order it to perform. It was her suggestion that a plan be written for how the engine might calculate Bernoulli numbers, which is now regarded as the first "computer program."

After Math

Lovelace made no other significant contribution in mathematics after the publication of her work on Babbage's engine. Although it was unacceptable for a woman to write scientific or technical papers, she was determined to receive credit for her hard work. Her intellectual ability was proved when she definitively signed herself "A.L.L." (Ada, Lady Lovelace).

On November 27, 1852, Lovelace succumbed to internal cancer; she died at thirty-six years of age, like her father. During the last year of her illness, she was able to put aside the

The Analytical Engine

Charles Babbage designed and drew plans for the calculating engine that would be the forerunner of the modern computer. Lovelace encouraged his attempts to design and construct it and made extensive notes on its workings.

The Analytical Engine had four basic parts. The first was the "store" in which the numerical data would be placed. Second was the "mill," the part in which arithmetical operations would be carried out by the rotation of gears and wheels. Third was a device, a collection of gears and levers that transferred numbers back and forth between the mill and the store. Finally, there was a mechanism for getting numerical data in and out.

The engine, in theory, would perform any arithmetic operation and string these operations together to solve any conceivable arithmetic problem. All operations would be mechanical and would involve the machinations of large collections of gears and cranks run by steam.

The method for getting data in and out of the machine was the use of punch cards, much like those used by the French inventor Joseph-Marie Jacquard for weaving patterns in rugs. The cards had patterns of holes to correspond to mathematical symbols. Thus, the Analytical Engine, in essence, wove algebraic patterns, just as the Jacquard loom wove patterns of flowers and leaves. By means of the cards, the machine could be programmed to do most of its operations automatically.

It was the conjecture of Babbage that this engine could foresee and then act on what it foresaw. Any operation in the scope of mathematics could be performed by this engine, in the opinion of its designer. Babbage had a clear understanding of one of the most extraordinary and valuable abilities of automatic computers, the ability to perform the conditional operation. He also recognized the need for having special mathematical data stored in an external memory and accessible to the engine on demand. The Analytical Engine was equipped with a series of bells that would sound if a particular element of data was needed. A card would be displayed at the window of the engine asking for the special data. If the operator input the wrong data, another bell would ring even louder. Although nearly forty years was spent trying to build the Analytical Engine, it was never completed.

Bibliography

The Analytical Engine: Computers—Past, Present, and Future. Jeremy Bernstein. New York: William Morrow, 1981.

Charles Babbage: Father of the Computer. Daniel Stephen Halacy. New York: Crowell-Collier, 1970.

Charles Babbage: Pioneer of the Computer. Anthony Hyman. Princeton, N.J.: Princeton University Press, 1982.

Computers: The Machines We Think With. Daniel Stephen Halacy. New York: Harper & Row, 1962.

Passages from the Life of a Philosopher. Charles Babbage. London: Green, Longmans, Roberts, and Green, 1864.

hatred for her father. At her request, she was buried in the Byron family vault in Hucknall Torkard Church in Nottinghamshir, beside him.

The world forgot about Ada Byron Lovelace after her death. After computers became more valuable in science and technology, however, her work was reexamined. In tribute to her extraordinary work and insight into the future, a high-level universal computer programming language was developed in the early 1980's by the U.S. Department of Defense and named ADA.

Bibliography

By Lovelace

"Sketch of the Analytical Engine Invented by Charles Babbage, Esq., by L. F. Menabrea of Turin, Officer of the Military Engineers," *Taylor's Scientific Memoirs* 29, 1843 (as translator, with extensive notes)

About Lovelace

Ada, Countess of Lovelace: Byron's Legitimate Daughter. Doris Langley Moore. New York: Harper & Row, 1977.

Ada, the Enchantress of Numbers. Betty A. Toole. Sausilito, Calif.: Strawberry Press, 1992.

The Calculating Passion of Ada Byron. Joan Baum. Hamden, Conn.: Archon Books/The Shoe String Press, 1986.

(*Margaret A. Haines*)

Colin Maclaurin

Areas of Achievement: Algebra, calculus, and geometry

Contribution: Maclaurin made advances in the treatment of plane curves in geometry and also attempted to prove Isaac Newton's "fluxions" rigorously. One unintended result of his defense of Newton was that other mathematicians turned from analytical techniques to solely geometric methods in doing calculus.

Feb., 1698	Born in Kilmodan, Argyll, Scotland
1709	Enters the University of Glasgow
1715	Receives a master's degree
1717	Appointed a professor of mathematics at Marischal College
1719	Meets Isaac Newton in London
1719	Elected a Fellow of the Royal Society of London
1722	Becomes a tutor to Lord Polworth's son
1724	Receives a prize from the French Académie des Sciences
1725	Named the chair of mathematics at the University of Edinburgh
1733	Marries Anne Stewart
1740	Shares the Académie des Sciences prize with Daniel Bernoulli and Leonhard Euler
1745	Helps with the defense of Edinburgh against Bonnie Prince Charlie
Jan. 14, 1746	Dies in Edinburgh, Scotland

Early Life

Colin Maclaurin (pronounced "muh-KLOHR-un") was the son of a minister who died six weeks after Colin's birth. Maclaurin's mother

(Library of Congress)

passed away when he was only nine years old, leaving him to be raised by his uncle, Daniel. In his uncle's household, Maclaurin grew up to have an appreciation of nature and a belief in God's perfection.

At the age of eleven, Maclaurin entered the University of Glasgow. He learned ancient Greek geometry and Isaac Newton's natural philosophy from Robert Simson. Maclaurin earned a master of arts degree for his thesis, "On the Power of Gravity," in which he defended the work of Newton. Then, at the unusually young age of nineteen, he was appointed professor of mathematics at Marischal College in Aberdeen, Scotland. During this time, Maclaurin traveled to London, where he met Newton and other important British natural philosophers (scientists). In 1722, even though he was still a professor in Aberdeen, Maclaurin began to travel with the son of Lord Polworth as the boy's tutor.

A Disciple of Newton

Lord Polworth's son died suddenly in 1724, but Maclaurin's absence from Marischal had led college officials to declare his chair vacant. Through the help of his friends in science, Maclaurin began to assist the professor of mathematics at the University of Edinburgh, replacing him when he died the next year. Maclaurin proved to be an excellent lecturer with well-attended classes.

Maclaurin's mastery of Newton's results in geometry had already been shown in his first book, the *Geometrica Organica* (1720), in which he improved Newton's treatment of plane curves. Maclaurin also vigorously defended Newton's development of the calculus and its notation, which he called "fluxions."

In 1734, Bishop George Berkeley published a tract called *The Analyst*, which argued that the calculus was no less based on faith than religion was. In part as a response to Berkeley, Maclaurin authored the first systematic account of fluxions in *The Treatise of Fluxions*, published in 1742. He included a number of new results in this work, such as the integral test for convergence of an infinite series. Yet, the most important feature of this treatise may be that it laid out the geometrical foundations of fluxions so well that it influenced British mathematicians to neglect the analytic notation for calculus for the next one hundred years.

Maclaurin's work in calculus and geometry earned for him international recognition. He won two prizes from the French Académie des Sciences, and, since his death, he has been considered the outstanding British mathematician of the eighteenth century.

In spite of his achievements in geometry, Maclaurin is perhaps most famous for the Maclaurin series. This series, however, is only a special case of the Taylor series, published by Brook Taylor in 1715 and also known by other mathematicians. Maclaurin himself stated that this particular theorem was not original to him, so it is somewhat an accident of history that he was credited with a separate formula.

Final Works

Maclaurin spent much of his life writing an extension of Newton's work on algebra. One of Maclaurin's more unique developments was the method of using determinants to solve simultaneous equations, which later became known as Cramer's rule after Gabriel Cramer. Although Maclaurin began working on *A Treatise of Algebra* around 1729, the book was not published until 1748, after his death. The last paragraphs of his final work, *An Account of Sir Isaac Newton's Philosophical Discoveries* (1748), were actually dictated from his deathbed.

Maclaurin had married in 1733. Seven children were born to the union, of which two sons and three daughters survived Maclaurin. He helped construct fortifications around Edinburgh in defense against Jacobite rebels in 1745. He later was forced to flee the city before the rebels were finally defeated, and the stress

The Foundations of the Calculus

In his exposition of Isaac Newton's "fluxions," Maclaurin made one of the first attempts to establish mathematical rigor for the calculus.

Mathematicians need to know how and why mathematical techniques work, so they try to demonstrate that mathematical statements have logical soundness. Although standards of rigor have changed over time, the necessity of some sort of proof in mathematical writings has remained the same. Thus, Maclaurin's *The Treatise of Fluxions* (1742) can be seen as an effort to give Newton's fluxions sound mathematical foundations.

Maclaurin's approach was to show that fluxions were based on constructions from ancient Greek geometry that had stood the test of time, especially the method of exhaustion. For example, he appealed to the geometry and algebra related to the accompanying diagram in order to demonstrate the validity of the differential triangle.

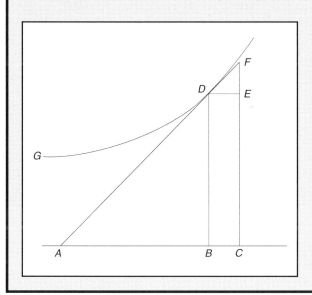

DF is tangent to the curve G at D. DE is parallel to AC, and EF is parallel to BD. Maclaurin proved by contradiction that the increase in the curve G from D to F was neither less than nor greater than EF. In other words, the increase in the curve is equal to EF. This means that Maclaurin used the fluxion (the rate of change for a function) of the area under the curve to determine the function describing the curve. Thus, in this example, he proved a special case of the fundamental theorem of the calculus.

Maclaurin's in-depth, geometrical treatment proved to be too tedious for most eighteenth century mathematicians, who preferred the ease and power of the algebraic tools associated with the differential notation for the calculus. Maclaurin also used definitions that are no longer accepted by mathematicians for some of the key terms, such as "tangent." When the foundations of analysis again became of general concern in the nineteenth century, mathematicians such as Augustin-Louis Cauchy approached the problem with different methods, most notably the theory of limits. By the twentieth century, mathematicians used even more sophisticated standards of rigor based on the work of Bernhard Bolzano and Karl Weierstrass, among others.

Bibliography
Advanced Calculus: An Introduction to Analysis. Watson Fulks. 3d ed. New York: John Wiley & Sons, 1978.
Foundations of Analysis: The Theory of Limits. Herbert S. Gaskill and P. P. Narayanaswami. New York: Harper & Row, 1989.
The Higher Calculus: A History of Real and Complex Analysis from Euler to Weierstrass. Umberto Bottazzini. Translated by Warren Van Egmond. New York: Springer-Verlag, 1986.

of this trip helped to bring on his final illness. He died in January, 1746.

Bibliography
By Maclaurin

Geometrica Organica, sive descriptio linearum curvarum universalis, 1720

The Treatise of Fluxions, 1742 (2 vols.)

An Account of Sir Isaac Newton's Philosophical Discoveries, 1748

A Treatise of Algebra, 1748

The Collected Letters of Colin Maclaurin, 1982 (Stella Mills, ed.)

About Maclaurin

Bi-Centenary of the Death of Colin Maclaurin (1698-1746). Herbert Westren Trumbull. Aberdeen, Scotland: The University Press, 1951.

"The Controversy Between Colin MacLaurin and George Campbell over Complex Roots, 1728-1729." Stella Mills. *Archive for History of Exact Sciences* 28 (1983): 149-164.

The Development of Newtonian Calculus in Britain, 1700-1800. Niccolo Guicciardini. Cambridge, England: Cambridge University Press, 1989.

"Was Newton's Calculus a Dead End?: The Continental Influence of Maclaurin's Treatise of Fluxions." Judith V. Grabiner. *American Mathematical Monthly* 104, no. 5 (May, 1997): 393-410.

(Amy Ackerberg-Hastings)

Benoit B. Mandelbrot

Area of Achievement: Applied math
Contribution: Mandelbrot introduced the notion of fractals to describe many of the chaotic phenomena of the natural world.

Nov. 20, 1924	Born in Warsaw, Poland
1936	Moves to Paris with his family
1952	Receives a Ph.D. in mathematics from the University of Paris
1953-1954	Studies at the Institute for Advanced Study in Princeton, New Jersey
1955-1957	Teaches at the University of Geneva
1958	Joins IBM's Thomas B. Watson Research Center
1975	Publishes *Les Objets fractals*
1982	Publishes *The Fractal Geometry of Nature*, a revised edition of *Fractals*
1985	Receives the Barnard Medal for Meritorious Service to Science
1986	Receives the Franklin Medal for Original and Eminent Service to Science
1987	Given the Alexander von Humboldt Prize
1993	Awarded the Wolf Prize

Early Life

Benoit B. Mandelbrot (pronounced "MAN-dehl-broht")—the "B." does not stand for anything—was born in Warsaw, Poland, as the descendent of a Lithuanian Jewish family. His father was a clothing wholesaler, and his mother was a dentist. Because of the increasing political turmoil in Poland, his family moved to Paris in 1936. Mandelbrot's uncle, Szolem Mandelbrojt, a professor of mathematics at the Collège de France and the successor of

Jacques-Salomon Hadamard in this post, took charge of his education. When Paris fell to the Nazis, his family fled to Tulle, a town in southern France.

Following the liberation of Paris, Mandelbrot passed the admission examinations for the École Normale and the École Polytechnique. After studying in France and in the United States, Mandelbrot received the Ph.D. in mathematics in 1952 with the thesis *Contribution à la théorie mathématique des jeux de communications* (1953; contribution to the mathematical theory of games of communication).

Cotton Price Fluctuations

In 1960, Hendrick Houthakker, a professor of economics at Harvard University, invited Mandelbrot to give a lecture. At that time, Mandelbrot was interested in studying the distribution of large and small incomes in an economy. When he entered Houthakker's office, he was surprised to see on the blackboard a chart that very much reflected his own findings.

Actually, the diagram represented the fluctuations of cotton prices over a period of eight years. The standard model used in statistics for plotting variation is Carl Friedrich Gauss's bell-shaped curve, the normal distribution. In the middle, where the hump of the curve is rising, most of the data tend to accumulate around an average value (μ), whereas measurements that are far from the average value are less likely to occur.

The cotton prices, however, did not obey the normal law. When he came back to New York, Mandelbrot fed the computers with data representing cotton prices over a span of sixty years. The results were surprising. The fluctuations were indeed random and unpredictable, but the sequence of changes was the same, whether they were daily or monthly changes.

How Long Is the Coast of Britain?

In 1961, Mandelbrot came across an article by an English meteorologist, Lewis Fry Richardson, in which the author was mentioning discrepancies of 20 percent in the estimated length of Great Britain's west coast and the Spanish-Portuguese land frontier. Richardson remarked that the measurements depended heavily on the scale of the map used.

Mandelbrot's analysis revealed that any coastline is in a sense infinite in length. No matter how small is the chosen length unit, some twists and turns will always be skipped. If the shape were regular, like a circle, the sums of finer straight-line approximations would converge, but Mandelbrot found that as the scale of the measurement becomes smaller, a more complex and irregular shape is revealed.

Fractal Geometry

In the winter of 1975, while he was preparing the manuscript of his first book, Mandelbrot thought about a name for his shapes. Looking into his son's Latin dictionary, he came across the adjective *fractus*, from the verb *frangere*, meaning "to break." He decided to name his shapes "fractals."

In 1945, Mandelbrot's uncle introduced him to an article published in 1918 by the French mathematician Gaston Julia. More than thirty years later, his uncle had tried to generalize the Julia sets. With the aid of computer graphics,

(Hank Morgan/Science Source)

Fractals

A fractal is a geometrical figure that has an identical motif repeating itself endlessly on an ever-diminishing scale. This property is called self-similarity.

In 1904, the Swedish mathematician Helge von Koch gave an example of a curve that had no tangent anywhere. The Koch curve is a prototype of a large group of fractals. Start with an equilateral triangle whose sides have a length of 1. At the middle of each side, draw a new triangle whose sides are one-third the original length. If this process is continuously repeated, the resulting shape is a fractal, the Koch snowflake.

In order to understand the complex structure of a fractal, Mandelbrot introduced the fractional dimension as a means of measuring the degree of roughness or irregularity in an object. According to Mandelbrot, the natural world is fractal in shape: Mountains are not cones, clouds are not spheres, and lightning does not travel in a straight line.

Fractal descriptions found immediate applications. Several cardiologists discovered that the frequency spectrum of heartbeat timing, like earthquakes and economic phenomena, follows fractal laws. The fractal dimension of the surface of a metal provides information about its

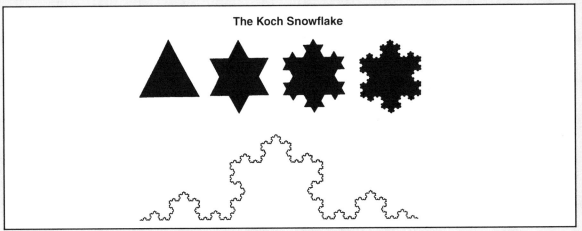

The Koch Snowflake

The four pictures on top represent the first three steps in the iteration process.

The Koch snowflake is an interesting example of a shape with infinite contour enclosing a finite area. Indeed, the area is smaller than the area of the circle circumscribing the original triangle, whereas the length is "$3 \times \frac{4}{3} \times \frac{4}{3} \ldots = \infty$."

Many fractal shapes can be defined by iterating a function in the complex plane. To obtain a Mandelbrot set, consider the function $f(z) = z^2 + c$, where c is a fixed complex number. Start with $z = 0$. The first iteration produces $f(0) = c$, the second $f(c) = c^2 + c$, the third $f(c^2 + c) = c^4 + 2c^3 + c^2 + c$, and so on. The number c is in the Mandelbrot set if the points obtained through iterations remain near the origin. It has been proved that if the distance from the origin becomes greater than 2, the set will grow without limit and the point is attracted to infinity.

strength. One consequence of the fractal geometry of surfaces is that surfaces in contact do not touch everywhere. In addition, the beauty of fractals has made them a key element in computer graphics. Fractals have also been used to compress video images on computers.

Bibliography

Fractal Geometry: Mathematical Foundations and Applications. Kenneth Falconer. New York: John Wiley & Sons, 1990.

Fractals: Endlessly Repeated Geometrical Figures. Hendrik Adolf Lauwerier. Translated by Sophia Gill-Hoffstadt. Princeton, N.J.: Princeton University Press, 1991.

Fractals Everywhere. Michael Barnsley. San Diego: Academic Press, 1988.

Mandelbrot was able to show how Julia's work was a source for creating amazing fractal shapes.

Teaching Career and Awards

Over the years, Mandelbrot held a variety of jobs. He taught economics at Harvard University, engineering at Yale University, physiology at the Albert Einstein College of Medicine, and mathematics in Paris and Geneva. In 1958, he began working as an IBM fellow at the Thomas B. Watson Research Center in New York. He also served as Professor of the Practice of Mathematics at Harvard. Once, after being introduced for a lecture, he jokingly said: "Very often when I listen to the list of my previous jobs I wonder if I exist. The intersection of such sets is surely empty."

The publication of his book *Les Objets fractals: Forme, hasard, et dimension* (1975), translated as *Fractals: Form, Chance, and Dimension* (1977), and its refined and improved version, *The Fractal Geometry of Nature* (1982), brought him international recognition and celebrity. In 1985, Mandelbrot was awarded the Barnard Medal for Meritorious Service to Science. The following year, he received the Franklin Medal. He was honored with the Alexander von Humboldt Prize in 1987, the Steinmetz Medal in 1988, the Nevada Medal in 1991, and the Wolf Prize in 1993.

Bibliography
By Mandelbrot
Contribution à la théorie mathématique des jeux de communications, 1953

"The Pareto-Lévy Law and the Distribution of Income," *International Economic Review* 1, 1960

"The Role of Sufficiency and of Estimation in Thermodynamics," *The Annals of Mathematical Statistics* 33, 1962

"How Long Is the Coast of Britain?: Statistical Self-Similarity and Fractional Dimension," *Science* 155, 1967

"Fractional Brownian Motions, Fractional Noises and Applications," *SIAM Review* 10, 1968 (with John W. van Ness)

"A Fast Fractional Gaussian Noise Generator," *Water Resources Research* 7, 1971

Les Objets fractals: Forme, hasard, et dimension, 1975 (*Fractals: Form, Chance, and Dimension*, 1977)

The Fractal Geometry of Nature, 1982 (rev. ed. of *Fractals*)

About Mandelbrot
Chaos: Making a New Science. James Gleick. New York: Viking Press, 1987.

From Newton to Mandelbrot: A Primer in Theoretical Physics. Dietrich Stauffer and H. Eugene Stanley. New York: Springer-Verlag, 1990.

(Anda Gadidov)

Pierre-Louis Moreau de Maupertuis

Area of Achievement: Applied math
Contribution: Maupertuis measured the terrestrial distance of one degree of arc of longitude.

Sept. 28, 1698	Born in Saint-Milo, France
1723	Elected to the Académie Royale des Sciences
1728	Travels to London
1732	Writes *Discours sur les différentes figures des astres*, in favor of Isaac Newton
1736	Sent to Lapland to measure the distance of a degree of arc of the meridian of longitude
1738	Visits Berlin and meets Frederick the Great
1739	Speaks before the Académie des Sciences to announce the results of the Lapland trip
1743	Elected to the Académie Française
1744	Publishes *Dissertation physique à l'occasion du nègre blanc*, concerning heredity
1745	Publishes *Vénus physique* (*The Earthly Venus*, 1966), also concerning heredity
1746	Becomes president of the Berlin Academy of Sciences
1750	Publishes *Essai de cosmologie*
1751	Publishes *Système de la nature*, also dealing with heredity
1752	Attacked by Voltaire
July 27, 1759	Dies in Basel, Switzerland

Early Life

Born on September 28, 1698, in Saint-Milo, France, Pierre-Louis Moreau de Maupertuis (pronounced "moh-pehr-TWEE") demonstrated such precocious ability in science and mathematics that he was elected to the Académie Royale des Sciences at the age of twenty-five. Short, abrasively contentious, and disheveled, Maupertuis was nevertheless capable of great charm and social grace. Unfortunately, his bold opinions, brusque manner, and arrogant bearing inspired vengefulness among many of his colleagues in the world of eighteenth century European science.

Like most French scholars, Maupertuis revered René Descartes, but, during a visit to London in 1728, he embraced the cosmology of Descartes's rival, Isaac Newton. Maupertuis's conversion resulted in *Discours sur les différentes figures des astres* (1732), which was popular among the reading public but not among French scientists. Moreover, he became fast friends with one of the towering figures of the French Enlightenment, François-Marie Arouet, known as Voltaire, who was foremost among French champions of Newton.

Expedition to Lapland

In 1736, to prove the Newtonian contention that the earth is slightly flattened at the poles because of gravity and to discredit the contrary theory of Jacques Cassini, Maupertuis journeyed to Lapland near the Arctic Circle. He intended to measure the terrestrial distance of a degree of arc of the meridian of longitude.

Upon his return to France in 1737, Maupertuis provoked the ire of many French scholars with his unabashed Newtonianism. In 1739, he deepened the bitterness of his critics when he announced before the Académie des Sciences that his calculations proved Newton's position conclusively. Having substantiated Newton's hypothesis, Maupertuis was said to have flattened not only the earth but his chief rival Cassini as well.

To his detractors' frustration, Maupertuis was rewarded with election to the Académie Française in 1743. Thereafter, he published one of his most influential works, *Dissertation physique à l'occasion du nègre blanc* (1744), in which he denounced another prevailing scientific orthodoxy, that of preformation or preexistence. This theory claimed that the human embryo resided in fully formed miniature in the reproductive cells of a single parent (usually reputed to be the male). In its place, he argued that inheritable traits descend from both parents, each of which is a necessary and equal partner in propagation. For this view, Maupertuis has been regarded by some as a forerunner of Charles Darwin.

Career in Berlin

At King Frederick the Great's invitation, Maupertuis moved to Berlin in 1745. He married and was elevated to the presidency of the Berlin Academy of Sciences. Under his leadership, the academy enticed some of the leading scientists of the age to the bleak Prussian capital. Continuing his research, Maupertuis elaborated his Newtonian ideas in *Essai de cosmologie* (1750) and returned to questions of genetics in *Système de la nature* (1751).

Although productive, Maupertuis's stay in Berlin was not, however, a period of unalloyed happiness. He found himself unexpectedly attacked by his longtime friend Samuel König, whom he had recently helped win appointment to the academy and who now ungraciously accused him of plagiarizing from Gottfried Wilhelm Leibniz.

Measuring Longitude

Maupertuis measured the terrestrial distance of a degree of arc of the meridian of longitude. He pioneered modern geodesy, a category of applied mathematics concerning the surveying and mapping of the earth.

When Maupertuis led an expedition to Lapland in 1736 to determine the length of a degree of arc of longitude, his purpose was both theoretical and practical: to prove Sir Isaac Newton's mathematical hypothesis that the earth is flattened at the poles and to improve mapmaking (cartography). His team employed transit telescopes for observing the time of a star's movement from one location to another, a pendulum for telling time, quadrants for measuring altitude, long wooden rulers for measuring terrestrial distances, and a zenith sector for observing stars close to their highest point in the sky.

Maupertuis's task required coordinating several different kinds of calculations. He measured angles between the horizon and specific stars to establish two latitudes a degree apart. After plotting the terrestrial location of each latitude, he intersected each latitude with a perpendicular line. He then measured the length of the line by standard surveying techniques, mainly by triangulation. The result was the terrestrial distance of a degree of arc of the meridian of longitude.

This relatively simple set of procedures was complicated by an arduous voyage to a terrain and climate hostile to the performance of careful scientific field trials and by the need to repeat observations many times and in different locations. Maupertuis's expedition to Lapland took a year to accomplish, while a similar expedition to Peru took an exhausting three years.

In the end, Maupertuis showed that a longitudinal degree of arc was longer near the poles than a degree near the equator, thus validating Newton's hypothesis that the earth is not a perfect sphere but an oblate spheroid (a sphere slightly flattened at the poles and bulging minutely at the equator). His empirically derived ratio of $^{177}/_{178}$, however, corrected Newton's conjecture of $^{229}/_{230}$ for the ratio of polar-to-equatorial diameter.

Bibliography

"'Aplatisseur du monde et de Cassini': Maupertuis, Precision Measurement, and the Shape of the Earth in the 1730's." Rob Iliffe. *History of Science* 31, part 4, no. 94 (December, 1993): 335-375.

Cartography in France, 1660-1848: Science, Engineering, and Statecraft. Josef W. Konvitz. Chicago: University of Chicago Press, 1987.

"Degrees of Longitude and the Earth's Shape: The Diffusion of a Scientific Idea in Paris in the 1730's." John L. Greenberg. *Annals of Science* 41., no. 2 (March, 1984): 151-158.

"The Measurement of the Earth." John L. Greenberg. *Annals of Science* 44, no. 3 (May, 1987): 289-295.

(Library of Congress)

Attacks from Voltaire

Even worse, considering their prior cordial relations and intellectual compatibility, Voltaire and Maupertuis came to swords' points in 1752. Mocking the expedition to Lapland, charging him with plagiarism and faulty science, as well as despotic rule over the Berlin academy, Voltaire barraged Maupertuis with insults and humiliations.

Stunned and demoralized, Maupertuis withered before Voltaire's invectives. Unable to marshal an effective defense, he retreated to France to regain his strength and his spirits. At the urging of the Prussian king, he returned to Berlin in 1754 but abandoned the city, exhausted and frail, in 1756. After nearly three years of meandering toward his hometown of Saint-Milo, Maupertuis collapsed, his health devastated, and died in Basel, Switzerland, on July 27, 1759.

Bibliography

By Maupertuis

Discours sur les différentes figures des astres, 1732 (discourse on the different shapes of stars)

Dissertation physique à l'occasion du nègre blanc, 1744 (physical dissertation on the subject of the white Negro)

Vénus physique, 1745 (*The Earthly Venus*, 1966)

Essai de cosmologie, 1750

Système de la nature, 1751

Lettre sur le progrès des sciences, 1752

About Maupertuis

Maupertuis: An Intellectual Biography. David Beeson. Oxford, England: Voltaire Foundation, 1992.

"Maupertuis and the Eighteenth-Century Critique of Preexistence." Michael H. Hoffheimer. *Journal of the History of Biology* 15, no. 1 (Spring, 1982): 119-144.

"Maupertuis: Pioneer of Genetics and Evolution." Bentley Glass. In *Forerunners of Darwin, 1745-1859*. Baltimore: The John Hopkins University Press, 1959.

"Salon, Academy, and Boudoir: Generation and Desire in Maupertuis's Science of Life." Mary Terrall. *Isis* 87, no. 2 (June, 1996): 217-229.

(David Allen Duncan)

Menaechmus

Area of Achievement: Geometry

Contribution: Menaechmus discovered conic sections (the parabola, hyperbola, and ellipse) and derived properties for them, geometrically, yielding their defining equations in analytic geometry.

c. 375 B.C.E.	Born on the island of Proconnesus (now Marmara, Turkey)
c. 355 B.C.E.	Becomes a pupil of Eudoxus in his school at Cyzicus
c. 350 B.C.E.	Travels with Eudoxus to Athens and stays on as a member of Plato's Academy
c. 340 B.C.E.	Succeeds Eudoxus as the director of the mathematical seminar at Cyzicus
c. 330 B.C.E.	Becomes a tutor to Alexander the Great
c. 325 B.C.E.	Dies

Early Life

Little is known about the life of Menaechmus, and specific dates are hard to come by. Furthermore, knowledge of his work comes from later commentators. Menaechmus was born about 375 B.C.E. on Proconnesus, an island in the Sea of Marmara (historically Propontis) connecting the Aegean Sea with the Black Sea (in modern-day Turkey). Both he and his brother Dinostratus, also a geometer, became pupils of the renown mathematician Eudoxus of Cnidus in his school at Cyzicus on the east coast of Propontis.

Shortly before 350 B.C.E., both brothers accompanied Eudoxus, attracted by the scholars at Plato's Academy, to Athens. Shortly after their arrival, Eudoxus left for Cnidus, but the brothers stayed on as part of the Academy. While there, according to the later commentator Proclus, "they made the whole of geometry more perfect."

The Delian Problem

The following story is told of the geometers in the Academy by Eratosthenes of Cyrene in his dialogue *Platonikos* (c. 240 B.C.E.).

A group of inhabitants of Delos had come to Plato's Academy to ask for help in solving a serious problem. A plague was ravaging Delos. The inhabitants consulted the oracle of Apollo and were instructed to double the size of the cubical altar there. They placed a second identical cube on top of the altar, but the plague did not cease; the oracle accused them of not obeying Apollo's order: They were to construct a cube whose volume was twice that of the altar. The geometers of the Academy set out to build mechanical devices to accomplish the task, but they were accused of demeaning the "virtue of geometry" by using mechanics.

Geometrically, the purest solution would have been to construct the cube with the most basic of tools: the straightedge and compass. (In the nineteenth century, this method was shown to be impossible.) The next best thing, geometrically, was to produce curves with the correct properties needed to solve the problem. Menaechmus found such curves by cutting various cones with a plane—curves referred to by Eratosthenes and other commentators as the triads of Menaechmus. These conic sections are now called an ellipse, a parabola, and a hyperbola.

In using conic sections to solve the Delian problem (also known as the duplication of the cube), Menaechmus derived properties of conic sections that resemble the equations of these curves when drawn on coordinate axes (an x,y coordinate system). This fact has prompted some historians to maintain that Menaechmus discovered analytic geometry some two thousand years before its "invention" by Pierre de Fermat and René Descartes in the seventeenth century. Since the concept of an equation in unknown variables was alien to the Greeks of the time, however, other historians are reluctant to credit Menaechmus with this discovery. Nevertheless, this event does point out two facts about mathematics: Ideas usually evolve over periods of time and in the minds of more than one person, and mathematics is quite often created to solve a particular problem.

Conic Sections and the Duplication of the Cube

Menaechmus invented conic sections in an attempt to solve the duplication of the cube problem, otherwise known as the Delian problem.

The duplication of the cube requires a person to construct, by geometric means, a cube whose volume is double that of an existing cube. For example, a cube whose side is of length 1 inch would have a volume of 1 cubic inch. The problem is to construct a cube whose volume is 2 cubic inches. To accomplish this task, the new cube must have a side whose length is the cube root of 2.

Ideally, the phrase "by geometric means" would imply using only a straightedge and compass to construct a segment whose length is the cube root of 2. In 1837, Pierre Wantzel showed this to be impossible.

By using two parabolas, Menaechmus was able to construct the required length. This can be seen with analytic geometry. Using an x,y coordinate system, the equations of the two parabolas needed are "$y = x^2$" and "$y^2 = 2x$."

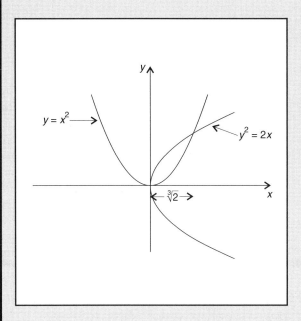

The key now is to find the coordinates of the point of intersection of the two parabolas. When squared, the first equation yields "$y^2 = x^4$," and this gives "$x^4 = y^2 = 2x$." Dividing by x now gives

"$x^3 = 2$," and x is equal to the cube of root 2, which is the length needed.

Menaechmus also gave a solution using the intersection of a parabola and a hyperbola that could be done as above, using the equations "$y = x^2$" and "$y = 2/x$." Although Menaechmus used properties of the parabola and hyperbola implied by the above equations, he did not use such modern notation. He did not even use the terms "parabola," "hyperbola," or "ellipse." Eratosthenes referred to the curves as the triads of Menaechmus cut from a cone (thus, the more modern term "conic sections").

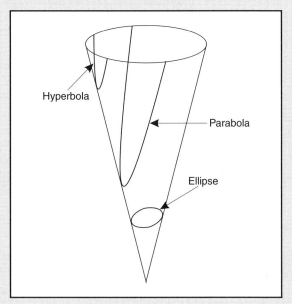

Using this formulation, Menaechmus was able to derive the properties given by the above equations.

Bibliography

Apollonius of Perga: Treatise on Conic Sections. Sir Thomas Little Heath. New York: Barnes & Noble, 1961.

A History of Geometrical Methods. Julian Lowell Coolidge. Oxford, England: Clarendon Press, 1940.

A History of Mathematics: An Introduction. Victor J. Katz. New York: HarperCollins, 1993.

Other Work

As with many of the mathematicians of the Academy, Menaechmus was concerned with the nature of mathematics. His views led away from the Platonic view of first principles such as points and lines as perfect objects and toward a view of them as undefined objects that one could use as a foundation upon which to build other mathematics. This emphasis away from first principles helped solidify a more modern view of axiomatic systems as modeled in Euclid's *Stoicheia* (c. 300 B.C.E.; known as *Elements*).

Eventually, Menaechmus succeeded Eudoxus as the director of the mathematical seminar at Cyzicus and became a tutor for Alexander the Great. Of the latter, there is an interesting anecdote. When told by Alexander that he wanted a shortcut to geometry, Menaechmus replied, "O King, for traveling over the country there are royal roads and roads for common citizens, but in geometry there is one road for all!"

Bibliography

By Menaechmus

None of his works has survived.

About Menaechmus

The Birth of Mathematics in the Age of Plato. François Lasserre. New York: American Research Council, 1964.

A History of Greek Mathematics. Sir Thomas Little Heath. Vol. 1. Oxford, England: Clarendon Press, 1921.

A History of Mathematics. Carl B. Boyer. New York: John Wiley & Sons, 1968.

Mathematics, Queen and Servant of Science. Eric Temple Bell. New York: McGraw-Hill, 1951.

(Robert R. Rogers)

Marin Mersenne

Area of Achievement: Number theory
Contribution: Mersenne launched the search for what have come to be known as Mersenne primes. In his day, he was Europe's most important disseminator of scientific knowledge.

Sept. 8, 1588	Born at La Soultière, near Oizé, Maine, France
1604	Enters the Jesuit college at La Flèche
1609	Begins studies in theology at the Sorbonne
1611	Joins a religious order, the Minims
1612	Ordained a priest at the Palace Royale
1614	Begins teaching philosophy and theology at the Minim convent at Nevers
1619	Returns to Paris to take up permanent residence at the Minim convent there
1635	Organizes the Academia Parisiensis
1636	Publishes *Harmonie universelle*, his major work on acoustics
1644	Publishes the list of numbers of the form "$2^p - 1$," which he claimed to be prime
Sept. 1, 1648	Dies in Paris, France

Early Life

Marin Mersenne (pronounced "mehr-SEHN") was born near Oizé, in Maine, France, on September 8, 1588. Little is known of his childhood until, at the age of sixteen, he entered the new college at La Flèche which was operated by the Jesuits, a Roman Catholic religious order of priests and brothers. The school was unusual in that, although it was in some sense a board-

(Library of Congress)

Continuing his dedication to the religious life, Mersenne was ordained a priest of the Catholic Church in October, 1612. Two years later, he began a five-year term teaching theology and philosophy at the Minim convent at Nevers, France. It was when he returned to the Minim house in Paris in 1619 that he began his astounding development as a scientist.

Mersenne and Music

Mersenne devoted himself to several areas of scientific study, not simply mathematics. He was famous in music, having learned much about the physics of sound. For example, he is credited with making the first absolute determination of an audible tone. Acoustics is a science of sound, and Mersenne is sometimes referred to as the founder of acoustics. He continued Galileo's work on acoustics and helped lead that famous scientist to further discoveries.

Some of his discoveries are now referred to in music as Mersenne's laws. These laws explain how a string vibrates in relation to the tension on the string and other factors. They are fundamental to the construction of stringed instruments like guitars and pianos.

Mersenne the Scientific Correspondent

In scientific circles, Mersenne is probably best known for his role as one who spread new scientific knowledge across Europe through his correspondence with the leading scientists of the day, including Blaise Pascal, René Descartes, Pierre de Fermat, and Galileo. In the seventeenth century, communication was very slow, but Mersenne had connections with so many people that he was able to spread word of new studies very quickly. Many of his correspondents even came to visit him and discuss scientific matters at his religious residence in Paris.

Throughout his work and discussion with others, Mersenne never forgot those two crucial lessons from his college years: There is truth that human beings can come to know through scientific inquiry, and scientists must never "cheat" by keeping inaccurate data or by performing imprecise experiments. He would insist on these two points all of his life.

In his work with other scientists, Mersenne

ing school, the students did not live at the school but in the town itself.

The five years at La Flèche proved formative for Mersenne. Living in town, the boys were exposed to many who tried to swindle or cheat them. This inspired in Mersenne a great loathing for dishonesty of any type. He also came to love learning and developed a great zeal for truth, both religious and scientific. He spent the rest of his life living the lessons he learned at La Flèche.

Theological Studies and the Priesthood

Upon leaving La Flèche, at the age of twenty-one, Mersenne entered the Sorbonne to study theology. After two years, he joined the Roman Catholic religious order known as the Minims; this name comes from the Latin root meaning "least." The Minims considered themselves the least and led a very simple lifestyle. The Minim brothers were called friars because the word "friar" comes from the Latin root meaning "brother." These friars were free to pursue scholarly interests, something Mersenne would soon excel in doing.

proved himself to be a scientist of many talents, and not only in acoustics. For example, his studies in optics led him to propose designs for telescopes that have been used for centuries. Because of this contribution, the lunar crater Mersenius was named in his honor.

Mersenne Primes

Four years before his death, Mersenne published what came to be his most famous mathematical statement. He studied numbers found by multiplying 2 by itself many times and then subtracting 1 from the result. These are now called Mersenne numbers. Some of these numbers are prime, called the Mersenne primes. His list of claimed Mersenne primes involved numbers so large that it took more than three hundred years for others to check them.

Mersenne died in 1648 just before his sixtieth birthday.

Bibliography
By Mersenne
Observationes et emendationes ad Francisci Georgii Venetii problemata, 1623
Questiones celeberrimæ in Genesim, 1623
L'Usage de la raison, 1623
L'Impiéte des deistes, athées, et libertins de ce temps, 1624
La Verité des sciences, 1625
Synopsis mathematica, 1626
Traité de l'harmonie universelle, 1627

Mersenne Primes

Mersenne primes are those prime numbers that are 1 less than a power of 2.

A prime number is a positive integer that has exactly two positive integer divisors. There are infinitely many such prime numbers, or primes. The first few of these are 2, 3, 5, 7, and 11. Thousands of years ago, people noticed that some prime numbers were only 1 less than a power of 2. A power of 2, symbolized mathematically by 2^n, is 2 multiplied by itself n times. Thus, for example, 2^5 is 2 times itself five times, or 32. The first two primes which are 1 less than a power of 2 are 3 ($= 2^2 - 1$) and 7 ($= 2^3 - 1$). By the seventeenth century, it was known that "$2^p - 1$" was a prime number if p was replaced by 2, 3, 5, 7, 13, or 19.

It was at this stage, in 1644, that the French scientist and monk Marin Mersenne published *Cogitata physico-mathematica*, a work on various mathematical sciences. In his preface, Mersenne claimed that "$2^p - 1$" was prime if p was replaced by 31, 67, 127, or 257 and that, in addition to those smaller values for p already known, there were no other values for p up to 257 that would make "$2^p - 1$" prime.

The claim was astounding if for no other reason than the great size of these numbers and therefore the enormous difficulty involved in checking whether they in fact were prime. It was not until 1947, more than three hundred years after Mersenne's original claim, that the checking was complete. Mersenne had made five mistakes: "$2^p - 1$" is not prime if p is replaced by 67 or 257. It is prime, however, if p is replaced by 61, 89, or 107, three values that Mersenne had missed.

Because of the long and arduous task of checking Mersenne's claim, any prime number of the form "$2^p - 1$" has come to be called a Mersenne prime. The search for new Mersenne primes has continued, fueled by the explosion in computing power that began in the middle of the twentieth century. Since then, many of the largest known primes are Mersenne primes, some of which are hundreds of thousands of digits long.

Bibliography
"A Brief History of the Investigations on Mersenne's Numbers and the Latest Immense Primes." H. S. Uhler. *Scripta Mathematica* 18 (1952): 122-131.
"Mersenne's Numbers." R. C. Archibald. *Scripta Mathematica* 3 (1935): 112-119.
The New Book of Prime Number Records. Paulo Ribenboim. 3d ed. New York: Springer-Verlag, 1995.
In addition, visit www.svpal.org/~olle/prime. html, a website on Mersenne primes started by a seventh grader in Sweden.

*Traité des mouvemens et de la cheute des corps
    pesans et de la proportion de leurs différentes
    vitesses dans lequel l'on verra plusieurs expéri-
    ences très exactes*, 1633
Les Méchaniques de Galilée, 1634
Les Préludes de l'harmonie universelle, 1634
Questions harmoniques, 1634
Questions inouyës, 1634
*Les Questions théologiques, physiques, morales, et
    mathématiques*, 1634
Harmonie universelle, 1636-1637
Les Nouvelles Pensées de Galilée, 1639
L'Usage du quadran, 1639
Cogitata physico-mathematica, 1644
*Universæ geometriæ mixtaeque mathematicæ syn-
    opsis*, 1644
*Novarum observationum physico-mathematicarum
    tomus III*, 1647
Harmonicorum libri XII, 1648
L'Optique et la catoptique, 1651
*Correspondance du P. Marin Mersenne, religieux
    minime*, 1932-1988 (17 vols.)

About Mersenne

"Marin Mersenne." A. C. Crombie. In *Diction-
    ary of Scientific Biography*, edited by Charles
    Coulston Gillispie. New York: Charles Scrib-
    ner's Sons, 1974.
Mersenne and the Learning of the Schools. Peter
    Dear. Ithaca, N.Y.: Cornell University Press,
    1988.
*The Position of Marin Mersenne in the History of
    Music*. Frederick Bill Hyde. Ph.D. thesis. Yale
    University, 1954.

(Michael J. Caulfield)

Hermann Minkowski

Areas of Achievement: Applied math, geometry, and number theory
Contribution: Minkowski's work was foundational to modern functional analysis.
He worked with quadratic forms and developed the mathematical theory called
the geometry of numbers. He formed a
mathematical description of Albert Einstein's special theory of relativity that
helped Einstein to develop his general
theory.

June 22, 1864	Born in Alexotas, Russian Empire (now Kaunas, Lithuania)
1872	His parents return to Königsberg, Germany
1883	Receives the Grand Prix des Sciences Mathématiques from the French Académie des Sciences
1885	Receives a doctorate from the University of Königsberg
1885	Teaches at the University of Bonn
1894	Returns to Königsberg to teach
1896	Goes to the University of Zurich to work with Adolf Hurwitz
1902	Obtains a professorship at the University of Göttingen with the help of David Hilbert
1905	Publishes an important paper based on a "geometry of numbers"
1909	Publishes *Raum und Zeit* (space and time), demonstrating that relativity necessitates considering time as a fourth dimension
Jan. 12, 1909	Dies in Göttingen, Germany

Early Life

Hermann Minkowski (pronounced "mihng-
KAWF-skee") was born on June 22, 1864, in

Alexotas, Russia. His parents were German and returned to their home country in 1872, when Hermann was eight years old. They settled in Königsberg, where Minkowski received his early education.

Minkowski came from a science-oriented family. His older brother, Oskar, was a well-known physician and pathologist who discovered the role of the pancreas in diabetes and the role of the pituitary gland in acromegaly. He is sometimes referred to as "the grandfather of insulin." Minkowski's nephew, Rudolph, fled Germany during World War II. In the United States he became a well-known astronomer who did important research into radio astronomy and planetary nebulas.

Except for three semesters at the University of Berlin, Minkowski's higher education was at the University of Königsberg. There, he met several people who would later be instrumental in his career, including fellow student David Hilbert, who became his lifelong friend and a famous mathematician in his own right.

Even as a student, Minkowski showed considerable talent in mathematics. In 1881, the Paris Académie des Sciences announced a competition for the Grand Prix des Sciences Mathématiques. The subject of the competition was the number of representations of an integer as a sum of five squares of integers. The academy was unaware that British mathematician H. J. Smith had already published an outline of exactly that proof in 1867. Smith sent the academy a detailed description of his proof.

Independently, Minkowski, who was eighteen at the time, developed an entire theory of quadratic forms in n variables with integral coefficients. Minkowski's formulation was considered to be a more natural and more general approach to the problem. He described it in considerable detail in a 140-page manuscript. The academy was unable to make a decision and in 1883 finally awarded the prize to both Smith and Minkowski.

Developing the Geometry of Numbers
Minkowski received his doctorate from Königsberg in 1885. He held a variety of positions until he finally settled down. He moved to Bonn in 1885 and taught at the university there until 1894. He then returned to the University of Königsberg to teach for two years. In 1896, he went to teach at the University of Zurich. One of his colleagues at Zurich was Adolf Hurwitz, who is known for his theorem on the composition of quadratic forms. Hurwitz had been Minkowski's professor when he was a student at Königsberg.

During this time, Minkowski continued his work in the arithmetic of quadratic forms in n variables, usually known as n-ary forms. This work eventually became known as the geometry of numbers.

Final Years at Göttingen
Hilbert had encouraged the University of Göttingen to create a new professorship for Minkowski. Finally, in 1902, Minkowski accepted the invitation of his friend. He taught there until his death. Minkowski is probably not as well known as some of his students at Göttingen, who included such famous physicists as Albert Einstein and Max Born. Minkowski's influence was fundamental to much of their later work.

Minkowski became particularly interested in Einstein's special theory of relativity. He rec-

Space-Time Diagrams

Minkowski proposed a way of visualizing special relativity.

A basic premise of classical physics was that the laws of physics are the same in all reference frames. This Newtonian principle of relativity allows for transformations of coordinates and velocities from one reference frame to another using equations known as Galilean transformations.

Albert Einstein noted that although Isaac Newton's laws of motion are the same under Galilean transformations, Maxwell's equations, describing electromagnetism, are not invariant. In 1905, Einstein proposed his theory of special relativity. One of its basic assumptions is that space and time are not separate.

Minkowski, one of Albert Einstein's teachers, developed the space-time, or Minkowski, diagram as a way of visualizing special relativity. Both the coordinates and the time of the event must be given. The axes of a space-time diagram are the product of the speed of light and time, *ct*, versus the spatial coordinates. This is the origin of the idea of time as a fourth dimension.

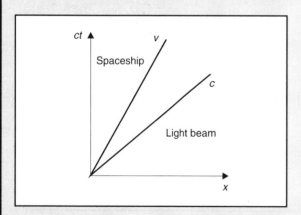

An event, such as a spaceship launching, is represented by points. The path from two points is depicted with a line called the worldline. A spaceship moving with some velocity *v* is represented by a straight line as shown. A light signal *c* sent out from the origin will be represented by a straight line at an angle of 45 degrees from the axes.

Any event that occurred before "*t* = 0" is called the past. Any event occurring after "*t* = 0" is called the future, as shown in figure 2.

The shaded areas of the graph are bordered by a worldline representing a light beam. Only the events within the shaded area can affect the pres-

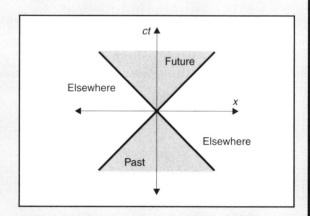

ent. Any object outside of this shaded region would have to be moving faster than the speed of light, which is not possible according to special relativity. The region outside the shaded area is referred to as "elsewhere." If the space-time diagram is expanded to include more than one spatial dimension, this shaded area becomes a cone called the light cone. All events within the light cone are related by cause and effect. The value of space-time diagrams lies in this ability to connect two events causally.

Bibliography

The Character of Physical Law. Richard P. Feynman. Cambridge, Mass.: MIT Press, 1965.

The Feynman Lectures on Physics. Richard P. Feynman, Robert B. Leighton, and Matthew Sands. Reading, Mass.: Addison-Wesley, 1963.

Gravitation. Charles W. Misner, Kip S. Thorne, and John Archibald Wheeler. New York: W. H. Freeman, 1973.

Modern Physics for Scientists and Engineers. Stephen T. Thornton and Andrew Rex. Fort Worth, Tex.: Saunders College Publishing, 1993.

Spacetime Physics: Introduction to Special Relativity. Edwin F. Taylor and John Archibald Wheeler. 2d ed. New York: W. H. Freeman, 1992.

ognized that one of the implications of special relativity is that space and time are no longer separate entities. As he wrote, "From now on, space by itself and time by itself are mere shadows and only a blend of the two exists in its own right." In 1908, Minkowski formalized this relationship using space-time, or Minkowski, diagrams. One axis of the diagram is the speed of light multiplied by a quantity that has the dimensions of a length. This gave rise to the idea of time as a fourth dimension of space. Nine years later, Einstein expanded on Minkowski's ideas in the development of his general theory of relativity.

Minkowski died on January 12, 1909, in Göttingen, Germany.

Bibliography

By Minkowski

Geometrie der Zahlen, 1896; 2d ed., 1910

Diophantische Approximationen eine Einfuhrung in die Zahlentheorie, 1907

Raum und Zeit, 1909 ("Space and Time" in *The Principle of Relativity: A Collection of Original Memoirs*, 1923)

Gesammelte Abhandlungen, 1911 (2 vols.; David Hilbert, ed.)

About Minkowski

Development of the Minkowski Geometry of Numbers. Harris Hancock. New York: Macmillan, 1939.

Relativity: An Elementary Explanation of the Space-Time Relations as Established by Minkowski and a Discussion of Gravitational Theory Based Thereon. Frederick W. Lanchester. London: Constable, 1935.

(Linda L. McDonald)

Richard von Mises

Areas of Achievement: Applied math, probability, and statistics

Contribution: Von Mises developed ideas related to probability, such as sample space.

Apr. 19, 1883	Born in Lemberg, Austro-Hungarian Empire (now Lvov, Ukraine)
1901	Publishes his first paper, on pure geometry
1907	Earns a doctorate in Vienna
1909	Begins a professorship of applied mathematics at Strassburg
1913	Gives the first university course on powered flight
1914	Begins a four-year service in the Flying Corps of the Austro-Hungarian army
1918	Publishes the von Mises distribution
1919	Publishes two works in probability
1920	Begins a professorship of applied mathematics in Berlin
1922	With Ludwig Prandtl, founds GAMM (Gesellschaft für Angewandte Mathematik und Mechanik), an organization for applied mathematicians
1933	Leaves Germany for a professorship in Istanbul, Turkey
1939	Leaves Europe for a professorship at Harvard University
1939	Formulates the birthday problem
1951	Publishes his book *Positivism*
July 14, 1953	Dies in Boston, Massachusetts

Early Life

Richard Martin Edler von Mises (pronounced "MEE-zehs") was born in Lemberg, Austro-Hungarian Empire, on April 19, 1883, to Arthur Edler von Mises and Adele von Landau. Arthur's job with the Austrian railways involved much traveling, which made Richard accustomed to living in many places. Richard's brother Ludwig would become a successful economist.

Richard von Mises's education in Germany turned him into a well-to-do intellectual young man with interests in poetry (especially that of Rainer Maria Rilke), philosophy, and sports. At the age of only eighteen, he published his first paper, in the area of pure geometry. At the age of twenty-four, he earned a doctorate in Vienna and two years later began his first professorship, in applied mathematics at the University of Strassburg. He stayed there through the end of World War I.

Military Activities

Von Mises's interest in fluid mechanics led to his interest in aerospace. In 1913, he gave the first university course on powered flight. The next year, he began a four-year service in the Flying Corps of the Austro-Hungarian army. In 1915, he made a huge, 600-horsepower plane with an original wing design for the Austrian army and actually piloted it during World War I. After the war, von Mises returned home to Berlin only to find that he had lost most of his material possessions during the war.

Mathematical Work

In addition to his applied work in aerospace, von Mises's contributions to other areas such as elasticity, plasticity, and turbulence led to deeper study of probability and statistics. Just after World War I ended, von Mises began publishing works on probability.

In 1920, he began a professorship of applied mathematics in Berlin. Two years later, he co-founded, with Ludwig Prandtl, the organization known as GAMM (Gesellschaft für Angewandte Mathematik und Mechanik). This organization of applied mathematicians promotes scientific development in applied mathematics and mechanics.

Although von Mises had become a Catholic, the fact that he had Jewish parents began to endanger his well-being in Nazi Germany. In 1933, at the age of fifty, he was forced to leave Berlin for a professorship in Istanbul, Turkey. In 1939, he left Europe for the United States, beginning a professorship in mathematics, probability, and fluid mechanics at Harvard University.

Von Mises contributed greatly to probability and statistics. A frequency theory of probability had been gaining popularity, in which the probability of a particular event was associated with the proportion of that event occurring in a set of trials under identical conditions. This theory was difficult to apply to realistic situations. Logician John Venn had refined the theory in the nineteenth century by introducing the concept of the probability "in the long run." Von Mises, in turn, combined this Venn limit with the idea of a random sequence of events. This idea was considered controversial and influential. Von Mises is also credited with the concept of sample space (possible outcomes of a probability experiment) and with posing a question involving the probability of matching birthdays among individuals in a given population.

Philosophy

Von Mises's many books and articles showed much breadth, ranging from philosophical foundations to practical computations. His work was also noted for its direct methods and for the consistent manner in which all the topics came from his philosophy of scientific research.

His scientific philosophy was called positivism. Positivism typically insists on value-free study of natural phenomena observable by the senses. To this day, many researchers struggle to reconcile positivistic and "postpositivistic" approaches. In a book published in 1951, von Mises maintained that positivism neither commits one to believing that all questions can be answered rationally nor excuses one from looking for answers that might not ultimately be achievable. Perhaps this steadfast open-mindedness helped him to explore so many areas of mathematics, science, and life successfully. On July 14, 1953, Richard von Mises died of cancer at the age of seventy in Boston, Massachusetts, but his contributions live on.

Bibliography
By von Mises
Probability, Statistics, and Truth, 1939
Theory of Flight, 1945
Positivism: A Study in Human Understanding, 1951
Selected Papers of Richard von Mises, 1963 (Philipp P. Frank et al., eds.)
Mathematical Theory of Probability and Statistics, 1964 (Hilda Geiringer, ed.)

Sample Space and the Birthday Problem

Von Mises helped introduce the probability term "sample space" and posed the famous problem of the probability of matching birthdays.

The sample space of a statistical experiment is the set of all possible outcomes. For example, the sample space for a flip of a coin has two outcomes, either heads or tails; one can state the set as {H,T}. The sample space for two-flip sequences, however, has four equally likely ordered pairs "(first flip, second flip)" in the sample space {(H,H), (H,T), (T,H), (T,T)}. Being able to list all elements of a sample space is important in calculating probabilities. For example, recognizing that the four elements in the above sample space are all equally probable, one can say that the probability of "one heads and one tails" is $\frac{2}{4}$, or 50 percent. Not listing the sample space, might make one incorrectly reason as follows: There are three possibilities—two heads, two tails, one head and one tail—so the probability of a head and a tail is $\frac{1}{3}$.

Von Mises posed the birthday problem in 1939. Its famous version is the following: How many people must there be in a room for the probability of at least one match in birthdays among them to be at least 50 percent? It would be too difficult to list the sample space for this question, because even a room of only two people produces a sample space of 365 × 365, or 133,225 equally likely ordered pairs such as (April 1, June 24). Since 365 of these outcomes are "matches" such as (May 1, May 1), the probability of a match with two people in the room is $^{365}/_{133,225} = ^{1}/_{365}$.

Using "product" and "complement" rules of probability, the probability of at least one match in a room of n people is "$1 - (^{364}/_{365})(^{363}/_{365}) \ldots [^{(366 - n)}/_{365}]$," an expression that exceeds .50 if there are at least twenty-three people in the room. A frequency interpretation of this probability is that if one went up and down the hall and checked for matches in a large number of classes with twenty-three students, then about half of the classes would have no matches and the rest would each have at least one match.

Bibliography
"The Birthday Problem Again?" Kevin Jones. *Mathematics Teacher* 86, no. 5 (1993).
"Methods for Studying Coincidences." P. Diaconis and F. Mosteller. *Journal of the American Statistical Association* 84 (December, 1989).
Probability and Inductive Logic. Henry E. Kyburg, Jr. New York: Macmillan, 1970.

About von Mises

"Richard von Mises." Norman T. Gridgeman. In *Dictionary of Scientific Biography*, edited by Charles Coulston Gillispie. Vol. 9. New York: Charles Scribner's Sons, 1974.

"Richard von Mises' Work in Probability and Statistics." H. Cramér. *Annals of Mathematical Statistics* 24 (1953): 657-662.

Studies in Mathematics and Mechanics Presented to Richard von Mises by Friends, Colleagues, and Pupils. New York: Academic Press, 1954.

"The Work of Richard von Mises: 1883-1953." P. Frank. *Science* 119 (1954): 823-824.

(Lawrence M. Lesser)

August Ferdinand Möbius

Areas of Achievement: Geometry and topology

Contribution: Möbius was a pioneer in the field of topology, which is a specialized branch of geometry. He is widely known for his discovery of the intriguing Möbius strip, which has a single surface without a reverse side.

Nov. 17, 1790	Born in Schulpforta, Saxony (now Germany)
1803	After home schooling, enters public school
1809	Becomes a student at Leipzig University
1813	Studies astronomy at the University of Göttingen and mathematics at the University of Halle
1814	Receives a doctorate from Leipzig
1815	Appointed to a faculty position at Leipzig
1818-1821	Makes renovations at the astronomical observatory
1820	Marries Dorothea Rothe
1827	Publishes *Der barycentrishce Calcul* (the calculus of centers of gravity)
1844	Receives a promotion to professor
1848	Becomes the director of the Leipzig Royal Observatory
1858	Discovers the one-sided Möbius strip
1865	Completes fifty years of teaching at Leipzig
Sept. 26, 1868	Dies in Leipzig, Saxony

Early Life

August Ferdinand Möbius (pronounced "MYOO-bee-oos") was born in 1790 in the small village of Schulpforta, not far from Leipzig, about one hundred miles southwest of Berlin. His father died when August was only three years old, and the family then was supported financially by his uncle. Möbius was educated at home until the age of thirteen, followed by six years in the public schools in Schulpforta. He was a good student with a special liking for mathematics.

At age nineteen, Möbius entered Leipzig University, where he concentrated on mathematics, physics, and astronomy. After four years, he received a traveling fellowship for further study at the Universities of Göttingen and Halle. He then returned to Leipzig, where he received a Ph.D. in 1814. Shortly thereafter, he was appointed to a faculty position at Leipzig, where he remained for the next fifty years.

Contributions to Astronomy

Möbius's duties at Leipzig University included being an observer at the astronomical observatory. After visiting several other observatories, he recommended improvements to modernize the apparatus at Leipzig. In 1823, he published his observations in the compilation *Beobachtungen auf der Königlichen Universitäts-Sternwarte zu Leipzig*.

Halley's comet, which has a seventy-five-year orbit around the sun, was due to reappear in 1835. In that year, Möbius published a popularization for the general public describing the path of the comet in nonmathematical terms. He published two other books on astronomy, *Die Hauptsätze der Astronomie* (1836; the principles of astronomy) and *Die Elemente der Mechanik des Himmels* (1843; the elements of celestial mechanics).

In 1844, Möbius was promoted to professor at Leipzig, and in 1848 he became director of the observatory. He had received job offers from several other academic institutions but preferred to remain at Leipzig, near where he had grown up.

Center of Gravity Calculations

Möbius earned his living as an astronomer, but his most important contributions were in the

(ARCHIV/Photo Researchers, Inc.)

field of mathematics. His book *Der barycentrishce Calcul* (1827; the calculus of centers of gravity) developed a new approach to analytic geometry. The center of gravity of two unequal weights is a mathematical point between them, closer to the heavier one. To calculate that point, one can use Archimedes' law of the lever, where the products of weight multiplied by distance on each side of the balance point are equal.

Suppose that several objects with different weights are placed at random locations in three-dimensional space. A center of gravity still exists, but calculating its location becomes complicated. Möbius developed a generalized method to solve such problems, using the three coordinates of each weight with appropriate numerical coefficients.

In 1837, Möbius published the two-volume *Lehrbuch der Statik* (textbook of statics). He gave illustrations to show how forces and torques

The Möbius Strip

The Möbius strip is a twisted strip of paper with only a single surface. The study of its unusual properties belongs to a branch of modern geometry called topology.

A Möbius strip is simple to construct. The reader is encouraged to make one and to discover its properties by carrying out the suggested experiments.

To make a Möbius strip, cut a strip of paper about 12 inches long and 1 inch wide, give it a half twist, and fasten the ends together with tape. Then, draw a line all along the center of the strip back to the starting point. Note that the line goes to all parts of the surface without crossing an edge. Möbius described this strip as a one-sided surface with no "other side."

Now, make a pencil mark anywhere along the edge of the strip and follow the edge around until you come back to the starting point. The Möbius strip has only one edge. A closed loop without the half twist would have had two surfaces and two edges.

For the next experiment, take a pair of scissors and cut the Möbius strip along its center line. One might expect to get two strips by cutting the original strip in half. The result, however, should be a longer single strip with a double twist, having two edges and two surfaces.

What would happen if a Möbius strip were cut into thirds? To try this experiment, make a new strip with a half twist, draw a continuous line that is one-third of the distance from the edge, and cut along this line. The result may be surprising: one long loop with a double twist intertwined with a new Möbius strip.

The work of Möbius was extended to three dimensions by another mathematician, Felix Klein. He conceived of a bottle that has only one surface and no edges, now called a Klein bottle. If the bottle were cut in half lengthwise, it would separate into two Möbius strips. The Möbius strip and the Klein bottle are objects with unusual topological properties that seem to challenge common sense.

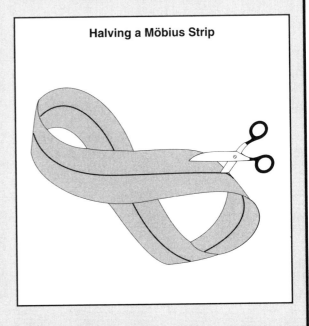

Halving a Möbius Strip

Bibliography

Experiments in Topology. Stephen Barr. New York: Thomas Y. Crowell, 1964.

"Topology." In *Mathematics,* edited by David Bergamini and the editors of *Life* magazine. New York: Time, 1963.

Topology: Exploring Mathematics on Your Own. William H. Glenn and Donovan A. Johnson. St. Louis: Webster, 1960.

both must be balanced to obtain equilibrium. He dealt with the special problem of force "couples," which involves pairs of equal and opposite forces acting at different points.

Topology

Topology has been called "the mathematics of distortion." For example, looking into a funhouse mirror at an amusement park produces a very distorted image. Each point on the image, however, corresponds to a point of the object, so that they are topologically equivalent.

A famous problem in the history of topology is the four-color map problem. It states that for any map drawn on a flat surface, four colors are sufficient to ensure that no two adjoining countries will have the same color. In 1840, Möbius posed a similar problem: How can a kingdom be divided into five regions so that every region borders on each of the other four? If this could be done, the map of the kingdom would require five colors, which would disprove the theorem.

The Möbius strip, which he discovered in 1858, is a narrow strip with a half twist, connected at its ends. It has some interesting topological properties, such as having a top surface with no "underneath." A map drawn on such a strip would require six colors rather than four.

Möbius died on September 26, 1868, in Leipzig. He was seventy-seven years old.

Bibliography

By Möbius
De Computandis Occultationibus Fixarum per Planetas, 1815 (concerning the calculations of the occultations of the planets)
Beobachtungen auf der Königlichen Universitäts-Sternwarte zu Leipzig, 1823 (observations at the Royal Observatory of Leipzig)
Der barycentrishce Calcul: Ein neues Hülfsmittel zur analytischen Behandlung der Geometrie, 1827 (the calculus of centers of gravity: a new method for analytic geometry)
Die Hauptsätze der Astronomie, 1836 (the principles of astronomy)
Lehrbuch der Statik, 1837 (2 vols.; textbook of statics)
Die Elemente der Mechanik des Himmels, 1843 (the elements of celestial mechanics)
"Über die Bestimmung des Inhaltes eines Polyëders," 1865 (determining the volume of a polyhedron)
Gesammelte Werke, 1885-1887 (4 vols.; collected works; Richard Baltzer, Christian Felix Klein, and Wilhelm Scheibner, eds.)

About Möbius
"August Ferdinand Möbius." In *Encyclopaedia Brittanica*. Vol. 8. 15th ed. Chicago: Encyclopaedia Brittanica, 1997.
"August Ferdinand Möbius." Michael J. Crowe. In *Dictionary of Scientific Bibliography*, edited by Charles Coulston Gillispie. Vol. 9. New York: Charles Scribner's Sons, 1980.
History of Mathematics. David Eugene Smith. Boston: Ginn, 1923.

(Hans G. Graetzer)

Abraham de Moivre

Area of Achievement: Probability
Contribution: De Moivre was the first mathematician to investigate the form and basic properties of the normal probability function and to demonstrate that it could be used to approximate other types of probabilities.

May 26, 1667	Born in Vitry, France
1678-1682	Studies classics at Sedan
1682-1684	Studies philosophy and logic at Saumur
1684-1685	Studies physics and mathematics, the University of Paris
1685	Jailed as a result of the Revocation of the Edict of Nantes
1688	Emigrates to England
1697	Elected a Fellow of the Royal Society of London
1710-1712	Serves on the Royal Society commission investigating a calculus priority dispute
1711	Reads his first paper on probability, "De mensura sortis," to the Royal Society of London
1718	Publishes *The Doctrine of Chances*
1725	Publishes *A Treatise of Annuities on Lives*
1730	Publishes *Miscellanea Analytica*
1733	Publishes a pamphlet on the normal probability function
1735	Elected to the Berlin Academy of Sciences
1754	Elected to the French Académie des Sciences
Nov. 27, 1754	Dies in London, England

(North Wind Picture Archives)

Early Life

Abraham de Moivre (pronounced either "duhm WAWVR" or "duh moy-VEHR") was the son of a Protestant surgeon of modest means. Wishing that his son receive a strong education, Abraham's father arranged for him to attend the Catholic village school in Vitry, followed by studies at a Protestant academy in Sedan. Abraham studied the standard classical curriculum of the time but also found time for mathematics on the side.

Continuing his studies at Saumur, de Moivre was introduced to probability upon reading Christiaan Huygens's *Tractatus de ratiociniis in aleae ludo* (1657; *Of the Games of Chance*, 1692). He completed his education at the University of Paris, where he studied physics and was tutored in mathematics by Jacques Ozanam.

In 1685, the Revocation of the Edict of Nantes put an end to religious toleration for French Protestants, and de Moivre was jailed. Upon his release in 1688, he fled to the more hospitable climate of Protestant England, where he would spend the remainder of his life.

Establishing a Scientific Reputation

Lacking contacts in his new homeland, de Moivre earned a precarious living by tutoring in mathematics and solving gambling and insurance problems for wealthy clients. He soon made the acquaintance of astronomer Edmond Halley, who encouraged him to read a paper to the Royal Society of London and supported his election as a Fellow. Through the society, de Moivre established relationships with many leading English scientists, including its president, Sir Isaac Newton. Because of his foreign birth, however, he could not obtain a university position and thus struggled to support himself.

De Moivre mastered Newton's famous work *Philosophiae Naturalis Principia Mathematica* (1687; *Mathematical Principles of Natural Philosophy*, 1729) by studying several pages at a time while walking to his tutoring duties. His relationship with Newton was such that he was appointed a foreign member of the Royal Society commission that ruled in Newton's favor in a dispute with Gottfried Wilhelm Leibniz over who invented the calculus. Despite his ties to Newton, de Moivre corresponded regularly with such supporters of Leibniz as Swiss mathematician Johann I Bernoulli.

Mathematical Work

De Moivre presented fifteen papers to the Royal Society of London during his career, but his reputation was based on his books. The most famous, *The Doctrine of Chances* (1718), was the first probability treatise written in English. It quickly surpassed the works of Huygens and Frenchman Pierre de Montmort as a standard text. In addition to analyzing games of chance, this work formulated important theoretical principles of probability, including the concepts of statistically independent events and conditional probability (the probability of an event occurring given that another event has occurred).

A Treatise of Annuities on Lives (1725) was a landmark in the mathematical theory of insurance. Drawing upon mortality data gathered by Halley, de Moivre derived mathematical formulas for the calculation of annuities, a considerable improvement upon existing practices.

The Normal Curve and the Normal Probability Function

De Moivre was the first mathematician to examine the form and basic properties of the normal probability function and to demonstrate that it could be used to approximate other types of probabilities.

The normal curve, more popularly known as the "bell-shaped" or error curve, is the graph of the normal probability function. The specific form of the curve is completely determined by the mean (μ), the point at which the curve peaks, and the standard deviation (σ), the distance from μ to the inflection points (the points where the curvature changes) on either side of the peak.

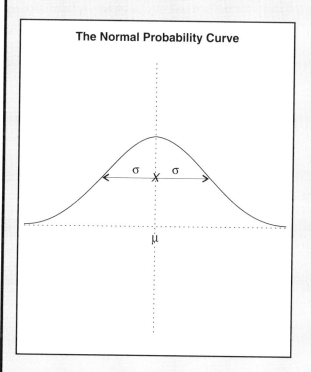

The Normal Probability Curve

The normal function models the behavior of many random phenomena, such as physical characteristics of a broad population. It also models the distribution of random errors when a quantity is measured repeatedly. More generally, it can be shown that the behavior of the sum of a large number of independently observed random quantities may be approximated by a normal function, no matter what probability model the individual quantities follow. This central limit theorem is a fundamental result in the theory of statistics.

In his 1733 pamphlet on approximating terms of the binomial expression "$(a + b)^n$," de Moivre showed that, for large n, the sum of the ratios of individual terms to the sum of all the terms may be estimated by determining the area under an appropriate normal curve. Since each such ratio corresponds to a binomial probability—that is, the probability of obtaining a certain number of successes in repeated trials when the probability of a success on each trial is known and does not vary—de Moivre's result represents a special case of the central limit theorem.

While de Moivre did not state an explicit formula for the normal function or sketch its curve, he recognized its essential form and demonstrated that the behavior of binomial probabilities could be described by a curve possessing the attributes of the normal curve. He also showed that the accuracy of the normal approximation of binomial probabilities increases as the square root of n increases. In calculating areas under the normal curve, de Moivre demonstrated that the percentages of observations lying one, two, and three units of σ to either side of μ are the same for all normal distributions.

De Moivre did not pursue results beyond the task of approximating binomial probabilities, but other mathematicians took up the question of whether other types of probabilities could be approximated by the normal function. In 1810, Pierre-Simon Laplace proved a more general form of de Moivre's result for sums of arbitrary random quantities.

Bibliography
A History of Probability and Statistics and Their Applications Before 1750. Anders Hald. New York: John Wiley & Sons, 1990.

The History of Statistics: The Measurement of Uncertainty Before 1900. Stephen M. Stigler. Cambridge, Mass.: The Belknap Press of Harvard University Press, 1986.

The Pleasures of Probability. Richard Isaac. New York: Springer-Verlag, 1995.

Miscellanea Analytica (1730) collected numerous results on recurrent series, trigonometry, and probability. De Moivre's formula, "$(\cos x + i \sin x)^n = \cos nx + i \sin nx$," remains a significant result in analytic trigonometry.

While de Moivre's published works featured many practical applications of mathematics, his most significant result was theoretical. In a pamphlet published privately in 1733, he examined the question of approximating terms of the binomial expression "$(a + b)^n$" for large values of n. His approximation method involved the first mathematical exploration of what would come to be known as the normal probability function. By showing that the normal function could be used to approximate other probabilities, de Moivre established its central importance as a tool in statistical analysis.

Final Years

Because of his financial status, de Moivre never married. He was protective of the material in his books because of the income that they provided, and he waged priority disputes with Montmort and English mathematician Thomas Simpson over some of his results. Nevertheless, he was generally well liked and respected by his colleagues. The aging Newton is said to have responded to a mathematical question with, "Go to Mr. de Moivre; he knows these things better than I do."

In his later years, de Moivre supported himself by solving gambling problems in coffeehouses. As he aged, he grew increasingly inactive. According to a famous anecdote, upon discovering that he was sleeping fifteen minutes more each day, de Moivre calculated that he would die on the day that his sleeping time equaled twenty-four hours—and so it came to pass. He died in 1754 at the age of eighty-seven.

Bibliography
By de Moivre
"De mensura sortis" (on the measurement of chance), *Philosophical Transactions of the Royal Society* 27, 1711
The Doctrine of Chances, 1718; 2d ed., 1738; 3d ed., 1756
A Treatise of Annuities on Lives, 1725; 2d ed., 1743 (also in *The Doctrine of Chances*, 3d ed.)
Miscellanea Analytica, 1730
"Approximatio ad summam terminorum binomii $(a + b)^n$ in seriem expansi" (a method of approximating the sum of the terms of the binomial $(a + b)^n$ expanded into a series), 1733 (incl. in *The Doctrine of Chances*, 2d and 3d eds.; also in David Eugene Smith's *A Source Book in Mathematics*, 1929)

About de Moivre
"Abraham de Moivre." Ian Hacking. In *Dictionary of Scientific Biography*, edited by Charles Coulston Gillispie. New York: Charles Scribner's Sons, 1981.
"Abraham de Moivre." Helen M. Walker. *Scripta mathematica* 2 (1934).
A History of the Mathematical Theory of Probability: From the Time of Pascal to That of Laplace. Isaac Todhunter. 1865. Reprint. New York: Chelsea House, 1965.

(Christopher E. Barat)

Gaspard Monge

Area of Achievement: Geometry

Contribution: Monge developed descriptive geometry, which became the basis of the standard system of drawing in engineering.

May 10, 1746	Born in Beaune, France
1762	Enters the École Militaire de Mézières
1768	Becomes a professor of mathematics at the École Militaire de Mézières
1792	Named Minister of the Navy
1794	Made a member of the Commission of Public Works
1795	Helps found the École Polytechnique and named a professor there
1796	Begins a political association and close friendship with Napoleon Bonaparte
1798	Participates in Napoleon's mission to Egypt
1804	Named Count of Péluse by Napoleon
1816	Removed from his academic position by the Bourbons
July 28, 1818	Dies in Paris, France

Early Life

Gaspard Monge (pronounced "mohnzh") was born into humble surroundings on May 10, 1746, in Beaune, France. His father, Jacques Monge, was a knife grinder and peddler who encouraged and supported the education of his three sons, all of whom eventually became mathematicians and professors. All three attended a local school operated by a religious order, the Oratorians.

Gaspard was noted early in his life for his scholastic and practical abilities. When he was sixteen, he developed a detailed map of Beaune using surveying instruments that he had made himself. This map was so accurate and detailed that it attracted the attention of a military officer who later arranged for Monge to attend classes at a military school, the École Militaire de Mézières.

The Development of Descriptive Geometry

Because of his humble birth, Monge could not become a military officer and was therefore somewhat restricted in the classes that he could attend at the École Militaire de Mézières. While working on some complicated geometric problems important in the design of fortifications, however, he developed the foundations of his principal contribution to mathematics—descriptive geometry.

Using systematic, geometric methods, Monge found a way to avoid tedious arithmetic calculations in determining firing lines for cannon and the plans for fortresses. In fact, when he described how he had solved one particular problem, his instructor first refused to check the work, believing that the

(Library of Congress)

Descriptive Geometry

Monge developed a systematic means of representing and analyzing three-dimensional geometric objects on a flat, two-dimensional surface, such as a piece of drawing paper.

When Monge was a student, military engineers used tedious arithmetic methods to design and analyze fortifications. They computed distances from point to point in fortresses, the lines of sight of soldiers behind barricades, and the areas that could be either defended or attacked by cannon. Monge realized that by using a systematic graphical means, the three-dimensional geometric relationships that were part of these problems could be conveniently represented and analyzed.

Geometric relationships such as distances, angles, and areas can be determined conveniently from the resulting drawing. Other planes, known as auxiliary planes, that are perpendicular to either the plan or the elevation can be introduced and used in the same way to find such things as the true lengths of lines and the actual areas of planes. Complex spatial curves and surfaces also can be investigated and analyzed using the same principles.

With training, people can produce and interpret drawings such as these in a systematic fashion. The method is so simple and elegant that it is used almost universally by engineers in designing and depicting physical objects.

Representation of a Pyramid Using the Principles of Descriptive Geometry

A Pyramid Shown Projected onto
Plan and Elevation Planes

A Pyramid Represented in
Three Dimensions on a Flat Plane

The basis of his scheme is shown in the accompanying figure. In the left part of the figure, two perpendicular, intersecting planes are shown. Also shown is a geometric object—in this case, a pyramid. The two planes have come to be called the "plan" and "elevation." Lines and points on the object are projected onto the plan and elevation planes by rays that are perpendicular to them. In practice, the plan and elevation are constructed as if they were folded out into a single plane, as shown in the right part.

Bibliography
Descriptive Geometry. James H. Earle. Reading, Mass.: Addison-Wesley, 1971.
Graphic Science and Design. Thomas E. French, Charles J. Vierck, and Robert J. Foster. 4th ed. New York: McGraw-Hill, 1984.
A History of Engineering Drawing. Peter Jeffrey Booker. London: Chatto & Windus, 1963.
A History of Geometrical Methods. Julian Lowell Coolidge. New York: Oxford University Press, 1940.

problem could not be solved so quickly.

Once Monge convinced his skeptics, he was immediately directed to teach his methods to military engineers. At the time, descriptive geometry was deemed strategically important by the military, and students had to hold a certain military rank to be permitted to attend his classes. He was not allowed to teach his methods publicly until 1794, following the French Revolution.

Monge became known as a gifted and inspiring teacher. He was also a good administrator, and he participated in the founding of several French institutions of higher education, including the famous École Polytechnique, where he became a professor. He was not very interested in writing, but many of his students authored textbooks and other works that described and extended his work.

Political Life

Monge was a contemporary of several other famous French mathematicians, including the marquis de Condorcet, Lazare Carnot, Joseph Fourier, Joseph-Louis Lagrange, Pierre-Simon Laplace, and Adrien-Marie Legendre. Together with Carnot and Condorcet, Monge was politically active in the years leading up to the French Revolution and became deeply involved in governmental and military affairs. Probably because of his humble origins, his sympathies lay with the radical Jacobin faction. He oversaw the production of gunpowder, cannon, and other armaments for the revolutionary forces. For a time, he served as Minister of the Navy, and he was made a member of a Commission of Public Works in 1794. He participated in the French reform of weights and measures that introduced the metric system of units in 1799.

In 1796, Monge was drawn into Napoleon's inner circle of friends and advisers. Bold and adventurous, Monge accompanied him on an Egyptian incursion, eventually being forced to escape, along with Napoleon, from the English troops following the Battle of the Nile.

Monge became a senator in 1805. Late in his life, in retaliation for his political activities, he was removed from his academic position following the restoration of the Bourbons. This act affected him greatly, and his friends thought that it shortened his life.

Monge's life spanned the French Revolution and the Industrial Revolution. Both profoundly affected future events, and he contributed significantly to them. He was an active participant in the French Revolution, and the system of drawing for engineering that grew from his descriptive geometry was important in stimulating the explosion of machine building and manufacturing that inaugurated the Industrial Revolution. Following his death in 1818, his wife hoped to perpetuate his memory and worked to memorialize him. She need not have bothered, for Monge himself had created a legacy during his life.

Bibliography
By Monge
Géométrie descriptive, 1798 (*An Elementary Treatise on Descriptive Geometry*, 1851)
Application de l'algèbre à la géométrie, 1805 (with M. Hachette; application of algebra to geometry)

About Monge
A History of Mathematics. Carl B. Boyer. New York: John Wiley & Sons, 1968.
Men of Mathematics. E. T. Bell. New York: Simon & Schuster, 1937.
A Short Account of the History of Mathematics. W. W. Rouse Ball. 4th ed. New York: Macmillan, 1908.

(Cecil O. Huey, Jr.)

Cathleen Synge Morawetz

Area of Achievement: Applied math

Contribution: Morawetz worked on some famous problems involving waves, proving that it is impossible to design an airplane wing to avoid shock waves. She was the first woman in the United States to head a mathematics institute.

May 5, 1923	Born in Toronto, Ontario, Canada
1945	Earns a B.A. in mathematics and physics from the University of Toronto
Oct. 25, 1945	Marries Herbert Morawetz
1946	Earns a master's degree from the Massachusetts Institute of Technology (MIT)
1950	Becomes a naturalized citizen of the United States
1951	Earns a Ph.D. from New York University (NYU)
1952-1957	Works as a research associate at the Courant Institute of Mathematical Sciences at NYU
1958	Joins the faculty at NYU
1980-1996	Receives eight honorary degrees
1981-1998	Invited to deliver addresses and lectures, including the Gibbs Lecture for the American Mathematical Society in 1981
1984-1988	Works as director of the Courant Institute
1993	Named Outstanding Woman Scientist by the Association of Women in Science
1995-1996	Serves as president of the American Mathematical Society

Early Life

Cathleen Synge was born on May 5, 1923, in Toronto, Ontario, Canada. Her parents, John Lighton Synge and Elizabeth Allen, were Protestant immigrants from southern Ireland. Cathleen liked to play with the Meccano erector set and to go sailing with her father, an applied mathematician at the University of Toronto. She was also close to her multitalented mother, who had studied mathematics before turning to history.

Synge was a stubborn child, insisting on starting school at age three when her older sister started. She considered going into history, but in her last year in high school, one of her teachers encouraged her to concentrate on mathematics in preparation for a scholarship to the University of Toronto.

Education

At the university, Synge majored in mathematics and physics. After her junior year, she took a year off to work on the effort for World War II. At her job in Quebec City, she thought for the first time that science was fun. Before that, it had been a worry, the means of keeping a big scholarship.

She ended up in applied mathematics, liking the spirit better than in the tough program in pure mathematics. It was this happy year that she got to know Herbert Morawetz, a Jewish chemical engineer who was a refugee from Czechoslovakia.

Cecilia Kriege, a mathematician on the faculty, encouraged Synge to apply for a fellowship. When she won it and discovered that California Institute of Technology (Caltech) would not take women, she started working on a master's degree in engineering at the Massachusetts Institute of Technology (MIT). Her discovery that being weak in arithmetic and at experiments mattered, however, sent her back to applied mathematics. By the time that she obtained her master's degree, she and Herbert Morawetz were married.

Seeking a job, Cathleen Synge Morawetz felt the discrimination practiced against women at the time. Bell Labs would have put her in a pool of women with bachelor's degrees from anywhere. General Electric told her that "GE wives" do not work. In 1946, Richard Courant, whose daughter was having similar difficulties pursuing a career, gave Morawetz a job editing grammar and checking the accuracy of the formulas in Courant and Kurt Friedrichs's book *Supersonic Flow and Shock Waves*.

When Friedrichs offered a topology course, Morawetz decided to take it. The course was exciting and competitive, and she cried when she could not do the homework. She had learned at Toronto that competition was bad for her. She wrote her dissertation on imploding shock waves with Friedrichs as her adviser, receiving her Ph.D from New York University (NYU) in 1951.

Career and Family

From that point on, her life showed that a woman can have both a career and a happy family life. Her husband became an eminent polymer chemist. They had four children, all of whom became professionals. Morawetz supplied her grandchildren with math problems and enjoyed sailing with them. She observed that it was important to have had a supportive husband and hired help to take care of the house and the children.

Her own career blossomed. Morawetz went through the academic ranks and then was named the first woman in the United States to head a mathematics institute, the Courant Institute of Mathematical Sciences at NYU. She had been a nervous and unhappy teacher, but she found that administration suited her because she liked the relationship with human beings.

Morawetz directed about ten Ph.D. dissertations—two for women. She was responsible for the American Mathematical Society's formation of a committee on women. She was invited to give prestigious lectures. She was granted eight honorary degrees. She was made a member of both the American Academy of Arts and

Transonic Flow and Waves

The research of Morawetz, an expert in applied differential equations, focused on two types of questions—those dealing with transonic flow and those with waves. Her results had significant applications in aerodynamics, acoustics, and optics.

Morawetz proved that there was no way to design airplane wings to avoid shock waves as the plane approaches sonic speed but has not yet reached it. Shock waves are certain to develop and to increase the drag on the aircraft. Therefore, it will take more energy to keep the aircraft flying. It is possible for airplane wings to experience only small shocks; engineers now settle for this situation.

It is known that the shape of the wings and the speed of travel affect the size of shock waves. Morawetz studied speeds in the transonic range. These speeds, which vary according to the aircraft design, are roughly between 0.6 and 0.9 times the speed of sound. If a plane is going faster than sound, like the Concorde, big bow shocks occur, but they are predictable. At close to but less than the speed of sound, however, it is a different story. The shock not only increases the amount of energy needed but also leads to abrupt changes in momentum or even to shaking.

Another major interest in Morawetz's career was the scattering of waves. When a wave hits something, the wave can be reflected, absorbed, or transmitted. An important class of problems is inverse scattering. In such a problem, the wave that was sent is known, data are obtained on how it scattered, and information on what the wave hit is desired. The first such problem to be mastered involved X-ray diffraction.

Because high-frequency waves tend to bounce straight off their targets, they are the easiest to analyze. They are used in medicine to study internal organs and in geology to search for oil fields. Morawetz studied waves numerically and analytically and sought methods that would work for all frequencies. She amazed collaborators with her insight, her seemingly endless stock of new ideas, and her original way of approaching each problem from scratch.

Bibliography
"Transonic Flight." Richard Whitcomb. In *McGraw-Hill Encyclopedia of Science and Technology*. 7th ed. Vol. 18. New York: McGraw-Hill, 1992.

(Courtesy of Cathleen Synge Morawetz)

Sciences and the National Academy of Sciences and served as trustee for several organizations, both mathematical and nonmathematical, starting with Princeton University in 1972.

Retirement
In 1995-1996, Morawetz served as president of the American Mathematical Society. Her wisdom and common sense made her in demand. She found that the life of a mathematician need not be one of isolation. She liked using mathematics to describe natural phenomena but found that no excitement beat that of proving a theorem. As an emeritus professor, she continued her research and gave mathematical talks.

Bibliography
By Morawetz
"Non-Existence of Transonic Flow Past a Profile," *Communications on Pure and Applied Mathematics* 17, 1964

"Decay and Scattering of Solutions of a Nonlinear Relativistic Wave Equation," *Communications on Pure and Applied Mathematics* 25, 1972 (with Walter A. Strauss)

"Decay of Solutions of the Wave Equation Outside Nontrapping Obstacles," *Communications on Pure and Applied Mathematics* 30, 1977 (with James V. Ralson and Strauss)

Lectures on Nonlinear Waves and Shocks, 1981 (notes by P. S. Datti)

"The Mathematical Approach to the Sonic Barrier," *Bulletin of the American Mathematical Society* 6, 1982

"On a Weak Solution for a Transonic Flow Problem," *Communications on Pure and Applied Mathematics* 38, 1985

"Scattering by a Potential Using Hyperbolic Methods," *Mathematics of Computation* 52, 1989 (with Alvin Bayliss and Yanyan Li)

About Morawetz
"Cathleen Morawetz: Riding the Waves." Janice Hopkins Tanne. *New York* 25, no. 50 (December 21-28, 1992): 103-106.

"Cathleen Morawetz: The Mathematics of Waves." Gina Bari Kolata. *Science* 206 (1979): 206-207.

"Cathleen S. Morawetz." In *More Mathematical People: Contemporary Conversations*, edited by Donald J. Albers et al. Boston: Harcourt Brace Jovanovich, 1990.

"Nomination for Cathleen S. Morawetz." Andrew J. Majda. *Notices of the American Mathematical Society* 40, no. 7 (September, 1993): 816-817, 819.

(Elizabeth Magarian)

John Napier

Areas of Achievement: Algebra, arithmetic, and trigonometry
Contribution: Napier invented logarithms as a tool for solving multiplication and division problems by addition and subtraction.

1550	Born at Merchiston Castle, in Edinburgh, Scotland
1563	Enters St. Andrews University
1572	Marries Elizabeth Stirling
1593	Publishes a religious tract, *A Plaine Discovery of the Whole Revelation of St. John*
1594	Knows the principle upon which his logarithms would be based
1614	Publishes the first table of logarithms, *Mirifici Logarithmorum Canonis Descriptio* (*A Description of the Admirable Table of Logarithms*, 1616)
1615	Meets with Henry Briggs to plan the first table of common logarithms
1617	Publishes *Rabdologiae* (*Rabdology*, 1990), a description of mechanical calculating devices
Apr. 4, 1617	Dies at Merchiston Castle, in Edinburgh, Scotland
1619	Robert Napier publishes his father's *Mirifici Logarithmorum Canonis Constructio* (*The Construction of the Wonderful Canon of Logarithms*, 1889), explaining how the table of logarithms had been constructed

Early Life

John Napier was born at Merchiston Castle, on the outskirts of Edinburgh, Scotland, in 1550. This fortress, with walls 6 feet thick and a tower 60 feet high, once guarded the southwestern approach to Edinburgh and today is on the campus of Napier Technical University.

John was the eldest child of Sir Archibald Napier and the former Janet Bothwell. His father was a prosperous landowner who played a prominent role in the affairs of church and state. Unfortunately, no record of John's childhood at Merchiston has been preserved, but he most likely received his early education at home.

In 1563, Napier entered St. Andrews University, where he studied theology and philosophy. He left there without earning a degree and spent the next several years studying abroad. In 1572, he married Elizabeth Stirling, the daughter of a neighboring nobleman.

Work on Logarithms

Napier's major mathematical achievement—the invention of logarithms—was the culmination of many years of work. Sixteenth century improvements in navigation and astronomy made the multiplication and division of large numbers quite common. Any device that could reduce the labor involved in such computations would be welcomed. Some evidence exists that Napier had the main ideas of logarithms worked out by 1594, but two decades passed before they were published.

(Archive Photos)

In 1614, Napier's *Mirifici Logarithmorum Canonis Descriptio* was published, including ninety pages of tables and instructions for using them. An English translation by Edward Wright, entitled *A Description of the Admirable Table of Logarithms*, appeared two years later. After Napier's death, a second work appeared, explaining how his logarithm tables had been calculated and the reasoning on which they were based. Evidently, Napier coined the term "logarithm" to mean "ratio number."

Conceptually, Napier thought of a moving point that approaches a fixed point so that its velocity is proportional to the distance remaining from the fixed point. According to Napier's own definition, a logarithm is "that number which has increased arithmetically with the same velocity throughout as that with which the radius began to decrease geometrically." This means that, as the natural numbers decrease, Napierian logarithms increase. For example, Napier's logarithm of 10,000,000 is 0, the logarithm of 9,900,000 is 100,503, and the logarithm of 1,000,000 is 23,025,851. Unlike logarithms used today, Napierian logarithms have no base.

Credit for the development of common (base 10) logarithms belongs jointly to Napier and Henry Briggs, the first professor of geometry at Gresham College in London. Briggs became excited when he saw Napier's work and, in the summer of 1615, visited Napier at Merchiston, where the two men devised a system of logarithms in which log 1 = 0 and log 10 = 1. Since Napier was in poor health, it was left to Briggs to calculate the new tables. At the same time, Jobst (or Joost) Bürgi, a native of Liechtenstein, was working independently in Prague and published his own system of logarithms in 1620.

Other Work

Napier's concern for practical methods of computation led him to invent several elementary calculating devices, the most famous being the rods known as "Napier's bones." He is also credited with "Napier's rules" for right triangles in spherical trigonometry. Although he did not invent decimal fractions, the widespread adoption of his logarithm tables brought the decimal point into common use.

Not all of Napier's work was mathematical.

In 1593, fearing a Catholic invasion of Scotland, Napier wrote *A Plaine Discovery of the Whole Revelation of St. John*, in which he concluded that the pope was the Antichrist and that the world would end before the year 1700. Napier believed that his life's reputation would rest on this theological work, and it was indeed very popular in its day. Napier's concern for the military security of Scotland also led him to write prophetically about weapons that would be realized centuries later as the machine gun, submarine, and tank.

In many respects, John Napier was a typical sixteenth century Scottish landowner. He was active in the Church and in politics, became embroiled in quarrels over inheritance and land rights, and contributed to the advancement of agriculture. He had a reputation for cleverness and was believed by some to have magical powers. Napier was afflicted with gout for many years and died on April 4, 1617.

Bibliography

By Napier

A Plaine Discovery of the Whole Revelation of St. John, 1593

Mirifici Logarithmorum Canonis Descriptio, 1614 (*A Description of the Admirable Table of Logarithms*, 1616)

Rabdologiae: Seu, Numerationis per virgulas, 1617 (*Rabdology*, 1990)

Mirifici Logarithmorum Canonis Constructio, 1619 (*The Construction of the Wonderful Canon of Logarithms*, 1889)

De Arte Logistica, 1839 (the art of calculating; published by a descendant, Mark Napier, from manuscript fragments left by John Napier to his son, Robert)

About Napier

Great Moments in Mathematics (Before 1650). Howard Whitley Eves. Washington, D.C.: Mathematical Association of America, 1980.

"John Napier." Margaret E. Baron. In *Dictionary of Scientific Biography*, edited by Charles Coulston Gillispie. New York: Charles Scribner's Sons, 1970.

Napier Tercentenary Memorial Volume. C. G. Knott, ed. London: Longmans, Green, 1915.

(David E. Kullman)

Logarithms

Napier invented logarithms as a computational tool whereby the operations of multiplying or dividing numbers may be carried out by adding or subtracting their logarithms.

The fundamental idea underlying logarithms is a correspondence between terms of a geometric progression of powers (formed by multiplication) and the related arithmetic progression of their exponents (formed by addition). The pattern had been observed in antiquity and was well known to mathematicians of the sixteenth century.

and 3) $\log a^n = n \log a$.

Common logarithms are those to base 10. The natural logarithm (to base e approximately equal to 2.71828) of a may be defined geometrically as the area between the x-axis and the hyperbola $y = \frac{1}{x}$, from $x = 1$ to a. In calculus, logarithms are usually represented by integrals or by infinite series.

In Napier's day, it was said that logarithms "doubled the life of an astronomer" by making it possible to carry out long calculations in only half the time formerly needed. The slide rule, which was an indispensable tool for scientists

Geometric Progression (Powers)	1	2	4	8	16	32	64	128
Arithmetic Progression (Exponents)	0	1	2	3	4	5	6	7

By working with the exponents, rather than the numbers themselves, multiplication can be accomplished by addition and division can be accomplished by subtraction. For example, using modern exponential notation (which first appeared in René Descartes's *La Géométrie* in 1637 or 1638), $2^5 \times 2^2 = 2^{5+2}$ and $2^5 \div 2^2 = 2^{5-2}$.

Unfortunately, powers of 2 increase much more rapidly than their exponents, leaving wide gaps in the list of numbers that can be represented in this way. Napier overcame this problem by constructing a geometric progression in which the ratio of successive terms is 0.9999999, a number very close to 1.

Today, the logarithm of a to base b is defined algebraically as the exponent y in the expression $a = b^y$. This is equivalent to writing $y = \log_b a$. There are three fundamental laws of logarithms: 1) $\log ac = \log a + \log c$; 2) $\log \frac{a}{c} = \log a - \log c$;

and engineers until the latter part of the twentieth century, is really a device for physically adding and subtracting logarithms. Today, logarithms as a computational tool are obsolete, but the logarithm concept is essential for analyzing many real-world phenomena, including compound interest, population growth, radioactive decay, the loudness of sound, and the intensity of earthquakes.

Bibliography

e: The Story of a Number. Eli Maor. Princeton, N.J.: Princeton University Press, 1994.

A History of Numerical Analysis from the Sixteenth Through the Nineteenth Century. Herman Heine Goldstine. New York: Springer-Verlag, 1977.

Precalculus and Its Applications. Larry Joel Goldstein. Dubuque, Iowa: Wm. C. Brown, 1994.

Hanna Neumann

Areas of Achievement: Algebra and mathematical logic

Contribution: Neumann developed theories in pure mathematics, especially concerning varieties of groups.

Feb. 12, 1914	Born in Berlin, Germany
1922	Enrolled in a girls' grammar school
1932	Graduated from primary school and enrolls at the University of Berlin
1936	Begins studies at the University of Göttingen
1938	Marries Bernhard Neumann in Cardiff, Wales
1944	Receives a D.Phil. degree from Oxford University
1945	Begins a position as lecturer at Hull University that lasts twelve years
1955	Receives a D.Sc. degree from Oxford
1958	Accepts a teaching position at Manchester College of Technology
1961-1962	Conducts research at New York's Courant Institute of Mathematical Sciences
1963	Becomes head of the Department of Pure Mathematics at Australian National University
1966	Founds and is elected vice president of the Australian Association of Mathematics Teachers
1967	Serves as president of the Canberra Mathematical Association
Nov. 14, 1971	Dies in Ottawa, Canada

Early Life

Hanna Neumann was born in Berlin in 1914 as Hanna von Caemmerer, the daughter of Hermann and Katharina von Caemmerer. Her father was a historian who died during World War I. His war pension provided the family some financial support. By the age of thirteen, Hanna von Caemmerer worked as a tutor to raise money for her education.

She spent two years in a private school before enrolling at the Augusta-Victoria-Schule Grammar School for Girls in 1922. She was graduated ten years later. Hanna enjoyed botany, collecting many specimens, until mathematics interested her more. In the spring of 1932, she began studying mathematics at the University of Berlin.

College Student

At the University of Berlin, von Caemmerer was influenced by such talented mathematicians as Ludwig Bieberbach, Erhard Schmidt, and Issai Schur. She took classes in analytic geometry, calculus, and number theory and was a reviewer for the *Jahrbuch ber die Fortschritte der Mathematik*. Joining students in informal discussions, she met Bernhard H. Neumann. He transferred to Cambridge University in 1933 because he was Jewish and Nazi Germany was anti-Semitic. Von Caemmerer visited Neumann, and the couple became secretly engaged.

Returning to Berlin, von Caemmerer accepted a part-time position in the library of the Mathematical Institute, gaining access to valuable books and journals. She publicly criticized the German government and anti-Jewish protestors. As a result, she lost her job and was warned that she might fail her doctoral examinations because of her political beliefs. She chose to take the *Staatsexamen*, an alternate test, and to complete her doctorate elsewhere.

War Years

Von Caemmerer was accepted as a research student at the University of Göttingen. Because Germany annexed Austria and seized Czechoslovakia in 1938, Hanna decided to leave school and marry Bernhard. They married secretly in Cardiff, Wales, where Bernhard had a teaching position.

Considered aliens during World War II, they had to leave the coastal area and moved to Oxford, England. Bernhard was interned and then joined the British intelligence corps. Hanna rented a trailer because housing was limited as a result of bombings and refugees. She wrote her dissertation about a group theory problem by candlelight, submitting it in 1943 to her thesis director Olga Taussky-Todd. Hanna Neumann received her doctorate in 1944.

Professional Development

After the war, Neumann was an assistant lecturer at Hull University where her husband taught. Interested in her students, she spoke to the mathematical society and participated in the model building club. She hosted weekly coffee evenings in her home for students and professors, where they could discuss problems. She conducted her own research and also worked with her husband.

Neumann published papers from her thesis and one about mathematically resolving tied chess games. She earned a D.Sc. degree from Oxford in 1955 when she submitted a portfolio of her publications. In 1958, she accepted a teaching position at Manchester College of Technology.

In 1961, Neumann and her husband spent one year in New York at the Courant Institute of Mathematical Sciences. He was offered the opportunity to establish a research department at Australian National University at Canberra. She devoted one year at Manchester to help her students complete their research.

Educator

Moving to Australia in August, 1963, Hanna Neumann served as head of the Department of Pure Mathematics at Australian National University. She implemented her teaching ideas, such as take-home tests, and changed the curriculum from applied to pure mathematics. Neumann belonged to university committees and served as dean of students. She also focused on research about varieties of groups, writing a book that other mathematicians considered a classic; it was translated into Russian.

Neumann helped secondary school teachers learn new mathematical methods and spoke to

groups of parents, encouraging them to view mathematics positively, especially for their daughters. She also wrote letters to newspapers, demanding that Australian schools improve the quality of mathematics education. She helped found the Australian Association of Mathematics Teachers in 1966 and was elected its vice president. Neumann also served as president of the Canberra Mathematical Association. She lectured about group theory throughout Europe, the United States, and Canada, where she died in Ottawa on November 14, 1971.

Neumann had five children, several of whom became mathematicians. A Fellow of the Australian Academy of Science and the Australian College of Education, she posed mathematical puzzles that inspired further research.

Bibliography

By Neumann

"On the Elimination Rule," *Journal of the London Mathematical Society* 15, 1940

"Generalized Free Products with Amalgamated Subgroups I," *American Journal of Mathematics* 70, 1948

Pure Mathematics

Neumann promoted the research and teaching of pure mathematics by developing theories about varieties of groups and solving mathematical puzzles.

Pure mathematics is the study of mathematical laws and relationships that are abstract and have no specific applications. Many mathematicians state that pure mathematics is similar to the study of logic. They want to advance mathematical knowledge by developing theories and discovering new mathematical relationships. Pure mathematics includes such disciplines as arithmetic, algebra, theory of numbers, calculus, and geometry. These are either elementary pure mathematics (used in daily life) or higher pure mathematics (used for advanced mathematics such as matrix theory). These concepts, however, often do not represent physical reality. The need for applied mathematics to explain and resolve problems in fields such as chemistry and engineering sometimes motivates pure mathematicians to devise theories for practical uses.

Neumann encouraged schools to teach courses in mathematical theory work in addition to problem solutions. She hoped to make abstract ideas accessible to students by providing understandable examples and exercises. Neumann also applied mathematics to other fields, such as physics.

Her most notable theory work concerned varieties of groups that explain the properties of algebraic operations. Groups are sets of finite or infinite mathematical data that are combined by a binary operation such as addition or multiplication in which pairs of numbers become one figure. This operation must meet specific conditions.

Many mathematicians consider groups to be valuable tools in computing or understanding data. Neumann was interested in identifying classes of groups that were governed by similar mathematical laws or identity relations. She looked for groups that behaved according to specific mathematical laws when any group of elements was substituted. Neumann advanced varieties of group theory by posing unresolved questions. For example, she asked if each variety could be defined by a finite set of laws.

Her formal theories about varieties of groups, outlined in several books, intrigued other researchers. Solutions to her problems required complex calculations and intricate mathematical techniques. Neumann solved one of her most difficult problems only after years of work, thus contributing helpful information to pure mathematicians who were analyzing related abstract theories.

Bibliography

A Course of Pure Mathematics. G. H. Hardy. 10th ed. Cambridge, England: Cambridge University Press, 1993.

Group Theory and Physics. Shlomo Sternberg. Cambridge, England: Cambridge University Press, 1994.

Groups and Characters. Larry C. Grove. New York: John Wiley & Sons, 1997.

Groups and Geometry. Peter M. Neumann, Gabrielle A. Stoy, and Edward C. Thompson. Oxford, England: Oxford University Press, 1994.

"Generalized Free Products with Amalgamated Subgroups II," *American Journal of Mathematics* 71, 1949

"Embedding Theorems for Groups," *Journal of the London Mathematical Society* 24, 1949 (with Graham Higman and Bernhard H. Neumann)

"On Varieties of Groups and Their Associated Near-Rings," *Mathematische Zeitschrift* 65, 1956

Varieties of Groups, 1967

Schwartz Distributions, 1969

"The Hopf Property of Free Products," *Mathematische Zeitschrift* 117, 1970 (with I. M. S. Dey)

Selected Works of B. H. Neumann and Hanna Neumann, 1988 (6 vols.; D. S. Meek and R. G. Stanton, eds.)

About Neumann

"A Great Woman Mathematician from Down Under." Kailash Kumari Anand. *Association for Women in Mathematics Newsletter* 18 (1988): 10-13.

"Hanna Neumann." G. Higman. *Bulletin of the London Mathematical Society* 6 (1974): 99-100.

"Hanna Neumann." M. F. Newman. *Australian Mathematics Teacher* 29 (1973): 1-22.

"Hanna Neumann." M. F. Newman and G. E. Wall. *Journal of the Australian Mathematical Society* 17 (1974): 1-28.

(Elizabeth D. Schafer)

Sir Isaac Newton

Area of Achievement: Calculus

Contribution: Newton developed the calculus, which allows the slopes of curves and the areas under curves to be calculated.

Dec. 25, 1642	Born in Woolstorpe, Lincolnshire, England
1665	Graduated from Trinity College, Cambridge University
1665	Leaves London during the plague and works on problems in mathematics and physics on his mother's farm
1665-1666	Develops the basic principles of the calculus
1667	Returns to Cambridge
1668	Develops the refracting telescope
1669	Appointed Lucasian Professor of Mathematics at Cambridge
1671	Circulates a manuscript, entitled "Methodus Fluxionum et Serierum Infinitarum," describing his method of the calculus
1672	Elected to the Royal Society of London
1687	Publishes *Philosophiae Naturalis Principia Mathematica* (*Mathematical Principles of Natural Philosophy,* 1729)
1689	Elected a member of Parliament
1696	Appointed Warden of the Mint
1699	Promoted to Master of the Mint
1703	Elected president of the Royal Society of London
1705	Knighted by Queen Anne
Mar. 20, 1727	Dies in London, England

(Library of Congress)

Early Life

Isaac Newton was born in Woolstorpe, England, on Christmas Day, 1642, by the Julian calendar (or on January 4, 1643, by the Gregorian calendar now in use). His father had died on October 6, 1642. His mother remarried three years later, to the Reverend Barnabus Smith, and left Newton in Woolstorpe in the care of his grandparents. Newton attended the King's School, in nearby Grantham, where his performance was undistinguished. He showed interest, however, in such devices as water clocks and sundials.

Upon the Reverend Smith's death in 1653, Newton's mother returned to Woolstorpe and took Newton out of school to work on the family farm. Newton was urged by his uncle, William Ayscough, to attend a university and entered Trinity College, at Cambridge, in 1661. He was graduated in 1665.

The Calculus

In 1665, while at Trinity, Newton developed the binomial theorem, a rule allowing the square of the sum of two functions to be written as a series of terms. When the plague struck London and the surrounding area in 1665, he re-

turned to his mother's farm. During the next eighteen months, Newton worked on problems in mathematics, optics, and the orbits of the planets.

Newton's binomial theorem led him to develop a method to determine the sum of a power series with an infinite number of terms, which eventually led to his formulation of the calculus. The functions now called derivatives Newton called "fluxions," and in 1671 he circulated a manuscript entitled "Methodus Fluxionum et Serierum Infinitarum" describing his method. The manuscript was published, as *The Method of Fluxions and Infinite Series* (1736), only after his death.

Newton's apparent lack of interest in publishing his results led to controversy. While Newton was working on the problem, German mathematician Gottfried Wilhelm Leibniz was trying to formulate the same mathematics. Leibniz apparently read a copy of Newton's manuscript during a visit to London in 1676. Newton charged Leibniz with plagiarism, and a long, intense quarrel began. Among later mathematicians, general agreement exists that Newton and Leibniz developed the calculus independently; the notation employed by Leibniz is now preferred.

The calculus was essential to Newton's interest in understanding the behavior of the physical world. Given a mathematical equation for the position, the velocity, or the acceleration of an object as a function of time, he could derive the other two functions. He could also relate the force applied to an object to the acceleration that the object experienced.

In 1667, Newton returned to Trinity as a Fellow, and, in 1669, at the age of twenty-six, he was appointed Lucasian Professor of Mathematics.

The Motion of Planets and Comets

During Newton's absence from London to escape the plague, he recognized that the same force, gravity, which causes objects to fall to the surface of the earth is responsible for holding the planets in their orbits around the sun. He developed the mathematics describing the motion of the planets under the attraction exerted by the sun.

In the 1680's, astronomer Edmond Halley asked Newton what path a comet would take moving in the sun's gravitational field. Newton quickly replied, "An ellipse," explaining that he had worked out this problem twenty years earlier. Halley arranged for the publication of this important result and paid the costs involved. The work was titled *Philosophiae Naturalis Principia Mathematica* (1687); an English translation, *Mathematical Principles of Natural Philosophy*, appeared in 1729. Despite his invention of the calculus, Newton used geometrical arguments in this book, which codified what are now called Newton's laws of motion.

In 1668, Newton invented the reflecting telescope, which focuses light by reflection from mirrors rather than refraction through lenses. The large telescopes used by modern astronomers, including the Hubble Space Telescope, use this reflection principle.

The Development of the Calculus

Newton changed the way in which mathematicians looked at the small increments required to determine a derivative.

A fundamental problem of mathematics in the seventeenth century was finding the quadrature of a function—that is, determining the area between the curve represented by the function and the horizontal axis. Prior to Newton, other mathematicians had developed techniques to determine the area under a semicircular curve. Newton recognized that this area could be represented by an infinite series, a continuing sequence of numbers that follows a well-defined pattern. Newton further recognized that the problem could be extended to allow the area of a part of this circle to be represented by a similar infinite series.

Newton's major breakthrough was his recognition that the fixed upper limit in the quadrature problem could be replaced with a variable, or unknown value, and that the general problem could be solved in terms of this variable. The area under any segment of the curve defined by the function could then be determined simply by substituting a fixed value for the variable. This recognition represented the beginning of integral calculus, the branch that determines areas under curves.

By 1666, Newton had reformulated the way to determine the derivative, the slope of a curve at any point along its length. Prior to Newton, mathematicians simply used a geometrical concept to calculate the derivative. In this technique, the derivative is simply the change in value of the function divided by the very small, but finite, interval over which that change occurs.

Newton rejected the idea of an indefinitely small but finite interval in favor of what he called the "fluxion." The fluxion represented the value of the change in the function divided by the size of the interval over which the change occurred when Newton let the interval shrink to zero. This concept represented the development of differential calculus, the branch that determines the slope of the tangent to a curve at any point or the rate of change of the function.

Newton developed an important principle allowing the determination of the maximum or minimum value of any function. He observed that, at the point where a function reaches an extreme—that is, it reaches a local maximum or minimum—the numerical value of the derivative of that function must be zero. If the function has a local maximum, then the slope of a line tangent to the curve is increasing on one side of that maximum and decreasing on the other side. At the point where the maximum occurs, the tangent line is horizontal. This recognition was critical to the use of the calculus to solve problems of practical interest, which frequently involve determining the maximum or minimum points of a function.

Bibliography

"The Discovery of Infinitesimal Calculus." H. W. Turnbull. *Nature* 167, no. 4261 (June 30, 1951): 1048-1050.

The History of the Calculus and Its Conceptual Development. Carl B. Boyer. New York: Dover, 1959.

Later Life

Despite Newton's insights into mathematics and physics, he spent much in unsuccessful attempts at alchemy, the transmutation of base metals into gold. He also wrote at length on theology and interpretations of mystical passages in the Bible.

In 1687, he defended the rights of Cambridge University against King James II. In 1689, after the king was forced into exile, Newton was elected to Parliament, but he never made an important speech in the legislature. Newton's politically influential friends had him appointed Warden of the Mint in 1696; he rose to Master of the Mint in 1699. He enthusiastically reorganized the minting process and developed techniques to detect counterfeit coinage.

Newton's research in science and mathematics dwindled with his role as Warden of the Mint, and he resigned his professorship in 1701. He did publish *Opticks* (1704), describing his experiments on light, prisms, and lenses in the late 1660's.

Newton was knighted by Queen Anne in 1705. He died in London on March 20, 1727 (March 31 by the Gregorian calendar), at the age of eighty-four. He was buried in Westminster Abbey alongside many heroes of England.

Bibliography

By Newton

"Methodus Fluxionum et Serierum Infinitarum," circulated in 1671 (*The Method of Fluxions and Infinite Series, with Its Application to the Geometry of Curve-Lines*, 1736)

Philosophiae Naturalis Principia Mathematica, 1687 (commonly known as the *Principia*; trans. as *Mathematical Principles of Natural Philosophy*, 1729)

Opticks, 1704

Arithmetica Universalis, 1707 (*Universal Arithmetick*, 1720)

About Newton

Isaac Newton: Adventurer in Thought. Alfred Rupert Hall. Cambridge, Mass.: Blackwell, 1992.

The Life of Isaac Newton. Richard S. Westfall. New York: Cambridge University Press, 1993.

The Newton Handbook. Derek Gjertsen. London: Routledge & Kegan Paul, 1986.

A Portrait of Isaac Newton. Frank Edward Manuel. Cambridge, Mass.: The Belknap Press of Harvard University Press, 1968.

Sir Isaac Newton. Herbert Douglas Anthony. London: Abelard-Schuman, 1960.

(George J. Flynn)

Emmy Noether

Area of Achievement: Algebra
Contribution: Noether made numerous advances in the development of abstract algebra.

Mar. 23, 1882	Born in Erlangen, Germany
1900-1902	Audits classes at the University of Erlangen
1903	Studies at the University of Göttingen
1904	Returns to Erlangen, earning a doctoral degree
1908-1915	Conducts research, supervises students, and delivers lectures at the University of Erlangen, without pay
1915	Joins Felix Klein and David Hilbert at Göttingen, delivering lectures again without pay
1919	Designated a licensed lecturer
1922	Granted the honorary title "unofficial extraordinary professor"
1923	Awarded a teaching appointment in algebra, with a small salary
1928-1930	Serves as a visiting professor at the Universities of Moscow and Frankfurt
1933	Dismissed from Göttingen and emigrates to the United States
1933	Accepts a position at Bryn Mawr College, in Pennsylvania
1933-1935	Works at the Institute for Advanced Study in Princeton, New Jersey
Apr. 14, 1935	Dies in Bryn Mawr, Pennsylvania

Early Life

Amalie Emmy Noether (pronounced "NYOO-tur"), usually known as Emmy Noether, was born in Erlangen, a small university town in southern Germany, on March 23, 1882. Her father, Max Noether, was a professor of mathematics at the University of Erlangen. Her mother, Ida Amalia Kaufmann Noether, was a talented musician.

Noether began her formal education in 1889 at the Stadtischen Hoheren Tochterschule in Erlangen, where she excelled in the study of foreign languages. In 1900, she passed government examinations in French and English, entitling her to teach these subjects. Instead of pursuing a career as a teacher, however, she turned to the study of mathematics.

Women could not enroll in German universities in 1900, but Noether was allowed to audit classes at the University of Erlangen from 1900 to 1902. She also audited classes at the Univer-

(Courtesy of Bryn Mawr College Archives)

sity of Göttingen for one semester in late 1903 and early 1904. In 1904, she returned to Erlangen, which had recently begun accepting female students. She studied under mathematics professor Paul Gordon, a family friend, and earned a doctorate in 1907.

The Struggle for Recognition

Noether worked at the University of Erlangen without pay from 1908 to 1915. She conducted research, published papers, supervised doctoral students, and occasionally delivered lectures for her ailing father. She also joined international mathematical organizations and gave talks at meetings in Germany and abroad.

In 1916, the noted mathematicians Felix Klein and David Hilbert invited Noether to join them at the University of Göttingen. Despite Hilbert's efforts to win for her an official position, she was still ineligible to receive a salary because of her sex. Instead, she taught classes that were officially listed under Hilbert's name, again without pay. During this time, she made important contributions to the mathematics of Albert Einstein's theory of relativity.

The defeat of Germany in World War I in 1918 led to government reforms, including an increase in the rights of women. In 1919, Noether was designated as a licensed lecturer, allowing her to receive fees directly from students but without payment from the univer-

---

Basic Concepts of Abstract Algebra

Noether's ability to deal with mathematical concepts in a highly generalized way was critical to the development of abstract algebra.

Abstract algebra can be thought of as a more general form of algebra. Algebra deals with specific sets of numbers and specific mathematical operations. Abstract algebra, on the other hand, deals with the properties of sets and operations in general. Although many mathematicians contributed to the development of abstract algebra, Noether was particularly noted for her ability to think about mathematical concepts in highly abstract ways.

One of the fundamental concepts of abstract algebra is the definition of a group. A group consists of a set S and an operation * with the following properties:

1. For any two elements A and B belonging to S, the value of $A * B$ is also an element belonging to S. This property is known as closure.

2. For any three elements A, B, and C belonging to S, $(A * B)\ C = A * (B * C)$. This property is known as associativity.

3. There exists an element I belonging to S such that $A * I = A$ for any element A belonging to S. I is known as the identity element.

4. For any element A belonging to S, there exists an element N belonging to S such that $A * N = I$. Element N is known as the inverse of element A.

Depending on its properties, a combination of a set and two operations may be known as a field, a ring, or an ideal. Noether was particularly noted for her pioneering work in the study of ideals.

An important property studied in abstract algebra is commutativity. An operation * is said to be commutative in the set S if $A * B = B * A$ for any two elements A and B belonging to S. Noether made important contributions to the study of noncommutative operations.

Although abstract algebra is usually studied only by advanced students of mathematics, its basic ideas have been incorporated in the concept of "new math" first introduced into elementary schools in the 1950's.

Bibliography

Abstract Algebra: An Introduction. Thomas W. Hungerford. Philadelphia: Saunders College Publishers, 1990.

Basic Abstract Algebra. P. B. Bhattacharya, S. K. Jain, and S. R. Nagpaul. New York: Cambridge University Press, 1986.

A First Course in Abstract Algebra. John B. Fraleigh. 5th ed. Reading, Mass.: Addison-Wesley, 1994.

sity. In 1922, she was given the honorary title of "unofficial extraordinary professor." In 1923, she was awarded a teaching appointment in algebra, providing her with a small salary.

Years of Triumph

During her years at Göttingen, Noether made her most important contributions to mathematics. From 1920 to 1933, she published several papers that were critical to the development of the relatively new field of abstract algebra. In addition to her publications, Noether also had a profound effect on the work of her colleagues and students.

She served as a visiting professor at the University of Moscow in late 1928 and early 1929. She also served as a visiting professor at the University of Frankfurt during the summer of 1930. In 1931, many of her ideas were incorporated into the highly influential book *Moderne Algebra* by Bartel L. van der Waerden.

In 1932, Noether shared the Alfred Ackerman-Teubner Memorial Prize with Emil Artin for their advancement of mathematics. The same year, she became the first woman invited to make a major address to a general session of the International Mathematical Congress.

Leaving Germany

The rise to power of the Nazis in Germany in 1933 meant the end of Noether's career at the University of Göttingen. On April 7, she and five other Jewish professors were dismissed and prohibited from teaching at any German university. For a few months, she held informal classes in her apartment.

In the fall of 1933, Noether left Germany for the United States. She accepted a position at Bryn Mawr College in Pennsylvania and also worked at the Institute for Advanced Study in Princeton, New Jersey. On April 10, 1935, she had surgery to remove a large ovarian cyst.

Her first few days of recovery from the surgery went well, but on April 14 she suddenly developed a high fever, lost consciousness, and died. She was fifty-three.

Bibliography

By Noether

Über die Bildung des Formensystems der ternären biquadratischen Form, 1908 (dissertation; on complete systems of invariants for ternary biquadratic forms)

"Moduln in nichtkommutativen Bereichen, insbesondere aus Differential- und Differenzenausdrücken," *Mathematische Zeitschrift*, 1920 (with Werner Schmeidler; moduli in noncommutative fields, particularly in differential and difference terms)

"Idealtheorie in Ringbereichen," *Mathematische Annalen*, 1921 (theory of ideals in ring fields)

"Hyperkomplexe Grössen und Darstellungstheorie," *Mathematische Zeitschrift*, 1929 (hypercomplex number systems and their representation)

"Nichtkommutative Algebren," *Mathematische Zeitschrift*, 1933 (noncommutative algebras)

Gesammelte Abhandlungen, 1983 (Nathan Jacobson, ed.; collected papers)

About Noether

Emmy Noether: A Tribute to Her Life and Work. James W. Brewer and Martha K. Smith, eds. New York: Marcel Dekker, 1981.

Emmy Noether, 1882-1935. Auguste Dick. Translated by Heidi Blocher. Boston: Birkhäuser, 1981.

Women in Mathematics. Lynn M. Osen. Cambridge, Mass.: MIT Press, 1974.

(Rose Secrest)

Olga Oleinik

Areas of Achievement: Algebra, applied math, and geometry

Contribution: Oleinik developed complex mathematical theories regarding differential equations that had scientific applications.

July 2, 1925	Born in the Soviet Union
1947	Graduated from Moscow State University and begins graduate studies and teaches mathematics
1950	Completes a master's degree at Moscow State University
1954	Receives a Ph.D. from the Institute of Mathematics of Moscow State University and continues teaching there
1973	Chosen head of the Department of Differential Equations at Moscow State University
1993	Lectures about her research in Rome
1996	Presents the Association for Women in Mathematics Emmy Noether Lecture
1997	The Partial Differential Equation Conference is hosted by Iowa State University in her honor

Early Life

Olga Arsenievna Oleinik (pronounced "ul-YEH-nick") was born on July 2, 1925, in the Soviet Union. Not much is known about her parents or her childhood. She probably attended schools near her home, where her mathematical talents were identified and encouraged.

Although World War II forced the members of the mathematics faculty at Moscow State University to evacuate in 1940, they returned to the school in the spring of 1943 to assist with necessary defense work. Oleinik may have be-

gun her undergraduate studies at the university later that year. She received her degree in 1947 and began graduate studies and the teaching of mathematics courses at Moscow State University.

Oleinik was influenced by Ivan G. Petrowsky, a gifted mathematician and university leader who became her academic mentor. He introduced his seminar students to current topics in mathematics, posing unusual problems for them to solve from journals and conferences. Petrowsky's seminar was considered the center of Soviet differential equations work; he discussed new theories and unique approaches for complex mathematical puzzles.

Petrowsky assigned Oleinik a research topic about developing a mathematical theory for shock waves, and she completed her master's degree in 1950. Four years later, she finished her Ph.D. from the Institute of Mathematics of Moscow State University and continued teaching there.

Professional Development

Collaborating with Petrowsky, Oleinik conducted research in algebraic geometry, partial differential equations, and mathematical physics. She developed numerous theories about equations and began prolifically publishing her work. Oleinik produced approximately three hundred technical papers and eight books. Many of her works were translated into other languages.

For many years, she served on the editorial board of the *Moscow University Mathematics Bulletin*. Oleinik wrote a brief biographical essay about Petrowsky, which she included in a collection of his papers that she edited.

Considered a charming, good-natured, and empathetic person by her scholarly colleagues, Oleinik guided fifty-eight graduate students through their theses. In 1973, she was selected as head of Moscow State University's Department of Differential Equations. By 1996, she was affiliated with the university's Department of Mathematics and Mechanics.

An able academician and professor, she pursued her own research to develop intricate mathematical theories while instructing students about fundamental procedures. Especially interested in applied problems, she provided mathematical solutions used to improve the filtration of liquids and gases in porous materials, to distribute heat more efficiently, and to understand elasticity.

Memberships and Awards

Oleinik received recognition from numerous Russian and international scientific organizations. She was a member of the Russian Academy of Sciences and a foreign member of three Italian groups, the Accademia Nazionale dei Lincei, the Italian Academy of Sciences in Palermo, and the Italian Academy of Sciences in Milan. Oleinik was also invited to membership in Germany's Sachsische Academie of Sciences and was designated an honorary member of the Royal Society of Edinburgh in Scotland.

The University of Rome granted her an honorary doctorate. Oleinik received the medal of

Differential Equations

Oleinik expanded knowledge of differential equation theory and its application to physical sciences including engineering.

Differential equations are mathematical expressions that describe an amount and rate of change. In mathematics, equations are like sentences in a book, providing symbols instead of words. An equation connects two expressions with an equal sign to show that they represent the same quantity; each side often contains variables, quantities sometimes symbolized by a letter that can change values, which are important for solving differential equations. For example, a problem might have variables representing the varying speeds of an accelerating car.

In 1676, Gottfried Wilhelm Leibniz introduced the term "differential equation" to describe a technique that he used to study mechanics and geometry problems. A basic differential equation is one that contains the derivatives of one or more dependent variables with respect to one or more independent variables. A derivative is the rate of change of the function, which is the set of operations performed on each value inserted. Sir Isaac Newton and other mathematicians of the late seventeenth century considered differential equations useful in explaining physical phenomena.

Since that time, mathematicians have studied differential equations and expanded the mathematical knowledge and uses of these equations. Working on problems to establish new theories, Oleinik focused on partial differential equations, which are partial derivatives of a function with one or more variables. Second-order partial differential equations, such as the wave equation and heat equation, are crucial in physics.

Differential equations can be applied as useful tools to solve practical mathematical physics problems, especially in engineering and physical science. This branch of mathematics can also be applied to the humanities, particularly the fields of economics and statistics. Laws describing natural processes can be written mathematically. Differential equations have been used to analyze the rate of radioactive decay of paintings and detect forgeries, to predict population patterns, and to gauge the spread of epidemics. Engineers use differential equations to determine vibration, oscillation, satellite trajectories, and airplane stability. These equations can also explain the behavior of pendulums, springs, and electrical circuits.

Mathematicians such as Oleinik attempt to advance abstract theories regarding differential equations and their applications to technology.

Bibliography

Differential Equations and Their Applications: An Introduction to Applied Mathematics. Martin Braun. 3d ed. New York: Springer-Verlag, 1983.
The Differential Equations Problem Solver. Research and Education Association. Piscataway, N.J.: Author, 1991.
Differential Equations with Applications to Mathematical Physics. William F. Ames, Evans M. Harrell II, and J. V. Herod. eds. Boston: Academic Press, 1993.
Elementary Differential Equations with Linear Algebra. David L. Powers. Boston: Prindle, Weber & Schmidt, 1986.

the Collège de France and the medal of the first degree from Charles University in Prague. Within Russia, she earned the State Award and recognition from the Russian Academy of Sciences, as well as the Petrowsky, Chebotarev, and Lomonosov Prizes.

Throughout her career, Oleinik was recognized for her mathematical expertise and invited to present papers internationally. In 1993, she discussed the use of partial differential equations in mathematical physics to understand waves, flame propagation, and combustion at lectures sponsored by the Accademia Nazionale dei Lincei and Foundazione IBM Italia in Rome, Italy.

The Association for Women in Mathematics in the United States selected her as an Emmy Noether Lecturer, a prestigious honor. In January, 1996, Oleinik traveled to Orlando, Florida, where she presented the speech "On Some Homogenization Problems for Differential Operators." Oleinik returned to the United States in November, 1997, when Iowa State University hosted a Partial Differential Equation Conference in her honor. She stressed that she wanted to establish new mathematical theorems and methods, specifically using differential equations, to apply to science and technology.

Bibliography

By Oleinik

"O zadache Koshi dlya nelineynykh uravneniy v klasse razryvnykh funktsiy," *Doklady Akademii Nauk SSSR* 95, 1954 ("The Cauchy Problem for Nonlinear Equations in a Class of Discontinuous Functions" in *Fifteen Papers on Differential Equations*, American Mathematical Society Translations, 2d ser., vol. 42, 1964)

"O povedenii resheniy zadachi Koshi dlya nekotorykh kvazilineynykh uravneniy pri neogranichennom vozrastanii vremeni," *Doklady Akademii Nauk SSSR* 120, 1958 (with A. M. Il'in; "Behavior of the Solutions of the Cauchy Problem for Certain Quasilinear Equations for Unbounded Increase of the Time" in *Fifteen Papers on Differential Equations*, American Mathematical Society Translations, 2d ser., vol. 42, 1964)

"O edinstvennosti i ustoychivosti obobshchennogo resheniya zadachi Koshi dlya kvazilineynogo uravneniya," *Uspekhi Matematicheskikh Nauk* 14, 1959 ("Uniqueness and Stability of the Generalized Solution of the Cauchy Problem for a Quasi-Linear Equation" in *Nine Papers on Differential Equations, Two on Information Theory*, American Mathematical Society Translations, 2d ser., vol. 33, 1963)

A Boundary Value Problem for Linear Elliptic-Parabolic Equations, 1965

"O lineynykh uraveniyakh vtorogo poryadka s neotritsatel'noy kharakteristicheskoy formoy," *Matematicheskiy Sbornik* 69, 1966 ("Linear Equations of Second Order with Nonnegative Characteristic Form" in *Nine Papers on Partial Differential Equations and Functional Analysis*, American Mathematical Society Translations, 2d ser., vol. 65, 1967)

Trudy seminara imeni I. G. Petrovskogo, nos. 1-5, 1975-1979 (as editor; *Topics in Modern Mathematics: Petrovskii Seminars*)

Matematicheskie zadachi teorii sil'no neodnorodnykh uprugikh sred, 1990 (*Mathematical Problems in Elasticity and Homogenization*, 1992)

Usrednenie differentsial'nykh operatorov, 1993 (with Vasilii V. Zhikov and Sergei M. Kozlov; *Homogenization of Differential Operators and Integral Functionals*, 1994)

Some Asymptotic Problems in the Theory of Partial Differential Equations, 1996

I. G. Petrowsky: Selected Works, 1996 (as editor)

About Oleinik

Profiles of Women in Mathematics: The Emmy Noether Lecturers. Association for Women in Mathematics. College Park, Md.: Author, 1996.

Recent Soviet Contributions to Mathematics. J. P. LaSalle and Solomon Lefschetz, eds. New York: Macmillan, 1962.

Soviet Secondary Schools for the Mathematically Talented. Bruce Ramon Vogeli. Washington, D.C.: National Council of Teachers of Mathematics, 1968.

(Elizabeth D. Schafer)

Omar Khayyám

Areas of Achievement: Algebra and geometry

Contribution: Omar Khayyám provided geometric solutions of cubic equations. He also discovered the binomial expansion.

May, 1044	Born in Nishapur, Persia (now Iran)
c. 1050-1060	Educated by renowned teacher Imam Mowaffak
c. 1075	Appointed to supervise an astronomical observatory
1079-1120	Publishes a treatise on algebra and a commentary on Euclid's fifth postulate and writes a collection of poems
Dec., 1131	Dies in Nishapur, Persia

Early Life

Abu'l-Fath Umar Ibn Ibrahim Al Khayyami, who is better known as Omar Khayyám (pronounced "oh-mawr ki-YAWM"), was born in May, 1044, in Nishapur. He spent most of his life there, except for brief visits to Baghdad, Mecca, and Merv.

It is said that as a boy, Khayyám befriended two schoolmates, Nizam Al-Mulk and Hassan Ibn Sabah. The two friends would later became very influential politicians of the region: Nizam as vizier (prime minister) to the sultan and Hassan as the leader of a rebellious group called the Ismailists that was opposed to the established government. Nizam helped Khayyám financially and encouraged him to devote himself to the advancement and pursuit of knowledge.

Scholarly Activities

Omar Khayyám was an accomplished and creative scholar who made contributions to several disciplines, including astronomy, mathematics, philosophy, and poetry.

As an astronomer, he headed an observatory for eighteen years. When the sultan commissioned him to reform the Islamic solar calendar, he came up with a very accurate calendar (named Jalali, after the sultan) that required a correction of one day every 3,770 years. The modern Gregorian calendar requires a correction of one day every 3,330 years. Since the Islamic tradition is based upon lunar rather than solar cycles, Khayyám's calendar has never been adopted.

As a poet, Khayyám composed quatrains. Some were translated from Persian into English by Edward FitzGerald, in 1859, as *The Rubáiyát of Omar Khayyám*. The poems provide glimpses of the philosophy of their author. Some readers see in them an Epicurean philosophy of life. Others see an atheistic and materialistic philosophy. While for others, they represent Sufi mystic lore.

Mathematical Work

It is only after translations of ancient Arabic manuscripts, in the 1930's, that Omar Khayyám was introduced and recognized in the Western world as an individual who made sig-

A Geometric Solution of the Cubic Equation

Omar Khayyám discovered a geometric method for solving cubic equations.

A cubic equation is an equation of the form "$x^3 + ax^2 + bx + c = 0$," where a, b, and c are given real numbers and x is an unknown. Khayyám interpreted cubic equations as relations between volumes of rectangular boxes. For example, the terms in the equation "$x^3 = 2x^2 + 27$" can be viewed as the volume of a cube with a side of x (that is, x^3); the volume of a parallelepiped (a solid with six faces that are parallelograms) with a square base of x^2 and a height of 2 (that is, $2x^2$); and the volume of cube with a side of 3 (that is, 27). For this reason, Khayyám sought only positive solutions, although his method can be applied to find negative solutions.

During Khayyám's time, an algebraic formula for the solution x of the cubic equation in terms of the coefficients a, b, and c was not known. To solve the equation, Khayyám transformed the algebraic problem into a geometrical problem. More precisely, instead of finding a formula for x, he associated with each equation a pair of curves (conics). The abscissa (the horizontal coordinate of a point in a Cartesian plane parallel to the x-axis) of the intersection point of the two curves turns out to be exactly the solution of the equation. For some type of equations, he had to find the intersection of a circle and a hyperbola; for another type, the intersection of a parabola and a hyperbola; and for another type, the intersection of two hyperbolas.

For example, for cubic equations of type "$x^3 + b^2x + a^3 = cx^2$" (with a, b, and c positive), Khayyám had to use a circle and a hyperbola. With the modern notation and the use of rectangular coordinates, these two curves can be written as "$(b - y)x = -a^3/b$" for the hyperbola and "$y^2 = -(x + a^3/b^2)(x - c)$" for the circle (see accompanying figure).

The two curves intersect at a point P with coordinates (x_0, y_0). It follows that "$y_0 = (b/x_0)(x_0 + a^3/b^2)$," since P is on the hyperbola. After substituting this value of y_0 into the equation of the circle, one finds the equation "$[(b/x_0)(x_0 + a^3/b^2)]^2 = -(x_0 +$

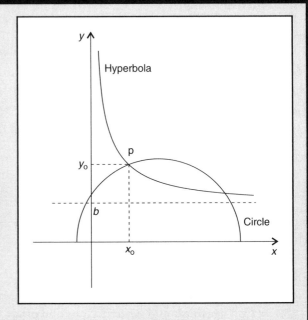

$a^3/b^2)(x_0 - c)$." After simplification, one obtains "$x_0^3 + b^2x_0 + a^3 = cx_0^2$."

This means that the abscissa of the intersection point P satisfies the desired cubic equation. For example, to find geometrically a solution of "$x^3 + \frac{1}{2}x + 1 = \frac{5}{2}x^2$," one must find the coordinates of the intersection point of the hyperbola and the circle given, respectively, by "$y = \frac{1}{\sqrt{2}} + \frac{\sqrt{2}}{x}$" and "$(x - \frac{1}{4})^2 + y^2 = \frac{81}{16}$." One such intersection point has coordinates $(1, \frac{3}{\sqrt{2}})$. Thus "$x = 1$" is a solution of the given equation.

Omar Khayyám tried to find an explicit formula for the solution of the cubic equation, but he did not succeed. Such a formula was subsequently found when a breakthrough was made by sixteenth century algebraists in Italy.

Bibliography

Historical Topics for the Mathematics Classroom. John K. Baumgart et al., eds. 2d ed. Reston, Va.: The National Council of Teachers of Mathematics, 1989.

A History of Mathematics: An Introduction. Victor J. Katz. New York: HarperCollins College, 1993.

The Mathematics of Great Amateurs. Julian Lowell Coolidge. Oxford, England: Clarendon Press, 1949.

nificant contributions to the mathematics of his time. Careful studies of the texts show that Khayyám provided geometric solutions to cubic equations, discovered the binomial expansion, and helped in the understanding of irrational numbers and the parallel postulate.

One of the major problems of medieval mathematics was the solvability of polynomial equations. By Khayyám's time, the linear equation ($ax + b = 0$), the quadratic equation ($a^2 + bx + c = 0$), and particular cases of the cubic equation ($ax^3 + bx^2 + cx + d = 0$) were well understood. A general method for solving cubic equations, however, was not known. Around 1079, Khayyám published a manuscript about cubic equations. He managed to solve every type of cubic equation that admits a positive solution. The solution that he gave is obtained geometrically by intersecting two conics (an ellipse, hyperbola, or parabola).

Another of Khayyám's accomplishments—one that was probably related to his astronomical work—was the discovery of the relation between the coefficients of the binomial expansion ($a + b)^n$, where $n = 1, 2, 3, \ldots$. The combinatorial formula that he obtained

$$C_n^k = C_{n-1}^k + C_{n-1}^{k-1}$$

was rediscovered in seventeenth century Europe and is now known as the Pascal triangle.

Another important problem that drew the attention of Khayyám deals with the parallel, or fifth, postulate of Euclid: From a point exterior to a line passes a unique parallel. For generations, mathematicians had tried to prove that the postulate is a theorem that follows from other Euclidean axioms. The discovery in the nineteenth century of non-Euclidean geometries put an end to these efforts,

Khayyám's study of the parallel postulate led him to construct a quadrilateral ABCD with right angles at A and B and with equal sides AD and BC. After he proved that angles at C and D are equal, he went on to consider three hypotheses: on acute, obtuse, and right angles. Using Aristotelian principles, Khayyám showed that the first two hypotheses lead to contradictions. Although Khayyám's aim was not to discover new geometries, the hypotheses that he considered appears to have been of fundamental importance in the development of non-Euclidean geometries.

Omar Khayyám died in December, 1131. His poetic wish to be buried in a garden was fulfilled. Admirers of the poet-mathematician still visit his adorned grave in Nishapur.

Bibliography

By Omar Khayyám
Risala fi'-I Barahin ala masa'-il al-jabr wa'l-muqabala (*The Algebra of Omar Khayyam*, 1931)
Sharh ma ashkala min musadarat kitab Uqlidis (partial trans. as "Discussion of Difficulties in Euclid," *Scripta Mathematica* 24, 1959)

About Omar Khayyám
Classics of Mathematics. Ronald Calinger, ed. Englewood Cliffs, N.J.: Prentice Hall, 1995, pp. 204-211.
Great Moments in Mathematics (Before 1650). Howard Eves. Dolciani Mathematical Expositions 5. Washington, D.C.: Mathematical Association of America, 1980, pp. 148-159.
A History of Mathematics: An Introduction. Victor J. Katz. New York: HarperCollins College, 1993, pp. 223-265.
"Omar Khayyam, Mathematician." Dirk Jan Struik. *The Mathematics Teacher* 51 (April, 1958): 280-285.

(Abdelhamid Meziani)

Nicole Oresme

Area of Achievement: Geometry
Contribution: Oresme developed a two-dimensional graphing system.

c. 1325	Born, possibly in Allemagne, France
c. 1342	Begins studies leading to a master's degree in the arts from the University of Paris
1348	Enters the College of Navarre, at the University of Paris, to study theology
1348-1351	Writes *Quaestiones Super Geometriam Euclidis*
1351-1355	Writes *Tractatus de configurationibus qualitatum et motuum*
July, 1356	Receives a doctorate in theology from the College of Navarre
Oct., 1356	Appointed headmaster of the College of Navarre
1362	Leaves Navarre to become canon at the Cathedral in Rouen, France
1363	Becomes a canon at La Sainte Chapelle, Paris
1364	Becomes the dean of the Cathedral in Rouen
1377	Named the bishop of Lisieux, France
1377	Completes his last work, a translation from Latin to French of Aristotle's *De caelo et mundo* (the heavens and the world)
July 11, 1382	Dies in Lisieux, France

Early Life

Nicole Oresme (pronounced "aw-REHM") was born in the Normandy region of France, near the city of Caen, possibly in the village of Allemagne. Since Oresme received his doctor-ate degree in 1356 and the age requirement for this degree was thirty-five years, his year of birth is estimated to be after 1320, perhaps in 1325.

Oresme probably began the six-year program leading to the master's degree in the arts at the University of Paris in 1342. There, he studied under Jean Buridan, a prominent philosopher. There is evidence that Oresme had brothers named Henry and Guillaume and a nephew named Henry.

The College of Navarre

In 1348, Oresme entered the theology program at the College of Navarre, at the University of Paris. The college was founded in 1304 by Jeanne de Navarre, the wife of Philip IV, king of France from 1285 to 1314. At the college were close ties between scholars and royalty. Oresme developed a friendship with the younger Prince Charles, son of King John II.

While a theology student, Oresme taught in the College of Arts, where he lectured on his analysis of the many works of the Greek philosopher Aristotle. In 1356, Oresme received a doctorate in theology, becoming headmaster of Navarre in the same year.

Training and Writings

During the Middle Ages, the arts studied at universities consisted of the trivium (grammar, logic, rhetoric) and the quadrivium (arithmetic, music, geometry, astronomy). Universities discouraged the study of the more practical subjects in the quadrivium. The study of theology and philosophy within the trivium led to a more distinguished career than the study of the sciences. Hence, like Oresme, mathematicians of the time were often trained in theology and philosophy.

Oresme wrote more than thirty works in the areas of philosophy, theology, mathematics, physics, astronomy, magical arts, economics, and politics. These works included "questions" on works of earlier writers, including Aristotle and the Greek geometer Euclid. Oresme wrote primarily in Latin, the language of scholarly writing throughout Europe during the Middle Ages. Since the printing press was not invented until about 1450, most of Oresme's works remain unpublished in manuscript form, making it difficult to determine the exact year that they were originally written.

Mathematical Work

Oresme's mathematical writings included work on ratios, proportions, fractional exponents, and two-dimensional graphing. In his day, mathematical descriptions were still "rhetorical"—that is, completely written out in words. Algebraic notation would not be developed until the 1630's. Oresme's graphing system helped to explain further ideas that had previously been described rhetorically.

Between 1348 and 1355, while at the College of Navarre, Oresme completed his principal writings on a two-dimensional graphing system. *Quaestiones Super Geometriam Euclidis* (questions on Euclid's geometry) was followed by *Tractatus de configurationibus qualitatum et motuum* (treatise on the configurations of qualities and motions).

Oresme's graphing system further developed the study of motion done at Merton College in England between 1280 and 1340. The work of Oresme and the Merton scholars was theoretical. They did not perform experiments to reach conclusions about the relationship between time, velocity, and the distance that an object travels. In the early seventeenth century, Galileo used some of Oresme's geometric techniques but performed experiments to arrive at his conclusions about the acceleration of freely falling objects. Oresme's work was also a precursor to analytic geometry, developed in the 1630's, and to integral calculus, developed in the 1670's.

Later Career

Oresme left Navarre in 1362 to become canon (a clergyman) at the cathedral in Rouen and subsequently canon at La Sainte Chapelle in Paris. He was named dean of the Rouen cathedral in 1364.

In 1364, Prince Charles, a friend of Oresme's from the College of Navarre, became King Charles V. Oresme became the king's chaplain and counselor. During the 1370's, at the king's request, Oresme translated works by Aristotle from Latin into French, adding commentaries. Completed in 1377, *Le Livre du ciel et du monde* (the book of the heavens and the world), a

translation of Aristotle's *De caelo et mundo*, was probably the last work by Oresme. In 1377, King Charles V appointed Oresme the bishop of Lisieux. Oresme died in Lisieux on July 11, 1382.

Bibliography

By Oresme

Quaestiones Super Geometriam Euclidis, 1348-1351 (questions on Euclid's geometry; English translation, 1961)

Ad pauca respicientes, 1350's (English translation, 1966)

De commensurabilitate sive incommensurabilitate motuum celi, 1350's (the commensurability or incommensurability of celestial motions; English translation in *Nicole Oresme and the Kinematics of Circular Motion*, 1971)

De proportionibus proportionum, 1350's (on the ratio of ratios; English translation, 1966)

Algorismus proportionum, 1351-1355 (algorithm of ratios)

Tractatus de configurationibus qualitatum et motuum, 1351-1355 (treatise on the configurations of qualities and motions; English translation in *Nicole Oresme and the Medieval Geometry of Qualities and Motions*, 1968)

Two-Dimensional Graphs

Oresme developed a two-dimensional graphing system to illustrate the relationship between time, velocity, and the total distance traveled by an object.

Oresme used a horizontal line to represent time. Line segments erected perpendicular to this time line represented the velocity of an object at each particular point in time. In the Middle Ages, no distinction was made between velocity and speed. The line, or curve, connecting the endpoints of these perpendicular line segments was called the summit line. This created a two-dimensional figure whose area was the total distance traveled by the object. A rectangle represented an object traveling with a constant velocity over the time period.

Uniform acceleration is motion for which there is a constant rate of increase in velocity. A right triangle represented an object that started from rest and uniformly accelerated over the time period. If the acceleration was uniform but not from rest, the resulting figure was a right trapezoid. If the acceleration was not uniform, the summit line

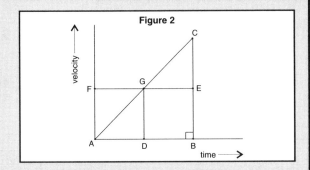

Figure 2

period at the constant mean speed, which occurs at the middle point in time (D). To prove that the distance traveled by the object is the same in both cases, the area of triangle ABC is shown to be the same as the area of rectangle ABEF. This is done by proving that right triangle GEC is congruent to right triangle GFA.

With the horizontal axis representing time and the vertical axis representing speed, Oresme's summit line represents the graph of speed as a function of time. The area of the figure, the total distance traveled, is referred to as the "area under the curve" in integral calculus.

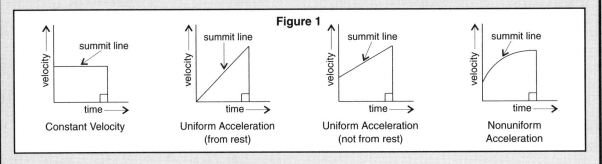

Figure 1

Constant Velocity

Uniform Acceleration (from rest)

Uniform Acceleration (not from rest)

Nonuniform Acceleration

was a curve and various other figures resulted (see figure 1).

Using the geometry of Euclid, Oresme proved the mean speed theorem developed by scholars at Merton College in England between 1280 and 1340. This theorem states that the distance an object travels with uniform acceleration is the same as the distance the object would have traveled if it had moved at the constant velocity of the middle point in time.

In figure 2, right triangle ABC represents a uniformly accelerated object. Rectangle ABEF represents the object moving over the same time

Bibliography

"Geometric Kinematics: The Method of Nicole Oresme." Robert C. Fleck, Jr. *Physics Teacher* 29, no. 6 (September, 1991): 410.

Geometry. The University of Chicago School Mathematics Project. Arthur Coxford, Zalman Usiskin, and Daniel Hirschhorn. Glenview, Ill.: Scott, Foresman, 1993.

McDougal, Littell Integrated Mathematics, Course I. Brendan Kelly, Bob Alexander, and Paul Atkinson. New York: McDougal, Littell, 1991. Chapter 9.

Le Livre du ciel et du monde d'Aristote, by Aristotle, 1377 (as translator, from Latin into French, of *De caelo et mundo*; the book of the heavens and the world; English translation, 1968)

About Oresme

"Nicole Oresme." In *Classics of Mathematics*, edited by Ronald Calinger. Englewood Cliffs, N.J.: Prentice Hall, 1995.

"Nicole Oresme." Marshall Clagett. In *Dictionary of Scientific Biography*, edited by Charles Coulston Gillispie. Vol. 10. New York: Charles Scribner's Sons, 1974.

Nicole Oresme: Highlights from His French Commentary on Aristotle's Politics. Albert D. Menut, trans. Lawrence, Kans.: Coronado Press, 1979.

(*Sharon O'Donnell*)

Blaise Pascal

Areas of Achievement: Geometry, number theory, and probability

Contribution: Pascal advanced the study of conic sections and the cycloid. He also investigated the arithmetic triangle and developed the foundations of probability.

June 19, 1623	Born in Clermont-Ferrand, France
1626	His mother dies
1631	His family moves to Paris
1640	Writes *Essai pour les coniques* (treatise on conic sections)
1644	Demonstrates his first calculating machine
1646	Becomes convinced of the truth of Jansenism
1651	His father dies
1654	Corresponds with Pierre de Fermat on the foundations of probability and the arithmetic triangle
Nov. 23, 1654	Undergoes an intense religious conversion experience
1656	Begins writing the *Les Provinciales* (1656-1657; *The Provincial Letters*, 1657) and notes that will become the *Pensées* (1670;)
1658	Investigates the cycloid
1662	Helps implement an omnibus transportation system in Paris, the first in Europe
Aug. 19, 1662	Dies in Paris, France

Early Life

Blaise Pascal (pronounced "pahs-KAHL") was the son of Étienne Pascal, a high-ranking civil servant skilled in mathematics. Pascal's mother died when he was three years old. Five years later, his father left his job, moved the family to Paris, and committed himself to the education

(Library of Congress)

of Blaise and his two sisters, as well as the pursuit of his own intellectual interests.

Étienne's plan was to have Blaise study languages first and then introduce the boy to mathematics later. When the boy discovered on his own that the sum of the angles of a triangle was always equal to two right angles, however, Étienne decided that Blaise was ready for the study of geometry.

Early Scientific Work

Blaise Pascal accompanied his father to meetings of a group of intellectuals in Paris. When Pascal presented his paper *Essai pour les coniques* (1640; treatise on conic sections), they were impressed. Not long afterward, he developed a calculating machine, in part to help his father with his work in the tax office.

Pascal conducted numerous experiments concerning vacuums. One result was that he disproved the traditional view that "nature abhors a vacuum." He discovered Pascal's principle: Pressure applied to a contained fluid is transmitted equally throughout the fluid irrespective of the area over which the pressure is applied. Practical developments from his

investigations included the syringe, an improved barometer, and the hydraulic press.

The Church or the World?

In 1646, the Pascal family was influenced by Jansenists, reformers within the Roman Catholic Church who sought a more genuine spiritual experience associated with a revival of Saint Augustine's doctrines of sin and grace. Blaise Pascal was converted doctrinally to their position, but his lifestyle was only somewhat affected. During the next several years, he had alternating periods of scientific exploration, severe illness, and pleasure-seeking that was apparently prescribed by his doctors to divert his attention from the exhausting work of science.

Pascal's gambling friends posed some questions that led to his now-famous correspondence with Pierre de Fermat. In the process of solving the problems posed, Pascal pursued extensive study of the arithmetic triangle, now often referred to as Pascal's triangle in honor of his investigations (although the triangle itself was certainly known to Chinese mathematicians before Pascal's time). The end result was the development of the foundations of probability.

Tension between the spiritual and the worldly, however, was weighing heavily on Pascal. A crisis was brewing.

Spiritual Conversion

During the evening of November 23, 1654, Pascal had a mystical experience of God and Jesus Christ that completely altered the course of his life. He recorded the experience on a piece of paper that he sewed into a piece of his clothing so that it would be always with him. He resolved to renounce the world and totally submit to Christ. As a result, he became an adamant supporter of the Jansenist movement. His mental talents were now focused on serving Christ.

An early result of this resolve were eighteen pamphlets collectively known as *Les Provinciales* (1656-1657; *The Provincial Letters*, 1657). These tracts were intended to sway public opinion in support of the Jansenists against their opponents, the Jesuits. Written anonymously to protect the author, they were an immediate success. Combining skill in persuasion with a commitment to the highest morality, Pascal used stinging satire and concise argumentation to critique his opponents effectively. *The Provincial Letters* marked the beginning of modern French prose.

Soon thereafter, Pascal decided to write a work that would provide an apologetic for Christianity. Unfortunately, his illness and early death resulted in only fragments in a variety of states of completion. Their compilation has come to be known as the *Pensées* (1670), or thoughts; an English-language compilation was published as *Monsieur Pascal's Thoughts, Meditations, and Prayers* (1688). In the *Pensées*,

---

The Arithmetical Triangle

Pascal derived numerous properties of the arithmetical triangle and applied these results to number theory and probability.

The arithmetical triangle is a triangular arrangement of numbers that are binomial coefficients. Pascal's name is often attached to the triangle, not because he was its discoverer but because of his extensive study and application of it. The triangular arrangement allows one to see conveniently many of the relationships among the binomial coefficients.

In modern notation, the triangle is often oriented so that the numbers in the nth row are the coefficients in the expansion of the binomial $(x + y)^n$, starting with $n = 0$. For example, "$(x + y)^2 = x^2 + 2xy + y^2$," and the coefficients 1, 2, 1 appear in

```
                1
            1       1
        1       2       1
    1       3       3       1
  1     4       6       4     1
1     5     10      10      5     1
```

the second row. A position in the triangle can be calculated as the sum of the two numbers diagonally above it. For example, in the accompanying figure, the bold **10** is the sum of the **4** and the **6**. A common notation for the rth number (again starting with $r = 0$) in the nth row is $C(n,r)$. For example, $C(5,2) = 10$.

Pascal derived a number of identities from the triangle. This method of calculating the entries suggests that "$C(n + 1,r) = C(n,r) + C(n,r - 1)$." The evident symmetry of the triangle implies that "$C(n,r) = C(n,n - r)$. Every entry is the sum of the entries on a diagonal above it; for example, the **10** above equals "$4 + 3 + 2 + 1$." By letting $x = y = 1$, Pascal derived the sum of the coefficients in any binomial expansion: $C(n,0) + C(n,1) + C(n,2) + \ldots + C(n,n) = 2^n$. He also derived the explicit formula

$$C(n,r) = \frac{n!}{r! \, (n - r)!}$$

Pascal's method is probably more significant than the result itself. To introduce his proof, Pascal wrote explicitly the two steps in the method now called mathematical induction. Historically, his was the first instance known of such a clear statement of this principle.

Pascal also recognized that the binomial coefficient $C(n,r)$ is the number of combinations of n objects taken r at a time. Finally, Pascal applied his discoveries about combinations to determine how the stakes should be divided between two players playing for a set of games. The resulting calculations and concepts helped to lay the foundations of probability.

Bibliography
The History of Mathematics: An Introduction. David M. Burton. 3d ed. New York: McGraw-Hill, 1997.

"Pascal and the Invention of Probability Theory." Oystein Ore. *American Mathematical Monthly* 67, no. 5 (1960): 409-419.

Pascal's Arithmetical Triangle. A. W. F. Edwards. New York: Oxford University Press, 1987.

Pascal's Triangle. V. A. Uspensky. Translated by David Sookne and Tim McLarnan. Chicago: University of Chicago Press, 1974.

Pascal sees human beings as both created by God for greatness and at the same time hopelessly lost in the vastness of the universe and the vanity of evil. As translated in *Great Books of the Western World* (1952), Pascal graphically expresses the misery and hope of humankind: "the infinite abyss [in a person] can only be filled by an infinite and immutable object, that is to say, only by God Himself."

The sickly Pascal died on August 19, 1662, at the age of thirty-nine.

Bibliography

By Pascal

Essai pour les coniques, 1640 (treatise on conic sections)

Expériences nouvelles touchant le vide, 1647 ("New Experiments Concerning the Vacuum" in *Great Books of the Western World*, 1952)

Récit de la grande expérience de l'équilibre des liqueurs, 1648 ("Account of the Great Experiment Concerning the Equilibrium of Fluids" in *Great Books of the Western World*, 1952)

Les Provinciales, 1656-1657 (*The Provincial Letters*, 1657)

Traité général de la roulette, 1658 (general treatise on the cycloid)

Traité du triangle arithmétique, 1665 ("Treatise on the Arithmetical Triangle" in *Great Books of the Western World*, 1952)

Pensées, 1670 (*Monsieur Pascal's Thoughts, Meditations, and Prayers*, 1688)

About Pascal

Blaise Pascal. Hugh M. Davidson. Boston: Twayne, 1983.

Blaise Pascal: Mathematician, Physicist, and Thinker About God. Donald Adamson. New York: St. Martin's Press, 1995.

Making Sense of It All: Pascal and the Meaning of Life. Thomas V. Morris. Grand Rapids, Mich.: Wm. B. Eerdmans, 1992.

Pascal. A. J. Krailsheimer. New York: Hill & Wang, 1980.

Pascal: The Emergence of Genius. Emile Cailliet. 2d ed. New York: Harper & Brothers, 1961.

(Walter D. Stangl)

Giuseppe Peano

Areas of Achievement: Calculus and mathematical logic

Contribution: Peano developed a set of five axioms for the natural numbers, known as the Peano postulates. His contributions to the development of the calculus include the discovery of counterexamples to accepted theory, the most well known being a space-filling curve.

Aug. 27, 1858	Born in Spinetta, Italy
1876	Enters the University of Turin to study mathematics
1880	Graduated from the University of Turin with high honors
1880	Named university assistant to Enrico D'Ovidio
1881	Named university assistant to Angelo Genocchi
1884	Publishes his first major work, a calculus textbook
1886	Appointed a professor at the Royal Military Academy while continuing his duties at the University of Turin
1887	Marries Carola Crosio
1889	Publishes the first statement of the Peano postulates
1890	Publishes his discovery of a space-filling curve
1890	Named a professor of calculus at the University of Turin
1908	Publishes the final volume of the *Formulario mathématico*
1915	Completes a comparative vocabulary for an international language project
Apr. 20, 1932	Dies in Turin, Italy

Early Life

Giuseppe Peano (pronounced "pay-AWN-oh") was the second son of Bartolomeo Peano and Rosa Cavallo. The family, later to include two younger brothers and a sister, lived on the small farm of Tetto Galant in the village of Spinetta, near Cuneo, northwestern Italy. Later, the family moved to Cuneo to be closer to schools. Around the age of twelve, Giuseppe went to live with his uncle, about sixty miles north in Turin. After receiving private lessons and teaching himself, he passed the lower secondary examination of the Cavour School in 1873.

In 1876, Peano completed the upper secondary program as a regular student and won a room-and-board scholarship that enabled him to attend the University of Turin. There, in 1876, he began what was to be a long association with the mathematics department. In 1880, he completed his final examination with high honors and was one of only two students to receive a degree in mathematics from the university that year.

Early Career

Peano remained at the University of Turin as university assistant to Enrico D'Ovidio, his former professor during the 1880-1881 academic year. The following academic year, he began serving as university assistant to Angelo Genocchi, the chair of infinitesimal calculus and another of Peano's professors. Genocchi's health was beginning to fail, so Peano began serving as a substitute for Genocchi in 1882. After Genocchi's death in 1889, Peano assumed full responsibility for his calculus course. Peano subsequently became professor and chair of infinitesimal calculus in 1890.

From 1886 until 1901, Peano also served as a professor, teaching calculus, at the Royal Military Academy, which was located near the University of Turin. The extra income enabled him to marry Carola Crosio in 1887. They never had children.

Mathematical Logic

Peano's first publication in mathematical logic was a chapter on the operations of deductive logic in an 1888 geometrical calculus book. It was based on his study of the works of others, including the English logician George Boole. The following year, Peano published the *Arithmetices principia, nova methodo exposita* (the principles of arithmetic, presented by a new method) where he introduced new symbols and concepts. This book includes Peano's first statement of the Peano postulates for the natural numbers.

Work in the Calculus

During his career, Peano published more than two hundred works. Although he is best known for his work in mathematical logic, much of his work was in the calculus.

Peano's first major work created a controversy. Angelo Genocchi was approached about writing a calculus text. Since Genocchi was ailing and Peano was substituting for him, Peano obtained Genocchi's permission to write the text based on Genocchi's calculus course. When *Calcolo differenziale e principii di calcolo integrale, pubblicato con aggiunte dal Dr. Giuseppe Peano* (differential calculus and fundamentals of integral calculus, published with additions by Giuseppe Peano) was published in 1884, Peano attributed the authorship to Genocchi.

Either because Genocchi was upset that the text and additions were better than his own lessons or because he thought that Peano was trying to use Genocchi's well-known name to get the work published, Genocchi renounced any involvement with the text. In 1915, the text was listed among the nineteen most important calculus texts since the time of Leonhard Euler and Augustin-Louis Cauchy.

Throughout his works, Peano produced many counterexamples—that is, examples that prove statements are not true. His most famous was a space-filling curve, published in 1890. Peano found equations that describe a curve that goes though every point in the unit square. This was contrary to the idea that any continuous curve in two-dimensional space could be enclosed in a region of arbitrarily small area.

Later Years

The Formulario project, initiated by Peano in 1882, was intended to produce a collection of all known propositions in the various branches of mathematics, expressed with logical symbols. Five volumes of the *Formulario mathématico* appeared between 1895 and 1908.

In 1903, Peano proposed the development of an international language. The result of his

---

The Peano Postulates

Peano developed a set of postulates for the natural numbers and used them to prove the theorems of arithmetic. These five postulates became known as the Peano postulates.

Peano wrote most of his work using symbols of logic and set theory. He was the first to make a distinction between a member of set and a subset of a set. For this purpose, he introduced the symbol $\in$ to indicate set membership—that is, $b \in A$ read as "b is an element of set A"—and the symbol $\supset$ to indicate inclusion—that is, $B \supset A$, which evolved into $B \subseteq A$, read "set B is a subset of set A."

Before introducing the postulates of the natural numbers, Peano identified four undefined terms: natural number (N), unity (1), the successor ($n + 1$) of n, and equal to (=). The Peano postulates can then be stated as follows:

1. $1 \in N$ (1 is a natural number.)

2. If $n \in N$, then $n + 1 \in N$ (The successor of any natural number is a natural number.)

3. $n = m$ if and only if $n + 1 = m + 1$ (If two natural numbers are equal their successors are equal. Also, if the successors of two natural numbers are equal, the natural numbers are equal.)

4. If $n \in N$, then $n + 1$ does not equal 1. (1 is not the successor of any natural number.)

5. S is any set. If $1 \in S$ and for any natural number n, $n \in S$ implies $n + 1 \in S$, then S contains the set of all natural numbers. (This is the principle of mathematical induction. If a property holds for 1, and if the property holds for some natural number n it also holds for $n + 1$, then the property holds for every natural number n.)

The set of postulates is consistent—that is, none of them contradicts the others. Peano also showed that the set of postulates is independent—that is, each postulate is not a result of the others. He did this by creating a model in which a particular postulate is false while the remaining postulates are true. Finally, the system is categorical—that is, any two systems that satisfy all the postulates are essentially the same.

With this axiomatic system, Peano proved theorems about the natural numbers, including their commutative, associative, and distributive properties. He was also able to develop definitions for rational and irrational numbers.

Bibliography

Frege, Dedekind, and Peano on the Foundations of Arithmetic. Douglas Angus Gillies. Assen, the Netherlands: Van Gorcum, 1982.

Introduction to the Foundations of Mathematics. Raymond Louis Wilder. 2d ed. New York: John Wiley & Sons, 1965.

Selected Works of Giuseppe Peano. Hubert C. Kennedy, trans. and ed. London: Allen & Unwin, 1973, chapter 7.

efforts was the publication of a vocabulary, completed in 1915, consisting of more than fourteen thousand entries from more than ten languages. Peano continued to publish papers and to teach at the University of Turin until his death from a heart problem on April 20, 1932.

Bibliography
By Peano

Calcolo differenziale e principii di calcolo integrale, pubblicato con aggiunte dal Dr. Giuseppe Peano, by Angelo Genocchi, 1884 (partial trans. as "Differential Calculus and Fundamentals of Integral Calculus [published with additions by Giuseppe Peano]" in *Selected Works of Giuseppe Peano,* 1973)

Applicazioni geometriche del calcolo infinitesimale, 1887 (partial trans. as "Geometrical Magnitudes" in *Selected Works of Giuseppe Peano,* 1973)

Calcolo geometrico secondo l'Ausdehnungslehre di H. Grassmann, preceduto dalle operazioni della logica deduttiva, 1888 (partial trans. as "The Geometrical Calculus According to the Ausdehnungslehre of H. Grassmann, Preceded by the Operations of Deductive Logic" in *Selected Works of Giuseppe Peano,* 1973)

Arithmetices principia, nova methodo exposita, 1889 ("The Principles of Arithmetic, Presented by a New Method" in *Selected Works of Giuseppe Peano,* 1973)

"Sur une courbe, qui remplit toute une aire plane," *Mathematische Annalen* 36, 1890 ("A Space-Filling Curve" in *Selected Works of Giuseppe Peano,* 1973)

Lezioni di Analisi infinitesimale, 1893 (lessons on infinitesimal analysis)

Formulario mathématico, 1895-1908 (5 vols.)

Aritmetica generale e Algebra elementare, 1902

Vocabulario commune ad linguas de Europa, 1909

Vocabulario commune ad latino-italiano-français-english-deutsch, 2d ed., 1915

Giochi di aritmetica e problemi interessanti, 1924 (games in arithmetic and interesting problems)

About Peano

"Giuseppe Peano." Hubert C. Kennedy. In *Dictionary of Scientific Biography,* edited by Charles Coulston Gillispie. Vol. 10. New York: Charles Scribner's Sons, 1974.

"Giuseppe Peano at the University of Turin." Hubert C. Kennedy. *The Mathematics Teacher* 61, no. 7 (November, 1968).

Peano: Life and Works of Giuseppe Peano. Hubert C. Kennedy. Dordrecht, the Netherlands: D. Reidel, 1980.

(Sharon O'Donnell)

Roger Penrose

Area of Achievement: Applied math
Contribution: Penrose provided mathematical understandings for such astrophysical phenomena as black holes. He is famous for Penrose tiles, two geometric shapes that can cover a two-dimensional plane without any repeating pattern.

Aug. 8, 1931	Born in Colchester, Essex, England
1955	Awarded a Ph.D. in mathematics, Cambridge University
1957	Appointed a research fellow at St. John's College
1959	Receives a NATO Research Fellowship to the United States
1964	Appointed a Reader at Birbeck College, London
1965	Suggests the idea of singularities
1966	Awarded the Adams Prize by Cambridge
1967	Elevated to Professor of Applied Mathematics at Birbeck
1971	Awarded the Dannie Heineman Prize for Physics
1972	Elected to the Royal Society of London
1973	Named Rouse Ball Professor of Mathematics at Oxford University
1975	Shares the Royal Astronomical Society's Eddington Medal with Stephen Hawking
1980	Named Edgar Odell Lovett Professor of Mathematics at Rice University
1988	Shares the Wolf Foundation Prize in Physics with Hawking
1989	Publishes *The Emperor's New Mind*

Early Life

Roger Penrose, the second of four children, was born on August 8, 1931, in Colchester, England. His father, Lionel S. Penrose, was a prominent genetics professor at University College, part of the University of London. His mother, Margaret Newman, was a physician, although Penrose believed that his father did not let her practice often. An uncle, Sir Roland Penrose, was a well-known painter who wrote a biography of Pablo Picasso. All three Penrose brothers distinguished themselves in various pursuits. Roger's older brother, Oliver, became a mathematics professor. His younger brother, Jonathan, became a grand master in chess and a psychology professor.

As a boy, Roger was interested in both nature and mathematics. He made cardboard models of geometric figures, developing a skill in visualizing shapes. Despite an avid interest in mathematics, however, Penrose read little beyond the required school assignments while growing up. The family spent World War II in the United States and Canada, where his father introduced him to the calculus.

Penrose loved devising geometry problems to stump his teachers. He and his father made a game of creating novel geometry problems. Ultimately, they invented a series of geometric figures that appeared to be possible but could not truly exist in three dimensions. Penrose sent one of these figures, a "tribar" of three beams, to Dutch artist M. C. Escher, whom he had met at a conference as an undergraduate. Escher used it as a motif in his famous lithograph "Waterfall."

University Studies

While at Cambridge University studying pure mathematics, Penrose was introduced to one of his brother's friends, Dennis Sciama, a professor of applied mathematics and theoretical physics at the university. Penrose had been listening to a series of BBC radio talks about modern cosmology by the famous astronomer Fred Hoyle. He asked Sciama to explain Hoyle's remark about "galaxies disappearing off the edge" of the universe. Penrose noted that he could not see how that was possible geometrically since if one draws light cones back from these distant objects, they all cross

Penrose with his diagram of a "twistor." (Anthony Howarth/Science Photo Library)

the cone. Sciama had never thought about it that way, and it made a lasting impression upon him.

Penrose was progressively drawn by the allure of physics, coming to realize through lectures at Cambridge by Paul Dirac in quantum theory and Hermann Bondi on general relativity that at its core, physics was about creating novel applications of mathematics. While continuing his work in pure mathematics, graduating with a Ph.D. in 1957, he was thinking about how his abilities in mathematics could be applied to cosmological problems.

Sciama frequently conversed with Penrose about both physics and cosmology and invited him to hear a lecture by David Finkelstein on the so-called Schwarzschild solution. This was Penrose's first exposure to the possibility of black holes in the universe, a phenomenon predicted by Karl Schwarzschild in 1917. A black hole is a star that has collapsed to such a degree that matter is increasingly drawn into it, warp-

ing the structure of space and not allowing even light to escape.

Penrose was determined to master physics and to apply his considerable mathematical talents to the mysteries of the universe. For the next two years as a research fellow at Cambridge, he enjoyed interactions with Sciama and the talented doctoral students working with him, including Stephen Hawking and Martin Rees.

Distinction as a Mathematical Physicist

Penrose's first major contribution to cosmology was to explain the peculiar behavior of black holes, entities whose existence flowed out of Albert Einstein's relativity theory but for which there had been no observational evidence. Penrose coauthored a paper with Hawking in 1964 in which they showed mathematically how black holes could collapse.

His next major contribution was to develop a new way to explain the origins of the universe using complex numbers that he termed

Penrose Tiling

One of the important and intriguing mathematical concepts that Penrose developed is that of Penrose tiling. After some of his original ideas in this area were proposed in 1974, the concept became a mathematical teaser regularly featured in recreational mathematics books and columns.

One of the long-standing issues about geometric shapes concerns how to repeat patterns in such a way that symmetry is maintained and to achieve it with the fewest possible geometric shapes repeated to make the pattern. It was thought that only threefold, fourfold, or sixfold symmetry was possible with two figures, since all attempts at achieving fivefold symmetry resulted in a crack in the pattern at key points.

Penrose found a new way out of the classic dilemma that the problem posed by considering a figure that consisted of two rhombuses that could be constructed in such a way that fivefold symmetry was possible (see the accompanying figure). By carefully placing the figures throughout the plane, a nearly perfect fivefold symmetry could be attained. The resulting forms, however, did not make a repeating pattern; they were "nonperiodic." In fact, when creating a Penrose tile, the creator often must stand some distance away from the developing tile to determine where to place the next figure.

Ten years later, Penrose's discovery moved out of the theoretical and into the real world when Dany Schechtman and his colleagues at the National Bureau of Standards reported such a shape in a aluminum-manganese alloy that they had heated and then rapidly cooled. They did not realize its connection to Penrose's work. That connection was made by physicist Paul Steinhardt and crystallographer Alan MacKay. The resulting quasi-crystals opened up an entirely new research field in crystallography. These were not true crystals but halfway between crystals and glasslike structures. Building upon Schechtman's original work, scientists soon discovered alloys with sevenfold, ninefold, and elevenfold symmetry.

In 1988, Steinhardt and ceramics expert George Onoda devised rules for how to build a Penrose tile. The practical hope is that these alloys prove to be harder than crystals and could be used in a variety of industrial applications. As is typical of much of Penrose's work, his original ideas opened up new mathematical and practical vistas for work in a wide range of scientific fields.

Bibliography

Penrose Tiles to Trapdoor Ciphers. Martin Gardner. New York: W. H. Freeman, 1989.

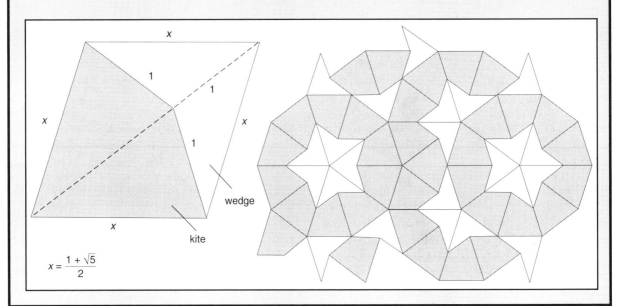

$$x = \frac{1 + \sqrt{5}}{2}$$

tensors. At the time, all mathematics of large-scale phenomena in the universe (such as general relativity) used real numbers and the world of atoms (quantum theory) used complex numbers. Penrose was committed to the idea that complex numbers must be used to account for everything in the universe. His theory of complex numbers required a reinvention of the laws of physics and the nature of space-time as explained by general relativity.

An early proponent of Hoyle's steady-state model of the universe, Penrose came to reject that model, largely because Sciama rejected it in light of more recent observational data. At the end of the twentieth century, Penrose remained uncommitted to the big bang theory and believed that the universe is open. He was unimpressed by such cosmological ideas as cosmic strings and the inflationary universe, believing that cosmology has been too heavily influenced by particle physicists with little appreciation or understanding of the mathematics surrounding relativity. Penrose was acknowledged by his colleagues as one of the most mathematically gifted individuals contributing to general relativity and cosmology.

Bibliography
By Penrose
Spinors and Space-Time, 1984-1986 (with Wolf-gang Rindler; vol. 1, *Two-Spinor Calculus and Relativistic Fields*, and vol. 2, *Spinor and Twistor Methods in Space-Time Geometry*)
The Emperor's New Mind: Concerning Computers, Minds, and the Laws of Physics, 1989
Shadows of the Mind: A Search for the Missing Science of Consciousness, 1994
The Nature of Space and Time, 1996 (with Stephen Hawking)

About Penrose
"The Artist, the Physicist, and the Waterfall." John Horgan. *Scientific American* 268 (February, 1993): 30.
"Quantum Consciousness: Polymath Roger Penrose Takes on the Ultimate Mystery." John Horgan. *Scientific American* 261 (November, 1989).
"Roger Penrose." Alan Lightman and Roberta Brawer. In *Origins: The Lives and Worlds of Modern Cosmologists*. Cambridge, Mass.: Harvard University Press, 1990.
"Roger Penrose." C. D. Lord. In *Notable Twentieth Century Scientists*, edited by Emily J. McMurray. Vol. 3. New York: Gale Research, 1995.

(Dennis W. Cheek)

Plato

Area of Achievement: Geometry

Contribution: Although Plato probably did not do much original work in mathematics, his enthusiasm for it and the preeminent place that he gave it in his theory of knowledge and reality influenced its development during and after his lifetime.

c. 427 B.C.E.	Born in Athens, Greece
399 B.C.E.	His mentor, Socrates, is executed
399 B.C.E.	Withdraws to Megara
399-388 B.C.E.	Writes the first dialogues and the *Apology*
c. 390-388 B.C.E.	Travels to the West, including Italy
388 B.C.E.	Returns to Athens
c. 386 B.C.E.	Founds the Academy
366-365 B.C.E.	Invited to Sicily to educate the prospective ruler of Syracuse
362 B.C.E.	Makes a third trip to Sicily
361 B.C.E.	Leaves Sicily, with some political difficulty
347 B.C.E.	Dies in Athens, Greece

Early Life

Plato (pronounced "PLAYT-oh") was born with the name Aristocles; Plato is a nickname meaning "broad forehead." He was the son of Ariston and his wife Pericitone. No reliable information exists about his father's family, but his mother's ancestors were distinguished. Plato's father died young, and his mother married Pyrilampes, the son of a close associate of Pericles, the great Greek general. References in Plato's writings indicate that he had two brothers, a sister, and a half brother.

Because of his distinguished family, Plato could have entered public affairs, but his maternal relatives became reactionary extremists during the Pelopponesian War with the reign of the Thirty Tyrants. The situation became more favorable to entering public life when democracy was restored. Plato had become a student of the philosopher Socrates. Under the democratic government, however, Socrates was tried and executed on trumped-up charges of impiety.

Plato founded the Academy, a school for male students, mainly over the age of thirty. He found the government more distasteful as he aged, and he wrote theoretical works on political reform.

Mathematics in Education

The most famous of Plato's thirty dialogues is the *Politeia* (c. 388-368 B.C.E.; *Republic*, 1701). In this dialogue, he described a utopian state ruled by philosopher kings. The education of these rulers was carefully explained. Years of study of mathematics were prerequisite to the study of philosophical argument, allowing rulers to understand how to govern with justice.

The education of rulers paralleled Plato's theory of knowledge. He believed that relying on the senses gave only opinion. True knowledge was based on reasoning, which studied mathematical realities, and on understanding, which focused on the so-called Forms, or generalized ideas. By studying geometry, which dealt with eternal shapes, the mind learned a method useful for determining philosophical truths.

The Use of Mathematical Examples

Plato's work reveals the strong influence of Pythagorean mathematicians. He often used mathematical examples to illustrate his philosophical ideas. For example, in the dialogue *Menon* (c. 388-368 B.C.E.; *Meno*, 1804), he tried to show that learning is an act of remembering. A slave boy in this dialogue figured out by himself how to form a square of twice the area of a given square by using the diagonal of the given square as the side of the larger square.

For Plato, numbers also represented various qualities. For example, there was a number for marriage. To establish the population of his ideal state, Plato searched for a special number. He settled on 5,040, which has sixty divisors, including all the numbers 1 through 12, except 7, which goes into 5,038 (=5,040 − 2).

The Geometric Nature of the Four Elements

Plato used existing knowledge of the five regular solids to construct a theory of the Greek elements.

The ancient Greeks believed that there were four elements—earth, air, fire, and water. Empedocles, an early philosopher, named the four elements and considered each to be totally different. Plato came up with a more economical conception of the elements. He associated each element with one of the regular solids: earth with the cube (6 equal square faces), fire with the tetrahedron (4 equal triangular faces), air with the octahedron (8 equal triangular faces), and water with the icosahedron (20 equal triangular faces). The dodecahedron (12 equal pentagonal faces) was implicitly associated with the perfect element that formed the celestial bodies.

Plato observed that drawing two diagonals on the face of a square produces four isosceles right triangles, while the triangular faces of the tetrahedron, octahedron, and icosahedron are all equilateral triangles and can be divided into six half equilateral triangles. Plato was aware that the pentagonal face of the dodecahedron cannot be divided into equal triangles.

Because the triangular faces of the tetrahedron, octahedron, and icosahedron are the same, Plato believed that one element could be transmuted into another. For example, an octahedron of air (8 faces) could be divided into two tetrahedrons of fire (4 + 4 faces), and an icosahedron of water (20 faces) could be split into two octahedrons of water and one tetrahedron of fire (8 + 8 + 4 faces). Similarly, particles of one element (or two) could combine to form another element. Plato never explained, however, how the primary bodies could disassemble and reassemble.

There were three grades of earth, with the faces of the square composed of two, four, or eight isosceles right triangles. The cube did not submit to change into another element. If broken, it produced smaller particles of earth. Various combinations of the four elements produced the many complex substances.

This idea had a great influence on Aristotle, who accepted the interchangeability of all four elements, although not of the geometric figures. The idea that one substance can transmute into another provided the theoretical basis for alchemy.

Bibliography

Early Greek Science: Thales to Aristotle. Geoffrey Ernest Richard Lloyd. London: Chatto & Windus, 1970

The History of Mathematics: A Reader. John Fauvel and Jeremy Gray, eds. Basingstoke, England: Macmillan Education, 1987.

Plato's Universe. Gregory Vlastos. Seattle: University of Washington Press, 1975.

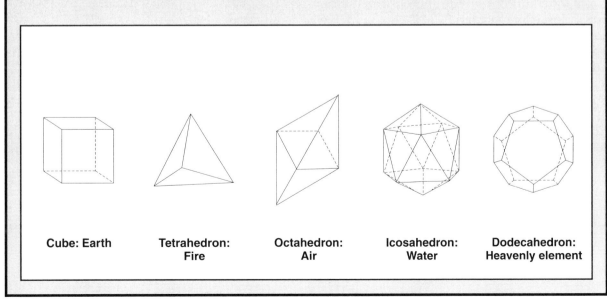

Cube: Earth   Tetrahedron: Fire   Octahedron: Air   Icosahedron: Water   Dodecahedron: Heavenly element

(Library of Congress)

Mathematics in Plato's Astronomy

In the *Timaeos* (c. 360-347 B.C.E.; *Timaeus*, 1804), Plato asserted that the world or universe must be a sphere because the sphere is the most perfect and uniform geometrical figure, with every part of its surface equidistant from the center. At the center was the world-soul, which was divided into harmonic intervals, including both the arithmetic series 1, 2, 4, 8 and the geometric series 1, 3, 9, 27. The fabric of the universe was divided further, resulting in a number of circles that accounted for the movement of the planets.

Plato also presented a geometric conception of matter. He represented each of the four ancient elements with a regular solid. The face of each solid was formed of triangles. The fifth regular solid represented the matter that composed the celestial bodies.

Influence

The Academy attracted important scholars of the day, including Eudoxus and Aristotle.

Through this institution, knowledge from the philosophical schools in Sicily reached Greece. For nine centuries, Plato's followers met at the Academy, until Emperor Justinian closed it and other pagan academies in 529.

Plato was also famed outside the Academy. While in Italy to study with Archytus of Tarentum, a Pythagorean mathematician skilled in number theory and geometry, he made the acquaintance of Dion, the brother-in-law of the tyrant Dionysius the Elder of Syracuse. After Dionysius's death, Dion invited Plato back to Syracuse to help determine a government for the city-state and to educate Dionysius the Younger, whom Dion planned to install as a constitutional monarch. A war interrupted the plan, and several years later Plato returned to Syracuse in a failed attempt to institute Dion's plan. Plato lived out the rest of his life in Athens, dying in 347 B.C.E.

Bibliography
By Plato
Apologia Sokratous, c. 399-390 B.C.E. (*Apology*, 1701)
Menon, c. 388-368 B.C.E. (*Meno*, 1804)
Politeia, c. 388-368 B.C.E. (*Republic*, 1701)
Symposion, c. 388-368 B.C.E. (*Symposium*, 1701)
Timaeos, c. 360-347 B.C.E. (*Timaeus*, 1804)

About Plato
From Thales to Euclid. Thomas Little Heath. Vol. 1 in *A History of Greek Mathematics*. Oxford, England: Clarendon Press, 1921.
Plato's Cosmology: The "Timaeus" of Plato Translated with a Running Commentary. Francis MacDonald Cornford. New York: Humanities Press, 1952.
Plato's Mathematical Imagination: The Mathematical Passages in the Dialogues and Their Interpretation. Robert Sherrick Brumbaugh. Bloomington: Indiana University Press, 1954.
Plato's Philosophy of Mathematics. Anders Wedberg. Stockholm: Almqvist & Wiksell, 1955.

(Kristen L. Zacharias)

Henri Poincaré

Areas of Achievement: Algebra, applied math, calculus, mathematical logic, number theory, and topology

Contribution: Poincaré was a true universalist in mathematics, making contributions to all aspects of the field. Among his most lasting contributions were advances in celestial mechanics and the early aspects of relativity theory.

Apr. 29, 1854	Born in Nancy, Lorraine, France
1873	Begins studies at the École Polytechnique
1875	Transfers to the École des Mines
1879	Receives an engineering degree from the École des Mines and a doctorate from the University of Paris
1879	Begins teaching at the University of Caen
1881	Accepts a faculty position at the University of Paris
1887	Elected to the Académie des Sciences
1889	Awarded a mathematics prize by King Oscar II of Sweden
1904	Travels to the United States as an invited lecturer for the St. Louis Exposition
1906	Elected to the presidency of the Académie des Sciences
1908	Elected to the Académie Française
July 17, 1912	Dies in Paris, France

Early Life

Jules-Henri Poincaré (pronounced "pwahn-kaw-RAY") was born on April 29, 1854, in Nancy, France. He was the son of Léon Poincaré, a physician and professor of medicine at the University of Nancy. Throughout his childhood, Henri Poincaré was physically awkward, with poor motor skills, perhaps the result of a bout with diphtheria at the age of five. This impairment kept him from playing with other children as much as most boys did. He turned his attention to his studies instead. Poincaré was always a good student, exhibiting a perfect memory for things that he had heard.

In 1870, during the Franco-Prussian War, his hometown of Nancy was occupied by enemy forces. Helping his father tend the wounded and dying, Henri and his cousin Raymond saw the horrors of the war, and they developed a deep-seated distaste for the German people. This may have influenced Poincaré late in his career to be slow to acknowledge Albert Einstein's work on the special theory of relativity. Raymond Poincaré eventually came to be elected as president of France, a position in which he served during World War I.

Education

Henri Poincaré was always good at mathematics, in most cases doing almost all the work on math problems in his head. He entered the École Polytechnique in 1871. In 1875, he enrolled in the École des Mines to pursue an engineering degree.

(Library of Congress)

Poincaré became interested in mathematical research, particularly in the area of differential equations. In 1879, he received his engineering degree from the École des Mines. In the same year, he presented his mathematical work to the University of Paris for a doctorate in mathematics.

In 1879, Poincaré accepted a teaching position at the University of Caen. In 1881, he received a promotion and a position as professor at the University of Paris. He remained at the University of Paris until his death in 1912.

Mathematical Works

Poincaré studied and contributed to almost all areas of mathematics. Few mathematicians have been able to contribute to so many different areas of mathematics. One odd note to his work, however, is that Poincaré seemed to do very little literature research before tackling mathematical problems. As a result, he frequently repeated the works of others. Nevertheless, he made an amazing number of new contributions to mathematics.

Poincaré was frequently satisfied when he had worked out the general ideas and framework of a problem. He was less interested in the details that were needed to apply his work to nature. He left the working out of the details to others as he moved on to study other things of interest to him.

Some of Poincaré's most important contri-

Relativity

Poincaré developed many of the initial ideas leading ultimately to the special theory of relativity.

While Albert Einstein's work on the special theory of relativity is well known, Poincaré had begun developing his own theory of relativity a decade earlier. Collaborating with Hendrik Antoon Lorentz to develop electromagnetic theory from the work of James Clerk Maxwell, Poincaré realized the need for a theory of relativity.

Poincaré began his work with studies of the synchronization of clocks. He realized that the finite value of the speed of light would make synchronization problematic for moving observers. This situation argued for some sort of theory of relativity to account for the effects of motion.

Like Einstein, Poincaré argued that a moving observer would be unable to determine motion relative to light. Poincaré argued that the difficulties of timekeeping for moving observers would result in the clocks of the moving observer apparently running slower than the clocks of a stationary observer. Poincaré further argued that all physical laws would appear the same for an observer moving at uniform velocity and an observer at rest.

Poincaré's ideas seem very similar to those proposed a few years later by Einstein, with a few major differences. Poincaré was locked into a belief in the ether, the mythical medium through which light waves were supposed to propagate. An observer at rest, to Poincaré, was an observer at rest relative to the ether.

Einstein discarded concepts of the ether and thus discarded the concept of an absolute reference frame. Einstein's assumption that there is no absolute reference frame meant that clocks really do run slower for moving objects, rather than simply appearing to run slower, as Poincaré had assumed.

Although Poincaré was the first to propose that a universal principal of relativity must exist to explain observations in electromagnetism, he did not truly develop a theory of relativity as Einstein did. Poincaré's work was an effort to fix electromagnetic theory with a generalization of ideas of relativity from classical mechanics. His ideas were close to those of Einstein, and he may have ultimately arrived at the same ideas had he discarded the ether as a medium for light. Poincaré's untimely death, however, prevented his understanding of relativity in the same way that Einstein did.

Bibliography

"Henri Poincaré and the Principle of Relativity." Charles Scribner, Jr. *American Journal of Physics* 32, no. 8 (1964): 672-678.

Understanding Relativity: Origin and Impact of a Scientific Revolution. Stanley Goldberg. Boston: Birkhäuser, 1984.

Celestial Mechanics

One of Poincaré's most lasting contributions in the area of applied mathematics was his discovery that some of the differential equations of celestial mechanics have divergent solutions. This discovery ultimately led to the development of the chaos theory in mathematics.

To a mathematician, chaos is not random. Rather, the term "chaos" denotes a complexity having an underlying order not readily apparent. The precise behavior of a chaotic system cannot be computed accurately, although limits on that behavior may be determined.

One of the principal problems of celestial mechanics is the restricted three body problem. It involves calculating the motion of a small object orbiting a very large body. A third body—small compared to the very large body but large compared to the small object—also orbits the very large body. The gravitational force between the small object and the mid-sized body provides a perturbation to the orbit of the small object. An example of the restricted three body problem would be the motion of asteroids about the sun with Jupiter's gravity acting as a perturbation on the orbits of the asteroids.

In studying the restricted three body problem, Poincaré discovered that the differential equations of the problem have divergent solutions. In other words, the solutions involve an infinite series of terms that do not converge to any single value. He found, however, that unlike many divergent systems, these solutions were asymptotically convergent; that is, the summations tend to approach functions for large numbers of terms. As a result, solutions to the equations can be used to predict behavior for a limited time, but these solutions fail for long time intervals.

One of the chief reasons that the solutions fail is that infinitesimally small differences in the initial conditions of the problem lead to exceedingly large differences in the final calculated positions because of the divergent nature of the solutions. This is the essence of chaos theory.

Chaos theory states that tiny changes in the initial conditions result in large unpredictable changes in the final results of calculations. Poincaré's work with celestial mechanics and divergent solutions led later mathematicians to develop chaos theory and to extend applications of chaos beyond celestial mechanics into almost every aspect of the physical world.

Bibliography

Chaos: Making a New Science. James Gleick. New York: Viking Press, 1988.

Methods of Celestial Mechanics. Dirk Brouwer and Gerald M. Clemence. New York: Academic Press, 1961.

Newton's Clock: Chaos in the Solar System. Ivars Peterson. New York: W. H. Freeman, 1993.

One Hundred Years of Mathematics: A Personal Viewpoint. George Temple. New York: Springer-Verlag, 1981.

"Urey Prize Lecture: Chaotic Dynamics in the Solar System." Jack Wisdom. *Icarus* 72, no. 2 (1987): 241-275.

butions came from his studies of differential equations. These equations are particularly important in applied mathematics, as in the areas of physics and engineering. Poincaré's work in celestial mechanics, particularly his study of the three body problem, began the whole field of study that was later called chaos theory.

Popular Works

In addition to his professional work in mathematics, Poincaré wrote several books on mathematics and the philosophy of science for the general public. These books were immensely popular throughout France.

Mathematics was always so easy and obvious to Poincaré that he was genuinely puzzled that some people did not understand it. Since logical thought and deduction are such an important part of mathematics, Poincaré believed that all adults should be able to understand the essentials of mathematics. His popular works were written to further this public understanding of mathematics.

Later Years

Illness prevented Poincaré from presenting a paper at the International Mathematical Congress of 1908 in Rome. Italian surgeons performed prostate surgery to alleviate his problems. By 1911, however, Poincaré was again experiencing health problems, which became severe the following spring. On July 9, 1912, he underwent another operation. He died suddenly on July 17, 1912, of an embolism.

At the time of his death, Poincaré was at the peak of his career. He was the preeminent mathematician of his time and one of the best of all time.

Bibliography

By Poincaré

Notice sur les travaux scientifiques de Henri Poincaré, 1884

Electricité et optique, 1890-1891

Les Méthodes nouvelles de la mécanique céleste, 1892-1899 (3 vols.; *New Methods of Celestial Mechanics*, 1960)

La Science et l'hypothèse, 1902 (*Science and Hypothesis*, 1905)

La Valeur de la science, 1905 (*The Value of Science*, 1907)

Science et méthode, 1908 (*Science and Method*, 1913)

Leçons sur les hypothèses cosmogoniques professees à la Sorbonne, 1911

Œuvres de Henri Poincaré, 1916-1954 (11 vols.)

About Poincaré

Asimov's Biographical Encyclopedia of Science and Technology. Isaac Asimov. 2d ed. Garden City, N.Y.: Doubleday, 1982.

A History of Mathematics. Carl B. Boyer. New York: John Wiley & Sons, 1968.

Men of Mathematics. E. T. Bell. New York: Simon & Schuster, 1937.

Newton's Clock: Chaos in the Solar System. Ivars Peterson. New York: W. H. Freeman, 1993.

(*Raymond D. Benge, Jr.*)

Siméon-Denis Poisson

Areas of Achievement: Applied math, calculus, and probability

Contribution: Poisson demonstrated that physics, especially electrostatics and magnetism, could be explained and described mathematically.

June 21, 1781	Born in Pithiviers, France
1798	Enters the École Polytechnique
1800	Publishes a memoir on the number of integrals of an equation of finite differences
1806	Appointed a professor at the École Polytechnique
1809	Appointed a professor of pure mathematics at the Faculty of Sciences, the University of Paris
1811	Publishes *Traité de méchanique* (*A Treatise of Mechanics*, 1842)
1812	Begins theoretical studies to describe electrical phenomena mathematically
1825	Awarded the title of baron for his work in higher mathematics
1833	Publishes a second, enlarged volume of *Traité de méchanique*
1837	Publishes *Recherches sur la probabilité des jugements en matière criminelle et en matière civile* (inquiry on the probability of judgment in criminal and civil matters)
Apr. 25, 1840	Dies in Sceaux, France

Early Life

Siméon-Denis Poisson (pronounced "pwah-SOHN") was born in 1781. He was the son of the head of local government at Pithiviers. After completing his elementary education, Poisson was sent to an uncle, a surgeon, at Fountainebleau for training in the medical arts. The first lessons were in bleeding and blistering, then common treatments for a variety of ailments. Poisson showed little interest in the curative arts, but he did demonstrate a genuine talent for mathematics.

Success at the École Polytechnique

Poisson was admitted to the École Polytechnique in Paris. He quickly attracted the notice of the instructors at the school because of his skills in higher mathematics. Recognizing Poisson's reasoning abilities in mathematics, the faculty members wisely allowed him to follow studies that were intellectually satisfying to him.

In 1800, less than two years after he entered the school, he wrote two mathematical memoirs critically examining the methodologies and soundness of logic in two papers by the mathematician E. Bouzout. One memoir, on the number of integrals of an equation of finite differences, drew the attention of senior faculty members, who were so impressed that they recommended the paper be published. This was looked on as a major honor for the young Poisson, who was still a student.

Other honors soon came his way. Well-known mathematicians drew him into their circle and invited him to attend special lectures in higher mathematics. His peers often gathered in Poisson's room after an unusually difficult lecture on some complex theorem to have him repeat it and explain it to them. The officials at the school recognized the value of his volunteer services and appointed him to an official post to carry on, with a stipend, the duties that he had performed as an unpaid volunteer.

Academic promotions came rapidly to Poisson after he had completed his course of study at the École Polytechnique. In 1802, he was appointed the equivalent of an assistant professor, and, in 1806, he was made a full professor. He is said to have once stated that life is good for only two things: to do mathematics and to teach it. He enjoyed a reputation as an excellent instructor and was sought out by students eager to learn the theories and workings of higher mathematics.

In addition to his teaching position at the École Polytechnique, Poisson held a number of positions in French government institutions. In 1808, he was appointed astronomer to the Bureau des Longitudes and in 1827 became geometer to the bureau.

Mathematical Works

Early in his career, he embarked on studies to make the study of electricity and magnetism a branch of mathematical physics. New discoveries in these fields by researchers including Carl Friedrich Gauss, Charles-Augustin Coulomb, and André-Marie Ampère intrigued Poisson, who sought to derive mathematical models to describe the phenomena that were taking place in the physics laboratories. His contributions to various fields of applied mathematics include the Poisson constant in electricity and the Poisson ratio in elasticity.

Despite the demands of teaching and his many official duties, Poisson found time to write and publish between three hundred and four hundred works in mathematics. Many of them dealt with esoteric branches of pure and applied mathematics. His most famous publications include *Traité de méchanique* (*A Treatise of Mechanics*, 1842), published in 1811 and in an

(Library of Congress)

A Probability of the Occurrence of Events

Poisson computed with elegant mathematics the probability of the occurrence of some event over a specified interval, such as time or distance.

The Poisson distribution is a mathematical model describing the probability distribution for the arrivals of entities requiring some service or attention. Examples would include the distribution of automobiles arriving at a service station or airplanes arriving at an airport. A characteristic Poisson distribution curve results when the time interval between new arrivals is plotted against the number of times that the interval occurs. As the time interval increases from zero, the distribution curve rises rapidly to a peak, to fall off exponentially toward infinity.

The Poisson distribution has been used to describe and understand the use of new words by published poets. Researchers examining the works of William Shakespeare, William Wordsworth, Edgar Allan Poe, and Robert Frost discovered that the use of new words in a poem could be described statistically by the Poisson distribution. This distribution results when the poet seeks the innovative inclusion of a new word in a poem. The longer the poet delays deriving a new word, the probability increases that the next word will be a new one.

The Poisson distribution has also been used to describe the randomly dispersed distribution of commercially exploited fish in the ocean. With marine fish (or other wildlife), individuals of the same species tend to be distributed in clumps. The clumps, in turn, are distributed randomly, in an arrangement of underdispersion. Such a distribution conforms mathematically to the Poisson distribution. The distribution of the exploitable fish population depends in large part on the fish arriving at a particular location as a result of the attraction of, for example, preferred water temperatures or a food source. Thus, the individual fish would be behaving in a manner similar to the automobiles at a gas station. As the gap between "customers" increases and the frequency of the gaps increases, an increase occurs in the urgency of new arrivals to exploit the resource (that is, food for the fish or fuel for the automobiles).

That a Poisson distribution can be used to describe these events does not enhance an opportunity to take advantage of the situation. Without additional pumps, the gasoline station cannot plan a more efficient way of serving the random influx of passengers and commercial fishers or fish managers cannot plan a way to increase the useable catch, given the random distribution of the fish.

Bibliography

A History of Mathematics. Carl B. Boyer. New York: John Wiley & Sons, 1968.

"Patterns of Distribution." William F. Royce. In *Introduction to the Fishery Sciences.* New York: Academic Press, 1972.

"Shall I Compare Thee to Poisson Curve?" Geoff Lowe. *New Scientist* 144, no. 1947 (October 15, 1994).

enlarged edition in 1833, and *Recherches sur la probabilité des jugements en matière criminelle at en matière civile* (inquiry on the probability of judgment in criminal and civil matters), published in 1837, toward the end of his brilliant career.

Politics

Throughout his life, Poisson held, and expressed, strong political beliefs. He inherited his father's hatred of aristocrats but refused to hold Napoleon in great esteem. He was faithful to the Bourbons, the extremely conservative, even reactionary, political faction. The Revolution of July 1830 threatened to strip Poisson of all of his honors. The intervention of friends, however, led to an invitation to dine with Louis Philippe and reconciliation with this "Citizen King." Thus, Poisson's position was made secure. Shortly afterward, he was made a peer of France—not, his supporters assured him, for political reasons, but as a representative of French science.

Nothing is available about Poisson's personal life—whether he was married, produced heirs, or established a lineage. His posterity seems to be the great works that he conceived and that stand as his memorial. He died on April 25, 1840.

Bibliography
By Poisson
"Sur les inégalities séculaires des moyens mou- vemens des planètes," *Journal de l'École Polytechnique* 8, 1809
Traité de méchanique, 1811 (2 vols.; *A Treatise of Mechanics*, 1842)
Traité de méchanique, 1833, 2d enlarged ed.
Recherches sur la probabilité des jugements en ma- tière criminelle at en matière civile, 1837

About Poisson
A Concise History of Mathematics. Dirk Jan Struik. 2d ed. New York: Dover, 1948.
A History of Mathematics. Carl B. Boyer. New York: John Wiley & Sons, 1968.
History of Mathematics, Volume I. David Eugene Smith. New York: Ginn, 1958.

(*Albert C. Jensen*)

George Pólya

Areas of Achievement: Applied math, cal- culus, geometry, number theory, and probability

Contribution: Pólya was known for his work in mathematics education. His teaching style—sometimes referred to as the "Pólya style"—is recorded on tape and presented as an example of masterful teaching to students at teachers' colleges. Pólya also contributed to the language of mathematics. He was the first to introduce the random walk and the central limit theorem.

Dec. 13, 1887	Born in Budapest, Austro-Hungarian Empire (now Hungary)
1912	Receives a Ph.D. in mathematics from the University of Budapest
1914	Obtains his first teaching position at the Swiss Federal Institute of Technology in Zurich
1940	Moves to the United States
1945	Publishes *How to Solve It*, a popular book about mathematical problem solving
1963	Receives the Mathematical Association of America award for distinguished service to mathematics
1968	Receives the Educational Film Library award for his lecture series "Let Us Teach Guessing"
Sept. 7, 1985	Dies in Palo Alto, California

Early Life
George Pólya (pronounced "POHL-yaw") at- tended a college preparatory school in Buda- pest. He studied, mathematics, physics, and lit- erature and received a literary prize for translating the works of one of his favorite authors, Heinrich Heine, into Hungarian.

In 1905, Pólya's academic achievements enabled him to attend the University of Budapest tuition-free. Upon his mother's insistence, Pólya spent his first semester in law school, which he found boring. He studied the works of Charles Darwin and was interested in biology. When his brother cautioned him that biology was not lucrative, Pólya turned to languages and literature, receiving Latin and Hungarian teaching certificates that he never used.

As part of his philosophy studies, Pólya took physics and mathematics. His physics course was taught by Loránd Eötvös, a distinguished physicist known for his devotion to the sciences and teaching. Pólya attributed his penchant for physics to Eötvös's memorable lessons.

Another professor who greatly influenced Pólya was Lipót Fejér, a well-known mathematician. Fejér would meet with his students in a café to work on problems and discuss mathematicians he had known. Pólya joined teachers and friends such as Fejér and both Frigyes Riesz and Marcel Riesz in a flourishing group of Budapest mathematicians. Pólya decided to become a mathematician himself.

Pólya was awarded a Ph.D. at the University of Budapest after spending a year at the University of Vienna. His degree was in mathematics, with a minor in physics and chemistry. Pólya did postdoctoral work at the Universities of Göttingen and Paris. He was in contact with other famous mathematicians, such as David Hilbert and Hermann Weyl.

The War Years and After

Pólya's first teaching position was at the Swiss Federal Institute of Technology in Zurich. Because of a childhood soccer injury that resulted in blood poisoning and a leg operation, Pólya was rejected by the Hungarian army when he tried to sign up. When World War I escalated, the army called him to report. Pólya had examined the works of mathematician-philosopher Bertrand Russell and concluded that war is wrong. He decided not to return to Hungary.

In Zurich, Pólya befriended Adolf Hurwitz and later edited Hurwitz's collected works. They shared a style of mathematical communication characterized by clarity and depth. Pólya produced papers on series, number theory, combinatorics, and voting systems. In 1918, he married a Swiss woman, Stella V. Weber; they remained married for sixty-seven years. In 1919, he published papers on astronomy and probability and did research on integral functions. Pólya spent 1924 in England working with G. H. Hardy and John E. Littlewood. Their joint work, *Inequalities*, was published in 1934.

The European political situation forced the Pólyas to leave for the United States in 1940. George Pólya taught as a visiting professor at Brown University in Rhode Island. He then received an appointment at Stanford University and settled in Palo Alto, California.

Pólya spoke Hungarian, French, German, and English fluently. He was an outstanding lecturer and writer. His masterful teaching was based on the principle that students should be helped to rediscover for themselves the material that they were taught.

Pólya poses with various translations of his book How to Solve It. *(AP/Wide World Photos)*

Approach to Problem Solving

Pólya encouraged students to become more capable and independent problem solvers. He developed the famous Pólya model, which utilizes common-sense questions and strategies that would naturally occur to the best problem solvers.

His 1945 book *How to Solve It* provides Pólya's outline of his problem-solving framework. The outline indicates the four phases of the problem-solving process: understanding the problem, devising a plan, carrying out the plan, and looking back. Pólya also provided important heuristics or general techniques for solving problems. Pólya's heuristics serve to guide and encourage students to develop an organized approach to the problem-solving process.

The accompanying summary is taken from *How to Solve It*.

Pólya drew upon his extensive experience as a master teacher and problem solver in providing this model for students. He also advised teachers concerning the use of the model. He urged them to pose key suggestions and questions carefully and to provide appropriate practice so that students gain more experience and confidence in problem solving. The Pólya model has become an integral part of mathematics-teacher education courses in colleges throughout the world.

Bibliography

"George Pólya's Influence on Mathematics Education." Jeremy Kilpatrick. *Mathematics Magazine* 60, no. 5 (1987): 299-300.

"Pólya, Problem Solving, and Education." Alan H. Schoenfeld. *Mathematics Magazine* 60, no. 5 (1987): 283-291.

1. UNDERSTANDING THE PROBLEM
   - What is the unknown? What are the data? What is the condition?
   - Is it possible to satisfy the condition? Is the condition sufficient to determine the unknown? Or is it insufficient? Or redundant? Or contradictory?
   - Draw a figure. Introduce suitable notation.
   - Separate the various parts of the condition. Can you write them down?
2. DEVISING A PLAN
   - Find the connection between the data and the unknown.
   - Have you seen it before? Or have you seen the same problem in a slightly different form?
   - Do you know a related problem? Do you know a theorem that could be useful?
   - Here is a problem related to yours and solved before. Could you use it? Could you use its result? Could you use its method? Should you introduce some auxiliary element in order to make its use possible?
   - Could you restate the problem? Could you restate it still differently? Go back to definitions.
   - Did you use all the data? Did you use the whole condition? Have you taken into account all essential notions involved in the problem?
3. CARRYING OUT THE PLAN
   - Carrying out your plan of the solution, check each step. Can you see clearly that the step is correct? Can you prove that it is correct?
4. LOOKING BACK
   - Examine the solution obtained.
   - Can you check the result? Can you check the argument?
   - Can you derive the solution differently? Can you see it at a glance?
   - Can you use the result, or the method, for some other problem?

Before leaving for the United States, Pólya wrote a draft of the book *How to Solve It* in German. He tried four publishers before finding one to publish it in English in 1945. It became a best-seller. Pólya's other great work in mathematics education, *Mathematics and Plausible Reasoning* (1954), reflected his knowledge and interest in philosophy.

Honors

Pólya wrote or coauthored more than 250 books and papers on problem solving as well as applied mathematics, calculus, geometry, number theory, and probability. His name describes many of the mathematical ideas that he developed. Among the theorems, methods, and concepts named for him are Pólya's algorithm, Pólya's counting theorem, Pólya's function, Pólya matrices, Pólya polynomials, Pólya sequences, and the Pólya series. Pólya Hall, which houses the Department of Numerical Analysis at Stanford, was named in his honor.

Pólya was an honorary member of the Hungarian Academy, the London Mathematical Society, the Swiss Mathematical Society, and the Society for Industrial and Applied Mathematics (SIAM). The Pólya Prize, established in 1969, is the SIAM award for extraordinary application of combinatorial theory. Pólya was also a member of the National Academy of Sciences and the American Academy of Arts and Sciences. He was a corresponding member of the Académie des Sciences.

In 1963, Pólya received the award for distinguished service to mathematics from the Mathematical Association of America. In 1968, he won an award at the Educational Film Library Association's film festival for his lecture series "Let Us Teach Guessing."

Pólya was an active member of the mathematics community for most of his life. He taught at Stanford until 1978 and gave lectures around the country. Pólya died in 1985 at the age of ninety-seven.

Bibliography
By Pólya
Aufgaben und Lehrsatze aus der Analysis I, 1925 (with Gabor Szegö; *Problems and Theorems in Analysis*, 1972-1976, 2 vols.)

How To Solve It: A New Aspect of Mathematical Method, 1945

Isoperimetric Inequalities in Mathematical Physics, 1951

Induction and Analogy in Mathematics, 1954

Mathematics and Plausible Reasoning, 1954

Mathematical Discovery: On Understanding, Learning, and Teaching Problem Solving, 1962-1965 (2 vols.)

Location of Zeros, 1974

Singularities of Analytic Functions, 1974

About Pólya
"A Conversation with George Pólya." Agnes A. Wieschenberg. *Mathematics Magazine* 60, no. 5 (1987): 265-268.

"George Pólya (1887-1985)." M. M. Schiffer. *Mathematics Magazine* 60, no. 5 (1987): 268-270.

Mathematical People: Profiles and Interviews. Donald J. Albers and Gerald L. Alexanderson, eds. Boston: Birkhäuser, 1985, pp. 245-254.

"Obituary: George Pólya." Gerald L. Alexanderson and Lester H. Lange. *Bulletin of the London Mathematical Society* 19, no. 6 (1987): 559-608.

(June Lundy Gastón)

Jean-Victor Poncelet

Area of Achievement: Geometry
Contribution: Poncelet developed projective geometry as a separate branch of mathematics.

July 1, 1788	Born in Metz, France
1807	Enters the École Polytechnique, Paris
1810	Graduated from École Polytechnique and admitted to the French military corps of engineers
1812	Serves as a lieutenant in Napoleon's campaign into Russia
1812	Taken prisoner at battle of Krasnoi
1814	Released from a Russian prison in Saratov
1822	Publishes *Traité des propriétés projectives des figures*
1824	Accepts a professorship at the École d'Application de l'Artillerie et du Génie, Metz
1848	Appointed commandant of the École Polytechnique
1862-1864	Publishes the two-volume work *Applications d'analyse et de géométrie*
Dec. 22, 1867	Dies in Paris, France

Early Life

Jean-Victor Poncelet (pronounced "pohn-SLEH") was the son of Claude Poncelet, a wealthy landowner and government lawyer, and Anne-Marie Perrein. Because Poncelet was illegitimate, he was sent to live with a family in the small town of Saint-Avold, where he began his earliest education. At sixteen, he returned to Metz and was recognized and provided for by his father. He attended a city school to further his education. Poncelet was quite successful at school, enabling him to join the École Polytechnique in 1807. In 1810, he

was admitted to the French corps of military engineers.

After an assignment on the Dutch island of Walcheren, he participated in Napoleon's campaign in Russia. During the battle of Krasnoi, he was left for dead until Russian soldiers found him quite alive and subsequently imprisoned him at Saratov. While in prison for two years, Poncelet resumed his study of mathematics. Using what he recalled about geometry from his earlier studies with Gaspard Monge at the École Polytechnique, Poncelet researched and wrote extensively. This work served as the basis for his subsequent research on projective geometry: *Traité des propriétés projectives des figures*, published in 1822.

Poncelet was released from prison in 1814 and returned to Metz, where he was appointed captain in the engineering corps, a position that he held until 1824. He managed various projects in fortification, mastered industrial mechanics, and developed a new model of a

(Collection Viollet)

counterweight drawbridge. Poncelet continued to pursue his research on projective geometry concurrent with his work as a military engineer.

A New Branch of Mathematics

Poncelet presented his paper "Essai sur les propriétés projectives des sections coniques" to the Faculty of Sciences at Metz in 1820. It was not well received, especially by Augustin-Louis Cauchy, who believed that Poncelet had not contributed anything different than the current analytical geometry approach. (Analytical geometry had been developed over the previous one hundred years as a new approach to classical geometry.)

Disheartened by this harsh criticism, Poncelet continued to refine his theories and used his original essay in *Traité des propriétés projectives des figures*. This text opened the way for the development of projective geometry as a separate branch of mathematics, as it presented the fundamental ideas of perspective, duality, and the circular points at infinity.

Teaching and Applied Mechanics

After devoting many years to the study of geometry, Poncelet shifted his attention to teach-

---

The Road to Projective Geometry

Poncelet developed projective geometry as a separate branch of mathematics.

After the development of algebra in the seventeenth century, René Descartes and Pierre de Fermat created what was referred to as coordinate geometry, based on algebraic analysis. This technique for analyzing geometric shapes was dominant until the early nineteenth century.

Poncelet altered the course of geometrical study by developing projective geometry as an independent branch of mathematics. Although preliminary work on projective geometry was discovered in the seventeenth century, largely by Girard Desargues, this work was neglected and lost until Poncelet reintroduced it. In 1820, he presented his paper "Essai sur les propriétés projectives des sections coniques" to the Académie des Sciences in Metz, France, showing that the concepts of geometry could be generalized—that is, made independent of algebraic analysis. Poncelet wanted to replace the extensive use of algebraic formulas with an alternative description based on his self-titled "principle of continuity."

Through his principle of continuity, Poncelet demonstrated that if any general shape is changed in a continuous way, such as through translation, projection, or cross section, then all resulting shapes are related to each other. For example, if a square hole is cut in a window shade and the sun is shining through the hole onto the floor, the hole in the shade and the shape of the light on the floor must be related because one is created from the other. As the sun moves, the shape that the sunlight makes on the floor changes, looking unlike the square through which it is projected.

Through this idea of projection, Poncelet was able to analyze figures using a new approach. He looked at a complicated shape and imagined a simpler shape from which the complicated shape could be derived through projection. By studying the two figures, he found the unchanging properties of the simpler shape. He then projected these properties onto the more complicated figure. Previously, mathematicians adhered to the use of separate algebraic formulas for each individual shape in their study of geometry, unless the shapes were obviously similar.

The resulting ideas based on projection forced a redefinition of fundamental principals regarding geometry. Parallel lines were assumed to join at infinity; obvious was the existence of imaginary lines, points, and circles. A whole new mathematics developed based on understanding concepts rather than corresponding real values.

Bibliography

A History of Mathematics. Carl B. Boyer. New York: John Wiley & Sons, 1968.

Mathematical Thought from Ancient to Modern Times. Morris Kline. New York: Oxford University Press, 1972.

The Non-Euclidean Revolution. Richard J. Trudeau. Boston: Birkhäuser, 1987.

ing and applied mechanics. He accepted a teaching position at the École d'Application de l'Artillerie et du Génie at Metz in 1825. He devoted his time to updating the course that he was teaching in mechanics applied to machines. The previous year, he was awarded a prize for an innovative design and construction of an undershot waterwheel with curved paddles that doubled the efficiency of the device.

Poncelet was chosen scientific reporter for the Committee of Fortifications and editor of the *Memorial de l'Officier du Génie*. Unfortunately, these appointments required him to move to Paris in 1834; he wanted to remain in his hometown of Metz. Once in Paris, Poncelet happily agreed to create and teach courses on physical and experimental mechanics at the Faculty of Sciences, a position that he held for more than ten years. While in Paris, Poncelet married Louise Gaudin.

In 1848, he was given the post of commandant at the École Polytechnique, the very school where he had studied geometry with Monge. After retiring from the École Polytechnique, he accepted the chair of industrial machines and tools at the International Exposition of London in 1851 and Paris in 1855. For these expositions, he prepared extensive, and historically valuable, reports on origins and different types of tools and machines used in industry.

During the last several years of his life, Poncelet edited the whole of his published and unpublished mathematical work, bringing out four volumes of his writings on geometry, two volumes of *Applications d'analyse et de géométrie* (1862, 1864), and two updated volumes of *Traité des propriétés projectives des figures*. He began a similar project on his theory of machines and on industrial, physical, and experimental mechanics but was unable to finish this final project before his death in 1867.

Bibliography

By Poncelet
"Problèmes de géométries" *Correspondance sur l'École Polytechnique* 2, 1811
Traité des propriétés projectives des figures, 1822
Applications d'analyse et de géométrie, 1862-1864 (2 vols.)

About Poncelet
A History of Mathematics. Carl B. Boyer. New York: John Wiley & Sons, 1968.
Journey Through Genius: The Great Theorems of Mathematics. William Dunham. New York: John Wiley & Sons, 1990.
Mathematical Thought from Ancient to Modern Times. Morris Kline. New York: Oxford University Press, 1972.

(*Karen Elting Brock*)

Freda Porter-Locklear

Area of Achievement: Applied math
Contribution: Porter-Locklear is a mathematician with research interests in environmental contamination and the predictive modeling of biodegradation rates of contaminants. She is an advocate for American Indians and women within the scientific community.

Oct. 14, 1957	Born in Lumberton, North Carolina
1975	Marries Milton Edward Locklear
1978	Receives a B.S. from Pembroke State University
1981	Earns a M.S. from North Carolina State University
1990	Becomes affiliated with the American Indian Science and Engineering Society (AISES)
1991	Earns a Ph.D. from Duke University
1991	Joins the mathematics faculty at Pembroke
1991	Founds an AISES Chapter at Pembroke and becomes its adviser
1994	Establishes Sonya Kovalesky High School Mathematics Day at Pembroke State University
1996	Wins a North Carolina Equity Carpathian Award for Speaking Out
1996	Featured in the PBS documentary series *BreakThrough*
1996	Becomes Project Director of the AISES Comprehensive Enrichment Program for the eastern portion of the United States
1996	Becomes president of Pembroke Waste Collections

Early Life

Freda Porter-Locklear was the second of five daughters born to James L. Porter, a sharecropper with a seventh-grade education, and Fannie Jacobs. While her older sister helped with domestic chores, Freda toiled in fields of wheat, soybeans, and tobacco alongside her father.

Porter began to hone her quantitative skills, and her father drew upon her computational ability. By the second grade, she was figuring the amount of seeds and fertilizer needed and computing crop yields. She discovered the necessity of mathematics and its many applications in everyday life.

Although Porter loved work in the fields, she loved school even more. She was an excellent student, graduating at the top of her high school class. She was also a normal teenager: popular with her classmates, president of the student government association, and involved in varsity basketball and softball.

On September 14, 1975, she married Milton Edward Locklear; they had two sons, Brian James and Dwayne Allen. Throughout her postsecondary education, Freda Porter-Locklear combined motherhood and her role as scholar quite successfully. According to Porter-Locklear, this challenging situation kept her focused and grounded in reality.

Her fine academic performance and diverse extracurricular activities helped Porter-Locklear win a scholarship to Pembroke State University in North Carolina. She started college in the summer after her high school graduation. There was no question as to what field of study Porter-Locklear would pursue in college: Mathematics was her love. She completed college in two and a half years, graduating magna cum laude with a bachelor of science degree in applied mathematics and a minor in computer science.

Within a month of graduation, Porter-Locklear landed a job in data processing with the ACME Electronic Corporation. After seven months, she won a National Science Foundation Fellowship and returned to school to pursue a master of science degree in applied mathematics at North Carolina State University. Upon completion of her master's degree, she worked briefly as a management information technician. Her job involved establishing computer records for all American Indian students in Robeson County, North Carolina.

Career as a Teacher

In 1994, Porter-Locklear began her teaching career as an instructor at Pembroke, where she taught mathematics and computer science courses. After two years, she was awarded the Board of Governor's Fellowship.

In 1986, Porter-Locklear began working on her doctorate at Duke University under the tutelage of Michael Reed and Carl Gardner. While in graduate school, she could combine research with teaching. She completed her dissertation, "A Numerical Study of Propagation of Singularities for Semilinear Hyperbolic Systems," and received her Ph.D. in applied mathematics in 1991.

Research Interests

Porter-Locklear became one of a handful of American Indian women who had earned a doctorate in mathematical sciences. Her background as a Lumbee has had a great influence on her career. Traditionally, American Indians have a profound reverence for the earth. Porter-Locklear shares this philosophy, and her mathematical research interests include the study of the natural biodegradation of contaminants, specifically gasoline spills.

An Advocate for American Indians and Women

Porter-Locklear has been instrumental in developing mentoring programs and workshops for girls to encourage and support women and American Indians entering the fields of mathematics, engineering, and other sciences.

Often, girls and American Indians are discouraged in school from taking the science and mathematics courses that they need to be competitive in contemporary society. American Indians and women frequently encounter bias in the classroom. They are called upon to answer questions less frequently than boys. Language, tests, and textbooks frequently stereotype and ignore women and American Indians. This shortchanging of girls has an impact on the number of women who pursue college-level and graduate-level study in mathematics. Porter-Locklear attempts to reverse this trend.

Because she is a sensitive female mathematician who happens to be an American Indian, Porter-Locklear is an especially effective role model and advocate for American Indians and women. She is active professionally, mentoring and conducting workshops to promote mathematics for women and American Indians. Her participation in the American Indian Science and Engineering Society (AISES) allows her to reach young American Indian students throughout the United States through a variety of precollege and college mathematics enrichment projects.

Porter-Locklear recognizes the need to promote mathematics to the American Indian population in the United States. By the mid-1990's, her persistent and committed effort and that of other mathematicians like her was gradually making a difference in the representation of women and American Indians in mathematics and the sciences.

Bibliography

Everybody Counts: A Report to the Nation on the Future of Mathematics Education. Mathematical Sciences Education Board and Board on Mathematical Sciences, Committee on the Mathematical Sciences in the Year 2000, National Research Council. Washington, D.C.: National Academy Press, 1989.

Growing Smart: What's Working for Girls in School. The American Association of University Women Educational Foundation. Washington, D.C.: Author, 1995.

How Schools Shortchange Girls: The AAUW Report. The American Association of University Women Educational Foundation. New York: Marlowe, 1995.

"Profile of a Field: Mathematics, Heroism Is Still the Norm." Paul Selvin. *Science* 255 (March 13, 1992).

"Time for Advancement." Mary Beth Ruskai. *Focus* (December, 1994).

She describes her work as the "development of a risk management tool that relies on natural biological processes to contain the spread of contamination from fuel spills." Porter-Locklear's research involves the analysis of mathematical models of mass conservation and the design and implementation of efficient numerical algorithms that predict the extent of contamination. Part of her research has focused on mathematical modeling of both the intrinsic bioremediation at Superfund sites and the bioremediation of JP-4 jet fuel. Another area of research for Porter-Locklear is the measurement of natural bioattenuation of ground water contaminants.

An Advocate

Gentleness and sensitivity are attributes that make Porter-Locklear an especially effective role model and advocate for American Indians and women. After becoming affiliated with the American Indian Science and Engineering Society (AISES) in 1990, Porter-Locklear established an AISES chapter at Pembroke State University and became the chapter adviser.

Her skill as a teacher and her expertise in mathematical modeling of the environment quickly propelled her to new endeavors as a teacher-trainer for AISES and as a director for the AISES comprehensive enrichment program (CEP) in North Carolina. Porter-Locklear's creative leadership makes this program a vital precollege experience for young American Indians from all over the United States.

Promoting women in mathematics and science fields is a passion for Porter-Locklear. After successfully writing a small grant in 1994, she established Sonya Kovalesky High School Mathematics Day at Pembroke. The American Association of University Women (AAUW) decided to continue sponsoring this event on an annual basis because it so effectively promotes mathematics to young women.

Porter-Locklear is most proud of the North Carolina Equity Carpathian Award for Speaking Out, which she received in 1996. It recognizes her leadership, commitment, dedication, and promotion of women and minorities.

Bibliography

By Porter-Locklear
"A Numerical Study of Propagation of Singularities for Semilinear Hyperbolic Systems," 1991 (Ph.D. thesis)
Educating American Indian/Alaskan Native Elementary and Secondary School Students: Guidelines for Mathematics, Science, and Technology Programs, 1994
Benchmark Problems in Computational Aeroacoustics, NASA Contractor Report 194972, 1994
Large Eddy Simulations of Compressible Turbulent Flows, NASA Contractor Report 198210, 1995

About Porter-Locklear
"BreakThrough: The Changing Face of Science in America." Lara Evans. *Winds of Change* (Spring, 1996).
BreakThrough: The Changing Face of Science in America. PBS documentary video. Produced by Blackside Corporation, Boston, 1996.
"Positive Energy." Teri Johnson. *The Alumni Magazine of North Carolina State University, Red Wolf Rising* (Fall, 1995).

(Bernadette A. Berken)

Ptolemy

Areas of Achievement: Geometry and topology

Contribution: Ptolemy compiled an astronomical and mathematical encyclopedia and catalog of 1,022 stars. He developed an influential model of the solar system.

c. 100	Born, possibly in Ptolemais Hermii, Egypt
c. 127-151	Completes the astronomical observations and calculations for his star catalog
c. 150	Publishes the value of π as 3.1416
c. 178	Dies, possibly in Egypt

Early Life

Claudius Ptolemaeus, or Ptolemy (pronounced "TAHL-uh-mee"), is widely known as an astronomer, geographer, and mathematician. His work influenced Western thought for nearly fourteen thousand years. Yet his life is almost entirely unknown. What little is recorded about his personal history has been gleaned from careful scrutiny of his writings.

Astronomical Calculations

Ptolemy's fame as an astronomer is based on his multivolume work *Almagest*. In addition to his own observations, the book includes the work of astronomers who had preceded him. Thus, most of what is known about ancient astronomy is available as a result of its preservation by Ptolemy. Ptolemy's own descriptions and measurement of "fixed stars" and the "wanderers" (*planetae*) were gathered during the period from 127 to 151. He cataloged 1,022 celestial objects and declared the earth to be the center of the universe.

The Earth-centered (geocentric) model of the universe and the solar system featured the known planets moving around the motionless Earth in circular orbits. (The Greeks considered the circle to be a perfect geometric shape.) The

sun, also orbiting Earth, was placed in a position between Venus and Mars. The apparent backward (retrograde) motion of the planets, observed against the background of the fixed stars, was not easily explained by the ancient astronomers. Ptolemy derived a model that seemed to account for this anomaly, again using circular motions.

Ptolemy's astronomical observations, measurements, and calculations were gathered in a thirteen-volume work, *Mathematike syntaxis*, or *The Mathematical Composition of Claudius Ptolemy*. This comprehensive treatise of Greek astronomy is the oldest systematic collection of star descriptions, their brightness, and their numerical position in the celestial sphere. Arab astronomers accepted Ptolemy's work and subsequently retitled it *Almagest* (meaning "the greatest" in Arabic).

Almagest includes basic assumptions of the science of astronomy and Ptolemy's contributions to it. He considered the earth to be at the center of a crystal sphere, with the fixed stars attached to the interior surface. The planets were attached to smaller, concentric spheres

(Library of Congress)

A Model of the Universe

Ptolemy defined a model of the universe and Earth's solar system based on observations, measurements, computations, and logical analysis. Widely accepted, the Ptolemaic system survived until the sixteenth century.

Early Greek astronomers were divided primarily into two camps regarding Earth and its place in the solar system. One group held that Earth rotates on its axis and, with the other planets, orbits the sun; this is a sun-centered, or heliocentric, model. The other group argued that Earth is fixed in space and that the sun, moon, and other planets orbit Earth; this is an earth-centered, or geocentric, model.

In the first book of the *Almagest*, Ptolemy reasoned that since all objects fall to the center of the universe, Earth must be fixed there at the center. If Earth were rotating on a vertical axis, an object thrown directly upward should not fall back to the same place, as was observed. Rather, it would fall back to a different place as Earth moved beneath the thrown object.

Ptolemy demonstrated that no contradictory observations had been made by others. Thus, the geocentric model, known as the Ptolemaic system, was accepted and dominated Western thought for nearly fifteen hundred years.

In the Ptolemaic system, celestial bodies were arranged about the earth in the following order: the moon, Mercury, Venus, the sun, Mars, Jupiter, and Saturn. These bodies moved about the earth in large circles called deferents. Epicycles were small circles whose centers moved around the circumferences of the deferents. To account for observed deviations in planetary motions, Ptolemy located Earth a short distance from the center of the deferents.

Ptolemy's geocentric model was accepted dogmatically by Christianity because it located Earth in a place of importance. Because biblical references stressed the significance of Earth, it was only logical that it should be at the center of not only the solar system but also the universe. In 1543, risking punishment from the Inquisition, the Polish astronomer Nicolaus Copernicus published his heliocentric model. Ptolemy's model was soon discarded.

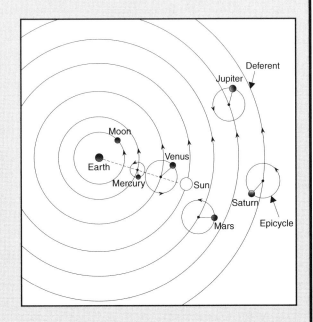

Bibliography

Claudius Ptolemy: The Geography. Edward Luther Stevenson, trans. and ed. New York: Dover, 1991.

"That Also the Earth, Taken as a Whole, Is Sensibly Spherical." Claudius Ptolemy. In *Almagest, Book One: Great Books of the Western World*. Translated and annotated by R. Catesby Taliaferro. Chicago: Encyclopaedia Britannica, 1952.

"That the Earth Is in the Middle of the Heavens." Claudius Ptolemy. In *Almagest, Book One: Great Books of the Western World*. Translated and annotated by R. Catesby Taliaferro. Chicago: Encyclopaedia Britannica, 1952.

moving at different speeds. This latter concept helped explain the different movements of the planets compared to the fixed stars. Ptolemy also established the earth as a sphere, its size relative to the sphere of the fixed stars.

Other Studies

Ptolemy's extensive studies in and around Alexandria led to the writing of a number of other books. One of these was *Opticae thesaurus* (*Optics*), which was concerned with the geometry of mirrors and the physics of vision. He also developed a calendar that, like an almanac, included weather forecasts and the rising and setting of stars in the morning and evening twilights.

His star charts located these bodies by latitude and longitude on the inside surface of the celestial sphere. He wrote of the ideal situation in which each place on Earth could be located scientifically according to its latitude and longitude. The result was *Geographike hyphegesis*, or the *Geography*. He introduced the system of latitudes and longitudes in use in modern maps and charts. He is also credited with establishing the cartographic principle of placing north at the top of a map or other projection. His guide to geography described cartographic methods and details about nearly eight thousand cities, rivers, mountains, and other important features of the earth's surface. It was used well into the fifteenth century by such European explorers as Christopher Columbus.

The *Geography*, however, is rife with errors. Ptolemy placed the equator farther north than it is. His calculations for the diameter of the earth yielded a value nearly one-third less than had earlier been determined. As a result, it placed eastern Asia closer to Europe. This is believed to have led Columbus to expect to find a short route to India simply by sailing westward.

Ptolemy also devised the armillary sphere, an apparatus to calculate celestial coordinates. He constructed the mural quadrant, an instrument for measuring the distance to the sun.

As with all of his life, nothing is known of Ptolemy's last years. It seems reasonable to assume that he was held in high esteem by his contemporaries and died an honored man. His accomplishments during his eighty-year lifetime, especially his major works *Almagest* and the *Geography*, stand as his only known memorials.

Bibliography

By Ptolemy

Mathematike syntaxis, c. 150 (commonly known as the *Almagest*; English trans. as *Almagest*, 1948)

Geographike hyphegesis (commonly known as the *Geography*; *The Geometry of Ptolemy . . .* , 1732)

Harmonika (partial trans. as *Ptolemy's Treatise on Music*, 1974)

Opticae thesaurus, 1572 (commonly known as the *Optics*; *Ptolemy's Theory of Visual Perception*, 1996)

About Ptolemy

"Biographical Note, Ptolemy, A.D. c. 100-c. 178." Translated by R. Catesby Taliaferro. In *The Almagest*. Vol. 16 of *Great Books of the Western World*, edited by Robert Maynard Hutchins. Chicago: Encyclopaedia Britannica, 1952.

The Crime of Claudius Ptolemy. Robert R. Newton. Baltimore: The Johns Hopkins University Press, 1977.

A History of Mathematics. Carl B. Boyer. New York: John Wiley & Sons, 1968.

An Introduction to the History of Mathematics. Howard Whitley Eves. 3d ed. New York: Holt, Rinehart and Winston, 1969.

"Some Puzzles of Ptolemy's Star Catalogue." Owen Gingerich and Barbara L. Welther. *Sky & Telescope* 67, no. 5 (May, 1984).

(Albert C. Jensen)

Pythagoras

Areas of Achievement: Algebra, arithmetic, geometry, and number theory

Contribution: Pythagoras was the first mathematical-physicist. He and his disciples sought to understand the world in terms of abstract relationships between numbers.

c. 580 B.C.E.	Born on Samos, Ionia, Greece
c. 550 B.C.E.	Possibly studies under Anaximander or Thales
c. 540 B.C.E.	Possibly studies abroad in Egypt and Babylonia
c. 530 B.C.E.	Emigrates to Croton, southern Italy
c. 530 B.C.E.	Founds the Pythagoreans, a religious and philosophical society
511 B.C.E.	Uses music to aid the armies of Croton in defeating the armies of Sybaris
c. 500 B.C.E.	Dies in Metapontum, Lucania (now Metaponto, Italy)

Early Life

Few details of the life of Pythagoras (pronounced "pi-THAHG-uh-rus") are known with certainty. He was born on the island of Samos in the Aegean sea. His mother's name is given as Parthenis or Pythais. His father, Mnesarchus, is said to have been a merchant or possibly a gem engraver. Mnesarchus seems to have been wealthy enough to give Pythagoras an education and allow him to travel.

Tradition has it that Pythagoras studied under either the great philosopher Thales or his pupil Anaximander, but there is no certain evidence. Pythagoras probably visited Egypt, especially if his father was a merchant, and he may have visited Babylonia, but it is unlikely that he traveled to India as some have claimed. At any rate, he obtained an excellent, broadly based education.

The Pythagoreans

Pythagoras took part in the Greek religious revival of the sixth century B.C.E. Extolling a simple life and perhaps as a protest against the excesses of Polycrates, king of Samos, Pythagoras left Samos for Croton, a Greek settlement in southern Italy. A charismatic leader, Pythagoras gathered a community of followers who became known as the Pythagoreans. Women were included in the Pythagorean Order, an unusual step then.

The Pythagoreans believed in reincarnation and that living a moral life enabled one to obtain a more favorable state in the next incarnation. A moral life included living simply, abstaining from meat and alcohol, and purifying the mind through learning. They found great virtue in striving to understand the hidden laws of nature, and it is in this manner that they forged their legacy to science.

Pythagorean Science

The cornerstone of Greek science was the notion that everything was made from a fundamental substance and that, if the properties of that substance were understood, the workings of the universe could be understood. Pythagoreans supposed that "number" was the underlying stuff from which the universe was made. The Greek word *kosmos* denotes the proper, or ordered, array of numbers, a term that has been adopted today to mean the universe.

Pythagoras is credited with relating numbers and music. Upon considering the vibrating strings of a harp, he showed that if a vibrating string of 12 units (centimeters, inches, or whatever) length produced a tone, then strings of 8 units length and of 6 units length would produce tones that were pleasing or harmonious with the first tone. In modern terms, the intervals between those tones are called a fifth and an octave. Pythagoras called the numbers 6, 8, and 12 a harmonic progression, and he saw a further example in the geometry of a cube, since it has 6 sides, 8 corners, and 12 edges.

His interest in music is said to have led him to an ingenious defense of Croton when it was attacked by the well-drilled calvary of Sybaris. This calvary was often featured in spectacles in which the horses pranced to music. Pythagoras

Abstract Numbers

Where others used numbers for counting and measuring things, the Pythagoreans were fascinated with the properties of the numbers themselves.

Pythagoras found it useful to represent numbers with dots and to arrange these dots into simple patterns. The top row of figure 1 shows that the numbers 1, 3, 6, 10, 15, 21, and so on, can be represented with triangular patterns of dots. The nth triangular number is equal to the sum of the first n numbers; for example, the fifth triangular number is 15, and "15 = 1 + 2 + 3 + 4 + 5." Pythagoreans believed that the number 10 was especially significant. It is the fourth triangular number (which has four dots along each edge), it is the sum of the first three triangular numbers, and it is the sum "1 + 2 + 3 + 4."

Consequently, they supposed that the universe consisted of ten concentric, crystalline spheres, each turning at its own rate about the central fire (not the sun). Beginning with the outermost sphere, these spheres carried the fixed stars, Saturn, Jupiter, Mars, the sun, Venus, Mercury, the moon, Earth, and the "Counter-earth." The Counter-earth was invented so that there would be ten spheres.

All odd numbers can be arranged in the shape of a carpenter's square, as shown by the middle row of figure 1. The Greeks called this shape a *gnomon*, or gnomen, which means "one who knows" or an "indicator." The bottom row of figure 1 shows square numbers. These numbers equal the square of the number of dots along one side.

Figure 2 shows that a gnomen can always be added to a square number to make another square number. Figure 3 shows that 4^2 plus the gnomen 9 equals 5^2. Since 9 is also 3^2, this means that "$3^2 + 4^2 = 5^2$." This is a special case of the Pythagorean theorem, "$a^2 + b^2 = c^2$," where a and b are the lengths of the two sides of a right triangle and c is the length of the hypotenuse (the long slanted side opposite the right angle). The theorem holds for any odd number that is also a square number. Later, the Pythagoreans showed that the theorem holds for a right triangle of any size or shape.

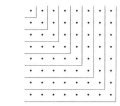

Figure 2. A gnomen can always be added to a square number to make another square number.

Figure 3. A simple case of the Pythagorean theorem: The square number 16 plus the gnomen 9 equals the square number 25.

Bibliography

A History of Mathematics. Carl B. Boyer. New York: John Wiley & Sons, 1968.

A History of Western Science. Anthony M. Alioto. Englewood Cliffs, N.J.: Prentice Hall, 1987.

The Number of Things: Pythagoras, Geometry, and Humming Strings. Evan G. Valens. New York: E. P. Dutton, 1964.

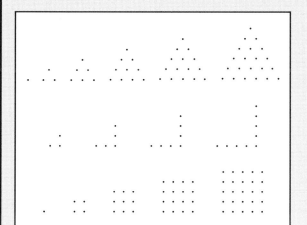

Figure 1. The top row shows the first six triangular numbers, the middle row shows the first four gnomens, and the bottom row shows the first five square numbers.

(Smithsonian Institution)

had flute players play parade tunes during the battle. As the Sybarite horses began to prance instead of fight, the Crotons gained the advantage and won.

Pythagoreans profoundly influenced astronomy. Pythagoras held the sphere to be the perfect shape, harmonious and complete. The perfect two-dimensional shape was obviously a circle, since it had no irregularities. The moon and the sun resemble spheres, and it was only a small mental leap for the Pythagoreans to suppose that the earth was also a sphere and that the planets and stars moved in circular orbits. Because of Pythagorean influence, astronomy remained the most mathematical of all the physical sciences until Galileo made the laws of motion mathematical.

The Death of Pythagoras
Pythagoras initially favored rule by the local aristocracy, which delighted them. As time passed, Pythagorean societies were founded in several cities, but as their influence grew, they made powerful enemies. Pythagoras was forced to flee Croton for the neighboring city of Metapontum, where he remained until his death in about 500 B.C.E. Some texts refer to a wife and daughters, but there is no strong evidence that Pythagoras ever married or had children.

Although the Pythagorean Order was eventually exterminated, many of their mathematical ideas influenced Plato and Aristotle and have come down through time to today.

Bibliography
By Pythagoras
Only fragments of his works survive. They may be found in collections such as *The Pythagorean Writings*. Robert Navon, ed. Kew Gardens, N.Y.: Selene Books, 1986.

About Pythagoras
Pythagoras and Early Pythagoreanism. J. A. Philip. Toronto: University of Toronto Press, 1966.
"Pythagoras of Samos." Kurt Von Fritz. In *Dictionary of Scientific Biography*, edited by Charles Coulston Gillispie. Vol. 11. New York: Charles Scribner's Sons, 1975.
A Short Account of Greek Philosophy from Thales to Epicurus. G. F. Parker. New York: Barnes & Noble, 1967.

(Charles W. Rogers)

Srinivasa Aiyangar Ramanujan

Areas of Achievement: Algebra and number theory

Contribution: Ramanujan contributed enormously to elementary algebra, continued fractions, power series, number theory, hypergeometric series, Bernoulli and Euler numbers, and in many other advanced areas of mathematics.

Dec. 22, 1887	Born in Erode, Madras (now Tamil Nadu), India
1903	Passes the matriculation exam of the University of Madras
1904	Joins Government College with a Subrahmanyam Scholarship
1905	Discontinues his studies
1907	Appears for his First Examination of Arts (FA) privately and fails
1911	Publishes his first paper, on Bernoulli numbers
1912	Joins the Madras Port Trust Office as an accounting clerk
1913	Writes to British mathematician G. H. Hardy with a set of results, including 120 theorems
1914	Joins Hardy at Trinity College, Cambridge University
1915	Publishes a paper on highly composite numbers
1916	Receives a B.A. "by research" from Trinity
1917	Contracts tuberculosis
1918	Elected a Fellow of Royal Society of London and a Fellow of Trinity College
1919	Sails back to India
Apr. 26, 1920	Dies in Chetput, Madras, India

Early Life

Srinivasa Aiyangar Ramanujan (pronounced "raw-MAWN-oo-jun") was born into a Brahmin Hindu family in Erode near Kumbakonam, a small town in the southern part of India. His father was a clerk in a cloth merchant's shop who maintained his family with a small income. His mother was a devoted housewife who had strong religious beliefs.

At the young age of seven, Ramanujan was admitted to high school. He was soon found to be an extraordinary student. By the age of twelve or thirteen, Ramanujan was recognized as truly brilliant. By this time, he already mastered Sidney Luxton Loney's *Plane Trigonometry* (1893). The book that is known to have stimulated Ramanujan to pursue mathematics was George Shoobridge Carr's *A Synopsis of Elementary Results in Pure and Applied Mathematics* (1880-1886). Upon borrowing this book from a friend, Ramanujan intensively studied it for several days. He simultaneously verified many results in the book quickly and discovered many new results.

Ramanujan passed the matriculation examination of the University of Madras in 1903. In

1904, he joined the First Examination of Arts (FA) class in the Government College. As a result of his great devotion to mathematics and consequent neglect of other subjects, he failed to get promoted to the senior class. In 1907, he appeared for the FA examination as a private student, but unfortunately he failed again. Although he was disappointed, he continued his research in mathematics independently.

Devotion to Mathematics

The years from 1907 to 1911 appeared to be the first period of intense activity in the life of Ramanujan. The depression caused by his failure of the FA examination, his inability to obtain employment, and poverty could not prevent him from doing mathematics. Initially, he studied on magic squares, continued fractions, the partition of numbers, elliptic integrals, Bernoulli and Euler numbers, representations of numbers as sums of squares, and several other areas of mathematics. Ramanujan had an unusually systematic habit of recording results in a notebook.

Marriage in 1909 brought the necessity of seeking a permanent job. Eventually, with a

Work on Partitions and Pi

Two areas of mathematics to which Ramanujan made significant contributions were the theory of partitions and efficient ways of computing pi (π) to many decimal places.

Ramanujan's technical forte was manipulating algebraic expressions involving infinite series, products, continued fractions, and integrals. This manipulative skill combined with an astonishing insight about numbers and their properties led him to discover startling and beautiful results in number theory and their connection to various representations of functions by means of infinite processes.

Some of Ramanujan's deepest and most original work is in the area of partitions. A partition of a positive integer n is a representation of n as a sum of positive integers. For example, the partitions of 4 are

$$4 = 1 + 1 + 1 + 1$$
$$= 1 + 1 + 2$$
$$= 2 + 2$$
$$= 1 + 3$$

Let $p(n)$ denote the number of partitions of n. The value of $p(n)$ increases very rapidly with n. Thus, $p(200) = 3,972,999,029,388$.

Computing $p(n)$ by trying to list all the partitions of n is infeasible. Ramanujan discovered several remarkable identities satisfied by $p(n)$. These identities equate an infinite series, whose coefficients are $p(n)$ for certain values of n, with certain infinite products. They provide a feasible method for evaluating $p(n)$. Together, Ramanujan

and G. H. Hardy worked on asymptotic formulas for $p(n)$—that is, formulas approximating $p(n)$ that increase in accuracy as n gets larger. One of their truly remarkable results is an asymptotic formula that predicts the value of $p(n)$ efficiently and with high accuracy.

There is great interest in computing pi (π) to millions of decimal places. One reason is that such calculations have become a benchmark computation, serving as a measure of the capability of the computers that carry out the calculations. The algorithms used for the calculations are based on mathematical formulas. In 1914, Ramanujan gave an infinite series for $1/\pi$ that has proved to be extraordinarily efficient for computing π. Each successive term of Ramanujan's series adds roughly eight more correct digits. His approach is now incorporated in computer algorithms to yield millions of digits of π.

Bibliography

An Introduction to the Theory of Numbers. G. H. Hardy and Edward Maitland Wright. 4th ed. Oxford, England: Clarendon Press, 1962.

Pi and the AGM: A Study in Analytic Number Theory and Computational Complexity. Jonathan M. Borwein and Peter B. Borwein. New York: John Wiley & Sons, 1987.

"Ramanujan and Pi." Jonathan M. Borwein and Peter B. Borwein. *Scientific American* 258, no. 2 (February, 1988): 112-117.

The Theory of Partitions. George E. Andrews. Reading, Mass.: Addison-Wesley, 1976.

great effort, Ramanujan joined the Madras Port Trust Office as a clerk in the accounts departments. Now that he had a steady job, he found time to do original research in mathematics.

In 1913, at the suggestion of his office manager, Ramanujan wrote a letter to the famous British mathematician G. H. Hardy at Cambridge University with a set of mathematical results and 120 theorems. Hardy was amazed by Ramanujan's results and immediately decided to bring Ramanujan to Cambridge.

The Cambridge Years and After

Despite his family's strong objections, Ramanujan departed for Cambridge in March, 1914. During the next five years, Hardy and Ramanujan worked together. The blend of Hardy's technical expertise and Ramanujan's raw talent produced an unparalleled collaboration. They published a series of papers on the properties of various arithmetic functions, laying the groundwork to answer such questions as "How many prime divisors is a given number likely to have?" and "How many ways can one express a number as a sum of smaller positive integers?"

In 1917, Ramanujan fell ill with tuberculosis and spent some time in a nursing home. In 1918, at the age of thirty, he was elected a Fellow of the Royal Society of London and a Fellow of Trinity College. The British climate seemed to delay his recovery, however, and he departed for India in February, 1919.

Even upon his return to India, his condition did not improve. In spite of his deteriorating health, he was always busy doing mathematics and jotting down formulas in his notebook. He died on April 26, 1920, at age of thirty-two, in Chetput, a suburb of Madras.

When Ramanujan died, he left behind three famous notebooks, which were later edited and published. The results and ideas appearing in these notebooks continue to amaze mathematicians and stimulate research. Ramanujan was a self-taught mathematician whose genius places him among the ranks of the greatest mathematicians.

Bibliography

By Ramanujan

Collected Papers of Srinivasa Ramanujan, 1927 (G. H. Hardy, P. V. Seshu Aiyar, and Bertram Martin Wilson, eds.)
Notebooks, 1957 (2 vols.)

About Ramanujan

The Man Who Knew Infinity: A Life of the Genius, Ramanujan. Robert Kanigel. New York: Maxwell Macmillan International, 1991.
"Ramanujan—For Lowbrows." Bruce C. Berndt and S. Bhargava. *American Mathematical Monthly* 100, no. 7 (August/September, 1993): 644-656.
Ramanujan: The Man and the Mathematician. Shivali Ramamrita Ranganathan. Calcutta: Asia, 1967.
Ramanujan: Twelve Lectures on Subjects Suggested by His Life and Work. G. H. Hardy. Cambridge, England: Cambridge University Press, 1940.

(Subhash C. Bagui and Rohan Hemasingha)

Regiomontanus (Johann Müller)

Area of Achievement: Trigonometry
Contribution: Regiomontanus was the first European to systematize plane and spherical trigonometry as a discipline independent of astronomy.

June 6, 1436	Born in Königsberg, Archbishopric of Mainz (now Kaliningrad, Russia)
1448	Matriculates at the University of Leipzig
1450	Begins studies at the University of Vienna under Georg von Peuerbach
1452	Awarded a bachelor's degree
1457	Appointed to the faculty as a master of the arts
1461	Travels to Rome to learn Greek under Cardinal Bessarion
1463	Completes translation work begun with Peuerbach
1464	Writes *De triangulis omnimodis libri quinque* (*Five Books on Triangles of All Kinds*, 1976; also as *Regiomontanus on Triangles*, 1967)
1467	Goes to Hungary to join the faculty of the University of Pressburg
1471	Receives permission to live in Nuremberg
1472	Observes a comet
1474	Publishes *Ephemerides*, a navigational table
July 6, 1476	Dies in Rome, Papal States (now Italy)

Early Life

Johann Müller (pronounced "MYOOL-ur") was the son of a prosperous miller. Since his birthplace, Königsberg, means "king's moun-tain," Johann sometimes wrote his name in Latin as "Joannes de Regio monte" (John from king's mountain). It is from this name that the pseudonym Regiomontanus (pronounced "ray-gee-oh-mawn-TAY-noos") was later derived.

The gifted boy entered the University of Leipzig at the age of eleven and produced his first astronomical almanac when he was twelve. He earned the bachelor's degree at the age of fifteen but, because of university regulations, had to wait until he was twenty-one to join the faculty as a master of arts. At the age of fifteen, he received a commission to cast the horoscope of Leonora of Portugal. The false-ness of such predictions was often ascribed to inaccurate knowledge of the positions of the heavenly bodies.

Astronomical Work

Much of Regiomontanus's work focused on the calculation of the positions of planets and stars. Cardinal Bessarion, who was interested in bringing knowledge of ancient Greek authors to the Latin West, persuaded Regiomontanus's teacher and colleague Georg von Peuerbach to translate Ptolemy's *Mathematike syntaxis* (c. 150; commonly known as the *Almagest*). Peuerbach died before finishing, and in 1463 Regiomontanus completed *Epytoma Joannis De monte regio In almagestum ptolomei* (known as the *Epitome*), including new obser-vations, improved computations, and criti-cisms showing the inaccuracies of Ptolemy's earth-centered solar system. His work on the *Epitome* inspired Regiomontanus to write a book devoted solely to triangles.

Regiomontanus went with Cardinal Bes-sarion to Rome to learn Greek, which enabled him to work with the originals of many impor-tant ancient texts in both astronomy and mathematics. He also studied the works of Muslim scholars, many of whom had known and amended ancient Greek works. Familiar with various astronomical tables, Regiomon-tanus noted that the predicted position of plan-ets did not agree with his observations. Thus, in 1467, he calculated *tabula directionum* (tables of direction), which provided the longitudes of celestial bodies in relation to the apparent daily rotation of the heavens.

While Regiomontanus was in Hungary, he

constructed a number of observational instruments for the king and archbishop. He also fashioned an instrument for himself and used it to ascertain the planets' angular distances from the sun at their last sighting near the sun. In 1512, the library of Friedrich, elector of Saxony, acquired a large astrolabe believed to have been built by Regiomontanus for the king of Hungary.

Mathematical Work

Regiomontanus's interest in mathematics derived from astronomical observations and calculations. He adopted Arabic numbers, first introduced into Europe during the previous century. He also assumed the practice of representing unknown mathematical quantities with letters.

Prior to Regiomontanus, sine tables were based on the sexagesimal (60) system. He abandoned this system, setting the value of sin 90° at 100,000. He also calculated tables of tangents, although he did not use that term, for angles up to 45 degrees in 1 degree intervals, with tan 45° = 100,000. These became the model for modern tables.

Later Life

When Regiomontanus left Hungary, he chose to settle in Nuremberg. Setting up a printing

---

Systematizing Trigonometry

In systematizing trigonometry as a subject independent of astronomy, Regiomontanus provided the laws of sines and of cosines for spherical triangles.

Trigonometry originated in ancient astronomy and in the subsequent development of spherical trigonometry and plane trigonometry. During the Middle Ages, Muslim scholars developed trigonometry. Abul Wefa generalized the sine law to spherical triangles, and al-Biruni formulated the sine law for plane triangles. In the second half of the thirteenth century, Nasir ad-Din systematized plane and spherical trigonometry as a discipline independent of astronomy.

In Western Europe, however, mathematics was not quite as advanced as it was in the East. In his wanderings, Regiomontanus came across works by Hindu and Muslim scholars and accomplished for the West what Nasir ad-Din had for the East. In his studies for the preparation of the *Epitome* of Ptolemy, Regiomontanus realized the need for a survey of the rules for triangles to facilitate astronomical calculations. The result was *De triangulis omnimodis libri quinque* (*Five Books on Triangles of All Kinds*, 1976), published in 1533. He states the law of sines in book 2, theorem 1: In every right triangle, the ratio of two sides is as that of the right sine of the angle opposite one of the sides to the right sine of the angle opposite the other side, or, in modern notation,

$$\frac{a}{\sin A} = \frac{b}{\sin B} = \frac{c}{\sin C}$$

Book 2, theorem 26 provides the first implicit statement of the trigonometric formula for the area of a triangle. In book 4, theorem 16, Regiomontanus provides the law of sines for spherical triangles: The ratio of the sines of all the sides to the sines of the angles that the sides subtend is the same, or

$$\frac{\sin a}{\sin A} = \frac{\sin b}{\sin B} = \frac{\sin c}{\sin C}$$

Book 5, theorem 2 contains the law of cosines for spherical triangles, expressed in terms of the versed sine. In modern notation, it states

$$\text{Cos } A = \frac{\cos a - \cos b \cos c}{\sin b \ \sin c}$$

Regiomontanus's book on triangles influenced a number of scholars in the sixteenth century, including Rheticus, the teacher of the great astronomer Nicolaus Copernicus.

Bibliography

The Development of Trigonometry from Regiomontanus to Pitiscus. Mary Claudia Zeller. Ann Arbor, Mich.: Edwards Brothers, 1946.

The History of Mathematics: A Reader. John Fauvel and Jeremy Gray, eds. Basingstoke, England: Macmillan/The Open University, 1987.

Mathematical Thought from Ancient to Modern Times. Morris Kline. New York: Oxford University Press, 1972.

press in his house, he became the first publisher of astronomical and mathematical works. To aid the production of accurate texts, he introduced the use of the Latin alphabet and used simplified letters for material written in German. His first published work was *Theoricae novae planatarum Georgii Purbachii astronomici de sole* (1474; new theory of the planets by George von Peuerbach). The second work was his own *Ephemerides anni 1475* (1474), which gave the daily positions of the heavenly bodies from 1475 to 1506. On his fourth voyage, Christopher Columbus took along a copy of this work and frightened hostile Jamaican Indians into submission by predicting a lunar eclipse on February 29, 1504.

In 1475, Pope Sixtus IV invited Regiomontanus to Rome to correct the highly inaccurate Church calendar. Regiomontanus never accomplished this task: He died within a year, perhaps from the plague or perhaps, as some believe, from poisoning by the sons of a man whose translations of Ptolemy Regiomontanus had promised to expose for their worthlessness.

Bibliography
By Regiomontanus
De triangulis omnimodis libri quinque, wr. 1464, pub. 1533 (*Five Books on Triangles of All Kinds*, 1976; also as *Regiomontanus on Triangles*, 1967)
Ephemerides anni 1475, 1474
Joannis Regiomontani opera collectanea, 1972 (Felix Schmeidler, ed.)

About Regiomontanus
"Planetary Latitudes, the *Theorica Gerardi*, and Regiomontanus." Claudia Kren. *Isis* 68 (1977).
Regiomontanus: His Life and Work. Ernst Zinner. Translated by Ezra Brown. Amsterdam: North-Holland, 1990.
"Regiomontanus on the Critical Problems of Astronomy." Noel M. Swerdlow. In *Nature, Experiment, and the Sciences: Essays on Galileo and the History of Science in Honour of Stillman Drake*, edited by Trevor H. Levere and William R. Shea. Dordrecht, the Netherlands: Kluwer Academic, 1990.

(Kristen L. Zacharias)

Bernhard Riemann

Areas of Achievement: Calculus, geometry, and number theory

Contribution: Riemann introduced the concepts of geometric spaces with different curvatures and the properties needed to define the integral operator of integral calculus. Perhaps his most significant contributions were criteria for deciding when complex valued functions of a complex variable are differentiable and the Riemann hypothesis, which is used in the study of prime numbers.

Sept. 17, 1826	Born in Breselenz, Hanover (now Germany)
1846	Switches from theology and philology to mathematics at the University of Göttingen
1847	Studies in Berlin under Karl Gustav Jacob Jacobi, Peter Gustav Lejeune Dirichlet, Jakob Steiner, and Ferdinand Gotthold Eisenstein
1849	Returns to Göttingen to complete his Ph.D. under Carl Friedrich Gauss
1851	Submits a dissertation on functions of a complex variable
1854	Delivers a probationary lecture on the foundation of geometry
1860	Publishes *Über eine Frage der Wärmeleitung* (concerning a question of heat conduction)
1862	Appointed a full professor at Göttingen
1862	Marries Elise Koch
July 20, 1866	Dies in Selasca, Italy

Early Life

Georg Friedrich Bernhard Riemann (pronounced "REE-mawn") was born in Breselenz, in Hanover, on Sunday, September 17, 1826. His father was a Lutheran minister and his mother, Charlotte Ebell, was the daughter of a court councillor. Because of his father's position at a small village church, the family did not have an abundance of financial resources. In spite of these humble means, the family was happy. Bernhard's father moved from Breselenz to a pastorate in Quickborn, where the elder Riemann began to teach his son.

Bernhard was an eager student who had an excellent teacher for a father. At ten, Riemann received advanced training in arithmetic and geometry from a professional teacher. As a teenager, he later moved to Hanover to live with his grandmother and to attend the Gymnasium, the equivalent of high school. Riemann was in the upper third of his class but exhibited shyness that made it difficult to socialize with classmates. He sought comfort in his studies.

When his grandmother died, Riemann transferred to the Gymnasium at Lüneburg. From there, he entered the University of Göt-

(Library of Congress)

tingen, where he studied theology and philology. It soon became apparent that mathematics would be how Riemann would serve God, rather than the pulpit. In 1846, at his matriculation, Riemann asked his father for permission to change from pursuing a career in the ministry to studying mathematics. Because mathematics was not one of the strengths at Göttingen at the time, Riemann transferred to the University of Berlin. There, he met Peter Gustav Lejeune Dirichlet, under whom Riemann studied analysis.

Riemann's Career

In 1850, Riemann returned to Göttingen to study physics under Wilhelm Eduard Weber. Riemann wrote his doctoral dissertation, "Grundlagen für eine allgemeine Theorie der Functionen einer veränderlichen complexen Grösse" (1851; foundations for a general theory of a complex variable), under Carl Friedrich Gauss, who was a part of the faculty in Göttingen in 1851.

In 1854, Riemann gave a lecture, "Über die Hypothesen, welche der Geometrie zu Grunde liegen" (1858; "On the Hypotheses Which Lie at the Foundations of Geometry," 1929), to the philosophical faculty as a part of the qualifications for becoming a privatdocent (lecturer) at Göttingen.

A lecture on a research topic was unusual in such a situation, and Riemann had to leave out some of the analytic details. Nevertheless, this lecture pointed toward the geometric ideas that are realized in differential geometry and the idea of a geodesic (the path of the shortest route) as the way to define what is meant by a line. The concepts of geodesic and curvature introduced as basic geometric concepts by Riemann were used by Albert Einstein to explain the geometry of space in his general relativity theory.

The position of privatdocent was approved by the faculty, but it was unpaid by the university. Riemann was dependent on students paying for his lectures. He was pleased when eight students showed up for his first lecture in the fall of 1854. What he could earn from student fees varied so greatly, however, that Riemann's friends talked the administration into paying him the equivalent of two hundred dollars a year. In 1857, he received an assistant professorship, and his salary increased by 50 percent to the equivalent of three hundred dollars per year. He shared his meager earnings with his three sisters. In 1862, Riemann received a full professorship, which provided enough money that he could marry Elise Koch.

Final Years

Riemann suffered from tuberculosis after contracting pleurisy in 1862, a month after his marriage. Friends helped Riemann obtain funds to spend the winter in the mild climate of Italy. Afterward, he moved back and forth between Göttingen in the summer and Italy in the winter. In 1866, Riemann's illness grew worse, and he remained in Selasca, Italy, into the summer. He died on Friday, July 20, 1866.

The inscription on his tombstone reveals his attitude toward life. It is a biblical quote from verse 28 of chapter 8 of Paul's letter to the Romans: "all things work together for those who love God and are called according to His purpose." The work that Riemann did with geometry and complex numbers had deep connections with other parts of mathematics such as the theory of numbers. He was indeed gifted to illuminate many areas of mathematics and physics.

Bibliography
By Riemann
"Allgemeine Voraussetzungen und Hülfsmittel für die Untersuchung von Functionen unbeschränkt veränderlicher Grössen," *Journal für die reine und angewandte Mathematik* 54, 1857 (partial trans. as part 1 of "On Riemann's Surfaces and Analysis Situs" in *A Source Book in Mathematics*, 1929, David Eugene Smith, ed.)
"Lehrsätze aus der analysis situs für die Theorie der Integrale von zweigliedrigen vollständigen Differentialien," *Journal für die reine und angewandte Mathematik* 54, 1857 (partial trans. as part 2 of "On Riemann's Surfaces and Analysis Situs" in *A Source Book in Mathematics*, 1929, David Eugene Smith, ed.)
"Über die Hypothesen, welche der Geometrie zu Grunde liegen," *Abhandlungen der Königlichen Gesellschaft der Wissenschaften zu*

The Riemann Zeta Function

One of Riemann's claims to fame is a conjecture called Riemann's hypothesis, about a function called the Riemann zeta function. Riemann conjectured that the only complex numbers "x + iy" with a nonzero y where this function is zero are those such that "x = ½."

Positive real numbers have squareroots that are real numbers. An example is 81, whose non-negative square root is 9. Negative real numbers, however, do not have real number square roots. In order to provide square roots of negative numbers, a new kind of number, a complex number, was created. In particular, the number i is a complex number whose square is –1. Each complex number can be written as "$a + bi$," where each a and b is a real number. Riemann studied equations whose variables and coefficients could be complex numbers. In fact, he showed how to start with an equation that defines a function of real numbers and extend it in a consistent manner to a larger set of numbers that includes some complex numbers.

Riemann studied the extension of a special function, the zeta function. The zeta function is the infinite sum of a given power of each positive integer. When the input number is greater than 1, such as 2, the function's value is the infinite sum "$1/1^2 + 1/2^2 + 1/3^2 + \ldots = \pi^2/6$," which is approximately 1.644934068. In fact, if any value z greater than 1 is used, the infinite sum "$1/1^z + 1/2^z + 1/3^z + \ldots$" has a finite value. This value is represented by the value of Riemann's zeta function, $\zeta(z)$.

Riemann's technique for extending a function to a larger set of complex numbers defines the so-called analytic continuation of this function. While the zeta function is never zero when z is a real number greater than 1, there are some complex numbers of the form "$1/2 + xi$" such that "$\zeta(1/2 + xI)$" is zero. Riemann's hypothesis is that the only nonreal complex numbers that can make the zeta function zero are those for which the real part is ½.

The following graph shows a curve that represents the complex numbers produced by "$\zeta(0.5 + xi)$," where x is allowed to range from –20 to 20. This graph shows that there may be at least two

values of x where the zeta function is zero.

This is what happens for a case where the real

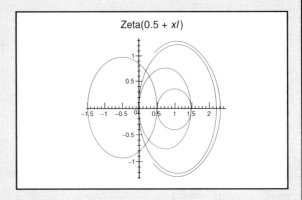
Zeta(0.5 + xI)

part is not ½:

This path does not have the origin "$(0 + 0i)$" as a

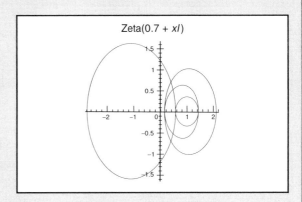
Zeta(0.7 + xI)

part of the graph.

If the Riemann zeta function conjecture is true, then the zeta function can be used to estimate the number of prime numbers less than a given number.

Bibliography

An Introduction to the Theory of the Riemann Zeta-Function. S. J. Patterson. Cambridge, England: Cambridge University Press, 1988.

The Little Book of Big Primes. Paulo Ribenboim. New York: Springer-Verlag, 1991, pp. 126-131.

p-adic Numbers, p-adic Analysis, and Zeta-Functions. Neal Koblitz. New York: Springer-Verlag, 1977, pp. 21-22.

Göttingen 13, 1858 ("On the Hypotheses Which Lie at the Foundations of Geometry" in *A Source Book in Mathematics*, 1929, David Eugene Smith, ed.)

About Riemann

A History of Mathematics. Charles B. Boyer and Uta C. Merzbach. 2d ed. New York: John Wiley & Sons, 1991, pp. 554-555.

The History of Mathematics: An Introduction. David M. Burton. 2d ed. Dubuque, Iowa: Wm. C. Brown, 1991, pp. 542-545.

A History of Mathematics: An Introduction. Victor J. Katz. New York: HarperCollins, 1993, pp. 642, 655-656.

An Introduction to the History of Mathematics. Howard Whitley Eves. 3d ed. New York: Holt, Rinehart and Winston, 1969, pp. 379-380.

Men of Mathematics. E. T. Bell. New York: Simon & Schuster, 1937, pp. 484-509.

(Paul R. Patten)

Frigyes Riesz

Areas of Achievement: Applied math, calculus, and topology
Contribution: With David Hilbert and Stefan Banach, Riesz created an important new division of mathematics called functional analysis.

Jan. 22, 1880	Born in Győr, Austria-Hungary (now Hungary)
1897	Enters the Polytechnic Institute in Zurich, Switzerland
1902	Earns a doctorate in mathematics from the University of Budapest
1907	Publishes a fundamental theorem on the theory of real functions, called the Riesz-Fischer theorem
1908	Presents a set of axioms for the abstract theory of topology to the Fourth International Congress of Mathematics in Rome
1911	Appointed to the University of Kolozsvár
1920	Moves to Szeged
1922	Creates, with Alfréd Haar, the journal *Acta Scientiarum Mathematicarum*
1936	Elected a member of the Hungarian Academy of Sciences
1946	Invited to the University of Budapest
1952	Publishes, with Béla Szőkefalvi-Nagy, a monograph on functional analysis
Feb. 28, 1956	Dies in Budapest, Hungary

Early Life

Frigyes Riesz (pronounced "REE-ehs") was born in the town of Győr, where his father, Ignácz, was a physician. His younger brother,

Marcel, moved to Stockholm and became one of Sweden's most influential mathematicians. His older brother became a lawyer in Budapest.

Frigyes was among the first problem solvers and problem posers for the *Középiskolai Matematikai Lapok*, a mathematics journal for secondary schools. It was founded in 1894 by Dániel Arany, a teacher of Györ, and inspired many generations of young mathematicians through the years.

Riesz began his university studies in 1897 at the Polytechnic Institute in Zurich but transferred to the University of Budapest in 1899 to pursue a doctorate in mathematics. Before receiving his degree, he had also studied in Göttingen for a year. He was influenced principally by Gyula König and József Kürschák at Budapest and by Hermann Minkowski and David Hilbert at Göttingen.

After receiving his teaching certificate, Riesz taught high school in Löcse and in Budapest from 1904 until 1911. His famous results from this period include the Riesz representation theorem and one, independently discovered by Ernst Fischer, called the Riesz-Fischer theorem. He also presented a set of axioms for the abstract theory of topology in 1908, which has been widely used since then.

In 1911, an opening occurred at the University of Budapest. Riesz and his friend and rival, Lipót Fejér, were the two best applicants. Fejér received the position. Riesz was then appointed to the position that Fejér had vacated on the progressive faculty of the University of Kolozsvár in Transylvania, which was at that time a part of Hungary.

After World War I, Transylvania was awarded by the Treaty of Trianon to Romania. The entire Hungarian administrative apparatus of Kolozsvár was moved into a small town in Hungary called Szeged.

The Years in Szeged

Beginning in 1920, Riesz worked in Szeged along with Alfréd Haar, who had also been a professor at Kolozsvár. Within a few years, the two of them established a mathematical center of international reputation by creating the Bolyai Institute and the journal *Acta Scientiarum Mathematicarum*, or *Acta*. The library of the university grew rapidly, since many mathematical journals were exchanged for the popular *Acta* and most publishers sent free books to the journal for review.

While in Szeged, Riesz served as provost from 1925 to 1926 and in 1945 and published more than forty articles, establishing and developing several new branches of modern analysis. He was first denied a full membership at the Hungarian Academy of Sciences, however, and was inducted only in 1936. He was also not allowed to work at the University of Budapest because, between the two world wars, no more than one Jewish person was permitted in each academic department there, and Fejér was also Jewish.

Years of Recognition

After World War II, Riesz was finally invited to the University of Budapest; he taught there until his death in 1956. He received several awards from the Hungarian government and became a member or honorary doctor of several European academies, societies, and universities. His monograph with Béla Szökefalvi-Nagy, entitled *Leçons d'analyse fonctionnelle* (1952; *Functional Analysis*, 1955), was widely used. It was translated from French into Rus-

Unifying Analysis, Geometry, Algebra, and Mathematical Physics

Riesz built a general theory of function spaces.

In analysis, the variable is a magnitude or a number; in functional analysis, the function itself is regarded as the variable. A collection of functions, characterized by a property, such as the collection of all continuous functions, forms a so-called function space. This transition from the consideration of separate functions to the investigation of a variable function allows the discussion of all curves on a surface or of all possible motions of a mechanical system.

When René Descartes started to use x and y as variables instead of unknown numbers, it empowered mathematicians to talk about an equation of a curve, unifying algebra and geometry into analytic geometry. The work of Riesz provided a uniform point of view to the discussion of the calculus of variation, problems of oscillations, the theory of integral and differential equations, and to the approximations of functions by unifying ideas from analysis, geometry, algebra, and mathematical physics.

In 1907, Erhard Schmidt and Maurice-René Fréchet found that the space of square summable (Lebesgue integrable) functions has a geometry analogous to the so-called Hilbert space of sequences. This analogy inspired Riesz to build a geometry of square summable functions by defining a distance between those functions in a way that generalized the distance formula of Euclidean geometry, which was based on the Pythagorean theorem. He was able to do so using the Riesz-Fischer theorem, which established a one-to-one correspondence between Lebesgue measurable square integrable functions and square summable sequences of real numbers.

The apparatus of functional analysis has developed rapidly and has been widely applied in almost all branches of mathematics, such as probability theory, partial differential equations, quantum mechanics, and the quantum theory of fields. Functional analysis also helped to realize many important connections among traditionally separate branches of mathematics. The concepts first invented and refined by Riesz continue to find ever-increasing applications in mathematics, physics, and engineering.

Bibliography
Elements of the History of Mathematics. Nicolas Bourbaki. Berlin: Springer-Verlag, 1994.

Mathematics: Its Content, Methods, and Meaning. Aleksandr Danilovich Aleksandrov, Andrei Nikolaevich Kolmogorov, and Mikhail Alekseevich Lavrent'ev, eds. Providence, R.I.: American Mathematical Society, 1962-1963.

One Hundred Years of Mathematics: A Personal Viewpoint. George Frederick Temple. New York: Springer-Verlag, 1981.

sian, German, English, Japanese, and Chinese. His lifelong effort at making complicated mathematical concepts accessible to his students was accomplished in this book.

Frigyes Riesz had a short, rather corpulent body. He was slow in motion and in speech. His friends said that his mind worked too fast for his tongue to keep up with it. Yet, he was a master of the written word in several languages. The ninety-five articles and books that he published in his life on functional analysis, real analysis, function spaces, topology, geometry, ergodic theory, and analytic, harmonic, and subharmonic functions were written in English, French, German, and Hungarian, all with the great elegance and clarity of a perfectionist.

Riesz never married; he devoted his entire life to research and to teaching mathematics. He was expert at finding the simplest, clearest explanations and at developing the ideas of others by finding the essence of arguments.

Bibliography
By Riesz
"Stetigkeitsbegriff und abstrakte Mengenlehre" in *Atti del IV Congresso Internazionale dei Matematici*, vol. 2, 1908 (Guido Castelnuovo, ed.)

Les Systèmes d'équations linéaires à une infinité d'inconnues, 1913

"Elemi módszerek a felsöbb matematikában," (elementary methods in higher mathematics) *Matematikai és fizikni lapok* 32, 1925

"The Integral Representation of Unbounded Self-Adjoint Transformations in Hilbert Space," *Transactions of the American Mathematical Society* 39, 1936 (with E. R. Lorch)

"Some Mean Ergodic Theorems," *The Journal of the London Mathematical Society* 13, 1938

"Sur quelques notions fondamentales dans la théorie générale des opérations linéaires," *Annals of Mathematics* 41, 1940

"On a Recent Generalisation of G. D. Birkhoff's Ergodic Theorem," *Acta Scientiarum Mathematicarum Szeged* 11, 1948

Leçons d'analyse fonctionnelle, 1952 (with Béla Szökefalvi-Nagy; *Functional Analysis*, 1955)

Riesz Frigyes összegyüjtött munkái, 1960 (collected works; 2 vols.; Ákos Császár, ed.)

About Riesz

"Frédéric Riesz: 1880-1956." *Acta Scientiarum Mathematicarum Szeged* 7 (1956).

History of Mathematics in Hungary Until the Twentieth Century. Barna Szénássy. Budapest: Akadémiai Kiadó, 1992.

"Szeged in 1934." Edgar R. Lorch. *The American Mathematical Monthly* 100, no. 3 (March, 1993): 219-230.

"A Visit to Hungarian Mathematics." Reuben Hersh and Vera John-Steiner. *The Mathematical Intelligencer* 15, no. 2 (Spring, 1993): 13-26.

(Agnes Tuska)

Julia Bowman Robinson

Areas of Achievement: Mathematical logic and number theory

Contribution: Robinson helped to solve Hilbert's tenth problem, which concerned finding a method to determine the solvability of Diophantine equations. She was the first woman to be elected to the National Academy of Sciences and to serve as president of the American Mathematical Society.

Dec. 8, 1919	Born in St. Louis, Missouri
1928	Contracts scarlet fever, followed by rheumatic fever, causing lifelong heart problems
1940	Earns an A.B. from the University of California, Berkeley (UCB)
1941	Receives an M.A. from UCB
1941	Marries mathematician Raphael M. Robinson
1948	Completes a Ph.D. at UCB and begins work on Hilbert's tenth problem
1949	Begins a year at the Rand Corporation
1970	With others, finally solves Hilbert's tenth problem
1976	Becomes the first woman to be elected to the National Academy of Sciences
1976	After years of serving as an occasional lecturer, offered a full professorship in the mathematics department at UCB
1983	Begins a term as the first female president of the American Mathematical Society
July 30, 1985	Dies in Oakland, California

(American Mathematical Society)

Early Life

Julia Bowman Robinson was born in St. Louis in 1919 to Ralph and Helen Hall Bowman. Helen Bowman died when Julia was only two, and she and her older sister Constance went to live with their grandmother in a small community near Phoenix. The following year, Ralph Bowman remarried, sold his company, and moved to Arizona to be with them. The community had no school, so the family moved to San Diego.

When Julia Bowman was nine, she contracted scarlet fever and rheumatic fever. She missed two years of school; the family moved to a new town so she would not be behind old schoolmates. Bowman received home tutoring and worked through the fifth-grade through eighth-grade curriculum in one year. When she reentered school, she was one of the youngest in her class.

One of her distinct memories of home tutoring was being told that the square root of 2 had a nonrepeating decimal expansion. Having learned the algorithm for extracting square roots, she spent one afternoon finding the square root of 2 to many places, looking for repeating digits. Bowman attributed her success in mathematics to her stubbornness.

College Years

In 1935, Bowman enrolled at San Diego College (now San Diego State University), majoring in mathematics. These were Depression years, and her father found his savings quickly dwindling, then gone. During her sophomore year, he committed suicide. The family moved to a modest apartment, but Bowman continued college with an aunt's financial help.

Bowman transferred to the University of California, Berkeley (UCB), in her senior year. She took a number theory course from a young professor named Raphael Robinson. They took walks during which he explained fascinating mathematical topics. She completed her A.B. after one year but did not find a job. A small stipend was arranged so that she could begin graduate work.

Marriage and a Doctorate

In December, 1941, Julia and Raphael were married. He provided her with financial support, encouragement, and access to the professional mathematics society. Julia Bowman Robinson completed her M.A. that year.

When Julia became pregnant, she was ecstatic and put her mathematics on hold. Unfortunately, she miscarried after a few months. Doctors discovered a buildup of scar tissue in her heart, a result of the rheumatic fever, and recommended that she not have children. Julia became despondent, but Raphael convinced her to work on a paper on general recursive functions, helping her toward the road to recovery.

Robinson began work on her doctorate at UCB under Alfred Tarski, a noted logician from Poland. She completed her degree in 1948 with a thesis showing that an integer can be defined arithmetically in terms of rational numbers and rational number addition and multiplication. Thus, rational number arithmetic is sufficient for formulating all problems in elementary number theory.

Solving Problems

At the Second International Congress of Mathematicians in 1900, David Hilbert, a foremost mathematician of the time, presented twenty-three problems to challenge mathematicians during the new century. In 1948, Robinson became interested in the tenth problem, which concerned finding a method using a finite number of operations to determine whether a given Diophantine equation is solvable in integers. She spent the next twenty years attempting to solve it.

In 1949, Robinson began work at the RAND Corporation in Santa Monica. The company ran a contest involving a game theory problem. She produced a correct solution but, as a company employee, did not win the prize. Her solution contained perhaps the most important theorem in elementary game theory.

Robinson avidly continued work on Hilbert's tenth problem. Each year, she wished as she blew out her birthday candles that a solution would be found. In 1970, young Russian mathematician Yuri Matijasevich discovered the missing piece for her proof. Instead of finding a finite step method, they showed that no method was possible.

The next year, Julia and Raphael traveled to

The Solvability of Diophantine Equations

Robinson searched for a solution to Hilbert's tenth problem, which concerned finding a method to determine the solvability of Diophantine equations.

A Diophantine equation is a polynomial equation with integer coefficients in any number of variables whose solutions are restricted to integers. For example, the equation "$4x^2 + 9y^2 - 36 = 0$" has an infinite number of solutions. If considered as a Diophantine equation, however, its only solutions will be the ordered pairs [(3,0), (–3,0),(0,2),(0,–2)].

Diophantine equations are named after Diophantus, who studied them during the third century. Since then, mathematicians have found solutions for many of these equations and also have found many others to be unsolvable.

The following is an example. A Pythagorean triple is a set of three integral lengths, such as (3,4,5) or (5,12,13), which could be used to form a right triangle. There are an infinite number of these triples, and the Pythagorean theorem assures that each would satisfy the Diophantine equation "$x^2 + y^2 = z^2$." On the other hand, the famous last theorem of the French mathematician Pierre de Fermat states that Diophantine equations of the form "$x^n + y^n = z^n$" have no solutions for values of n greater than 2— that is, there is no similar triple of integers that will satisfy an equation such as "$x^3 + y^3 = z^3$."

Hilbert's tenth problem questioned whether a universal method involving a finite number of operations could be developed that could determine whether a given Diophantine equation was solvable.

In 1960, Robinson, Martin Davis, and Hilary Putnam, making use of an extended form of Diophantine equations that allowed variable exponents, showed that if even one Diophantine equation could be found whose solutions behaved exponentially, Hilbert's tenth problem was unsolvable.

In 1970, Yuri Matijasevich, a young Russian mathematician who was only twenty-two at the time, was able to construct such an equation using Fibonacci numbers. Fibonacci numbers are those of the sequence 1, 1, 2, 3, 5, 8, 13, . . . , where each term is formed by adding the two preceding terms. For Matijasevich's work, the important property of Fibonacci numbers was that they grow exponentially.

It was thus proven that it is impossible to find a single procedure that can be applied to every Diophantine equation to determine whether it has integer solutions.

Bibliography

Fascinating Fibonaccis: Mystery and Magic in Numbers. Trudi Hammel Garland. Palo Alto, Calif.: Dale Seymour, 1987.

"Hilbert's Tenth Problem." Martin Davis and Reuben Hersh. *Scientific American* 229, no. 5 (November, 1973).

"Universal Diophantine Equation." James P. Jones. *The Journal of Symbolic Logic* 47, no. 3 (September, 1982).

Leningrad to meet Matijasevich. In the following years, Robinson, Matijasevich, Martin Davis, and Hilary Putnam published numerous papers on the problem, each giving the others credit for their contribution.

Recognition
In 1976, Robinson became the first woman elected to the National Academy of Sciences. Although she had taught occasional courses at UCB, she was not a regular faculty member. After her election, she was offered a full professorship. She was also elected to the American Academy of Arts and Sciences. In 1983, she became president of the American Mathematical Society, the first woman to serve in that position. Robinson died of leukemia in 1985.

Bibliography
By Robinson
"An Iterative Method of Solving a Game," *Annals of Mathematics* 54, 1951

"Existential Definability in Arithmetic," *Transactions of the American Mathematics Society* 72, 1952

"The Decision Problem for Exponential Diophantine Equations," *Annals of Mathematics* 74, 1961 (with Martin Davis and Hilary Putnam)

"Unsolvable Diophantine Problems," *Proceedings of the American Mathematical Society* 22, 1969

"Axioms for Number Theoretic Functions" in *Selected Questions of Algebra and Logic*, 1973 (A. I. Shirshov et al., eds.)

"Reduction of an Arbitrary Diophantine Equation to One in Thirteen Unknowns," *Acta Arithmetica* 27, 1975 (with Yuri Matijasevich)

"Hilbert's Tenth Problem" (with Davis and Matijasevich) in *Mathematical Developments Arising from Hilbert Problems*, 1976 (Felix E. Browder, ed.)

The Collected Works of Julia Robinson, 1996 (Solomon Feferman, ed.)

About Robinson
Julia: A Life in Mathematics. Constance Reid. Washington, D.C.: Mathematical Association of America, 1996.

"Julia Bowman Robinson." Joan Fisher Koppy. In *Celebrating Women in Mathematics and Science*, edited by Miriam P. Cooney. Reston, Va.: National Council of Teachers of Mathematics, 1996.

"Julia Bowman Robinson (1919-1985)." Constance Reid with Raphael M. Robinson. In *Women of Mathematics: A Biobibliographic Sourcebook*, edited by Louise S. Grinstein and Paul J. Campbell. Westport, Conn.: Greenwood Press, 1987.

(Linda G. Thompson)

Bertrand Russell

Area of Achievement: Mathematical logic
Contribution: Russell demonstrated that much, if not all, of mathematics can be obtained from a few primitive ideas and propositions that are intuitive concepts of logic.

May 18, 1872	Born in Trelleck, Monmouthshire, Wales
1890	Enters Trinity College, Cambridge University
1895	Obtains a six-year fellowship at Trinity
1903	Publishes *The Principles of Mathematics*
1910	Lectures in logic and philosophy of mathematics at Trinity
1910-1913	Publishes, with Alfred North Whitehead, *Principia Mathematica*
1916	Dismissed from Trinity and imprisoned for pacifist views and acts against conscription
1931	Becomes the third Earl Russell
1934	Awarded the Royal Society of London's Sylvester and De Morgan Medals
1944	Appointed a Fellow at Trinity
1945	Publishes *History of Western Philosophy*
1949	Awarded the Order of Merit by King George VI
1950	Wins the Nobel Prize in Literature for his body of writings
1950-1970	Protests against racial segregation, nuclear weapons, and U.S. involvement in Vietnam
Feb. 2, 1970	Dies near Penrhyndeudraeth, Wales

Early Life

Born to an aristocratic family, Bertrand Arthur William Russell was the son of Viscount Amberly and Kate Stanley. Orphaned by the age of four, he was raised by his grandmother and educated at home. His grandfather, who was the first Earl Russell and served as prime minister of England on two occasions, died when Bertrand was seven.

In his first autobiography, Russell describes his childhood as lonely but not unhappy. He also recounts his first experience with Euclid's geometry at age eleven. He had no difficulty mastering the theorems but objected to having to accept the axioms on trust. At eighteen, Russell entered Trinity College, where he took high honors in mathematics and philosophy.

The Logistic School of Mathematics

Russell believed that progress in mathematics went in two directions: toward the more com-

(The Nobel Foundation)

plex formulations and also toward the more general foundations. He viewed his meeting in 1900 with Giuseppe Peano at the International Congress of Philosophy in Paris as a turning point in his career. Peano was treating positive integers as objects of logic with five self-evident properties. Using a cumbersome symbolism, he was able to reduce much of mathematics to theorems in logic.

Russell modified Peano's methods in an attempt to create the positive integers as unique objects from primitive ideas and propositions of logic. The intent being to show that all mathematical results derivable from the integers could then be seen as theorems in logic. Russell's contention and the foundation of the logistic school is that mathematics is a branch of logic rather than logic being a tool of mathematics.

Within a year, Russell had written the first draft of *The Principles of Mathematics* (1903). By 1913, he and Alfred North Whitehead had completed the sequel to this five hundred-page work, the two thousand-page, three-volume *Principia Mathematica*. While Russell asserted to the end that mathematics and logic were identical, the *Principia Mathematica* fell short of its mark.

Russell's integers could not be used to define the real numbers as Richard Dedekind had been able to, unless Russell assumed the so-called axiom of reducibility. Most experts agree that reducibility or efforts to avoid its need amount to the introduction of mathematics into an axiomatic system of pure logic. As even Russell and Whitehead admitted, "This axiom has a purely pragmatic justification: it leads to the desired results and to no others." The *Prin-*

Russell's Paradox

During the 1890's, mathematicians began to discover contradictions in Georg Cantor's set theory. The most famous of these was discovered by Russell in 1901. It attacked Cantor's very definition of set.

Cantor defined a set to be any collection of things that can be real, imagined, or abstract. For example, the sun is a member of the set S of all stars in the universe. One can also consider the set A of all abstract ideas. The very notion of set is an abstract idea, so in the latter case one can say that A is a member of itself. On the other hand, a set of stars is not an individual star, so S is not a member of itself.

Russell asked, "Does the set X of all sets that do not contain themselves contain itself?" This obvious bit of double-talk requires some careful thinking. In the examples above, S is not a member of itself, so S would be a member of X, while A is a member of itself, so A would not belong to X.

What about X? If X belongs to itself, then the definition of membership in X says that X does not belong to itself. On the other hand, if X does not belong to itself, then the definition of membership in X says that X belongs to itself. Both statements are clearly impossible. What this means is that some sets cannot exist. Cantor's definition of a set was too broad.

Russell's paradox is often stated as the barber problem: In a certain village, the male barber shaves all the men who do not shave themselves and only them. Who shaves the barber? If he shaves himself, then he is shaving someone who does not shave himself. If he does not shave himself, then he will shave himself. Again, both statements are impossible.

Yet another example occurs if one writes "The sentence on the other side is false" on the front of a piece of paper and "The sentence on the other side is true" on the back. Such undecidable questions undoubtedly fueled Russell's need to create mathematics as a branch of logic that would be free from contradictions.

Bibliography

Classics of Mathematics. Ronald Calinger, ed. Englewood Cliffs, N.J.: Prentice Hall, 1995.
The History of Mathematics: An Introduction. David Burton. Boston: Allyn & Bacon, 1985.
An Introduction to the History of Mathematics. Howard Whitley Eves. 6th ed. Philadelphia: Saunders College Publishing, 1990.

cipia Mathematica suffered additional criticism in the 1930's when Kurt Gödel showed that Russell's system had merely circumvented all known paradoxes but could not be proven to be free of contradictions.

Russell's Other Life

Russell's philosophy, like his mathematics, shows his commitment to reason and common sense. He rejected the philosophy of idealism of his predecessors in favor of physical realism and rigorous argument. His views influenced many and changed the direction of philosophy in the twentieth century.

Russell wrote more than forty books in his lifetime. While many were scholarly, they were noted for their clarity and covered a wide range of topics, including education, sex, religion, marriage, psychology, and science. They were often controversial and widely read.

Russell states in his first autobiography that three simple but overwhelmingly strong passions governed his life: the longing for love, the search for knowledge, and unbearable pity for the suffering of humankind. He also rejected all guidance from his grandmother, with the exception of the inscription on the Bible that he inherited from her: "Do not follow a multitude to do evil." Much of Russell's life was lived as a social and political activist, which caused him some difficulties in his lifetime. He was dismissed from his position at Trinity College and imprisoned for four months in 1916 for his antiwar activities. His views on sex and marriage caused Mayor Fiorello Henry La Guardia to cancel Russell's appointment at the City College of New York in 1940. Healthy in mind and body until his death at ninety-seven, Russell was arrested and briefly imprisoned in his nineties for his participation at a demonstration against nuclear weapons.

Bibliography

By Russell
The Principles of Mathematics, 1903
Principia Mathematica, 1910-1913 (3 vols.; with Alfred North Whitehead)
The ABC of Relativity, 1925
On Education, 1926
Marriage and Morals, 1929
The Scientific Outlook, 1931
Freedom and Organization, 1934
History of Western Philosophy, 1945
Portraits from Memory, 1956
The Autobiography of Bertrand Russell, 1967-1968 (3 vols.)

About Russell
Bertrand Russell. Alfred Jules Ayer. New York: Viking Press, 1972.
Bertrand Russell and Trinity. G. H. Hardy. Cambridge, England: Cambridge University Press, 1942.
Classics of Mathematics. Ronald Calinger, ed. Englewood Cliffs, N.J.: Prentice Hall, 1995.
Russell Remembered. Rupert Crawshay-Williams. New York: Oxford University Press, 1970.

(Charles Waiveris)

Charlotte Angas Scott

Areas of Achievement: Algebra and geometry

Contribution: A lucid, thorough examiner of the geometry of her day, Scott introduced many, especially women, to the careful study of mathematics. Her research centered on the relationship between geometry and algebra.

June 8, 1858	Born in Lincoln, England
1876	Wins a scholarship to Girton College, England's first college for women
1880	Achieves eighth place (unofficially) in Cambridge University examinations
1882	Earns a B.Sc. (first class) from the University of London
1885	Earns a D.Sc. (first class) from the University of London
1885	Named founding department head at Bryn Mawr College
1891	Becomes the only woman elected to the Council of the American Mathematical Society
1894	Publishes *An Introductory Account of Certain Modern Ideas and Methods in Plane Analytical Geometry*
1899	Publishes "A Proof of Noether's Fundamental Theorem"
1906	Is the only female mathematician noted as outstanding in *American Men of Science*
1907	Publishes *Cartesian Plane Geometry*
1909	First Bryn Mawr endowed chair named for her
1924	Retires from Bryn Mawr
Nov. 10, 1931	Dies in Cambridge, England

Early Life

Charlotte Angas Scott was the second child of Caleb and Eliza Scott. Her father, a minister of the Congregational Church, was the principal of Lancashire Independent College. Little education was available to non-Anglicans, and still less for women. Her family members, especially her father, were essential for Charlotte's education.

Scott may have obtained her excellent literary style from her father's influence. She noted later in life that her family considered mathematical games a part of home entertainment. This early home schooling was of excellent quality: At eighteen, she won a scholarship to Girton College, which had opened in 1869 as England's first women's college.

University and Discrimination

Scott's tiny college class contained only eleven women studying under primitive conditions. In 1873, Girton College had been relocated near Cambridge University so that students could attend lectures of those professors who would permit it. Chaperones had to accompany them, or the women would be classed as prostitutes. To protect their "weak feminine nature," they were required to sit behind a screen.

These difficulties, however, did not inhibit Scott's education. In 1880, she received permission to take the tripos examination informally. Fifty hours were required, and the results determined who received honors with their degree. When the scores were read, the young gentlemen of Cambridge insisted that Miss Scott of Girton be recognized as taking the eighth position, even if she could not receive a degree.

The University of London had begun granting external degrees to women in 1876. By taking a second set of examinations, Scott was able to receive the B.Sc. degree with first-class honors in 1882. She continued to study at London, with the algebra specialist Arthur Cayley, and received her doctorate, also with first-class honors, in 1885. Her first publication concerning a binomial equation appeared the following year in the *American Journal of Mathematics*.

Life at Bryn Mawr

It was coincidental that, in 1885, Bryn Mawr College opened its doors in a suburb of Philadelphia. M. Carey Thomas, the first dean and later the college president, selected Scott to be the first head of the mathematics department as well as its sole faculty member. For the first three years, only four students studied mathematics, but, under Scott's able leadership, the reputation and size of the department grew. At the end of the nineteenth century, nine American women had earned doctorates in mathematics; three of them were Scott's students.

During her years on the faculty at Bryn Mawr, Scott carried a heavy teaching load in addition to working with graduate students as a thesis adviser. She was also a force in the development of the college beyond the mathematics department. She pressed for adequate library resources, even over the skepticism of President Thomas. Her correspondence shows a lifelong concern for her students. She assisted them whenever possible but would not support their desires when she judged them detrimental to their best interests.

Professional Activities

Outside the college, Scott served her profession well. She took an active part in converting the New York Mathematical Society into the American Mathematical Society. As the only female member of its first council, she served from 1891 to 1894 and was elected again in 1899 to 1902. She was vice president in 1905-1906. For twenty-seven years, beginning in 1899, Scott served as coeditor of the *American Journal of Mathematics*, an important research publication of its time. In 1938, while reviewing the first fifty years of that society, Thomas Fiske cited about thirty people—including one woman, Charlotte Angas Scott.

In addition to approximately thirty papers, published in a variety of journals, she wrote two textbooks. The first, in 1894, was entitled "introductory" but in fact took its students to the current edge of research in geometry. The book was used widely and revised twice. A second textbook on plane geometry, however, was poorly received.

Retirement

After 1906, acute rheumatoid arthritis obliged Scott gradually to withdraw from college life. Her interest in gardening helped compensate

(Bryn Mawr College Archives)

for this isolation. After her retirement in 1924, she remained for a year to help her last doctoral student. She then moved to England, close to Griton and Cambridge. She died there in 1931.

Bibliography

By Scott

"The Binomial Equation $x^p - 1 = 0$," *American Journal of Mathematics* 8, 1886

"On the Higher Singularities of Plane Curves," *American Journal of Mathematics* 14, 1892

"The Nature and Effect of Singularities of Plane Algebraic Curves," *American Journal of Mathematics* 15, 1893

An Introductory Account of Certain Modern Ideas and Methods in Plane Analytical Geometry, 1894

"On Plane Cubics," *Philosophical Transactions of the Royal Society of London* 185(A), 1894

"Note on Equianharmonic Cubics," *Messenger of Mathematics* 25, 1896

"Notes on Adjoint Curves," *Quarterly Journal of Pure and Applied Mathematics* 28, 1896

"On Cayley's Theory of the Absolute," *Bulletin of the American Mathematical Society* 3, 1897

"On the Intersections of Plane Curves," *Bulletin of the American Mathematical Society* 4, 1898

"Studies in the Transformation of Plane Algebraic Curves," *Quarterly Journal of Pure and Applied Mathematics* 29, 1898; 32, 1901

"A Proof of Noether's Fundamental Theorem," *Mathematische Annalen* 52, 1899

"The Status of Imaginaries in Pure Geometry," *Bulletin of the American Mathematical Society* 6, 1900

"Notes on the Geometrical Treatment of Conics," *Annals of Mathematics* 2, 1901

"Note on the Real Inflexions of Plane Curves," *Transactions of the American Mathematical Society* 3, 1902

"On a Recent Method for Dealing with the Intersection of Plane Curves," *Transactions of the American Mathematical Society* 3, 1902

"On the Circuits of Plane Curves," *Transactions of the American Mathematical Society* 3, 1902

Modern Views of Geometry

Scott's research centered on the relationship of geometry and algebra, a field later called analytic geometry.

For many years, geometry ended with the study of Euclid's *Stoicheia* (c. 300 B.C.E.; *Elements*); no other mathematical work has had such a profound influence for so many centuries. The essence of Euclid's method is to derive every new concept from strict logical argument based on the smallest number of axioms. These ideas, which he called common notions, are considered to be self-evident and to require no proof for acceptance. Examples of axioms are that the whole is greater than any of its parts and that things equal to the same thing are equal to each other.

In addition to the axioms are a small number of postulates. One accepts the idea that it is possible to draw a straight line between any two points and that all right angles are equal. Euclid included among his postulates one dealing with parallel lines, also known as the fifth postulate. This single idea has been among the most studied of all mathematical thoughts.

With his definition of parallel lines in terms of interior angles formed when a third line intersects the two lines in question, however, Euclid's postulate became longer and less easily accepted. Many mathematicians tried to prove the parallel postulate using the other axioms. Their attempts brought about profound changes in geometry, mathematics, and logic.

Suppose that Euclid's idea about parallel lines is not the only way to reach a reasonable geometry. The Russian mathematician Nikolay Ivanovich Lobachevsky assumed that through a point, not a part of a line, there are at least two lines parallel to that line. This basic assumption leads to a geometry as logical as that of Euclid's. In fact, the two geometric systems are identical except where the parallel postulate is involved. This hyperbolic geometry is one of several successful approaches to this fascinating new world.

While Scott's specific research area ceased to be popular, her work contributed to an increasingly creative approach to this very old mathematical subject. By understanding that, in mathematics, truth is not absolute, one can create a truly scientific approach. Science seeks explanations that best fit the experimental evidence. Such an expansion of the intellectual horizon, together with non-Euclidean geometries, allowed Albert Einstein to produce his theory of relativity.

Bibliography

An Introduction to the Foundations and Fundamental Concepts of Mathematics. Howard Whitley Eves and Carroll V. Newsom. Rev. ed. New York: Holt, Rinehart and Winston, 1965, chapter 3.

Mathematical Thought from Ancient to Modern Times. Morris Kline. New York: Oxford University Press, 1972, chapter 36.

Mathematics for College Students: Elementary Concepts. A. William Gray and Otis M. Ulm. 2d ed. Beverly Hills, Calif.: Glencoe Press, 1975, chapter 10.

"Elementary Treatment of Conics by Means of the Regulus," *Bulletin of the American Mathematical Society* 12, 1905

"Note on Regular Polygons," *Annals of Mathematics* 8, 1906

Cartesian Plane Geometry—Part I: Analytical Conics, 1907

"Higher Singularities of Plane Algebraic Curves," *Proceedings of the Cambridge Philosophical Society* 23, 1926

About Scott

"Charlotte Angas Scott." Marguerite Lehr. In *Notable American Women, 1607-1950.* Vol. 3. Cambridge, Mass.: The Belknap Press of Harvard University Press, 1971.

"Charlotte Angas Scott: An Appreciation." Isabel Maddison and Marguerite Lehr. *Bryn Mawr Alumni Bulletin* 12 (January, 1932): 9-12.

"Charlotte Angas Scott (1858-1931)." Patricia Clark Kenschaft. In *Women of Mathematics: A Biobibliographic Sourcebook*, edited by Louise S. Grinstein and Paul J. Campbell. New York: Greenwood Press, 1987.

(K. Thomas Finley)

Claude Elwood Shannon

Areas of Achievement: Algebra, applied math, and probability

Contribution: Shannon contributed to information theory and applied Boolean algebra to the theory of switching circuits.

Apr. 30, 1916	Born in Gaylord, Michigan
1932	Enters the University of Michigan
1936	Receives bachelor of science degrees in electrical engineering and mathematics
1940	Receives a master of science degree in electrical engineering and a Ph.D. in mathematics
1948	Publishes the seminal paper "A Mathematical Theory of Communication" while working at Bell Telephone Laboratories
1950	Writes a paper on programming a computer to play chess, a precursor to artificial intelligence
1957	Becomes a Fellow at the Center for the Study of the Behavioral Sciences in Palo Alto, California
1958	Becomes Donner Professor of Science at MIT
1966	Receives the Institute of Electronics and Electrical Engineers Medal of Honor and the National Medal of Science
1972	Receives the Harvey Prize, Technion, Haifa, Israel
1985	Receives the Kyoto Prize
1994	Receives the Norbert Wiener Centenary Medal of the International Association of Cybernetics

(MIT Museum)

Early Life

Claude Elwood Shannon was born on April 30, 1916. He spent the first sixteen years of his life in Gaylord, Michigan, and was graduated from Gaylord High School in 1932. He was quite adept at building mechanical and electrical gadgets. While still in school, he constructed models planes, a radio-controlled model boat, and a telegraph system. Among his childhood heroes was the famous inventor Thomas Edison, although years later as an accomplished scientist he admired more academic luminaries, such as Isaac Newton, Albert Einstein, and John von Neumann.

Shannon entered the University of Michigan in 1932. Four years later, he received bachelor's degrees in both electrical engineering and mathematics, two fields in which he maintained a lifelong interest.

Mathematical and Other Scientific Work

Shannon joined the electrical engineering program at the Massachusetts Institute of Technology (MIT) as a research assistant in 1936. He earned advanced degrees while participating in several research projects, including a differential analyzer and a complex relay circuit associated with it.

While Shannon worked on these projects, his interest in the design of switching circuits intensified. Following a summer at Bell Telephone Laboratories, he showed in his master's thesis that Boolean algebra could be used in the analysis and synthesis of switching circuits. His first paper on the subject, published in 1940, was awarded the Alfred Nobel Prize of the combined engineering societies of the United States (not to be confused with the more well-known prize awarded by the Nobel Committee) for the best paper written by a scientist under the age of thirty.

In September, 1938, Shannon changed his major from electrical engineering to mathematics at the suggestion of Vannevar Bush, then president of the Carnegie Institution in Washington, D.C. Encouraged by Bush, Shannon explored the possibility that algebra might be useful in organizing genetic knowledge. After working under geneticist Barbara Burks during the summer of 1939 in Cold Spring Harbor Laboratory, Shannon turned the subject into dissertation material under the title "An Algebra for Theoretical Genetics." Alongside his doctoral research, Shannon also developed ideas in computers and communication systems, including the trade-off between time, bandwidth, and noise in communication systems, as well as computer design using symbolic mathematical operations.

In the spring of 1940, Shannon received a master of science degree and a doctorate in electrical engineering and mathematics, respectively. He spent the academic year 1940-1941 as a National Research Fellow at the Institute for Advanced Study in Princeton, New Jersey, working under Hermann Weyl. Subsequently, he worked for fifteen years at Bell Laboratories, where his illustrious peers included signal theorist Harry Nyquist, feedback expert Hendrik Bode, and transistor inventors Walter Brattain, John Bardeen, and William Shockley.

It was during this period that Shannon made his most important scientific contribution. His development of information theory was published in 1948 as "A Mathematical Theory of Communication." At the 1981 International Symposium on Information Theory in Brighton, England, Irving Reed said, "Few other works of this century have had greater impact on science and engineering. By this landmark paper and his several subsequent papers on information theory he has altered most profoundly all aspects of communication theory and practice."

In subsequent years, Shannon made numerous contributions to the understanding of information theory and noise, and he devised a variety of other electrical and mechanical systems, including the maze-solving mouse Theseus.

Impact and Recognition

After working as a visiting professor at MIT in 1956 and as a Fellow at the Center for the Study of the Behavioral Sciences in Palo Alto, California, the following year, Shannon became a per-

---

Information Theory and Symbolic Computation

Shannon developed concepts of information theory and techniques for symbolic computation that ushered in the communications revolution.

In his most significant paper, "A Mathematical Theory of Communication," which has been described as the Magna Carta of the information age, Shannon showed that all information sources—including telegraph keys, human speech, and television cameras—have a source rate associated with them, which can be measured in bits per second. Communication channels such as free space, coaxial cables, and optical fibers have a capacity measured in the same units. The information can be transmitted over the channel if, and only if, the source rate does not exceed the channel capacity.

In his paper "Communication Theory of Secrecy Systems," Shannon related cryptography to communication in a noisy channel, the "noise" being the scrambling performed by the cryptographic system. In another problem investigated with Edward Moore, Shannon proposed that the reliability of relay circuits could be increased via redundancy of unreliable contacts. Once again, the problem may be equated to transmission over a noisy channel.

In 1953, Shannon devised a utilitarian device called THROBAC (*THrifty ROman numeral BAckward-looking* Computer), which performed all the arithmetic operations in Roman numerals. A maze-solving mouse named Theseus, built in 1950, consisted of a lifesize magnetic mouse that moved around a maze of twenty-five squares. The maze could be altered at will, and the mouse would search the passageways until it found the arbitrarily placed goal. In the process, the mouse added new knowledge to its memory. This was very likely the first learning device of its kind and a precursor to artificial intelligence.

Robert Lucky, executive director of research at Bell Laboratories, described Shannon's mathematical and engineering work as "the greatest in the annals of technological thought." International Business Machines (IBM) Fellow Rolf Landauer equated Shannon's pioneering insight with that of Albert Einstein.

Shannon's ideas were far ahead of their time, since vacuum tube circuits could not calculate the complex codes required. Only after high-speed integrated circuits became a reality in the 1970's was the information theory developed by Shannon utilized significantly. By the late 1990's, virtually all systems that stored, processed, or transmitted digital information—including such diverse devices as compact disks, computers, fax machines, and deep-space probes—were based on Shannon's concepts. Information theory had infiltrated other fields, including linguistics, economics, biology, and even the arts. According to Shannon, common principles underlie mechanical and living things. When asked if machines can think, he responded, "You bet. I'm a machine and you're a machine, and we both think, don't we?"

Bibliography

Claude Elwood Shannon: Collected Papers. Claude E. Shannon. Edited by N. J. A. Sloane and Aaron D. Wyner. New York: IEEE Press, 1993.

"Machine Aid for Switching Circuit Design." Claude E. Shannon and Edward F. Moore. *Proceedings of the Institute of Radio Engineers* 41, no. 10 (October, 1953).

"Programming a Computer for Playing Chess." Claude E. Shannon. *Philosophical Magazine*, 7th ser. 41 (March, 1950).

manent member of the MIT faculty as Donner Professor of Science. Many of his papers have been translated into various foreign languages.

Shannon has received numerous awards and other honors, including the Institute of Electronics and Electrical Engineers (IEEE) Medal of Honor and the National Medal of Science in 1966, the Harvey Prize from Israel in 1972, the Kyoto Prize in 1985, and the Norbert Wiener Centenary Medal in 1994. Shannon was named a Fellow of the IEEE and the Royal Society of London and a member of the National Academy of Sciences, the National Academy of Engineering, the American Mathematical Society, and the American Academy of Arts and Sciences.

Bibliography
By Shannon

"A Symbolic Analysis of Relay and Switching Circuits," *Transactions of the American Institute of Electrical Engineers* 57, 1938

"An Algebra for Theoretical Genetics," 1940 (dissertation)

"A Mathematical Theory of Communication," *The Bell System Technical Journal* 27, 1948

"A Simplified Derivation of Linear Least Square Smoothing and Prediction Theory," *Proceedings of the Institute of Radio Engineers* 38, 1950 (with Hendrik Wade Bode)

"Computers and Automata," *Proceedings of the Institute of Radio Engineers* 41, 1953

"Von Neumann's Contributions to Automata Theory," *Bulletin of the American Mathematical Society* 64, 1958

"Lower Bounds to Error Probability for Coding on Discrete Memoryless Channels I & II," *Information and Control* 10, 1967 (with R. G. Gallager and E. R. Berlekamp)

Claude Elwood Shannon: Collected Papers, 1993 (N. J. A. Sloane and Aaron D. Wyner, eds.)

About Shannon

"Claude E. Shannon: Unicyclist, Juggler, and Father of Information Theory." John Horgan. *Scientific American* 262, no. 1 (January, 1990).

The Computer—from Pascal to Von Neumann. Herman H. Goldstine. Princeton, N.J.: Princeton University Press, 1993.

(Monish R. Chatterjee)

Thoralf Albert Skolem

Areas of Achievement: Mathematical logic and number theory

Contribution: Skolem established that certain concepts in mathematics cannot have absolute meaning; they must be interpreted relative to the underlying structure. He also introduced the *p*-adic method in Diophantine analysis.

May 23, 1887	Born in Sandsvaer, Norway
1905	Enters the University of Oslo
1909-1914	Serves as an assistant to Kristian Birkeland and publishes his first scientific papers in physics
1913	Graduated in mathematics with highest honors
1915	Studies for one year in Göttingen, Germany
1918	Appointed docent (assistant professor) of mathematics at the University of Oslo
1920	Proves the Löwenheim-Skolem theorem
1922	Presents the Skolem paradox and the replacement axiom at the Fifth Scandinavian Math Congress
1926	Receives a Ph.D. in mathematics
1935	Publishes the *p*-adic method for Diophantine analysis
1936	Publishes a survey of his early work on lattice theory
1938	Appointed full professor of mathematics at Oslo
1950	Presents his finitistic construction of mathematics at the International Congress of Mathematicians
Mar. 23, 1963	Dies in Oslo, Norway

Early Life

Thoralf Albert Skolem (pronounced "SKOH-lum") was born on May 23, 1887, in Sandsvaer, Norway. He was the son of Even Skolem and Helene Vaal. His father was an elementary school teacher, but most of the family were farmers. Skolem passed the concluding examinations of the Norwegian Gymnasium in 1905 and immediately went to the University of Oslo to study mathematics and science. He was graduated with the highest distinction in 1913 after completing a dissertation on the algebra of logic.

By this time, he had already spent four years as an assistant to physicist Olaf Kristian Bernhard Birkeland, with whom he published his first scientific papers. Skolem spent another two years as Birkeland's assistant before going abroad to Göttingen, Germany, in 1915 to study for a year. From 1916 to 1918, he was a research fellow at the University of Oslo, and then he was appointed to a newly created position as assistant professor.

Mathematical Logic

Mathematical logic was in a state of chaos at the beginning of the twentieth century. Although the main concepts were already introduced and some interesting results were found, not enough was known to indicate which concepts were fundamental. Mathematics was thought of as an axiomatic system in which certain self-evident statements were taken as axioms and results were deduced by using logic. It was hoped that all the true mathematical statements could be derived by manipulating symbols according to explicit rules, but no one had the slightest clue how to prove that this was actually so.

In his early works, Skolem was one of the first to indicate that it may not be possible to derive all the true mathematical statements. He published an important paper in 1920; from it emerged what is now known as the Löwenheim-Skolem theorem. Skolem proved that if a countable set of sentences is satisfiable, then it is satisfiable within a countable domain. When he applied this theorem to the Zermelo axioms for set theory, he obtained a paradoxical result (now known as the Skolem paradox) and correctly deduced that certain concepts of mathematics must be interpreted relatively.

In this matter, he was ahead of his time; nearly a decade passed before the full significance of his ideas was recognized with the publication of Kurt Gödel's incompleteness theorems. In 1922, Skolem also extended and placed the Zermelo axioms on firmer footing by introducing the replacement axiom and by clarifying what Ernst Zermelo meant by subsets with "definite property." The replacement axiom was also introduced independently by Abraham Fraenkel at about the same time; because Fraenkel's paper of 1922 was better known, it is usually attributed to him. To be scrupulously fair, however, what is now known as the Zermelo-Fraenkel axioms should be more correctly referred to as the Zermelo-Fraenkel-Skolem axioms.

The Later Years

Skolem was a retiring man, almost entirely devoted to mathematical research. He wrote at least 180 scientific papers, and, unusual for a mathematician, most of them were written after he was forty. Skolem's early work in mathe-

The Skolem Paradox

Skolem established that certain concepts in mathematics are relative and can have no absolute meaning.

Skolem proved that if a countable set of sentences has a model, then it has a countable model. (A model is any mathematical structure in which all the sentences are satisfied.) This result was obtained five years earlier for the case of a single sentence by Leopold Löwenheim; therefore, this result is known as the Löwenheim-Skolem theorem.

A set is said to be countable if it can be mapped by a one-to-one function into the set of all natural numbers. A set that is not countable is called uncountable. Two sets A and B are said to have the same cardinality (or size) if there is a one-to-one function that maps A onto B (that is, there is a one-to-one correspondence between the elements of A and B). Using this notion of size, the uncountable sets can be partitioned into a transfinite hierarchy of larger and larger sets.

The Löwenheim-Skolem theorem implies that if the Zermelo-Fraenkel-Skolem (ZFS) axioms have a model, then they have a countable model (M). Georg Cantor had proved that the collection of all subsets of all natural numbers was uncountable. How can the countable model M contain uncountable sets? This is the paradox that Skolem found.

Skolem correctly pointed out that M will still contain uncountable sets—they will be uncountable because there will not be any one-to-one function in M that maps them into the natural numbers of M. The notion of uncountable thus must be relative to the model in question. The notion of a set also must be a relative concept. Not every concept must be relative; the concepts of 1 and 2 will be always be the same in all models of ZFS axioms. Such concepts are said to be absolute in set theory.

Bibliography

Formal Logic: Its Scope and Limits. Richard C. Jeffrey. 3d ed. New York: McGraw-Hill, 1990.

From Frege to Godel: A Source Book in Mathematical Logic, 1879-1931. Jean van Heijenoort, ed. Cambridge, Mass.: Harvard University Press, 1967.

Georg Cantor: His Mathematics and Philosophy of the Infinite. Joseph Warren Dauben. Cambridge, Mass.: Harvard University Press, 1979.

matical logic did not create much interest among his Scandinavian colleagues, so he turned, in the early 1920's, to more traditional areas such as number theory and algebra. He also made important contributions here—of significant note is his work on the *p*-adic method used in the study of integer solutions of equations.

Skolem was promoted to full professor in 1938 and returned with renewed vigor to his earlier research in logic. Most of his work was published in Norwegian journals, to the chagrin of his foreign colleagues, and so were often inaccessible. His frequent visits to the United States later in his career, however, went some way toward breaking down this barrier.

Age did not diminish Skolem's activities, and his death on March 23, 1963, was quite unexpected. He was in good health and as productive as always. In his best works, he always started from simple fundamental situations, and what he produced has remained basic for all further work.

Bibliography
By Skolem

"Einige Bemerkungen zur axiomatischen Begründung der Mengenlehre," *Wissenshaften Vorträge gehalten auf dem 5. Kongress der scandinavischen Mathematiker in Helsingsfors* 1922 ("Some Remarks on Axiomatized Set Theory" in *From Frege to Godel: A Source Book in Mathematical Logic, 1871-1931,* 1967, Jean van Heijenoort, ed.)

"Begründung der elementaren Arithmetik durch die rekurrierende Denkweise ohne Anwendung scheinbarer Veränderlichen mit unendlichem Ausdehnungsbereich," *Skrifter utgit av Videnskapsselskapet i Kristiania, I. Matematisk-naturvidenskabelig klasse,* no. 6, 1923 ("The Foundations of Elementary Arithmetic Established by Means of the Recursive Mode of Thought, Without the Use of Apparent Variables Ranging over Infinite Domains" in *From Frege to Godel: A Source Book in Mathematical Logic, 1871-1931*, 1967, Jean van Heijenoort, ed.)

Diophantische Gleichungen, 1938

"Sur la portée du théorème du Löwenheim-Skolem" in *Les Entretiens de Zurich sur les Fondements et la Méthode des Sciences Mathématiques, 6-9 Decembre, 1938*, 1941

"Some Remarks on the Foundation of Set Theory" in *Proceedings of the International Congress of Mathematicians, Cambridge, Massachusetts, USA, August 30-September 6, 1950*, vol. 1, 1952

"Peano's Axioms and Models of Arithmetic" in *Mathematical Interpretation of Formal Systems*, 1955

"Two Remarks on Set Theory," *Mathematica Scandinavica* 5, 1957

Selected Works in Logic, 1970 (Jens Erik Fenstad, ed.)

About Skolem

"Thoralf Albert Skolem, 1887-1963: A Biographical Sketch." Jens Erik Fenstad. *Nordic Journal of Philosophical Logic* 1, no. 2 (December, 1996): 99-106. Reprinted in Skolem's *Selected Works in Logic*, Jens Erik Fenstad, ed., Oslo: Universitetsforlaget, 1970.

(Taje I. Ramsamujh)

Duncan McLaren Young Sommerville

Area of Achievement: Geometry

Contribution: Sommerville made contributions to Euclidean and non-Euclidean geometry. He is best known for his research into tessellations, the study of how geometric shapes fit together to fill a plane; this work found applications in crystallography.

Nov. 24, 1879	Born in Beawar, Rajasthan, India
1899	Given a Ramsay Scholarship to the University of St. Andrews
1900	Receives a Bruce Scholarship to St. Andrews
1902-1914	Serves as a lecturer in mathematics at St. Andrews
1905	Publishes his first research paper, "Networks of the Plane in Absolute Geometry"
1911	Publishes the four hundred-page *Bibliography of Non-Euclidean Geometry*
1911-1912	Named president of the Edinburgh Mathematical Society
1912	Marries Louisa Agnes Beveridge
1914	Publishes his first textbook, *The Elements of Non-Euclidean Geometry*
1915	Accepts a position as professor of pure and applied mathematics at Victoria College, Wellington, New Zealand
1924	Publishes his text *Analytical Conics*
1929	Publishes *An Introduction to the Geometry of* n *Dimensions*
1934	Publishes *Analytical Geometry of Three Dimensions*
Jan. 31, 1934	Dies in Wellington, New Zealand

Early Life

Duncan McLaren Young Sommerville was born in Beawar, Rajasthan, India, on November 24, 1879. His father was the Reverend James Sommerville. Sommerville was educated in Scotland, attending Perth Academy and the University of St. Andrews. While at the university, he was awarded a Ramsay Scholarship in 1899 and a Bruce Scholarship in 1900.

Although his major field of study was in mathematics, specifically geometry, Sommerville was also interested in astronomy, anatomy, and chemistry, and particularly in crystallography. It was this interest in crystals and their structure that led him to research repetitive space-filling geometric patterns. Sommerville was also a skilled artist, painting watercolors of New Zealand scenes. His artistic ability served him well in the making of models that helped him to visualize his abstract ideas.

From 1902 through 1914, Sommerville taught in the mathematics department of the University of St. Andrews. In 1912, he married Louisa Agnes Beveridge, formerly of Belfast, Ireland. As a lecturer, Sommerville was admired by his students and colleagues alike for his teaching and research. Students valued his unobtrusive style.

Although he was shy and somewhat reserved, Sommerville's research was impressive. He investigated branches of geometry other than the Euclidean system. In 1911, he published the four hundred-page *Bibliography of Non-Euclidean Geometry*, which also included a bibliography of *n*-dimensional geometry. In 1911 and 1912, he found time to serve as the president of the Edinburgh Mathematical Society.

New Zealand

In 1915, Sommerville became professor of pure and applied mathematics at Victoria University College, in Wellington, New Zealand. He was a devoted teacher, and his students appreciated the time and dedication that he put into his teaching. At one time, the University of Otago was temporarily without a mathematics professor. Sommerville willingly filled the gap by providing a correspondence course in higher mathematics.

Sommerville was a founder of the Royal Astronomical Society of New Zealand and served as its first executive secretary. In 1924, he presided over the mathematics section of the Adelaide meeting of the Australasian Association for the Advancement of Science. In 1928, the Institute (Royal Society) of New Zealand awarded him its Hector Medal.

Publications and Research

Further evidence of Sommerville's skill as a teacher can be seen in his textbooks. His first text, *The Elements of Non-Euclidean Geometry* (1914), broke new ground in an area that few people knew anything about at the time. In 1924, he published a text called *Analytical Conics*. His text *An Introduction to the Geometry of* n *Dimensions* was published in 1929, followed by *Analytical Geometry of Three Dimensions* in 1934.

In addition to his textbooks, Sommerville published more than thirty original research papers. Most of them covered areas of geometry. One exception was a 1928 paper "Analysis of Preferential Voting"—which, however, he analyzed in terms of geometric concepts. In 1906, he published two papers that presented a purely mathematical approach to the statistical questions raised by Karl Pearson's research in biometrics. He also published papers on the connections between geometry and group theory and developed an original analysis of the musical scale.

Another area of particular interest to Sommerville was the study of tessellations and crystallography. Tessellations is the study of how geometric shapes fit together in a mosaic-like pattern to fill a plane, much the same way as tiles cover a bathroom floor. Sommerville extended this work to include the study of how three-dimensional space can be filled with cubes and other polyhedrons, as in honeycombs. He drew generalizations to spaces with four, five, and more dimensions, using both Euclidean and non-Euclidean geometries. This work was later fundamental to the study of the formation of crystals and the development of new ceramic materials.

In 1935, Sommerville's biographer, H. W. Turnbull, called him Scotland's leading geometer of the twentieth century. An unassuming scholar dedicated to his students and his research, Sommerville influenced a generation of mathematicians in both Scotland and New Zealand. He died on January 31, 1934, in Wellington, New Zealand.

Bibliography
By Sommerville
Bibliography of Non-Euclidean Geometry, 1911
The Elements of Non-Euclidean Geometry, 1914
Analytical Conics, 1924
An Introduction to the Geometry of n *Dimensions*, 1929
Analytical Geometry of Three Dimensions, 1934

About Sommerville
"Professor D. M. Y. Sommerville." H. W. Turnbull. *Proceedings of the Edinburgh Mathematical Society*, 2d ser. 4, part 1 (March, 1934).

(Linda L. McDonald)

Non-Euclidean Geometry

By redefining what is meant by parallel lines, a new type of geometry, known as non-Euclidean geometry, can be developed. Non-Euclidean geometry is no longer tied to the plane. Sommerville investigated these branches of geometry.

Until the nineteenth century, the only known system of geometry was Euclidean geometry, which deals with points, lines, and figures in a plane. The word "geometry" comes from two Greek words: *ge*, or "earth," and *metria*, meaning "measure." Since the earth was originally assumed to be flat, Euclidean geometry deals mainly with planes.

Euclidean geometry is based on five postulates and five axioms. The fifth postulate, the so-called parallel postulate, states that given a straight line and a point not on the line, only one line passes through the point and is parallel to the first line. The complexity and length of this postulate make it seem more like a theorem, which should be provable. Starting almost from the time of Euclid, efforts were made to prove this postulate, to no avail.

These efforts to prove the parallel postulate, however, led eventually to the new field of non-Euclidean geometry. The discovery of this new field was a revolution in geometry. Its discovery has had profound effects on other fields of mathematics, on physical science, and on philosophy. Non-Euclidean geometry demonstrated that a given set of explicitly stated assumptions could lead to different mathematical systems.

In 1829, Nikolay Ivanovich Lobachevsky published the first non-Euclidean geometry. In hyperbolic, or Lobachevskian geometry, it is assumed that there exist two parallels to a given line through an outside point. A model of hyperbolic geometry can be seen in the interior of a circle. The lines are defined as the circular arcs that meet the boundary of the circle at right angles. Since parallel lines are lines that never meet, then several parallel lines can be drawn for a given point.

In 1854, Bernhard Riemann suggested another type of non-Euclidean geometry. In elliptical, or Riemannian, geometry it is assumed that no parallels exist through the point. An example of elliptical geometry is spherical geometry, which is used to describe the surface of the earth. The shortest distance between any two points on a sphere is a great circle, which is the intersection of the sphere with a plane through its center, such as the meridian or the equator. Thus, a line is a great circle. Spherical geometry is non-Euclidean since all the great circles intersect; there can be no parallels.

Bibliography
Geometry. Harold R. Jacobs. San Francisco: W. H. Freeman, 1974.
Geometry. Vol. 2 in *Fundamentals of Mathematics*, edited by H. Behnke, F. Bachmann, K. Fladt, and H. Kunle. Cambridge, Mass.: MIT Press, 1983.
An Introduction to Non-Euclidean Geometry. David Gans. New York: Academic Press, 1973.
Non-Euclidean Geometry: A Critical and Historical Study of Its Development. Roberto Bonola. 1912. Reprint. New York: Dover, 1955.
Non-Euclidean Geometry: Or, Three Moons in Mathesis. Lillian R. Lieber. 2d ed. Lancaster, Pa.: Science Press, 1940.

Thomas Jan Stieltjes

Areas of Achievement: Calculus and number theory

Contribution: Stieltjes introduced a generalization of definite integrals that led to many advances in mathematics and statistics.

Dec. 29, 1856	Born in Zwolle, the Netherlands
1873	Begins studies at the Polytechnical School in Delft, the Netherlands
1876	Fails his examinations for the third time
1877	Appointed as an assistant for astronomical calculations at Leiden Observatory
1882	Writes his first letter to Charles Hermite, marking the beginning of a lifelong correspondence
1883	Marries Elizabeth Intveld
1884	Receives an honorary doctorate in mathematics and astronomy from Leiden University
1885	His family settles in Paris
1889	Appointed as professor of differential and integral calculus in Toulouse, France
1894	Publishes "Recherches sur les fractions continues," in which he introduces the Stieltjes integral
Dec. 31, 1894	Dies in Toulouse, France

Early Life

Thomas Jan Stieltjes (pronounced "STEEL-tyus") was the son of a civil engineer and member of parliament. He entered the Polytechnical School of Delft in 1873 and spent most of his time in the library studying only the works of Carl Friedrich Gauss and Karl Gustav Jacob Jacobi. Consequently, he failed his examinations three times.

After consultations with the director of Leiden Observatory, his father was able to persuade him to become an assistant for astronomical observations. It was during this time that Stieltjes began his correspondence with the famous mathematician Charles Hermite, which lasted until Stieltjes's death.

A New Integral

Ancient mathematicians knew formulas for calculating the areas of basic geometric figures such as rectangles, circles, and polygons. Some were even successful in obtaining formulas for areas bounded by parabolas and spirals, as well as volumes of cylinders and spheres. The special procedures devised to obtain these formulas, however, lacked generality.

A major breakthrough was made in the late seventeenth century when Isaac Newton and Gottfried Wilhelm Leibniz independently discovered a new branch of mathematics called the calculus. The methods of the calculus made it possible to find the rate of change of a function with respect to a given variable, via a process known as differentiation.

Another remarkable result was that areas could be obtained by reversing the process of differentiation. The German mathematician Bernhard Riemann later showed that the area under a positive curve can be obtained by the definite integral of the function representing the curve. The notion of the definite integral is presented in most modern-day basic calculus courses.

Stieltjes introduced a very clever particular generalization of the definite integral, now known as the Stieltjes integral. His integral arose from an unconventional yet important area of mathematics known as number theory. While this fact astonished some mathematicians, many were delighted when applications of the Stieltjes integral began sprouting up in various branches of mathematics. Stieltjes is fondly remembered as the founder of the analytic theory of continued fractions.

The Move to Paris

The beginning of a new period in the life of Stieltjes was marked by his resignation from the Leiden Observatory in 1883. He was now able to devote himself completely to mathe-

The Stieltjes Integral

Stieltjes discovered a particular generalization of the definite integral, which allows a function to be integrated not only with respect to a variable but also with respect to another function.

The areas of regular shapes such as squares, rectangles, circles, and triangles can be computed with ease. For example, to obtain the area of a rectangle, one needs to multiply its length and width; the area of a circle is pi (π) multiplied by the square of its radius. In three dimensions, the concept of area is replaced by volume. Once again, standard formulas exist for the volumes of regular objects, such as rectangular boxes, cylinders, and spheres.

The physical world contains myriad irregular objects. Throughout history, mathematicians have made attempts to find formulas for areas and volumes of given objects. It was the study of the calculus that finally provided a definitive answer. The fascinating solution to the area problem was a mathematical object called the definite integral. Intuitively, the definite integral of a function can be thought of as a sum of function values, as the input variable changes from a starting value to a final value. The shaded region in figure 1 has an area equal to the definite integral of the function f, with respect to the input variable x, as x varies from a to b.

The names of Bernhard Riemann and Henri-Léon Lebesgue are associated with the discovery and generalization of the definite integral. The early investigations of Stieltjes were in a branch of mathematics known as number theory, a field that was not directly linked to the calculus. While working with a mathematical object known as continued fractions, he was able to expound the Stieltjes integral for continuous functions. A basic example of a continued fraction is given in figure 2. The Stieltjes integral allows a function to be integrated not only with respect to a variable but also with respect to another function. In this sense, it became a valuable particular generalization of the definite integral.

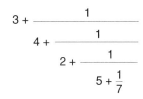

$$3 + \cfrac{1}{4 + \cfrac{1}{2 + \cfrac{1}{5 + \cfrac{1}{7}}}}$$

Figure 2. An example of a continued fraction.

A variety of concepts in mathematics such as density, volume, length, and probability have properties remarkably similar to that of area. The notion of the definite integral, and the Stieltjes integral in particular, has become an essential computational tool of mathematics that provides a means of efficient calculation.

Bibliography

A Concise History of Mathematics. Dirk J. Struik. 4th rev. ed. New York: Dover, 1987.

The Hitchhiker's Guide to Calculus: A Calculus Course Companion. Michael Spivak. Houston: Polished Pebble Press, 1995.

What Is Calculus About? Walter Warwick Sawyer. Washington, D.C.: The Mathematical Association of America, 1961.

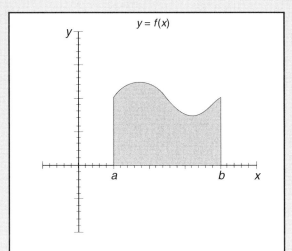

$y = f(x)$

Figure 1. The shaded area is the definite integral.

matics. During this period, his correspondence with Hermite grew in number and a lasting friendship was in the making. They appreciated each other's work. Hermite once wrote to Stieltjes: "You are always right and I am always wrong."

Stieltjes soon became recognized among his contemporaries for his meticulous mathematical thinking. His work gained recognition throughout Europe. His lack of formal qualifications, however, prevented him from obtaining a faculty position at Groningen University, in the Netherlands. Stieltjes was disappointed at the turn of events, and even the honorary doctorate conferred upon him by Leiden University in 1884 offered him little consolation. His subsequent move to Paris did not come as a surprise to many.

In recognition of his achievements and as a result of some influence by his friend Hermite, in 1889, Stieltjes was appointed a professor in Toulouse, France. His most important paper, "Recherches sur les fractions continues" ("Research on Continued Fractions," 1993), appeared in 1894; it was awarded a prize by the French Académie des Sciences. Stieltjes passed away the same year, after a brief illness, at the age of thirty-eight.

Thomas Stieltjes was a brilliant mathematician who made important contributions to number theory, to calculus, and via his integral, to statistics. His name is still revered in the two cities in which he spent most of his life; Leiden, the Netherlands, and Toulouse, France. Both cities have streets named after him. In 1992, a new Dutch research institute was named the Thomas Stieltjes Institute of Mathematics.

Bibliography
By Stieltjes

"Recherches sur les fractions continues," *Annales de la Faculté des Sciences de l'Université de Toulouse pour les sciences mathématiques et physiques* 8 J1-J122, 1894 ("Research on Continued Fractions" in *Collected Works*, 1993)

Œuvres Complètes, 1914-1918 (*Collected Works*, 1993; 2 vols., Gerrit van Dijk, ed.)

About Stieltjes

"Thomas Joannes Stieltjes: Honorary Doctor of Leiden University." Gerrit van Dijk. *The Mathematical Intelligencer* 16, no. 1 (Winter, 1994): 52-53.

(A. Bathi Kasturiarachi)

James Stirling

Areas of Achievement: Applied math, calculus, and geometry

Contribution: Stirling is best known for finding a formula that approximates $n!$, the product of the first n positive integers.

1692	Born in Garden, Stirling, Scotland
1711	Enters Balliol College, Oxford University
1716	Leaves Oxford for political reasons
1717	Publishes his first book, *Lineae Tertii Ordinis Neutonianae sive Illustratio Tractatus D. Neutoni De Enumeratione Linearum Tertii Ordinis*
1718	Publishes his first paper for the Royal Society of London, with the help of Sir Isaac Newton
1726	With Newton's help, obtains a fellowship in the Royal Society of London
1726	Teaches mechanics and experimental philosophy at the Little Tower Street Academy in London
1730	Publishes his main work, *Methodus Differentialis Sive Tractatus de Summatione et Interpolatione Serierum Infinitarum*
1735	Becomes a manager with the Scots Mining Company
1738	Elected to the Edinburgh Philosophical Society
1745	Invents the Stirling engine
1748	Elected to the Berlin Academy of Sciences
Dec. 5, 1770	Dies in Edinburgh, Scotland

Early Life

In 1692, James Stirling was born into the "Stirlings of Garden," one of the oldest landed families in Scotland. In 1180, a Stirling acquired the estate of Cawder, which has been in the family's possession ever since. In 1571, one of the Stirlings married John Napier, the inventor of logarithms; several other marriages between the Napier and Stirling families have been recorded.

James Stirling was the third son born to Archibald Stirling and Anna Hamilton. Archibald and Anna had four sons and five daughters, but the first son, also named James, died in infancy. Little is known about Stirling's childhood, but, at eighteen, he entered Oxford University, where he was described as studious and cheerful.

Loyal to the House of Stuart

Stirling lived in a time of political turmoil. In 1688, William of Orange and his army landed in England and asked to meet peacefully with his father-in-law, King James II, to settle their differences. James refused and fled England a month later. William and his wife Mary ruled England for five years, and William reigned alone for eight years after her death. His rule was followed by that of Queen Anne, who reigned for twelve years. When Queen Anne died in 1714, a group loyal to the House of Stuart called the Jacobites believed that the next king of England should be the son of King James II. The Stirlings were Jacobites and took part in demonstrations of protest when the throne went to King George of the House of Hanover instead.

When King George was crowned, Stirling was studying mathematics at Oxford. It is recorded that in 1715, Stirling was tried and acquitted for cursing the king in public. The next year, he lost his scholarship for refusing to take the oath of allegiance to King George. Stirling's father was tried for high treason but acquitted, and his uncle was imprisoned in a subsequent rebellion.

Relationship with Newton

When Stirling lost his scholarship at Oxford, Sir Isaac Newton helped him to obtain a position in Venice, Italy. Stirling thus earned the

Infinite Series, Coefficients, and Cubic Curves

Much of Stirling's work involves infinite series. He also studied the coefficients of polynomials and expanded on Sir Isaac Newton's theorems on cubic curves.

An example of an infinite series is "$1 + \frac{1}{2} + \frac{1}{4} + \frac{1}{8} + \ldots$." This series is said to converge to 2 because the sum of its first n terms, "$1 + \frac{1}{2} + \frac{1}{4} + \frac{1}{2^{n-1}} = 2 - \frac{1}{2^{n-1}}$," gets arbitrarily close to 2. Here, two numbers, a and b, are considered close if their difference, $a - b$, is close to zero. Thus, 999,900 and 1,000,000 are not considered very close, since "$1,000,000 - 999,900 = 100$" is not close to zero. In another type of closeness, a and b are considered to be close, written $a \approx b$, if $\frac{a}{b}$ is close to 1. In this case, 999,900 is considered close to 1,000,000, since "$\frac{999,900}{1,000,000} = .9999$" is close to 1. Stirling's series states that

$$n! \approx \left(\frac{n}{e}\right)^n \sqrt{2\pi n} \left[1 + \frac{1}{12n} + \frac{1}{288n^2} - \frac{139}{51,840n^3} - \cdots \right]$$

where $n! = 1 \times 2 \times 3 \ldots n$ and $e = 2.71828\ldots$, the base for the natural logarithm.

By taking only the first term of Stirling's series, one obtains

$$n! \approx \left(\frac{n}{e}\right)^n \sqrt{2\pi n}$$

known as Stirling's formula, even though it was first discovered by Abraham de Moivre. For $n = 10$, this approximation says

$$10! = 3,628,800 \approx \left(\frac{10}{e}\right)^{10} \sqrt{20\pi}$$
$$= 3,598,695.6$$

This is true because the ratio "$\frac{3,598,695.6}{3,628,800} = .99170\ldots$" is close to 1, even though the difference "$3,628,800 - 3,598,695.6 = 30104.4$" is not close to zero.

Stirling also studied the coefficients of polynomials such as "$x_{(4)} = x(x-1)(x-2)(x-3) = -6x + 11x^2 - 6x^3 + x^4$." The coefficients $(-6, 11, -6, 1)$ are called Stirling numbers of the first kind, written as

$$\begin{bmatrix} 4 \\ 1 \end{bmatrix} = -6, \ \begin{bmatrix} 4 \\ 2 \end{bmatrix} = 11, \ \begin{bmatrix} 4 \\ 3 \end{bmatrix} = -6, \ \begin{bmatrix} 4 \\ 4 \end{bmatrix} = 1$$

Stirling was also interested in how to express powers of x, such as x^4, in terms of these polynomials. For example,

$$x^4 = x(x-1)(x-2)(x-3) + 6x(x-1)(x-2) + 7x(x-1) + x$$
$$= x_{(1)} + 7x_{(2)} + 6x_{(3)} + x_{(4)}$$

The coefficients (1, 7, 6, 1) are called Stirling numbers of the second kind, written as

$$\left\{ \begin{matrix} 4 \\ 1 \end{matrix} \right\} = 1, \ \left\{ \begin{matrix} 4 \\ 2 \end{matrix} \right\} = 7, \ \left\{ \begin{matrix} 4 \\ 3 \end{matrix} \right\} = 6, \ \left\{ \begin{matrix} 4 \\ 4 \end{matrix} \right\} = 1$$

The number $\left\{ \begin{matrix} n \\ k \end{matrix} \right\}$ also counts the number of different ways of arranging n distinct objects into k piles. For example, there are seven possible ways to split the four objects A, B, C, and D into two piles: $A - BCD$, $B - ACD$, $C - ABD$, $D - ABC$, $AB - CD$, $AC - BD$, and $AD - BC$. Once again, $\left\{ \begin{matrix} 4 \\ 2 \end{matrix} \right\} = 7$. Some other Stirling numbers of the second kind are given in the accompanying table.

$\left\{ \begin{matrix} n \\ k \end{matrix} \right\}$	1	2	3	4	5
1	1				
2	1	1			
3	1	3	1		
4	1	7	6	1	
5	1	15	25	10	1

The work that first brought fame to Stirling was cubic curves. A cubic curve is the graph of the equation of the form "$y^3 + (ax + b)y^2 + (cx^2 + dx + e)y + (fx^3 + gx^2 + hx + i) = 0$," where $a, b, c \ldots, s$ are constants. Stirling proved that each equation representing a cubic curve can be reduced to one of the four forms "$(i) xy^2 + ky = 0$," "$(ii) y^2 = 0$," "$(iii) xy = 0$," or "$(iv) y = 0$," where y is of the form "$y = px^3 + qx^2 + rx + s$." Each of these forms has subcases; Newton missed six of them in his original theorems on cubic curves.

Bibliography

Combinatorial Problems and Exercises. László Lovász. 2d ed. Amsterdam: North-Holland, 1993.

A Course of Modern Analysis. Edmund Taylor Whittaker and George Neville Watson. 4th ed. Cambridge, England: Cambridge University Press, 1940.

James Stirling: A Sketch of His Life and Works, Along with His Scientific Correspondence. Charles Tweedie. Oxford, England: Clarendon Press, 1922.

name "the Venetian." Stirling's successful work in cubic curves impressed Newton, who, in 1704, published a paper describing (without proof) seventy-two different types of cubic curves.

In 1717, Stirling published his first book, entitled *Lineae Tertii Ordinis Neutonianae*, in which he proved all of Newton's theorems on cubic curves and found four new types that Newton had missed. (The two remaining types were discovered by François Nicole in 1731 and Nikolaus Bernoulli in 1733). This book made him famous throughout the European mathematical community, especially in Italy.

Stirling was devoted to Newton, who was instrumental in Stirling's publication of the *Lineae Tertii Ordinis Neutonianae* and his first paper for the Royal Society of London, on the method of differences.

Main Work and Later Life

Stirling's main work, *Methodus Differentialis*, appeared in 1730. In it appears the famous Stirling series for "$n! = 1 \times 2 \times 3 \ldots n$" and many results about infinite sums and products. Stirling's 1745 paper "A Description of a Machine to Blow Fire by the Fall of Water" describes his Stirling engine, which was used commercially through the nineteenth century.

In 1735, Stirling was asked to manage the Leadhills Mines of the Scots Mining Company. He did an excellent job, instituting managerial ideas well ahead of their time. He gave the miners a six-hour workday and encouraged them to read and to stay healthy. The library that he built for the miners in 1740 still stands today. Stirling offered each miner a free tract of land on which to plant a garden, and each miner was required to contribute to a fund for the sick and elderly.

Stirling was happy working at Leadhills and became quite successful there. He married Barbara Watson and had a daughter named Christian. Unfortunately, his letters to Leonhard Euler and Colin Maclaurin indicate that he had little time to spend on mathematics. In one letter to Stirling, Euler described a formula of his that Stirling had already seen in a letter from Maclaurin. Stirling told Euler about this, and Euler generously let Maclaurin lay claim to the formula. Both men eventually published the formula, which is now known as the Euler-Maclaurin summation formula. Stirling died in 1770 at the age of seventy-eight.

Bibliography
By Stirling
Lineae Tertii Ordinis Neutonianae sive Illustratio Tractatus D. Neutoni De Enumeratione Linearum Tertii Ordinis, 1717
Methodus Differentialis Sive Tractatus de Summatione et Interpolatione Serierum Infinitarum, 1730
"History of the Theory of Attraction and the Figure of the Earth," *Philosophical Transactions of the Royal Society of London*, 1735
"A Description of a Machine to Blow Fire by the Fall of Water," *Philosophical Transactions of the Royal Society of London*, 1745

About Stirling
James Stirling: A Sketch of His Life and Works, Along with His Scientific Correspondence. Charles Tweedie. Oxford, England: Clarendon Press, 1922.
Oxford in the Eighteenth Century. Alfred Denis Godley. London: Methuen, 1908.
Scotland and Scotsmen in the Eighteenth Century. John Ramsay. Edinburgh, Scotland: W. Blackwood & Sons, 1888.

(*Zachary M. Franco*)

Alicia Boole Stott

Area of Achievement: Geometry

Contribution: Stott contributed significantly to the understanding and visualization of certain four-dimensional geometric figures that she named polytopes.

June 8, 1860	Born in Cork, Ireland
1867	Develops an interest in geometric figures
1890	Marries Walter Stott
1895	Begins a collaboration with Pieter Hendrik Schoute on polytopes
1900	Publishes "On Certain Sections of the Regular Four-Dimensional Hypersolids"
1910	Publishes "Geometrical Deduction of Semiregular from Regular Polytopes and Space Fillings"
1914	Receives an honorary doctorate from the University of Groningen
1930	Begins a collaboration with mathematician Harold Coxeter
Dec. 17, 1940	Dies in London, England

Early Life

Alicia Boole Stott, known to those close to her as Alice, was born in Cork, Ireland, on June 8, 1860. Her mother, Mary Everest Boole, was the niece of Sir George Everest, after whom Mount Everest is named. Her father, George Boole, was a brilliant, self-taught mathematician and logician whose work formed the foundations for modern symbolic logic and early computer design. Before marrying Alicia's mother, Boole had founded his own school, joined the mathematics faculty at Queen's College, and received the Royal Medal from the Royal Society of London.

George and Mary Boole had five daughters: Mary, Margaret, Alicia, Lucy, and Ethel. Alicia was only four years old when her father died,

leaving the family destitute. Her mother took a position as matron of Queen's College and had to send her youngest three daughters elsewhere to live. During this time, Alicia lived with her grandmother and great-uncle John Ryall in Cork. Her relationship with her grandmother was stifled by the older woman's selfish and conventional ways.

When Alicia was thirteen, she went to London to live with her invalid mother and four sisters. The quarters they rented were dark and dingy and, for some time, the five sisters shared one small, sunless bedroom. Mrs. Boole, herself an eccentric author, had become good friends with James Hinton, the author of a book on suffering called *The Mystery of Pain* (1866). They hosted long nightly talks for a variety of unusual persons, including many unconventional psychologists and members of fringe religious groups. Alicia, Lucy, and Ethel were present at these discussions. They were too young to understand the strange subjects broached by their elders but often troubled by the heady talk.

Finding Her Life's Work

After working in a children's hospital in Cork, Alicia returned to London. Then, James Hinton's son Howard, a teacher at Uppingham School and the author of *Scientific Romances* (1884-1885), entered her intellectual life. Howard had been working with small wooden cubes in an attempt to understand the four-dimensional hypercube, or tesseract, which includes a fourth dimension not easily visualized. Having brought the cubes to Alicia's home, Howard asked the younger sisters to memorize the Latin names that he assigned to each cube. While her sisters took to the task with different degrees of interest and diligence, Alicia tried to "see" the hypercube that Howard sought.

Howard went on to marry Alicia's eldest sister, but Alicia was a changed person from her encounter with Howard and his cubes. Perhaps for the first time, she was inspired to learn. Furthermore, she was compelled to master the problem of constructing and conceptualizing the complex four-dimensional figures for which she ultimately coined the name "polytopes." She had found her life's work.

"Seeing" the Hypercube

Stott was particularly interested in the four-dimensional convex regular solids and invented the word "polytope" (meaning "many surfaces") to describe them.

Stott developed a remarkable ability to visualize four-dimensional figures. She was not limited to seeing only the figures that exist in the three-dimensional world but could also envision one more dimension for each figure. She would then go about constructing a three-dimensional figure that would represent the polytope, just as a two-dimensional sketch can be constructed as a cross section or representation of a three-dimensional figure. Stott went on to invent two processes called expansion and contraction that led to her discovery of many more polytopes.

An elementary attempt at understanding Stott's methods and visualizing the polytope called the tesseract, a four-dimensional cube, would entail considering the following figures and their construction. A single point would be considered a zero-dimensional figure. Moving the point one unit to the left or right would form a line segment, a one-dimensional figure. Moving the line segment one unit up or down and connecting the endpoints would form a square, a two-dimensional figure. Then, moving the square one unit outward or inward and connecting the endpoints would form a cube. The final step would entail moving the cube (one vertex at a time) one unit in a direction not previously traveled and away from the cube to form the hypercube.

Stott's uncanny ability to visualize and construct certain four-dimensional figures has inspired many geometers to construct and analyze similar figures. Her genius centered about the ease and clarity with which she could visualize and reproduce each polytope. While other mathematicians have focused on the analytical aspects of the fourth and higher dimensions,

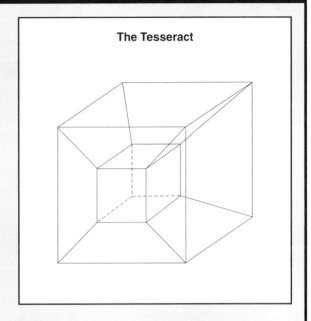

The Tesseract

Stott sought through purely Euclidean constructions to make her polytopes accessible to all who sought to "see" them.

Bibliography

"Alicia Boole Stott (1860-1940)." H. S. M. Coxeter. In *Women of Mathematics*, edited by Louise S. Grinstein and Paul J. Campbell, ed. New York: Greenwood Press, 1985.

"Geometrical Deduction of Semiregular from Regular Polytopes and Space Fillings." Alicia Boole Stott. *Verhandelingen der Koninklijke Akademie van Wetenschappen* 11, no. 1 (1910): 1-24.

The Joy of Mathematics: Discovering Mathematics All Around You. Theoni Pappus. Rev. ed. San Carlos, Calif.: Wide World Publishing/Tetra, 1989.

"On Certain Sections of the Regular Four-Dimensional Hypersolids." Alicia Boole Stott. *Verhandelingen der Koninklijke Akademie van Wetenschappen* 7. no. 3 (1900): 1-21.

Mixing Marriage and Mathematics

In 1889, while working as a secretary for Howard's friend, John Falk, Alicia met Walter Stott, her future husband. They were married in 1890 and had two children, Mary and Leonard. For several years, Alicia Boole Stott stayed home and raised her children. Money was tight, and Alicia was bored.

Perhaps because Walter was an actuary, he understood Alicia's need to work and to talk

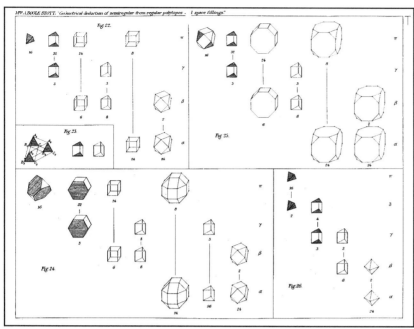

Drawings from Stott's paper "Geometrical Deduction of Semiregular from Regular Polytopes and Space Fillings." (Library of Congress)

about her mathematical findings with other mathematicians. Walter would encourage Alicia to write about her geometric findings. When he heard of Professor Pieter Hendrik Schoute's work with polytopes, he convinced his wife to write to the mathematician. The result was a wonderful collaboration, with Schoute traveling from the University of Groningen to London during several summer vacations to visit Alicia and persuading her to publish her work.

Stott had other interests. Because of her love for animals, she joined the London Zoological Society and would watch squirrels and birds eat food that she had left out for them. She also loved music. Her greatest loves, however, were polytopes.

After publishing two papers in Amsterdam, Stott spent the next several years doing further investigations into four-dimensional figures. In 1914, the University of Groningen awarded her an honorary doctorate and exhibited her geometric models at its tercentenary celebration. After the event, she remarked to her husband that the cardboard cylinder containing the degree would make a good place to store macaroni sticks, further demonstrating the intertwined nature of her dual roles of geometer and housewife.

Later Life

Stott would abandon her mathematical work for the next seventeen years, perhaps to concentrate on being a good housewife. Then, in 1930, she met the mathematician Harold Coxeter, and another happy and productive period of collaboration ensued. Over the next several years, Stott and Coxeter would discuss and write about her favorite subject, polytopes.

By 1938, both Alicia and Walter were in poor health and experiencing a general but normal lack of energy, considering their ages. She spent the last few weeks of her life peacefully residing in a Catholic nursing home before succumbing to medullary thrombosis, a fatal clotting of the blood in the heart. Alicia Boole Stott died in 1940 at the age of eighty.

Bibliography

By Stott

"On Certain Sections of the Regular Four-Dimensional Hypersolids," *Verhandelingen der Koninklijke Akademie van Wetenschappen* 7, 1900

"Geometrical Deduction of Semiregular from Regular Polytopes and Space Fillings," *Verhandelingen der Koninklijke Akademie van Wetenschappen* 11, 1910

About Stott

"Alicia Boole Stott (1860-1940)." H. S. M. Coxeter. In *Women of Mathematics*, edited by Louise S. Grinstein and Paul J. Campbell, ed. New York: Greenwood Press, 1985.

Classics of Mathematics. Ronald Calinger, ed. Englewood Cliffs, N.J.: Prentice Hall, 1995.

George Boole: His Life and Work. Desmond MacHale. Dublin, Ireland: Boole Press Limited, 1985.

A History of Mathematics: An Introduction. Victor J. Katz. New York: HarperCollins College, 1993.

(Pat Mower)

James Joseph Sylvester

Areas of Achievement: Algebra and number theory

Contribution: Sylvester, in collaboration with Arthur Cayley, is credited with developing the theory of invariants. He also discovered and coined the term "discriminant" for quadratic and higher-order equations. Sylvester was the first to use the term "matrix."

Sept. 3, 1814	Born in London, England
1829	Studies mathematics at the University of London under Augustus De Morgan
1831	Enters St. John's College, Cambridge University, but is not permitted to graduate
1838	Appointed professor of natural philosophy at London
1841	Appointed professor of mathematics at the University of Virginia but resigns abruptly
1843	Returns to London and begins work as an actuary
1846	Enters the Inner Temple to prepare for a legal career
1850	Called to the bar and meets Cayley
1854	Joins the faculty at the Royal Military Academy
1870	Publishes his book of poetry, *The Laws of Verse*
1876	Returns to America to teach at The Johns Hopkins University
1878	Founds the *American Journal of Mathematics*
1884	Accepts an invitation to join the faculty at Oxford University
Mar. 15, 1897	Dies in London, England

Early Life

James Joseph Sylvester, one of the most colorful mathematicians of the nineteenth century, was born on September 3, 1814 in London, England. He was the youngest of several siblings born to Jewish parents. It was not until his eldest brother immigrated to the United States and took the surname of Sylvester that the rest of the family did likewise.

Education and Religious Persecution

Sylvester's mathematical talent became apparent early. By the age of fourteen, he was studying mathematics at the University of London under Augustus De Morgan. By fifteen, he had been admitted to the Royal Institution at Liverpool and won the prize in mathematics at the end of his first year.

Nevertheless, Sylvester was quite unhappy in Liverpool. He had become the subject of much torment at the Royal Institution because of his Jewish faith. Eventually, he left Liverpool for Dublin, but he returned a short while later.

(Science Photo Library)

In 1831, at the age of seventeen, Sylvester became a student at St. John's College at Cambridge University. He was not permitted to graduate, however, for, in order to do so, he would have had to swear an oath to the Church of England. Sylvester, being Jewish, refused.

Nevertheless, in 1838 Sylvester landed his first professorial position, teaching natural philosophy at his old school, the University of London. Sylvester did not enjoy teaching the subject matter, and he left the university a few years later.

The American Misadventure

In 1841, Sylvester embarked on what was to become, perhaps, the greatest misadventure of his life. He set sail for America to become professor of mathematics at the University of Virginia.

Although his lectures were replete with his signature enthusiasm, Sylvester resigned

---

Mathematical Invariants

The development of the theory of invariants is credited to Sylvester, in collaboration with Arthur Cayley.

Although Sylvester and Cayley are both credited with the founding of this important mathematical field, the earliest referral to the idea of an invariant began with Joseph-Louis Lagrange, from whom it passed into the arithmetical works of Carl Friedrich Gauss. Furthermore, it was George Boole who is credited with discovering invariants. Nevertheless, none of these mathematicians seemed to realize fully the vast theoretical importance implied by this seemingly simple algebraic phenomenon.

Frequently in the history of mathematics, an important mathematical tool for some specific application is invented years before the science to which the mathematics is applied is even imagined. In particular, without invariant theory, the theory of relativity would have been impossible.

The theory of algebraic invariants, from which many extensions have emerged over the years, actually originated in a very simple observation. To outline the basic idea of an invariant, first observe that a necessary and sufficient condition for the equation "$ax^2 + 2bx + c = 0$" to have two equal roots is that the discriminant "$b^2 - ac$" equals zero. Now, if "$y = {}^{(px + q)}/_{(rx + s)}$," then upon solving for x, one obtains "$x = {}^{(q - sy)}/_{(ry - p)}$." This transforms the original equation "$ax^2 + 2bx + c = 0$" into a new equation in the variable y, such as "$Ay^2 + 2By + C = 0$," where

$$A = as^2 - 2bsr + cr^2$$
$$B = -aqs + b(qr + sp) - cpr$$
$$C = aq^2 - 2bpq + cp^2$$

Moreover, the new equation "$Ay^2 + 2By + C = 0$" has two equal roots if, and only if, its discriminant "$B^2 - AC = (ps - qr)^2(b^2 - ac) = 0$."

Thus, one can make the observation that the discriminant of the new equation is equal to the discriminant of the new equation multiplied by a (constant) factor of "$(ps - qr)^2$." Moreover, this constant depends only on the coefficients p, q, r, and s in the transformation. In other words, the discriminant of the transformed equation remains unchanged (invariant) except for a constant factor depending only on the coefficients of the transformation. This is the basic idea of an invariant.

Cayley set out to find uniform methods for discovering invariant expressions of linear transformations. Sylvester, on the other hand, focused his attention on deriving the characteristic forms of invariants pertaining to homogeneous polynomials in two or three variables.

Bibliography

A First Course in Abstract Algebra. John B. Fraleigh. 4th ed. Reading, Mass.: Addison-Wesley, 1989.

Linear Algebra. John B. Fraleigh and Raymond A. Beauregard. Reading, Mass.: Addison-Wesley, 1987.

Matrix Analysis. Roger A. Horn and Charles R. Johnson. Cambridge, England: Cambridge University Press, 1985.

abruptly after only a few months. It appears that he became infuriated over the administration's refusal to discipline a student who had insulted him. Being unable to locate a suitable position at another institution, Sylvester returned to England.

A Ten-Year Hiatus

Having had his fill of university teaching, Sylvester became an energetic actuary for a life insurance company. In 1846, he decided to prepare for a career in law. Four years later, he was called to the bar. It was at this time that he met mathematician Arthur Cayley.

Although quite a different personality from the exuberant Sylvester, Cayley was able to reinvigorate Sylvester's love for mathematics. The two became lifelong friends and collaborators in research. In fact, they eventually founded the field of invariant theory together.

Return to Teaching

After spending ten years away from pure mathematics, Sylvester desperately wanted to become a professional mathematician again. He initially encountered some difficulty in landing a professorship position, but, in 1854, he joined the faculty at the Royal Military Academy in Woolwich. He held this position for the next sixteen years, until he was forced to retire at the age of fifty-six for being "superannuated" (too old). In spite of his retirement, much of Sylvester's greatest work was still in the future.

Sylvester began his retirement in London writing verse, reading the classics, and playing chess. His great interest outside mathematics was poetry. In 1870, he published the poetry book *The Laws of Verse* and was quite proud of it. After its publication, he would sometimes sign himself "J. J. Sylvester, author of the Laws of Verse."

It is noteworthy to mention that throughout his career in mathematics, Sylvester's expositions tended to be eloquent, flowery, and at times seasoned with poetry and emotional expressions. Few mathematicians have so transparently revealed themselves through their writings and classroom lectures as Sylvester did.

In 1876, Sylvester was coaxed out of retirement to accept a prestigious position at the newly founded Johns Hopkins University in Baltimore. He demanded to be paid in gold and stayed there for seven years. During that time, he enthusiastically pursued research in pure mathematics, the first in the United States. Moreover, he also founded the *American Journal of Mathematics*, the first American periodical devoted entirely to mathematical research.

In 1884, Sylvester once again left America for England. This time, it was to accept a professorship at Oxford. He continued to work on mathematics until his death on March 15, 1897, at the age of eighty-two, after suffering a paralytic stroke.

Bibliography

By Sylvester
"On the Derivation of Coexistence," *Philosophical Magazine* 16, 1840
The Laws of Verse, 1870
The Collected Mathematical Papers of James Joseph Sylvester, 1904-1912 (4 vols.)

About Sylvester
A History of Mathematics. Carl B. Boyer and Uta C. Merzbach. 2d ed. New York: John Wiley & Sons, 1991.
Men of Mathematics. E. T. Bell. New York: Simon & Schuster, 1965.

(John H. Jaroma)

Richard A. Tapia

Area of Achievement: Applied math
Contribution: Tapia uses numerical analysis and optimization to apply computers to problem solving. He is an advocate for minority students and scientists.

Mar. 25, 1939	Born in Santa Monica, California
1961	Earns a B.A. in mathematics from the University of California, Los Angeles (UCLA)
1963-1966	Works at International Business Machines (IBM)
1967	Named acting assistant professor of mathematics at UCLA
1967	Earns a Ph.D. in mathematics from UCLA
1968-1970	Teaches at the University of Wisconsin, Madison
1970	Joins the faculty of Rice University, Houston, Texas
1978	His wife, Jean, is diagnosed with multiple sclerosis
1982	His daughter Circee is killed by a drunk driver
1990	Named one of the twenty most influential leaders in minority math education in the United States
1991	Named Noah Harding Professor
1992	Elected to the National Academy of Engineering
1996	Featured in the PBS documentary series *BreakThrough*
1996	Nominated to the National Science Board by President Bill Clinton
1996	Receives the Presidential Award for Excellence in Science, Mathematics, and Engineering

Early Life

Richard A. Tapia was born in Santa Monica, California, a city bordering Los Angeles, on March 25, 1939. His parents were Mexican immigrants who had become U.S. citizens. The need to support their families had not allowed them to finish high school. Richard learned early in life that hard work and sacrifice were needed to overcome economic and social obstacles. Some American children insulted his Mexican heritage. When he visited Mexico, however, people called him a *gringo*, or non-Hispanic. His mother taught him to be proud of his identity. Tapia would spend his career trying to encourage the dreams of minority students.

A high school counselor discouraged Tapia from continuing his education, but he went to a local junior college anyway. He found support there and transferred to the University of California, Los Angeles (UCLA). On July 25, 1959, he married while still in college; the couple's daughter Circee was born the following year. Tapia also developed a love for drag racing and set national and world records. He completed a bachelor's degree in mathematics in 1961.

Building a Career in Mathematics

Following his graduation from UCLA, Tapia found a job as a mathematician at Todd Shipyards, in San Pedro, California. A few years later, he began to work as a part-time scientific programmer at International Business Machines (IBM) Corporation in Los Angeles.

Tapia continued his education at UCLA, completing an M.A. in mathematics in 1966 and a Ph.D. the next year. His first academic appointment came in 1967 when he was named acting assistant professor of mathematics at UCLA. In 1968, Tapia left California to teach at the University of Wisconsin, Madison. That year, Richard and Jean Tapia had a second child, a boy named Richard. In 1970, he moved again, this time to Rice University, in Houston, Texas. By 1976, Tapia had worked his way up from assistant to associate to full professor. He served as chair of the Mathematical Sciences department at Rice from 1978 to 1983 and became the director of Education and Minority Programs and associate director of Minority

Affairs for the Office of Graduate Studies at the university in 1989. In 1991, he was named Noah Harding Professor of Computational and Applied Mathematics.

Struggles and Triumphs

In 1978, soon after he received tenure, Tapia's personal life met with a challenge. His wife, Jean, a professional dancer who also taught dance classes, was diagnosed with multiple sclerosis. This disease makes movement difficult, and she was forced to give up both dancing and teaching. They faced this situation together, and Jean found a new career running an exercise program for people with physical disabilities.

Tragedy struck in 1982 when their twenty-one-year-old daughter was involved in an automobile accident with a drunk driver and killed. The couple carried on in spite of their grief. The next year, they adopted a baby girl named Rebecca.

Activism and Recognition

Tapia knew all too well the struggles of women and minority groups in society, in education, and especially in the sciences. He began to travel around the United States lecturing to organizations, schools, and fellow mathematics professors about the importance of recruiting and encouraging African American, Latino, and American Indian students and women. His efforts brought many more female and minority students to Rice University and earned for Tapia many awards.

In 1990, he was named one of the twenty most influential leaders in minority mathematics education in the United States by the National Research Council. In 1994, he received the first Nico A. Habermann Award for his outstanding contributions to helping members of underrepresented groups in computing research. In 1996, Tapia was one of eighteen minority scientists featured in the PBS documentary television series *BreakThrough: The Changing Face of Science in America*. That same year, he was named Hispanic Engineer of the Year by *Hispanic Engineer Magazine*, nominated to the National Science Board by President Bill Clinton, and given the Presidential Award for Excellence in Science, Mathematics, and Engi-

(Tommy Lavergne/Rice University)

neering from the National Science Foundation.

In 1992, Tapia was elected to the prestigious National Academy of Engineering, the first Mexican American to be so honored. He also became a member of the American Mathematics Society, the Society for Industrial and Applied Mathematics (SIAM), the Mathematical Association of America, and the Society for the Advancement of Chicanos and Native Americans in Science (SACNAS).

Bibliography

By Tapia

"The Weak Newton Method and Boundary Value Problems," *SIAM Journal on Numerical Analysis* 6, 1969

"The Differentiation and Integration of Nonlinear Operators" in *Nonlinear Functional Analysis and Applications*, 1971 (L. B. Rall, ed.)

"A Characterization of Inner Product Spaces," *Bulletin of the American Mathematical Society* 79, 1973

"A General Approach to Newton's Method for Banach Space Problems with Equality Con-

Computational Optimization Theory

Tapia developed ways of programming computers to solve problems that arise in both academic research and real-world applications, such as industry and government. Within the field of computational mathematics, Tapia found his specialty in optimization theory.

Optimization theory is the branch of mathematics concerned with analyzing and solving problems in the field of mathematical programming. A basic problem in mathematical programming is the optimization of a real-valued function over a prescribed set, where optimization is the determination of the optimal values of a function, often subject to constraints of values. The solution to such a problem involves the establishment of the existence and characteristics of optimal points and the algorithms, or sets of instructions, to compute the optimum. The term "computational mathematics" denotes the use of computer programs to solve mathematical problems. Thus, computational optimization seeks the most efficient method to accomplish a task or to solve a problem using computers.

Tapia has employed computational optimization to help airlines find the most efficient routes. For this assignment, he was asked to balance such factors as consumer demand, personnel needs, fuel consumption, and wear and tear on aircraft. On such large matters, he prefers to use a method known as parallel processing, in which many smaller computers work simultaneously on different aspects of the same problem. Programming groups of computers to process information in tandem allows more efficient and effective problem solving.

Through his research into computational optimization, Tapia has made important contributions to the study of algorithms for constrained optimization problems and the theory of quasi-Newton methods for general nonlinear programming. He has received much international recognition for his involvement in the field of interior-point methods for both linear and nonlinear programming.

Bibliography

Computer Architecture: Pipelined and Parallel Processor Design. Michael J. Flynn. Boston: Jones and Bartlett, 1995.

Encyclopedia of Computer Science. Anthony Ralston and Edwin D. Reilley, ed. 3d ed. New York: Van Nostrand Reinhold, 1993.

"On the Formulation and Theory of the Newton Interior-Point Method for Nonlinear Programming." Richard A. Tapia, A. S. El-Bakry, T. Tsuchiya, and Y. Zhang. *Journal of Optimization Theory and Applications* 89 (1996): 507-541.

straints," *Bulletin of the American Mathematical Society* 80, 1974

"Newton's Method for Problems with Equality Constraints," *SIAM Journal on Numerical Analysis* 11, 1974

Nonparametric Density Estimation, 1978 (with J. R. Thompson; rev. as *Nonparametric Function Estimation, Modeling, and Simulation*, 1990)

"On the Role of Slack Variables in Quasi-Newton Methods for Constrained Optimization" in *Numerical Optimization of Dynamic Systems*, 1980 (L. C. W. Dixon and G. P. Szeg, eds.)

"On the Convergence Rate of Newton Interior-Point Methods in the Absence of Strict Complementarity," *Computational Optimization and Applications* 6, 1996 (with El-Bakry and Zhang)

"On the Formulation and Theory of the Newton Interior-Point Method for Nonlinear Programming," *Journal of Optimization Theory and Applications* 89, 1996 (with A. S. El-Bakry, T. Tsuchiya, and Y. Zhang)

About Tapia

"BreakThrough: The Changing Face of Science in America." Lara Evans. *Winds of Change* (Spring, 1996).

BreakThrough: The Changing Face of Science in America. PBS documentary video. Produced by Blackside Corporation, Boston, 1996.

"By the Numbers: It All Adds Up for Math Prof Richard Tapia." Cheryl Laird. *Houston Chronicle*, April 25, 1996.

(Tracy Irons-Georges)

Alfred Tarski

Areas of Achievement: Algebra and mathematical logic

Contribution: Tarski focused on establishing the equivalence between certain problems in logic and related problems in algebra. He then used mathematical rules to establish if the mathematical problem, and by implication the equivalent logical problem, was solvable or unsolvable.

Jan. 14, 1902	Born in Warsaw, Poland, Russian Empire (now Poland)
1922-1925	Serves as an instructor in logic at the Polish Pedagogical Institute in Warsaw
1924	Earns a Ph.D. in mathematics from the University of Warsaw
1925-1939	Serves as an adjunct professor of mathematics and logic at Warsaw and a faculty member at Zeromski's Lycée
1939	Remains in the United States when World War II breaks out while he is on a lecture tour
1939-1941	Works as a research associate in mathematics at Harvard University
1941-1942	Joins the Institute for Advanced Study in Princeton, New Jersey
1942-1968	Serves on the faculty of the University of California, Berkeley (UCB)
1953	Publishes *Undecidable Theories*
1968-1983	Named professor emeritus at UCB
Oct. 26, 1983	Dies in Berkeley, California

Early Life

Alfred Tarski was born Alfred Tajtelbaum in Warsaw, Poland, on January 14, 1902. His father, Ignacy Tajtelbaum, was a successful shopkeeper, and his mother, Rose Prussak Tajtelbaum, was a homemaker. Alfred Tajtelbaum was educated in Warsaw. His studies were interrupted by World War I, when he served briefly in the Polish army in 1918 and again in 1920.

Tajtelbaum studied mathematics and philosophy, a combination of interests that led him to the study of logic, at the University of Warsaw. He published his first mathematics paper, on the theory of sets, in 1921, and he received a doctorate in mathematics in 1924. From 1922 to 1924, he also served as an instructor of logic at the Polish Pedagogical Institute in Warsaw. Around 1924, Tajtelbaum changed his name to Tarski as protection from anti-Semitism, which was gaining strength in Europe.

Career in Mathematics and Logic

Tarski became an adjunct professor of mathematics and logic at the University of Warsaw in 1925. This was not a teaching position, but it allowed him to perform research. Therefore, at the same time, he accepted a teaching faculty position at Zeromski's Lycée in Warsaw. In 1929, he married Maria Witkowski; they had a son and a daughter. In 1939, Tarski visited the

Algebraic Methods and the Undecidability of Theories

Tarski performed research on the development of various forms of algebra as a tool for solving problems in logic, focusing on establishing the decidability of theories.

Logic is a field of study that links mathematics and philosophy, using principles of advanced forms of algebra and group theory to test the truth or falsity of various propositions. The idea is to determine if for a certain type of problem in logic, there is an algebra in which the equivalent mathematical problem can be formulated. This is called the problem of representability. As part of his research, Tarski investigated various types of algebras as a tool for studying logic. In particular, he was able to demonstrate that certain types of algebras could be used to represent specific logical problems.

Once the equivalence between a particular type of logical problem and an algebraic representation was established, Tarski could then determine if the algebraic problem could be solved or if it was unsolvable. In the simple case, if an algebraic equation contains three independent variables, two of these variables must be known from other conditions in the problem if the problem is to be solved. If fewer than two variables are known, the problem is unsolvable.

The conclusion about the decidability of the algebraic problem applies to the equivalent problem in logic as well. Tarski, working with Andrzej Mostowski, was able to establish that the classic theorem of incompleteness developed by Kurt Gödel could be represented using statements of first-order arithmetic. This result allowed Tarski to establish that a number of theories, whose decidability had not previously been established, were undecidable. He published his results in a monograph, *Undecidable Theories*, in 1953.

Bibliography
"Alfred Tarski and Decidable Theories." John Doner and Wilfrid Hodges. *Journal of Symbolic Logic* 53 (1988): 20-35.
"Alfred Tarski and Undecidable Theories." George F. McNulty. *Journal of Symbolic Logic* 51 (1986): 890—898.
"Tarski on Truth and Logical Consequence." John Etchemendy. *Journal of Symbolic Logic* 53 (1988): 51-79.

United States on a lecture tour and was still there when World War II broke out in Europe. He remained in the United States and became a naturalized citizen in 1945.

From 1939 to 1941, Tarski was a research associate in mathematics at Harvard University in Cambridge, Massachusetts. From there, he went to the Institute for Advanced Study at Princeton University in New Jersey. Because of the large influx of technically trained refugees from Europe during World War II, it was difficult to get a permanent teaching position. Finally, in 1942, he was appointed a lecturer at the University of California, Berkeley (UCB), where he spent the rest of his career, rising to the rank of professor.

During his entire career, Tarski's research focused on algebra, group theory, and logic, particularly the representation of logical statements in algebraic forms. His interest was the "decidability of theories," establishing by a rigorous mathematical proof that a particular question is answerable or not answerable.

Tarski demanded rigorous proofs. Often there was a long gap between the time that he formulated a result and the time that he finally published the result, with the intervening time being used to refine his proof. For example, his 1939 discovery, with Andrzej Mostowski, that a certain type of theory was decidable was not published until 1978. This long delay between discovery and publication resulted in many disputes between Tarski and other researchers over who had developed an idea first, since other researchers frequently developed a proof during the interval between Tarski's discovery and his publication of the result. His major publication was *Undecidable Theories* (1953), in which he established that numerous theories were undecidable.

Later Life

While a professor at UCB, Tarski supervised the Ph.D. dissertations of many important mathematicians and logicians of the next generation. Thus, his influence extended well beyond his own career. Tarski retired in 1968 but remained a professor emeritus at UCB until his death in 1983.

Bibliography

By Tarski
Geometry, 1935
A Decision Method for Elementary Algebra and Geometry, 1948
Undecidable Theories, 1953
Logic, Semantics, Metamathematics, 1956
Collected Papers, 1986 (4 vols.)

About Tarski
"Alfred Tarski." Wilfrid Hodges. *Journal of Symbolic Logic* 51 (1986): 866-868.
"Alfred Tarski's Work on General Metamathematics." W. J. Blok and Don Pigozzi. *Journal of Symbolic Logic* 53 (1988): 36-50.
"Philosophical Implications of Tarski's Work." Patrick Suppes. *Journal of Symbolic Logic* 53 (1988): 80-91.

(George J. Flynn)

Niccolò Fontana Tartaglia

Area of Achievement: Algebra
Contribution: Tartaglia discovered a formula to solve cubic equations.

1500	Born in Brescia, Republic of Venice (now Italy)
1512	Suffers saber cuts about the face and mouth, which cause a speech impediment
1535	Teaches mathematics in Venice
1535	Wins a public contest solving cubic equations
1537	Investigates the paths of cannon shots and publishes his findings in *Nova Scientia* (new science)
1543	Publishes editions of the works of Euclid and Archimedes
1545	His solution to the cubic equation is published in Girolamo Cardano's *Ars Magna*
1556-1560	His text *Trattato di numeri et misure* (treatise on numbers and measure) appears in print
Dec. 13, 1557	Dies in Venice, Republic of Venice

Early Life

Niccolò Fontana Tartaglia (pronounced "tawr-TAWL-yaw") was born to poor parents in Brescia, Italy, in 1500. His family name was Fontana, and his father was a postal messenger in Brescia. Niccolò was present at the taking of this city by the French in 1512. He, his father, and many others sought safety in a cathedral, but the soldiers found them and a massacre followed. His father was murdered and young Niccolò suffered a split skull and severe saber cuts about the face and throat.

When his mother found him alive in the cathedral, she carried him home but was unable to afford medical treatment. Under the care of

(Library of Congress)

One way to assure victory in one of these debates or contests was to discover something that no one else knew. No one had published a general solution for all types of cubic equations. It was the discovery of this solution that led to Tartaglia's fame.

In 1515, Scipione del Ferro claimed to have solved cubic equations of the form "$x^3 + ax = b$." Del Ferro died in 1526, however, before he published his solution. He had revealed the secret of his discovery to his student, Antonio Fior. About 1535, Tartaglia claimed to have found the algebraic solution to cubic equations of the form "$x^3 + ax^2 = b$."

Fior did not believe Tartaglia's claim, so he challenged Tartaglia to a public contest solving cubic equations. They issued each other questions to which the other had to answer within a specified time period. Shortly before the time limit expired, Tartaglia found a general solution to all cubic equations. He answered all of Fior's questions, but Fior could not answer any of Tartaglia's.

The Tartaglia-Cardano Dispute

Gerolamo Cardano, who taught mathematics in Milan, heard about Tartaglia's victory. Cardano then requested that Tartaglia give him this solution. Cardano wanted to include the solution in his publication. Initially, Tartaglia refused because he planned to reveal the procedure in a publication of his own at a later date. Cardano continued to pressure Tartaglia. Finally, he agreed to reveal his solution to Cardano under the condition that he would vow not to reveal it.

In 1545, Cardano published *Ars Magna*, a great Latin treatise on algebra. He included in this publication Tartaglia's solutions to cubic equations. Tartaglia responded by publicly speaking against Cardano's character and mathematical competence. Lodovico Ferrari, one of Cardano's star pupils, came to his defense, charging Tartaglia with plagiarism and challenging him to a public debate. After some time had elapsed, Tartaglia accepted, and, on August 10, 1548, the two met in Milan to debate. Cardano had conveniently left town. The debate quickly degenerated into a shouting match for which Tartaglia claimed the victory and left. His early departure left

his mother, the boy recovered. The damage inflicted upon his palate, however, caused a speech impediment that resulted in his nickname "Tartaglia," which means "stammerer" or "stutterer."

Tartaglia's formal education was very limited. His mother had saved a sum of money to hire a writing master to tutor her son. Unfortunately, the money ran out after about fifteen days. Refusing to end his education at this point, he stole his teacher's notebook and taught himself to read and write. When he and his mother could not afford to buy paper, Tartaglia would often go to the cemetery, where he could use the tombstones as writing slates.

The Debate with Fior

At the end of the Middle Ages, a renewed interest in scientific investigation took place. Universities were located in many of the larger cities. A university's prominence depended on the quality of its lecturers, which was determined by public debates and contests. Winners gained immediate recognition and were awarded academic positions at prestigious universities.

the opportunity for Ferrari to win by default.

Tartaglia died in 1557 without having published his solution to the cubic equation. Nevertheless, he was credited with being the first to apply mathematics to the investigation of the paths of cannon shots. He published these findings in *Nova Scientia* (1537; new science).

Bibliography
By Tartaglia
Nova Scientia, 1537 (new science; partial trans. in *Mechanics in Sixteenth-Century Italy: Selections from Tartaglia*, 1969)
Euclide Megarense, 1543
Opera Archimedis, 1543
Quesiti et inventioni diverse, 1546 (various queries and inventions; partial trans. in *Mechanics in Sixteenth-Century Italy: Selections from Tartaglia*, 1969)
General Trattato di numeri et misure, 1556-1560 (treatise on numbers and measure)

About Tartaglia
"The Cardano-Tartaglia Dispute." Richard W. Feldmann. *The Mathematics Teacher* 54, no. 3 (March, 1961): 160-163.
A Concise History of Mathematics. Dirk Jan Struik. 3d ed. New York: Dover, 1967.

Solving Cubic Equations

Tartaglia provided an algebraic solution to cubic equations.

The introduction to the art of printing inspired a renewed interest in mathematics, particularly in Italy. Many businesses, including banks, shops, mines, and military organizations, needed more in-depth mathematics to maximize the efficiency of their operations. Mathematical computations had to be done by retailers, shopkeepers, builders, doctors, and particularly by astrologers.

Consequently, advances made in mathematics had many benefits to society in general. Although there were practical needs for these advancements, often the inspiration for progress came from the benefits offered to those who made mathematical discoveries. It was customary for university professors to challenge their peers to public debates and contests. Winners were awarded cash, positions at prestigious universities, and invitations to lecture. Tartaglia's discovery of the solution to the cubic equation was the result of this drive among mathematicians to be the first to discover a mathematical "secret" that no one else knew.

In 1510, Scipione del Ferro found the solution to cubic equations that did not contain a squared term. The cubic equations that he could solve were of the form "$x^3 + ax = b$." Before his death, he passed this solution to one of his students, Antonio Fior. Tartaglia initially found the solution to cubic equations of the form "$x^3 + ax^2 = b$."

Upon hearing this information, Fior challenged Tartaglia to a public contest solving cubic equations. The rules consisted of each man giving his opponent thirty problems to solve within a forty-day time frame. Within two hours, Tartaglia successfully completed the problem set that Fior gave to him, and, eight days prior to the end of the contest, Tartaglia found the general method to solve all types of cubic equations. Fior was unable to solve any of the problems posed to him in this contest. Consequently, Tartaglia was declared the winner and was credited with the discovery of a formula to solve cubic equations.

Tartaglia's discovery of a formula to find solutions of cubic equations laid the foundation for finding a formula to solve quartic (fourth-degree) equations. In 1540, this formula was found by Lodovico Ferrari. These two discoveries in the sixteenth century inspired optimistic mathematicians to think that perhaps formulas could be discovered to solve equations of the fifth and even higher degrees.

Bibliography
From Five Fingers to Infinity: A Journey Through the History of Mathematics. Frank Swetz, ed. Chicago: Open Court, 1994.
History of Mathematics. David Eugene Smith. Vol. 1. New York: Dover, 1958.
The History of Mathematics: A Reader. John Fauvel and Jeremy Gray, ed. Basingstoke, England: Macmillan Press, 1988.

LIBRO
QVESITO SECONDO FATTO
dal medesimo Illust. Sig. Duca consequentemente
al precedente.

A page from a work by Tartaglia in which he applied mathematical principles to the use of cannons in battle. (Library of Congress)

History of Mathematics. David Eugene Smith. Vol. 2. New York: Dover, 1958.

An Introduction to the History of Mathematics. Howard Whitley Eves. Philadelphia: Saunders College Publishers, 1990.

Six Wings: Men of Science in the Renaissance. George Sarton. Bloomington: Indiana University Press, 1957.

(Marva Sullivan Lucas)

Olga Taussky-Todd

Areas of Achievement: Algebra and number theory

Contribution: Taussky-Todd modernized and popularized matrix theory for the resolution of mathematical problems involved in technological development.

Aug. 30, 1906	Born in Olmütz, Austro-Hungarian Empire (now Olomouc, Czech Republic)
1930	Earns a doctorate in mathematics, the University of Vienna
1931-1932	Edits *Hilbert's Collected Papers in Number Theory*
1934	Pursues postgraduate work at Bryn Mawr College
1935	Gains a fellowship at Girton College, Cambridge University
1943-1946	Works as a science officer at the National Physical Laboratory
1947	Immigrates to the United States
1948-1957	Conducts computer research at the National Applied Mathematics Laboratory
1955	Teaches at the Courant Institute of Mathematical Sciences, New York University
1957	Becomes an engineering professor, California Institute of Technology
1964	Named a Fellow of the American Association for the Advancement of Science
1965	Selected as a Fulbright Professor
1970	Wins the Mathematical Association of America's Ford Prize
1986	Named vice president of the American Mathematical Society
Oct. 7, 1995	Dies in Pasadena, California

Early Life
Olga Taussky-Todd (pronounced "TOW-skee tawd") was born Olga Taussky; she was the daughter of chemist Julius David Taussky and journalist Ida Pollach Taussky. During World War I, her family moved to Linz, Austria, where Taussky's father was director of a vinegar factory. Aware that his daughter was mathematically gifted, he asked her to figure out the proportions of water and vinegar the factory needed to combine, and he posted the formula that she devised.

During Taussky's final year of school, her father died, and she worked as a tutor to support her family. Despite this pressure, she was the outstanding student in her class. Taussky wrote an essay, "From the Binomial to the Polynomial Theorem," that her teachers praised, bolstering her confidence.

Intellectual Maturation
In 1925, Taussky enrolled at the University of Vienna, receiving a doctorate in mathematics five years later. Her dissertation about algebraic number theory was directed by Philip Furtwängler, a prominent number theoretician who frustrated Taussky with his aloofness.

At Göttingen University, she edited David Hilbert's work about number theory and Emil Artin's lectures about field theory. Taussky also served as an assistant for mathematician Emmy Noether. Taussky returned to Vienna because of political tensions in Göttingen. She continued to tutor students and to assist university mathematicians.

Advanced Education
Wishing to continue her education, Taussky applied for a fellowship and was accepted by Bryn Mawr College in Pennsylvania. Noether was teaching there while Taussky attended classes in 1934. They often traveled to Princeton University for meetings at the Institute for Advanced Study. Taussky met many scholars, including Albert Einstein, who proved crucial to her future mathematical career.

In June, 1935, Taussky accepted a fellowship to Girton College at Cambridge University, but she found few people there interested in her mathematical field. She began teaching at Westfield College for women at the University of London.

She met mathematician John ("Jack") Todd, marrying him in 1938. Because of World War II, they moved to his home in Belfast, Ireland, where Taussky-Todd concentrated on matrices. The couple returned to London in 1943, and she conducted aerodynamics research for the Ministry of Aircraft Production Flutter Group at the National Physical Laboratory. She applied matrix theory to supersonic stability problems.

The United States
In 1947, Jack Todd accepted a position with the National Bureau of Standards' Institute for Numerical Analysis at the University of California, Los Angeles (UCLA). Taussky-Todd joined the institute's staff and conducted research. After a brief return to London, they elected to work at the National Bureau of Standards' headquarters in Washington, D.C.

Taussky-Todd was a mathematical consultant for National Bureau of Standards director

(California Institute of Technology)

Matrix Theory

Matrix theory explores the use of arrangements of numbers, representing equations, in mathematical problems. Taussky-Todd investigated matrices throughout her mathematical career. Because of her contributions, matrix theory expanded into a field considered essential for advanced mathematics education.

A matrix is an array of numbers, usually displayed within brackets or parentheses, with each row of numbers corresponding to an equation. Definitions of matrices often indicate that the quantity of numbers and rows can be indefinite.

The word "matrix" is derived from Latin, literally meaning something that creates new forms. The Latin source originally referred to a pregnant woman, and mathematicians have compared matrices to wombs because both surround developments that eventually become independent.

In mathematical formulas, a matrix can be multiplied, added, and manipulated according to mathematical rules to resolve problems. Mathematicians used similar forms as early as the eighteenth century, and James Joseph Sylvester introduced the word "matrix" in 1850.

During her World War II work with the Ministry of Aircraft Production Flutter Group, Taussky-Todd discovered that matrices are crucial for aerodynamics research. She used matrices to solve difficult equations and calculate speeds that result in aircraft vibration. She then alerted designers about how to achieve aerospace stability.

Taussky-Todd continued exploring matrix theory, emphasizing the importance of matrices to mathematics. She promoted the advancement of matrix theory, collecting published references for mathematical texts and resolving complex number theorems. Matrices became as accepted algebraic structures as groups, lattices, and rings.

Taussky-Todd's matrix theory work became her best known and most influential contribution to analytic mathematical thought. She inspired and influenced matrix theorists worldwide by suggesting new ways to approach mathematical puzzles.

Internationally, matrix research centers have been established, and journals are devoted to modern matrix theory. Matrices permit new, efficient research strategies for mathematically saturated fields such as electrical engineering, quantum mechanics, and computer science, where researchers can rely on matrices instead of linear algebra.

Bibliography

Combinatorial Matrix Theory. Richard A. Brualdi with Herbert John Ryser. Cambridge, England: Cambridge University Press, 1991.

"How I Became a Torchbearer for Matrix Theory." Olga Taussky-Todd. *American Mathematical Monthly* 95, no. 9 (November, 1988): 801-812.

"Matrix Theory." I. Grattan-Guinness and W. Ledermann. In *Companion Encyclopedia of the History and Philosophy of the Mathematical Sciences.* 2 vols. London: Routledge, 1994.

Matrix Theory and Applications. Charles R. Johnson, ed. Providence, R.I.: American Mathematical Society, 1990.

Survey of Numerical Analysis. John Todd, ed. New York: McGraw-Hill, 1962.

Edward U. Condon, contributing three chapters for his book *Handbook of Physics.* She planned the bureau's first seminar on numerical aspects of matrix theory, which became a notable conference series known as the Gatlinburg meetings. Taussky-Todd also developed number theory problems for high-speed computers. She alerted mathematicians to obscure but significant concepts that otherwise might have been unknown.

She became a U.S. citizen in 1953, and two years later, she taught matrix theory at the prestigious Courant Institute of Mathematical Sciences at New York University. In 1957, Taussky-Todd was appointed the first female professor in the mathematics department at the California Institute of Technology (Caltech).

Accolades

Taussky-Todd retired in 1971. During her career, she reaped numerous professional honors. In 1948, she was invited to join the Institute for Advanced Study. The American Association for the Advancement of Science named her a Fellow, and the *Los Angeles Times* declared her "Woman of the Year" in 1964. She won the Mathematical Association of America's Ford Prize for her article "Sums of Squares" in 1970.

She served as vice president of the American Mathematical Society in 1986. Taussky-Todd wrote an estimated three hundred scholarly papers. She edited four journals: *Linear Algebra and Its Applications* (of which she was founding editor), *Linear and Multilinear Algebra, Journal of Number Theory*, and *Advances in Mathematics*.

Taussky-Todd returned to the University of Vienna as a Fulbright Professor in 1965. Her alma mater presented her with a Golden Doctorate in 1980, and the Austrian Republic bestowed its highest honor on her, the Golden Cross of Honor First Class. She died in 1995 at the age of eighty-nine.

Bibliography
By Taussky-Todd
"Infinite Powers of Matrices," *Journal of the London Mathematical Society* 17, 1942 (with John Todd)

"Commutativity in Finite Matrices," *American Mathematical Monthly* 64, 1957

"Sums of Squares," *American Mathematical Monthly* 77, 1970

"Composition of Binary Integral Quadratic Forms Via Integral 2 × 2 Matrices and Matrix Theory Composition of Matrix Classes," *Linear and Multilinear Algebra* 10, 1981

"History of Sums of Squares in Algebra" in *American Mathematical Heritage: Algebra and Applied Mathematics*, 1981 (Dalton Tarwater et al., eds.)

About Taussky-Todd
Number Theory and Algebra. Hans Zassenhaus, ed. New York: Academic Press, 1977.

"Olga Taussky-Todd: An Autobiographical Essay." Olga Taussky-Todd. In *Mathematical People: Profiles and Interviews*, edited by Donald J. Albers and G. L. Alexanderson. Boston: Birkhäuser, 1985.

"On Olga Taussky's Influence on Matrix Theory and Matrix Theorists: A Discursive Personal Tribute." H. Schneider. *Linear and Multilinear Algebra* 5 (1977-1978): 197-224.

(Elizabeth D. Schafer)

Brook Taylor

Areas of Achievement: Calculus and geometry

Contribution: Taylor developed a famous formula for expanding functions and a mathematical theory of perspective.

Aug. 18, 1685	Born in Edmonton, Middlesex, England
1701	Enters St. John's College
1708	Produces his first work on physics
1709	Receives an LLB from St. John's College at Cambridge University
1712	Publishes works on physics
1712	Elected a Fellow of the Royal Society of London
1714	Received a doctor of law degree from Cambridge
1714	Elected secretary of the Royal Society of London
1715	Publishes *Methodus incrementorum directa et inversa*, a major work on analysis
1715	Publishes *Linear Perspective*, his first work on perspective
1719	Publishes *New Principles of Linear Perspective*, a second work on perspective
1719	Stops his work in mathematics and continues to write on religion and philosophy
Dec. 29, 1731	Dies in London, England

Early Life
On August 18, 1685, Brook Taylor was born to the life of an English gentleman. Because his parents, John and Olivia Taylor, were members of the aristocracy, Brook Taylor was well educated. Even as a student, he showed exceptional talent in mathematics and physics, as

(Archive Photos)

well as promise in art, music, and writing. In 1701, he entered St. John's College at Cambridge University and was graduated with a bachelor of law degree in 1709.

By the time that he was twenty-three, Taylor had already solved a major problem in physics about vibrating strings. On the strength of this work and other papers presented to the Royal Society of London, he was elected a Fellow to the society at the age of twenty-seven.

Major Works

Taylor's thirtieth year was a significant milestone, for in that year he published two groundbreaking books. The first, *Methodus incrementorum directa et inversa* (1715), dealt with the calculus, the preeminent field of mathematics during Taylor's era. In this work, Taylor gave his famous formula for the expansion of a function f in terms of its derivatives f', f'', f''', and so on:

$$f(x + h) = f(x) + hf'(x) + \frac{h^2 f''(x)}{2!} + \frac{h^3 f'''(x)}{3!} + \ldots \cdot \frac{h^n f^n(x)}{n!} + \ldots$$

This formula is referred to as a Taylor series or a Taylor polynomial. His work on series did not have its major impact on mathematics, however, until it was used as the basis for Joseph-Louis Lagrange's extension of the calculus in 1755.

Taylor's formula was useful in computing tables for such well-known functions as $\sin(x)$, $\cos(x)$, $\log(x)$, and many others. One of Taylor's publications showed how to obtain a logarithm table. Although these tables are less commonly used since the development of good calculators, tables were very important up until that time. In fact, calculators and computers still use Taylor series to compute results for many functions.

Taylor's other work published in 1715, *Linear Perspective*, dealt with the mathematical theory of perspective. The concept of perspective, whereby a painting on a flat surface gives the illusion of depth, had been used by artists for years, but no mathematical theory of perspective had been developed. Using the principles of Euclidean geometry, Taylor coined the term "vanishing point" for the point in a painting that corresponds to the point on a line as it vanishes across the horizon. Although Taylor's theory of perspective was valid, it was unclear to some readers. Thus, Taylor published a second work on perspective in 1719 entitled *New Principles of Linear Perspective*.

Controversies

In his short career, Taylor was caught up in several controversies. A major controversy had to do with whether Sir Isaac Newton or Gottfried Wilhelm Leibniz should be given credit for the discovery of the calculus. This dispute in some ways pitted the mathematicians of England against those from the other European countries. To resolve this controversy, the Royal Society of London appointed a commission of which Taylor was a member. The commission ruled that Newton was the principal discoverer of the calculus, a ruling that mathematicians from other countries discounted because Newton was a member of the Royal Society and because Taylor and other members of the commission were friends and admirers of Newton.

Taylor was also embroiled in disputes of his

Perspective

Although many artists before Taylor had used perspective in their work, he was the first to develop a mathematical theory of perspective.

A painting is usually done on a two-dimensional surface such as a wall or a canvas. If the painting is to appear to have depth, the artist must use perspective. Perspective is the art of creating a three-dimensional illusion on a two-dimensional plane.

Taylor's mathematical theory of perspective was based on the idea that every point in a painting done in perspective corresponds to a point in the original scene. In figure 1, the scene to be painted lies in the horizontal plane H and the canvas lies in the vertical plane V. The artist's eye (or observation point) is point O. To represent point P from the scene in perspective, the artist must place the image of P (P′) on the canvas at the point where an imaginary line OP would intersect the canvas.

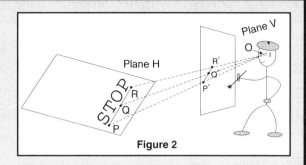

Figure 2

plane H, however, there is no point V corresponding to V′. The preimage of V′ is the point at which the ray vanishes into the horizon. Thus, point V′ in the painting is called the vanishing point.

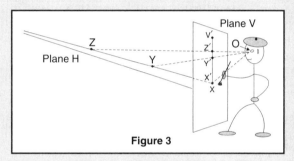

Figure 3

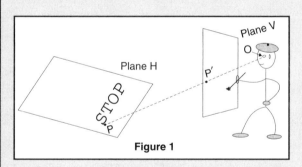

Figure 1

To represent PQR, a line segment parallel to the canvas, the artist must locate the images of P, Q, and R (P′, Q′, R′) by finding where the imaginary lines OP, OQ, and OR intersect the canvas (see figure 2). Taylor showed that the image of line segment PQR would be a line segment in V and that the original line segment and its image would be parallel.

An important concept in perspective is the vanishing point. Let X, Y, and Z be points on a ray in plane H, a ray perpendicular to plane V. The image of ray XYZ will be the line segment X′Y′Z′V′, where X′ and V′ are end points of the segment (see figure 3). Since ray XYZ intersects plane V at X, X and X′ are the same point. In

Taylor went on to show that every ray in H that extends from V away from O and that is not parallel to V also has a vanishing point. He also demonstrated that if all the vanishing points were connected, they would fall along a line called the vanishing line. Taylor's work was more general than the illustrations given above and was not restricted to horizontal and vertical planes.

Bibliography

Brook Taylor's Work on Linear Perspective: A Study of Taylor's Role in the History of Perspective Geometry. Kirsti Andersen. New York: Springer-Verlag, 1992.

Classics of Mathematics. Ronald Calinger, ed. Oak Park, Ill.: Moore, 1982.

Historical Topics for the Mathematics Classroom. John K. Baumgart et al., eds. Washington, D.C.: National Council for Teachers of Mathematics, 1969.

own with Johann I Bernoulli. Both Taylor and Bernoulli claimed credit for developing the Taylor series, for solving the problem of vibrating strings, and for discovering a procedure in the calculus called integration by parts. The conflict between Taylor and Bernoulli was aggravated by the fact that Taylor attributed the discovery of the calculus to Newton rather than to Bernoulli's friend Leibniz and, therefore, failed to cite Leibniz in any of his works.

Final Years

Taylor was very productive in the field of mathematics from 1712 to 1719. Although after that he published articles in art, religion, and philosophy, he published no further work in mathematics. It is not clear whether this drought was the result of the bitter disputes, of Taylor's poor health, or of losing two wives in childbirth—one in 1723 and one in 1730. Shortly after the death of his second wife, Brook Taylor himself died on December 29, 1731, survived by his only child, an infant daughter, Elizabeth.

Bibliography

By Taylor

Methodus incrementorum directa et inversa, 1715

Linear Perspective: Or, A New Method of Representing Justly All Manner of Objects as They Appear to the Eye in All Situations, 1715

"A New Method of Computing Logarithms," 1715

"De Seriebus infinitis Tractatus, a Method of Approximation in Extracting the Roots of an Equation," 1717

New Principles of Linear Perspective: Or, The Art of Designing on a Plane the Representations of All Sorts of Objects, . . . , 1719

About Taylor

Classics of Mathematics. Ronald Calinger, ed. Oak Park, Ill.: Moore, 1982.

The History of the Calculus and Its Conceptual Development. Carl B. Boyer. New York: Dover, 1959.

An Introduction to the History of Mathematics. Howard Eves. 5th ed. Philadelphia: W. B. Saunders, 1983.

(Jerry D. Taylor)

Valerie E. Taylor

Area of Achievement: Applied math

Contribution: A pioneering computer architect, Taylor applied mathematics to design high-speed computers.

May 24, 1963	Born in Chicago, Illinois
1981	Enters Purdue University
1982	Elected to the engineering honorary Tau Beta Pi
1983	Works for IBM's Disc Drive Department, Colorado
1984	Works as an electrical and instrumentation contact engineer at the Exxon refinery, Louisiana
1985	Earns a bachelor's degree in electrical engineering, Purdue
1985	Works in IBM's Software Assurance Department, Florida
1985	Begins graduate studies funded by an IBM fellowship and serves as a teaching assistant at Purdue
1986	Earns a master's in electrical engineering from Purdue
1987	Wins an award from the National Society of Black Engineers
1991	Completes a Ph.D. in electrical engineering and computer sciences at the University of California, Berkeley
1991	Accepts a computer science and engineering professorship at Northwestern University
1993	Wins the National Science Foundation's Young Investigator Award
1996	Featured in a PBS documentary about minority scientists

Early Life

Valerie Elaine Taylor was born on May 24, 1963. The daughter of Willie and Ollie Thompson Taylor, she grew up in Chicago, where her father owned an engineering company. Taylor credited her father with inspiring her to pursue a scientific career. She helped him with his work on weekends and decided that she wanted to be an engineer.

Taylor enrolled at Purdue University in 1981 and, although she was lonely as one of the few African Americans and women in her classes, she excelled in her studies, being elected to the engineering honorary Tau Beta Pi and serving as president of Purdue's student chapter from 1983 to 1984. She also was a campus and community leader, participating in programs to encourage minority students in high school and college to study science. Taylor led computer workshops to familiarize students with technology. During summers, Taylor worked for International Business Machines (IBM) and Exxon, gaining practical engineering experience.

She completed a bachelor's degree in electrical engineering in 1985 and began graduate work at Purdue, working on processor problems and presenting papers at conferences. In 1986, she earned a National Science Foundation Minority fellowship. Taylor joined the Institute of Electrical and Electronics Engineers and the National Society of Professional Engineers. She won a paper award from the National Society of Black Engineers in 1987.

Professional Development

After receiving her master's degree in electrical engineering from Purdue in 1986, Taylor moved to Oakland, California, to begin doctoral work at the University of California, Berkeley. By 1991, she finished her Ph.D. in electrical engineering and computer sciences, focusing on processors. In November, 1991, Taylor filed for a patent for a computer process that she designed for her dissertation. Patent #5,206,822, "Method and Apparatus for Optimized Processing of Sparse Matrices," was approved in 1993.

Although she had planned to work for industries, Taylor was persuaded to accept a professorship at Northwestern University, in

(Courtesy of Valerie E. Taylor)

Evanston, Illinois. One of her professors urged her to be a role model for African American students. At first, Taylor was unsure about an academic career, but then she realized how she wished she had been taught by black and female professors in college.

Career as a Professor

Taylor began teaching students and conducting research at Northwestern in 1991. The National Science Foundation awarded her grants and honored her with the Young Investigator Award in 1993. As an assistant professor of electrical and computer engineering, she focused on computer architecture, parallel processing, and hardware development and analysis for numerical computations. She and another faculty member directed the High Performance Computer Systems Laboratory, assisting graduate students with computer design problems.

Taylor's skills for computer architecture enabled her to design tools and computers for special uses and to enhance processing efficiency. The National Science Foundation awarded Taylor and a team of researchers a $100,000 grant to develop a high-speed supercomputer. Taylor's work improving the performance of computers processing parallel data resulted in her collaboration with the Urban Transportation Center at the University of Illinois at Chicago and the Mathematics and Computer Science Division at Argonne National Laboratory. Taylor also utilized virtual reality to simulate how molecules combine with body proteins, using three-dimensional computer models to assist pharmaceutical developments.

Work as a Mentor

Taylor served on faculty committees to address minority and women's issues on campus. She considered being a role model a serious responsibility. Taylor visited Chicago public schools to talk to children about her research, and she taught science and mathematics to residents of local housing projects. She wanted

Computer Architecture

Taylor applied mathematics to design parallel processing systems and high-speed computers to use for efficient problem resolution.

Computer architecture is the designing of computer systems to achieve specific purposes. Taylor developed methods for computer designers and programmers to use to improve and increase the performance of computers processing data. She specialized in parallel processing, designing computer programs to enable many computers to communicate and work together simultaneously on problems. By programming groups of computers to process information in tandem, problem resolution is achieved efficiently and effectively. The results then are applied to a variety of practical uses, such as urban transportation management.

When Taylor talked to students about her work, she used an easy example to explain the theory of parallel processing. She compared parallel processing to putting together a puzzle. Dividing the classroom into several groups, she gave each section a portion of the puzzle to piece together and then combine with other groups' sections to achieve a finished product. Sometimes, she gave another group a complete set of the same puzzle to demonstrate the time-saving benefits of dividing tasks between groups, comparing this to using many computers to tackle complex mathematical computations.

Parallel processing is essential in achieving high-speed computations. While in graduate school, Taylor developed a system to compress vast quantities of mathematical data into computer memory and then increase the performance of general processors by creating parallel processors to compute this information and

speed up results. Taylor then attempted to use similar techniques to develop an ultra-fast computer, called a petaflop, which would process information one thousand times faster than teraflop computers, which processed one trillion operations per second.

By using a hierarchical computer architecture, Taylor experimented with the placement of processors that transmitted information at varying speeds. Placing the fastest processors at the top, she connected them with slower-speed processors to create a cost-efficient design that enabled the processors to function together at high speeds.

Advances in computer architecture such as those developed by Taylor permitted the synchronization of high-performance computer networks to conduct parallel applications. Taylor's work in this specialty, designing computers to be quicker and more efficient, made possible technological procedures requiring intricate mathematical calculations and provided a technical design framework for future progress in computing.

Bibliography
Application Specific Processors. Earl E. Swartzlander, Jr., ed. Boston: Kluwer Academic, 1997.

Computer Architecture: A Designer's Text Based on a Generic RISC. James M. Feldman and Charles T. Retter. New York: McGraw-Hill, 1994.

Computer Architecture: Pipelined and Parallel Processor Design. Michael J. Flynn. Boston: Jones and Bartlett, 1995.

Encyclopedia of Computer Science. Anthony Ralston and Edwin D. Reilley, ed. 3d ed. New York: Van Nostrand Reinhold, 1993.

children to realize that they could succeed in any field that they wanted to, especially science. "I've gotten a lot from the community. Now I want to give back," Taylor explained, "to actually see a student have a spark and say, 'Yes, I can do that.'"

In April, 1996, PBS aired a program in its documentary series *BreakThrough: The Changing Face of Science in America* featuring Taylor and her parents visiting classrooms to talk about her experiences as a female, African American engineer. By the age of thirty-five, Taylor had achieved many professional goals and significantly influenced the designing of computers.

Bibliography
By Taylor
"Application-Specific Architectures for Large Finite Element Applications," 1991 (Ph.D. dissertation)

"Three-Dimensional Finite-Element Analyses: Implications for Computer Architectures" (with Abhiram Ranade and David G. Messerschmitt) in *Proceedings: Supercomputing '91*, 1991

"The Effects of Communication Overhead on the Speedup of Parallel 3-D Finite Element Applications" (with Bahram Nour-Omid and Messerschmitt) in *Proceedings of the Sixth International Parallel Processing Symposium*, 1992 (Victor K. Prasanna and Larry H. Canter, eds.)

"Sparse Matrix Computations: Implications for Cache Designs" in *Proceedings: Supercomputing '92*, 1992

"A Study of the Factorization Fill-in for a Parallel Implementation of the Finite Element Method," *International Journal for Numerical Methods in Engineering* 37, 1994 (with Nour-Omid)

"Modeling Processor Wait Time for 2-D Parallel Finite Element Applications" (with Michelle Hribar) in *Proceedings of the Mardi Gras 1994: Toward Teraflop Computing and New Grand Challenge Applications*, 1995 (Rajiv K. Kalin and Priya Vashishta, eds.)

"Practical Issues of 2-D Parallel Finite Element Analysis" (with Hribar) in *Proceedings of the 1994 International Conference on Parallel Processing*, 1994 (Jagdish Chandra, ed.)

"SPAR: A New Architecture for Large Finite Element Computations," *IEEE Transactions on Computers* 44, 1995 (with Ranade and Messerschmitt)

"Performance Models of Interactive, Immersive Visualization for Scientific Applications" (with Rick Stevens and Thomas Canfeld) in *Proceedings of the International Workshop on High Performance Computing for Computer Graphics and Visualisation*, 1996 (Min Chen, Peter Townsend, and John A. Vince, eds.)

"Balancing Load Versus Decreasing Communication: Exploring the Tradeoffs" (with B. K. Holmer, E. Schwabe, and Hribar) in *Proceedings of the Twenty-ninth Hawaii International Conference on System Sciences*, 1996

"Identifying and Reducing Critical Lag in Finite Element Simulations," *IEEE Computer Graphics and Applications* 16, 1996 (with Jian Chen, Milana Huang, Canfeld, and Stevens)

About Taylor
BreakThrough: Career Navigation Kit Activity Guide. Lauren Foley. Boston: Blackside, 1996.

BreakThrough: Teacher's Guide to the Series. Lauren Foley. Boston: Blackside, 1996.

"Taylor, Valerie Elaine." In *Outstanding Young Women of America*. Montgomery, Ala.: Junior Chamber of Commerce, 1987.

(Elizabeth D. Schafer)

Thales of Miletus

Areas of Achievement: Applied math, arithmetic, and geometry
Contribution: Thales was the first Western cosmologist to make practical discoveries by using applied mathematics.

c. 624 B.C.E.   Born in Miletus, Ionia, Asia Minor (now Turkey)

c. 548 B.C.E.   Dies in Miletus, Ionia, Asia Minor

Early Life

Precious little is known about the life and exploits of Thales (pronounced "THAY-leez"). Yet, what is known has served to immortalize him as a man of great vision and influence. There are no written works attributed to him, the central theme of Thales' teaching can be discovered in the writings of such great thinkers as Plato, Aristotle, Diogenes Laertius, and others.

Thales was born in the town of Miletus, which is located on the western end of modern-day Turkey. His national origin and culture were Greek, since Greek civilization had already predominated that region for more than four hundred years. That general area of western Turkey was called Ionia, and Thales was the founder of what came to be known as the Ionian School. In fact, after his death, Thales was proclaimed to be one of the Seven Great Wisemen of Greece.

The First Western Philosopher

According to all accounts Thales, is known as the first Western philosopher. More specifically, his philosophy comes under the heading of natural philosophy—that is, a philosophy of nature, or more properly, cosmology. Cosmology is a study that seeks to explain the order and workings of the universe in terms of scientific explorations that account for the structure and movement evident therein.

Although Thales was known as a philosopher, it must be noted that no clear distinction was made at this time between philosophy and science. The early philosophers were the first scientists. What is important, however, is that Thales was the turning point from explaining the forces of nature by an appeal to mythology and primitive deities to a systematic, rational approach in describing causal connections throughout the universe by means of mathematical formulations.

Unity Amid Diversity

It has often been stated that philosophy begins when one starts to wonder. At that critical point in development when humans are no longer satisfied merely to observe the world but rather probe, reflect, and critique, only then do people seek underlying answers to the mysteries of life and reality. It is precisely this probing attitude that brought Thales to speculate, for possibly the first time in Western civilization, on the underlying forces that propel all of nature.

The first question that confronted Thales is the so-called problem of the one and the many. Of all the various happenings and appearances that confront humans each day, is there one "stuff" or one material that underlies all the different qualitative manifestations exhibited by nature? Is the stuff in the acorn the same as the stuff in the oak tree from which it came? Is the stuff in the apple the same or different from the stuff in the human body when it metabolizes food?

The Source Is Water

Thales's answer to this vexing question was to state the following and most notable of all of his theories: All things are derived from and ultimately composed of water. Consequently, Thales theorized that all the changes evident in the universe are changes of quantity rather than quality. All things are exchanges of, by, and with water. For example, when water evaporates, it becomes air, wind, clouds, and rain, which, when it falls, comprises the vast oceans of the planet. When water freezes, it hardens to snow and ice, which under atmospheric conditions then become dirt, sand, glass, rock, and all other things.

Since Thales left no writings, one must rely exclusively on other sources to determine why he chose water as the unity amid all diversity. Aristotle claims that Thales reached this conclusion by observing simple events. Perhaps, thought Aristotle, Thales recognized the importance of moisture in the air to sustain all manner of living things. Water is an absolute prerequisite for the growth of plants as well as for the maintenance of animal and human existence. Furthermore, the seeds of plants, animals, and humans are viable only in moist conditions, and heat is generated in a moist atmosphere.

Probably the most significant legacy of Thales' theories is that he inspired all future philosophers to probe deeply into the question of the origin and ultimate reality of the universe.

Bibliography
By Thales
None of his works survive.

About Thales
Greek Philosophy, Thales to Plato. John Burnet. Reprint. London: Macmillan, 1932.

Mathematics as a Means for Discovery

Thales utilized mathematical skills in discovering practical advances in his quest to benefit society.

Being a learned and wise man, Thales directed his unique abilities toward benefiting the lives of his contemporaries by means of applying his vast mathematical skills to everyday situations.

According to many commentators, it is believed that Thales was the first person to propose the following axioms in geometry: that the base angles of an isosceles triangle are equal; that when two lines intersect one another the opposite angles at the point of intersection are equal (now known as vertical angles); that in any given circle a line drawn through its center (the diameter) necessarily bisects the circle into equal halves; and that two triangles are identical (congruent) when they both have a side equal to each other, with the adjacent angles of these respective sides equal in both triangles (now known as "a.s.a. = a.s.a.").

Probably the most significant episode in Thales' life occurred when he sailed to Egypt, which enabled him to come in contact with the rich tradition of Eastern science and mathematics. It was there that Thales devised a method for measuring the heights of the Great Pyramids, which until this point remained problematic to the Egyptians. Thales solved the problem by using the principle of proportionality. He measured the shadow of a person at the precise time of day when the shadow equaled the person's height. At the same time, the shadow of the pyramid was measured from tip to base in order to determine the exact height of each pyramid.

Another account of Thales' mathematical skill is said to have occurred when he predicted an eclipse of the sun on May 28, 585 B.C.E.; this solar eclipse was confirmed by the historian Herodotus, as well as by modern-day astronomy. The eclipse is reputed to have occurred during a war between Ionia's neighbors, the Lydeans, against the invading Persians. The prediction of this eclipse has been construed as having given the Lydeans a military advantage.

During this same war, Thales, acting as an adviser to King Croesus, enabled the king and his Lydean army to cross the impassable Halys River to gain a strategic military victory. He accomplished this by engineering a method to divert the river into two tributaries, at which time a bridge was constructed over the now-manageable river.

Bibliography
Greek Thought and the Origins of the Scientific Spirit. Leon Robin. London: K. Paul, Trench, Trubner, 1928.
A History of Greek Philosophy. W. K. C. Guthrie. Vol. 1. Cambridge, England: Cambridge University Press, 1962.
The Presocratic Philosophers: A Critical History with a Selection of Texts. Geoffrey Stephen Kirk and John Earle Raven. Cambridge, England: Cambridge University Press, 1957.

(Library of Congress)

A History of Philosophy. Frederick Charles Copleston. Vol. 1, part 1. New rev. ed. Garden City, N.Y.: Image Books, 1962.

"Thales." D. R. Dicks. *Classical Quarterly* 9, no. 2 (1960).

(*Joseph R. Lafaro*)

Evangelista Torricelli

Area of Achievement: Geometry
Contribution: Torricelli's work in geometry contributed to the development of integral calculus.

Oct. 15, 1608	Born in Faenza, Romagna (now Italy)
1624	Attends a Jesuit school in Faenza
1626	Becomes secretary to Benedetto Castelli, the head of the College at Sapienza in Rome
1632	Responds to a letter from Galileo to Castelli, introducing himself as a mathematician
1632-1640	Possibly serves as secretary to Monsignor Giovanni Ciampoli, a governor of several cities and a friend of Galileo
1641	Invited by Galileo to Arcetri to assist in developing additional days to his lecture
1642	Upon Galileo's death, appointed to the vacated post as mathematician to the grand duke of Tuscany
1643	Creates the first barometer
1644	Publishes his only work, the *Opera geometrica*
1646	Begins drafting a book on his role in the development of the geometry of the cycloid
Oct. 25, 1647	Dies in Florence, Tuscany (now Italy)

Early Life

Evangelista Torricelli (pronounced "tohr-ree-CHEHL-lee") was the eldest of three sons of Caterina Angetti and Gaspare Torricelli, a textile artisan. When he was a boy, his father sent him to study with an uncle, a Camaldolese monk named Jacopo. Torricelli was sent for further education to a school in Rome run by Benedetto Castelli, a mathematician, hydraulic engineer, and former pupil of Galileo. Taking a liking to Torricelli and recognizing his potential intellectual ability, Castelli engaged him as his secretary. Once when Castelli was away from Rome, Torricelli responded to a correspondence from Galileo, using the opportunity to introduce himself as a mathematician by profession.

In 1641, while in Rome, Torricelli asked Castelli his opinion on a treatise he had written that extended some of Galileo's work on motion. During his travels, Castelli submitted the treatise to Galileo and proposed that he engage Torricelli as an assistant. Galileo concurred and invited Torricelli to join him at Arcetri to draft additions to his lectures.

Torricelli took up residence at Galileo's home and remained there as a close friend until Galileo's death in 1641. Galileo's passing left open the post of mathematician and philosopher to which Grand Duke Ferdinando II of Tuscany appointed Torricelli.

Mathematical Work

Torricelli's early interest was in astronomy, but the condemning of Galileo's work by the Vatican in 1633 changed his direction. He was cautious of authority and unwilling to challenge the existing powers. Research occupied Torricelli's entire life, and, as a youth, he studied classic Greek geometry. At the end of the seventeenth century, more intuitive processes began to evolve with the works of Johannes Kepler, Bonaventura Cavalieri, Gilles Personne de Roberval, Pierre de Fermat, and René Descartes.

The new geometry of indivisibles developed by Cavalieri dealt with the concept of a plane as an infinite number of parallel lines. Every line was considered to be a rectangle of infinitesimal thickness. A plane would therefore be composed of an infinite number of infinitesimally small lines. Galileo named the infinitesimal lines the "indivisible," lines that became so small they could not become any smaller. Torricelli initially had a mistrust of this method but eventually used it in the development of new geometrical propositions.

Torricelli used a combination of both the in-

(Library of Congress)

divisibles and classical Greek geometrical methods in his only published work, *Opera geometrica* (1644). The first part contains a study of figures arising from the rotation of a regular polygon about a circle. The second volume discusses the motion of projectiles, and the third includes a study of various geometrical figures.

Torricelli's work came close to developing some of the principles of the calculus, including the concept of a maximum and minimum, the derivative, and the notion of the limit. Torricelli was considered one of the most promising mathematicians of his day, and, had his life not been cut short, he may have become the originator of the calculus.

Later Life

Torricelli remained in Florence until his death. These years are characterized as the happiest of his life, filled with scientific activity, research, lecturing, and writing. Although Torricelli is primarily known for his invention of the barometer, he also made contributions to mechanics, the motion of projectiles, the study of velocity and distance, military fortifications and architecture, the study of the centers of gravity of solid objects, and hydraulics. He also became known as a skilled lens grinder.

Torricelli became interested in the geometry of the cycloid (the figure resulting from the

Contribution to Geometry

Torricelli developed geometric principles that provided the basis for many calculus concepts, including the approximation of areas and the volumes of revolutions.

Torricelli extended the ideas of Bonaventura Cavalieri's "indivisibles" to curved surfaces and eventually solids. He demonstrated that the area of a figure can be described as the sum of many small intervals. Starting with a circle of radius r, a series of equal concentric circles are formed. Each concentric circle is then compared to equal and parallel "slats" on a triangle that has a base length equal to the circumference of the circle and an altitude equal to the radius.

The first slat of the triangle forms a trapezoid that has an area equal to "$A = \frac{1}{2}$ (the sum of the bases) $\times h$." Since "$h = r - r_1$," then

$$A = \tfrac{1}{2}(2\pi r + 2\pi r_1)(r - r_1)$$
$$= \pi(r + r_1)(r - r_1)$$
$$= \pi(r^2 - r_1^2)$$

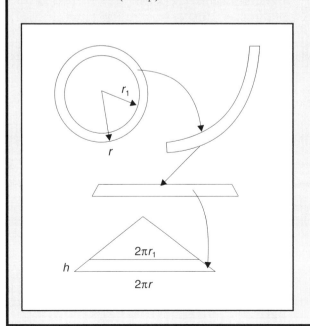

The area of the ring of the circle can be determined by subtracting the area of the inside circle of radius r_1 from the area of the entire circle of radius r, yielding "$A = \pi r^2 - \pi r_1^2$," which is exactly the same expression as derived from the area of the slat on the triangle. When all of the slats have been summed, they will equal the total area of the circle, which is πr^2. It can also be shown that the total area of the triangle is equal to "$\frac{1}{2}\ b \times h$," or "$\frac{1}{2}(2\pi r)r$." This is equivalent to πr^2, the area of the circle.

This same concept is then extended to include irregularly shaped curves, thereby determining their areas. The curves are similarly divided into curved slats, and the area of each is computed over the entire curved surface. When the number of slats are increased to infinity, the size of the slats becomes infinitesimally small, providing a closer and closer value to the actual area to be computed. In the calculus, the increasing of intervals in such a manner is the basis for the theory of the limit.

Torricelli also extended the idea to solids and demonstrated that a finite area can be computed for an infinite figure. He rotated a hyperbola about an axis and then divided the resulting solid into a series of cylindrical disks, which he called "barrels." The volume of each barrel could then be determined. By summing all the barrels contained in the solid, a value for the volume can be calculated.

Bibliography

History of Mathematics. David Eugene Smith. New York: Ginn, 1951.
"Torricelli's Correspondence on Ballistics." Michael Segre. *Annals of Science* 40, no. 5 (September, 1983).
"Torricelli's Infinitely Long Solid and Its Philosophical Reception in the Seventeenth Century." Paolo Mancosu and Ezio Vailati. *Isis* 82, no. 311 (March, 1991).

plot of a point on the circumference of a rotating circle) about the same time as did the mathematician Roberval. When Torricelli published his findings, he did not mention that Roberval had previously arrived at the same results and left them unpublished. Roberval accused Torricelli of plagiarism, and many subsequent letters were exchanged between the two mathematicians on the subject. Torricelli was in the process of publishing the letters in defense of his work at the time of his death.

Torricelli died at the young age of thirty-nine of a sudden and violent illness. Although undocumented, it is suspected that his death was a result of typhoid fever. As he instructed, he was buried in the Church of San Lorenzo in Florence; the location of his tomb remains unknown.

Bibliography
By Torricelli
Opera geometrica, 1644

About Torricelli
"Evangelista Torricelli." Jerzy Neyman and Niccolo Zucchi. In *Dictionary of Scientific Biography*. New York: Charles Scribner's Sons, 1991.
"Evangelista Torricelli." P. Robertson. *Mathematical Gazette* 78 (1994): 37-47.
General Survey of the History of Elementary Mathematics. David Eugene Smith. Vol. 1 in *History of Mathematics*. New York: Ginn, 1951.

(William M. and Corinne G. Casolara)

Alan Mathison Turing

Area of Achievement: Mathematical logic
Contribution: Turing established the impossibility of devising a mechanical procedure that could determine the truth or falsity of mathematical statements.

June 23, 1912	Born in London, England
1931	Enters King's College, Cambridge University
1935	Elected a Fellow of King's College
1936	Begins a two-year leave of absence to collaborate at Princeton University with Alonzo Church
1937	Publishes his first mathematical paper, "On Computable Numbers, with an Application to the *Entscheidungsproblem*"
1938	Receives a Ph.D. in mathematics from Princeton
1939	Begins work in cryptography at the British Foreign Office
1948	Appointed to the faculty of the University of Manchester
1950	Proposes a criterion for the identification of artificial intelligence
1951	Elected a Fellow of the Royal Society of London
1952	Publishes "The Chemical Basis of Morphogenesis"
June 7, 1954	Dies in Wimslow, Cheshire, England

Early Life
Alan Mathison Turing was the son of Julian Mathias Turing, an official in the Indian Civil Service, and Ethel Sara Stoney. Unwilling to subject their son to the rigors of life in India, the Turings arranged for Alan to lodge with a

(Smithsonian Institution)

retired military officer and his wife, although they frequently returned to England to spend time with Alan and his brother, John. Alan Turing was admitted to a private day school in 1918 and to boarding school in 1922. He entered Cambridge University in 1931 and was elected a Fellow of King's College after submitting a dissertation.

The Decidability Problem
Mathematical logic was in crisis at the beginning of the twentieth century. Set theory had suggested that all mathematical relationships could be expressed as membership in sets and relations between sets. This idea was threatened by the discovery of serious paradoxes inherent in the concept of membership. As British logician Bertrand Russell had pointed out, a set, such as the set of all infinite sets, could belong to itself, but the set of all sets not belonging to themselves could neither be said to belong to itself nor be said not to belong to itself.

One response to the crisis was to try to establish mathematical notions on the basis of state-ments in symbolic form. In this form, all the true mathematical statements could be derived by manipulating symbols according to explicit rules. Proving that this was so constituted the *Entscheidungsproblem*, or decidability problem, posed by the great German mathematician David Hilbert.

Turing published a paper on computable numbers in which he described an idealized machine, now called a Turing machine, the forerunner of the digital computer, that could execute computations. This would make it possible to equate a statement about whole numbers having particular properties to a claim that a certain machine would finish computing given a certain string of symbols as input. Turing showed that no machine could be built that would always accept a string of symbols describing the machine in question and its input string and then compute whether the other machine would halt, thus deciding the issue.

The War Years and After
Following a stay at Princeton University collaborating with Alonzo Church, Turing resumed his fellowship at King's College. He was soon hired, along with many other academics, by the British Foreign Office to break the secret codes used by Germany for military communications during World War II. These codes were based on a sort of computing machine called the "Enigma." Turing and his colleagues are credited with cracking several versions of the code, thus giving Britain and its allies a vital military advantage.

Following the German surrender, Turing decided not to return to the comfortable academic existence at King's College. Instead, he accepted the offer of a position at the University of Manchester, where one of the first electronic computers was being built. In 1950, he published an article in the philosophical journal *Mind* in which he proposed what has come to be known as the Turing Test for Artificial Intelligence. In simplified terms, Turing proposed that a machine be credited with artificial intelligence if a human, allowed to ask questions to both a machine and another human by appropriate means, could not tell which set of responses came from the machine.

Turing's last major contribution to applied mathematics was his paper "The Chemical Basis of Morphogenesis" (1952). Turing showed how an instability in the equations describing the exchange of substances between cells in an embryo could produce different concentrations of the substances in each cell, providing a basis for cell differentiation.

Turing's last years were not happy. He was openly homosexual and was convicted of committing "unnatural acts" with another man. He agreed to undergo chemical therapy to alter his behavior. Turing died of poisoning in 1954. Although the death was ruled a suicide, he left no indication of intent to kill himself. He was performing experiments to test his morphogenesis

Defining Computability

Turing provided a precise definition for the notion of computability and used it to show that there are numbers that cannot be obtained by computation.

A mathematical result is considered computable if it can be obtained from the statement of a problem in symbols, through manipulation of those symbols according to a prescribed sequence of operations. To make this notion more precise, Turing envisioned an idealized machine, something like a tape recorder, in which an essentially infinite tape, carrying symbols, was read one symbol at a time. The machine would contain a single register, or memory, that would remember one number from one step to the next. Depending on the number in the register, it would replace the old tape symbol with a new one, change the number in the register, and then move the tape one space to the right or left.

The claim that any computation a mathematician might be called on to perform could be ac-

complished by a machine of this type has come to be known as the Turing-Church thesis. A number is computable if it can appear as the output of a Turing machine—that is, as a string of digits written on the tape. Any number that can be written in a finite number of digits is computable. So are all rational numbers and some irrational numbers such as the square root of 2 or the geometer's π (= 3.14159 . . .), for which a procedure could be given to generate the successive digits.

Turing showed that for the vast majority of irrational numbers, no such procedure could exist. His argument was based on the fact that all the instructions that constituted a given machine could be encoded in a single symbol string, which could also be read as a number. One could list, in order, all the possible Turing machines and thus all the computable numbers. It would then be easy to construct a number that differed in the first decimal place from the first number on the list, in the second place from the second number, and so on, and thus would not be on the list and therefore not computable.

Bibliography

The Emperor's New Mind: Concerning Computers, Minds, and the Laws of Physics. Roger Penrose. New York: Oxford University Press, 1989.

Feynman Lectures on Computation. Richard P. Feynman. Edited by Anthony J. G. Hey and Robin W. Allen. Reading, Mass.: Addison-Wesley, 1996.

The (New) Turing Omnibus: Sixty-six Excursions in Computer Science. A. K. Dewdney. New York: Computer Science Press, 1993.

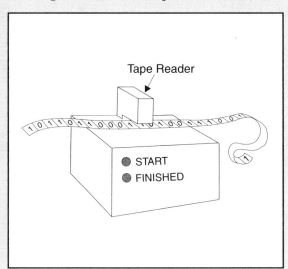

Tape Reader

START
FINISHED

theory and could have poisoned himself accidentally.

Bibliography

By Turing

On the Gaussian Error Function, 1935 (dissertation)

"Computability and λ-Definability," *Journal of Symbolic Logic* 2, 1937

"On Computable Numbers, with an Application to the *Entscheidungsproblem*," *Proceedings of the London Mathematical Society* 42, 1937

"Systems of Logic Based on Ordinals," *Proceedings of the London Mathematical Society* 45, 1939

"Computing Machinery and Intelligence," *Mind* 59, 1950

"The Chemical Basis of Morphogenesis," *Philosophical Transactions of the Royal Society of London* 227, 1952

About Turing

Alan M. Turing. Sara Turing. Cambridge, England: Heffers, 1959.

"Alan Mathison Turing." M. H. A. Newman. In *Biographical Memoirs of Fellows of the Royal Society 1955*. London: Burlington House, 1955.

Alan Turing: The Enigma. Andrew Hodges. New York: Simon & Schuster, 1983

(Donald R. Franceschetti)

Stanislaw Ulam

Areas of Achievement: Applied math, probability, set theory, and topology

Contribution: Ulam helped establish new branches of graph theory, probability, and biomathematics. He employed the Monte Carlo method to simulate the fission process in the hydrogen bomb using the first computer.

Apr. 13, 1909	Born in Lwów, Poland, Austrian Empire (now Lvov, Ukraine)
1914-1918	His family takes refuge in Vienna when Russian troops invade
1927	Enters the Polytechnic Institute
1929	Publishes his first research paper
1932-1934	Attends the International Mathematical Congress in Zurich and earns an M.A. and a D.Sc. from the Polytechnic Institute
1935	Joins the Institute for Advanced Study, Princeton, New Jersey
1936-1939	Joins the Society of Fellows at Harvard University
1939-1940	Works as a lecturer at Harvard
1940	Joins the University of Wisconsin
1941	Becomes a U.S. citizen
1944	Joins the Los Alamos National Laboratory to work on secret military projects
1945	Becomes an associate professor at the University of Southern California (USC)
1946	Returns to Los Alamos, remaining there until 1967
1965	Begins a professorship at the University of Colorado
May 13, 1984	Dies in Santa Fe, New Mexico

Early Life

Stanislaw Marcin Ulam (pronounced "EW-lawm") was born on April 13, 1909, in Lwów, Poland. At the time of his birth, the city was the capital of Galicia Province in the Austrian Empire; it is now Lvov, Ukraine. His father, Jozef Ulam, was an officer in the Austrian army and had to travel frequently. His mother, Anna, was from the relatively rich Auerbach family. Except for a little schooling, Stanislaw, until age ten, received his education through tutors and his parents and by reading books himself. His father taught him the game of chess.

In 1919, Ulam entered the Gymnasium, the equivalent of secondary school, and underwent eight years of thorough educational training. He was healthy except for one eye, which had been myopic (nearsighted) since childhood; the other eye became presbyopic (unable to focus on near objects) later in life. Except for penmanship and drawing, he was an A student. In 1927, he passed the matriculation examination of the Gymnasium and was at-

(Los Alamos National Laboratory)

tracted to university positions, which were rare and hard to obtain for people with Jewish backgrounds such as Ulam. He wanted to study mathematics, but electrical engineering seemed the second best choice for his future career.

Life at the Polytechnic Institute

Ulam entered the Polytechnic Institute in the fall of 1927 to become an electrical engineer. In his set theory class, the teacher, Kazimir Kuratowski, quickly spotted Ulam as a well-prepared student who could converse about groups, rings, ideals, and measures. In the spring semester of 1928, Kuratowski suggested to Ulam a set theory problem connected with the Bernstein theorem. Ulam solved it by devising a method in which decomposition of sets and corresponding transformations are represented by graphs. His solution, which appeared in *Fundamenta Mathematicae* in 1929, opened new avenues of graph theory and boosted Ulam's self-confidence.

It was a second problem, on the existence of subtractive set functions, that put his career at stake: If Ulam could solve it, he would continue as a mathematician; otherwise, he would change to electrical engineering. Using transfinite induction, this problem was also solved, and, by the end of his freshman year, Ulam had two research papers to his credit.

Ulam, a third-year student, began to participate in conversations and to produce papers in collaboration with Stanislaw Mazur, a well-read young assistant, and with Stefan Banach, a thorough pure mathematician of broad knowledge. They enriched the fields of set theory, the theory of functions of real variables, functional analysis, and the theory of infinite series of numbers. The degree of D.Sc. was awarded to Ulam in 1933.

Life in the United States

In 1935, John von Neumann, the youngest and best-known professor at the Institute for Advanced Study in Princeton, New Jersey, invited Ulam to spend a few months there, offering him a stipend of $300. Ulam sailed to America in December, 1935, and joined the institute, but he soon moved to Harvard University, where he spent his next four years.

The last time that Ulam visited his parents was in the summer of 1939. He departed Poland with his younger brother Adam, leaving behind his father, uncle, and other family members to suffer the atrocities of World War II.

In Madison, Wisconsin, Ulam married Françoise Aron, a French exchange student at Mount Holyoke College. In 1941, he became a U.S. citizen and wished to volunteer his services to the U.S. Air Force but was turned down because of his eyesight. In 1944, Ulam joined the group of scientists at the Los Alamos National Laboratory who were engaged in making the hydrogen bomb, as a pure mathematician, and spent, on and off, about twenty-three years with them. Ulam moved to Los Angeles as an associate professor at the University of Southern California (USC) in the fall of 1945. In January, 1946, he underwent brain surgery to relieve severe pressure, resulting from encephalitis, that caused him headaches and affected his speech. He then returned to Los Alamos. Ulam joined the University of Colorado in 1965 and stayed there for the rest of his life.

Ulam was elected a Fellow of the American Academy of Arts and Sciences and a member of the National Academy of Sciences, the American Philosophical Society, the Polish Mathematical Society, the American Mathematical Society, the American Physical Society, and the American Association for the Advancement of Science. He served as a consultant to President John F. Kennedy's Science Advisory Committee. He held honorary degrees from the Universities of New Mexico, Pittsburgh, and Wisconsin and was recipient of the Sierpinski Medal, the Heritage Award, and the Polish Millennium Prize. Ulam had a charming and charismatic personality. He died in Santa Fe, New Mexico, on May 13, 1984.

Bibliography

By Ulam

"Remark on the Generalized Bernstein's Theorem," *Fundamenta Mathematicae* 13, 1929

"Concerning Functions of Sets," *Fundamenta Mathematicae* 14, 1929

"On the Existence of a Measure Invariant Under a Transformation" *Annals of Mathematics*, 2d ser. 40, 1939 (with J. C. Oxtoby)

"Stefan Banach, 1892-1945," *Bulletin of the American Mathematical Society* 52, 1946

"Homage to Fermi," *Santa Fe New Mexican*, 1955

The Scottish Book: A Collection of Problems, 1957 (translated from a notebook kept at the Scottish Café for use by the Lwów section of the Polish Mathematical Society)

"John Von Neumann, 1903-1957." *Bulletin of the American Mathematical Society* 64, 1958

A Collection of Mathematical Problems, 1960

Mathematics and Logic: Retrospective Prospects, 1968 (with Mark Kac)

Sets, Numbers, and Universes: Selected Works, 1974 (W. A. Beyer, J. Mycielski, and Gian-Carlo Rota, eds.)

Adventures of a Mathematician, 1976

"Kazimierz Kuratowski, 1896-1980," *Polish Review* 26, 1981

About Ulam

"Iteration of Maps, Strange Attractors, and Number Therory—An Ulamian Potpourri." Paul R. Stein. *Los Alamos Science* 15 (1987): 91-106.

A Wide-Ranging Talent in Mathematics

Ulam helped build the foundations for several new branches of mathematics, including graph theory, probability, and biomathematics.

From the last quarter of the nineteenth century through the first quarter of the twentieth century, many mathematical structures were being created and several new mathematical branches were being started. The ideas of measure theory, transformations, space, and dimensionalities were generalized and applied to these new branches. The Polish school of mathematics in this period examined and contributed to a growth in topology, functional analysis, probability, measure theory, and new geometries. Ulam was one of the brilliant products of this school. He was a student of Stefan Banach, the creator of Banach algebras, and Kazimir Kuratowski, the set theorist.

In collaboration with Stanislaw Mazur, Banach, and others at Lwów and, using set theoretical and axiomatic schemes, Ulam examined and generalized the notions of space, points in Euclidean space, functions of real variables, spaces of functions, measure, continuity, and probability. Ulam's active collaboration with Mazur resulted in finding the proof of the theorem that in infinitely dimensional vector space, a distance preserving transformation is linear. Some of the results obtained by Ulam in measure theory, by solving certain set theoretical problems of Felix Hausdorff, Banach, Kuratowski, and others, are well known and have become as significant as the works of Kurt Gödel and Paul J.

Cohen. Ulam's work with semigroups is part of the mathematical literature.

In his second paper, Ulam established a maximum prime ideal for subsets in the infinite set by showing the possibility of defining a special measure. After a year, Alfred Tarski, an internationally known logician, published the same result in a long paper, unaware of Ulam's theorem. Tarski later acknowledged it in a footnote.

In the later part of his life, Ulam, a well-read scholar, had traversed the branches of biomathematics and life sciences and proved fundamental results. Under his tutelage, physicists such as Paul Skein were converted to mathematicians. Together, Ulam and Skein studied the evolution of large populations under the assumption of random mating. The mathematical results well justify the evolutionary theories. Ulam's work on the Monte Carlo method is of great importance to scientists working on the simulation of statistical problems.

Bibliography

"Measure-Preserving Homeomorphisms and Metrical Transitivity." Stanislaw Ulam and J. C. Oxtoby. *Annals of Mathematics*, 2d ser. 42 (1941): 874-920.

"The Monte Carlo Method." Stanislaw Ulam and Nicholas Metropolis. *Journal of the American Statistical Association* 44 (1949): 335-341.

"Some Ideas and Prospects in Biomathematics." Stanislaw Ulam. *Annual Review of Biophysics and Bioengineering* 1 (1972): 277-291.

"The Lost Café." Gian-Carlo Rota. *Los Alamos Science* 15 (1987): 23-32.
"Stan Ulam, John Von Neumann, and the Monte Carlo Method." Roger Eckhardt. *Los Alamos Science* 15 (1987): 131-143.

(Lakshmi N. Nigam)

John Venn

Areas of Achievement: Mathematical logic and probability

Contribution: Venn refined the use of geometrical figures to provide a visual representation for interpreting propositions of logic. These figures have become known as Venn diagrams.

Aug. 4, 1834	Born in Hull, Humberside, England
1853	Enters Gonville and Caius College, Cambridge University
1857	Receives a degree in mathematics from Gonville and Caius College and is elected a Fellow of the college
1859	Ordained a priest for the Church of England
1862	Returns to Cambridge as a lecturer in moral science
1866	Publishes *The Logic of Chance*
1881	Publishes *Symbolic Logic*
1883	Receives a Doctor of Science (Sc.D.) degree from Cambridge and is elected a Fellow of the Royal Society of London
1889	Publishes *The Principles of Empirical or Inductive Logic*
1897	Writes *The Biographical History of Gonville and Caius College, 1349-1897*
1903	Becomes the president of Gonville and Caius College
1922	Publishes the first volume of the history of Cambridge University with his son
Apr. 4, 1923	Dies in Cambridge, England

Early Life

John Venn was born in Drypool, Hull, in 1834 into a family with an evangelical background. His father was the Reverend Henry Venn, rector of the parish. His grandfather was the Reverend John Venn, rector of Clapham, a London suburb, and his great-grandfather was the Reverend Henry Venn, vicar of Huddersfield. Continuing in the family tradition, he studied to prepare himself for holy orders.

Venn entered Gonville and Caius College of Cambridge University in 1853, the eighth generation of his family to be admitted to, and subsequently to be graduated from, Cambridge or a sister university. In 1857, he received his degree in mathematics. The same year, he was elected a Fellow of his college, holding this membership until his death.

He was ordained a priest and was a curate at Cheshunt, Hertfordshire, and at Mortlake, Surrey. In 1862, Venn returned to Cambridge to study and lecture in moral sciences. His studies at this time led to his significant work in logic and probability theory.

Because of disagreements with the Church of England's orthodox dogma, he later resigned his clerical orders, but he remained a devout lay member of the church.

Mathematical Work

Venn's first published book was *The Logic of Chance* (1866). He redefined the classical definition of probability developed in the eighteenth century by Abraham de Moivre and critically discussed the work of fellow Britons Augustus De Morgan and George Boole.

Venn next focused his attention on the development of the symbolic language of logic. He studied the work of Gottfried Wilhelm Leibniz, Leonhard Euler, and Boole, and he clarified many inconsistencies. His lectures and published articles became the basis of his next book, *Symbolic Logic* (1881). In this work, he refined the use of geometric figures to provide a visual representation for interpreting propositions of logic. These figures have become known as Venn diagrams and are his chief contribution to logic.

In 1883, Venn received the Doctor of Science (Sc.D.) degree from Cambridge and was elected a Fellow of the prestigious Royal Society of London. His last book on logic, *The Principles of Empirical or Inductive Logic*, was published in 1889. All three of Venn's books became standard textbooks for students of logic. He edited and reprinted each one himself.

While studying logic, Venn collected scholarly books on the subject. He was unable to find many of the books he wanted in the libraries of England, so he purchased what he could from booksellers in London and made trips abroad to locate additional titles. His personal library on the subject of logic grew to more than one thousand volumes. Venn donated his collection to the Cambridge University Library, where it is held today in the rare books department.

Historical Work

Later in his life, Venn became interested in historical records. He published a three-volume work, the *Biographical History of Gonville and Caius College, 1349-1897* (1897). Together with his son, John Archibald Venn, he wrote the first two volumes of the history of Cambridge University, *Alumni Cantabrigienses* (1922). In addition to these works, he researched the Venn family history, the biography of John Caius,

Venn Diagrams

Venn diagrams are used in the study of set theory and logic. They provide a visual representation of the basic concepts of sets and propositions of logic through the use of interlocking circles with shading.

Without looking at the accompanying diagrams, consider the following definitions of three basic concepts of sets.

Let A and B be any sets. Then,

1. Set A is a subset of set B (written A ⊆ B) if every element of A is also an element of B.

2. The intersection of sets A and B (written A ∩ B) is the set of elements common to both A and B.

3. The union of sets A and B (written A ∪ B) is the set of all elements belonging to either of the sets.

Reading each definition again while looking at the corresponding Venn diagram in figure 1 should make the meaning of these concepts clearer.

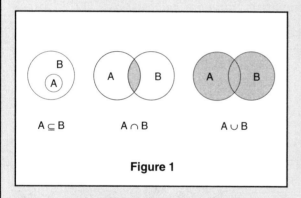

Figure 1

When one set is used in a Venn diagram, the plane is divided into two compartments. When two interlocking sets are drawn in a Venn diagram, the plane is divided into four compartments. Similarly, when three interlocking sets are drawn in a Venn diagram, they must be drawn so that each successive circle, or figure that represents a set, must intersect all the compartments already produced. Such a diagram divides the plane into eight compartments, and the diagram illustrating four sets divides the plane into sixteen compartments. Examples of the figures that Venn introduced are found in chapter 5 of his

book *Symbolic Logic* (1881). He found it necessary to use ovals instead of circles when representing four sets. The diagram for five sets is rather complicated, and thus he believed that the diagrams are no longer beneficial at this point.

Venn used his diagrams to illustrate propositions of logic. The formal idea of the null set, or empty set, was not accepted at this time, so he introduced shading to denote compartments that were unoccupied. Figure 2 is his representation of the following categorical syllogism:

No Y is Z.
All X is Y.
Therefore, no X is Z.

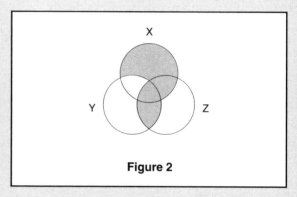

Figure 2

The logician Charles Lutwidge Dodgson (better known by his pen name, Lewis Carroll) wrote many interesting and humorous categorical syllogisms. He used his own style of diagrams, but it is Venn's diagrams that have become more popular. Even young students can be introduced to set concepts and logical thinking with Venn diagrams.

Bibliography
Fundamentals of Symbolic Logic. Alice Ambrose and Morris Lazerowitz. Rev. ed. New York: Holt, Rinehart and Winston, 1962.
Lewis Carroll's Symbolic Logic. Lewis Carroll. Edited by William Warren Bartley III. New York: Clarkson N. Potter, 1977.
Mathematical Ideas. 8th ed. Charles D. Miller, Vern E. Heeren, and E. John Hornsby, Jr. Reading, Mass.: Addison-Wesley, 1997.

and additional history associated with Cambridge University.

Venn's association with Gonville and Caius College lasted for seventy years. At the time of his death in 1923, he was its president. In remembrance of his life and work, a stained glass window in Caius Hall at Cambridge depicts a Venn diagram of three intersecting sets.

Bibliography
By Venn
The Logic of Chance: An Essay on the Foundations and Province of the Theory of Probability, 1866

"On the Diagrammatic and Mechanical Representation of Propositions and Reasonings," *The London, Edinburgh, and Dublin Philosophical Magazine and Journal of Science* 9, 1880

Symbolic Logic, 1881

The Principles of Empirical or Inductive Logic, 1889

The Biographical History of Gonville and Caius College, 1349-1897, 1897 (3 vols.)

Alumni Cantabrigienses, 1922 (vols. 1 and 2; with John Archibald Venn)

About Venn
"John Venn." T. A. A. Broadbent. In *Dictionary of Scientific Biography*, edited by Charles Coulston Gillispie. Vol. 13. New York: Charles Scribner's Sons, 1976.

"John Venn—1834-1923." In *Proceedings of the Royal Society of London* A110. London: Royal Society, 1926.

"John Venn (1834-1923)." John Archibald Venn. In *Dictionary of National Biography 1922-1930*, edited by J. R. H. Weaver. London: Oxford University Press, 1937.

"A Note on Venn, John, as a Collector and Bibliographer of Works on Logic." T. Boswell. *History and Philosophy of Logic* 16, no. 1 (1995).

(Mary Kathleen Simons)

François Viète

Areas of Achievement: Algebra and trigonometry

Contribution: Viète continued the development of algebra begun by Italian mathematicians, adding new techniques of solution of equations using trigonometry and a significant improvement in notation.

1540	Born in Fontenay-le-Comte, Poitou (now Vendée), France
1560	Receives a law degree from the University of Poitiers, France
1564	Becomes a tutor to Catherine de Parthenay
1571	Publishes his first mathematical work, a text on trigonometry
1573	Appointed counselor of the Parlement of Brittany
1584	Banished from the royal court in Paris by his enemies
1584-1589	Takes advantage of the enforced leisure to study mathematics
1589	Recalled to service under Henri III to crack Spanish codes
1600	Attacks the Copernican theory
1602	Attacks the Gregorian calendar reforms
Feb. 23, 1603	Dies in Paris, France

Early Life

François Viète (pronounced "vyeht"), also known by his Latin name Franciscus Vieta, was born in Fontenay-le-Comte, near the west coast of France, in 1540. His father was a lawyer, and his mother came from a prominent bourgeois family. Schooled locally, Viète advanced to the University of Poitiers, earning a law degree in 1560.

Diplomatic Career

Serving the wealthy and powerful Catherine of Parthenay as her legal adviser and tutor, Viète accompanied her to Paris in 1570, where he caught the attention of King Charles IX. In 1573, Charles appointed him counselor to the Parlement of Brittany, a judicial body in Rennes. Promotion to the office of *maître des requêtes* in 1580 took Viète back to Paris as the parlement's agent. There, he deftly negotiated a settlement between two fueding noble families; lingering enmities, however, precipitated his banishment from Paris in 1584. While in exile, he began advising and serving Charles's successor, Henri III, notably by decoding messages sent by the Spanish, with whom the French were at war. His success provoked the Spanish king to accuse Viète of sorcery. The codes were actually such simple ciphers that they hardly challenged the mathematically adept Viète.

When Henri III was killed in 1589, the new king, Henri IV, refused Viète's plea to retire, ultimately elevating him to privy counselor in 1594. Seriously ill, Viète was allowed to return to Fontenay-le-Comte but continued to handle delicate negotiations for the king up to his retirement in 1602. Viète died on February 23, 1603.

Time for Mathematics

During his politically active life, only twice was Viète able to devote himself at length to his beloved mathematics. From 1564 to 1568, while tutoring his patron Catherine, Viète undertook astronomical analyses, hoping to buttress the earth-centered Ptolemaic system against the new sun-centered Copernican theory. From these studies came most of his mathematical innovations. The second extended period of mathematical study was from 1584 to 1589, during his banishment from Paris, when he was able to develop the algebraic and trigonometric work that was his greatest contribution.

For the rest of his busy life, Viète could only snatch opportunities for his studies. In 1593, for example, after the Dutch ambassador sneered that no French mathematician could solve a problem posed by Adrian Romanus, Henri IV called for Viète. Viète looked at the problem for a few moments, gave one solution, and the next day returned with twenty-two more. The problem reduced to finding the roots of a polynomial equation of degree 45, and Viète had discerned in the equation's pattern an underlying trigonometric formula. When the delighted Romanus was shown Viète's solutions, he insisted on traveling to Fontenay to meet him. They became good friends and corresponded about mathematics for years.

Prized by sovereigns for the niceties of his diplomacy, and adroit in handling delicate affairs, Viète unleashed his passion and fervor in matters mathematical. For example, after his studies exposed errors in the Copernican system, he wrote a strongly worded attack on it. (The Ptolemaic inaccuracies that he found, he neatly mended.) He also strongly opposed the Gregorian calendar reform of 1582, probably because it was contrary to some suggestions of his own. A committee of scientists and clergymen appointed by Pope Gregory VIII decided to omit the days between October 4 and October 15 of that year, in order to correct the accumulated errors of centuries of the Julian calendar. Incensed and unreconciled, as late as 1600 Viète published a bitter attack on the astronomer who had proposed the change.

Viète's most lasting work was in algebra. He proposed denoting unknown quantities by

Algebra and Trigonometry

Viète broke new ground in the use of trigonometry to solve algebraic equations and also advanced the use of symbolic notation.

Modern readers of mathematical work done prior to 1600 are usually most struck by the lack of symbolic notation for algebraic computations. Like those who came before him, Viète often stated his results in words. He began, however, to use single letters, such as *A* and *B*, to represent unknown quantities. To distinguish between numbers ("roots"), areas ("planes") and volumes ("solids"), he writes, for example, the "square on *A*," or *A quadratum*, for an area. For example, he states: "The product of the difference of two roots and their sum is equal to the difference between their squares." He then explains with symbols: "Let the greater root be *A*, the smaller *B*. Multiply *A* − *B* by *A* + *B* and collect the individual planes [terms]. They will be *A quadratum* − *B quadratum*." The advantages of this system of abbreviation become obvious as he discusses equations of the third and higher degrees.

The idea of using numbers to represent powers was established in *L'Algebra* by Rafael Bombelli, published in Bologna, Italy, in 1572. Combined with Viète's use of letters improved slightly by others, the resulting notational system was championed by René Descartes and soon drove out all others.

The mathematical content of Viète's work grew from his study of astronomy, which led him to connect trigonometry and the solution of algebraic equations in fruitful ways. His solutions to cubic equations were in the spirit of the original solutions of Gerolamo Cardano but took advantage of his improved notation. Some cases of Cardano's solutions lead to extraordinarily complicated expressions involving cube roots and square roots, despite having as an actual solution a simple number such as 2. Viète used angular section analysis to simplify such equations before solving. For example, to simplify "*A cubum* − *3B quadratum A* equals *B quadratum D*"—that is, "$x^3 - 3b^2 x = b^2 d$"—he used a geometric version of the identity "$\cos\theta = 4\cos^3\theta - 3\cos\theta$."

Viète's work also included excellent tables of trigonometric values, useful in astronomy as well as in calculating the roots of equations after his identities were applied.

Bibliography
The Analytic Art: Nine Studies in Algebra, Geometry and Trigonometry. François Viète. Translated by T. Richard Witmer. Kent, Ohio: Kent State University Press, 1983.

A History of Mathematical Notation: Notations in Elementary Mathematics. Florian Cajori. Chicago: Open Court, 1928.

A History of Mathematics: An Introduction. Victor J. Katz. New York: HarperCollins College, 1993.

(North Wind Picture Archives)

vowels and known quantities by consonants. Following René Descartes's modification, unknowns are now commonly denote by x, y, and z and known quantities by a, b, c, d, and so on.

Viète's notation was a crucial step toward the modern power and economy of algebra. Oddly, Viète did not take the next step of effectively abbreviating powers of the quantities, still writing A quadratum or A quad. for A^2, for example.

Although no longer read today, Viète's books on the solution of equations and on trigonometry were studied carefully by Descartes and Sir Isaac Newton, thereby contributing to the development of modern mathematics.

Bibliography
By Viète
Canon mathematicus, seu ad triangula cum appendicibus, 1571

In artem analyticem isagoge, 1591 (The Analytic Art, 1983)

Supplementum geometriae, 1593

De aequationum recognitione et emendatione tractus duo, 1615

About Viète
"Viète, François." H. L. L. Busard. In Dictionary of Scientific Biography, edited by Charles Coulston Gillispie. Charles Scribner's Sons, New York, 1971.

(Daniel J. Curtin)

Vito Volterra

Areas of Achievement: Applied math and calculus

Contribution: Volterra developed the idea of functionals in differential calculus, made important contributions to integral calculus, and pioneered several mathematical applications.

May 3, 1860	Born in Ancona, Papal States (now Italy)
1878	Enters the University of Pisa
1881	Writes his first original papers on mathematics
1882	Graduated with a doctorate in physics from Pisa
1883	Becomes a professor of mechanics at Pisa
1887	Publishes his first paper on functionals
1892	Becomes a professor of mechanics at the University of Turin
1896	Publishes a series of important papers on a technique of integral calculus
1900	Accepts the Chair of Mathematical Physics in Rome
1905	Becomes a senator of the Kingdom of Italy
1909	Applies his integro-differential equations to the study of elastic materials
1926	Publishes the first of his papers on mathematical biology
1931	Refuses to take an oath of allegiance to Italy's Fascist government
1932	Moves abroad
Oct. 11, 1940	Dies in Rome, Italy

Early Life

Vito Volterra (pronounced "vahl-TEHR-raw") was the only child of Angelica and Abramo Volterra. When his father died when Vito was two years old, his mother moved in with her brother, Alfonso Almagià, a bank employee in Florence. Alfonso treated Vito well, but the family was always poor.

Vito's interest in mathematics and science became apparent early. At fourteen, he learned differential calculus from a textbook, then integral calculus without a book. His family wanted him to learn a trade, but a relative recognized his interest and ability in mathematics and science and encouraged him to continue those studies.

Volterra moved quickly through the University of Pisa, publishing several important papers as a student. He was employed by the university upon graduation and became a full faculty member at twenty-three. He had already made important contributions to mathematics.

Once established at Pisa, Volterra sent for his mother, who lived with him for the rest of her life. Volterra married Virginia Almagià after he moved to Rome; they had six children.

The Calculus and Its Applications

The two basic operations of the calculus are differentiation and integration. Both are used to solve mathematical relationships that are often related to problems in physics, engineering, economics, biology, and other fields. In fact, the calculus is often essential for the solution of practical problems.

The fundamental methods of both operations were well known before Volterra was born, but he developed techniques for solving more complex problems. He discovered methods for working out complex differential equations to solve relationships that came to be called functionals. He worked out new methods of integration. He developed a system of integro-differential methods, in which he combined integration and differentiation in the solution of complex problems. All these methods are used to solve theoretical and practical problems.

Volterra contributed directly to the practical application of the calculus in a number of ways. He worked out mathematical descriptions of the properties and characteristics of elastic materials. During World War I, he applied his methods to the development of military aircraft. Later, he developed the fundamental models for interaction among species in a biological community.

Italian and International Politics

In 1905, Volterra became an Italian senator. He could have moved into a career in politics, but he chose to remain a mathematician and scientist. Two critical periods in Italian history, however, drew him into the political arena—the first world war and the prelude to the second.

In World War I, Volterra worked hard, and successfully, to have Italy join the Allies. He also applied his mathematical genius to military problems, especially in the fledgling realm of military aviation.

When the Italian Fascist Party gained strength in the 1930's, Volterra recognized its dangers. He vigorously opposed Fascist activities and lost his university position as a result. Eventually, he was forced to leave Italy. He spent most of his last eight years abroad.

Vito Volterra died in Rome in 1940. He was not only a great mathematician but a pioneer-

ing scientist as well. He was instrumental in the application of mathematics to practical problems, including the development of mathematical biology. Volterra was also a great Italian—as demonstrated by his courageous behavior in the face of a world war and Fascism.

Bibliography
By Volterra
Leçons sur l'intégration des équations différentielles aux dérivées partielles, 1906; repub., 1912

Leçons sur les équations intégrales et les équations intégro-différentielles, 1913

The Theory of Permutable Functions, 1915

"The Generalization of Analytical Functions" and "On the Theory of Waves and Green's Method," *Rice Institute Pamphlet* 4, 1917

"Functions of Composition," *Rice Institute Pamphlet* 7, 1920

The Flow of Electricity in a Magnetic Field: Four Lectures, 1921

Teoria de los funcionales y de las ecuaciones integrates e integro-differenciales, 1927 (*Theory of Functionals and of Integral and Integro-differential Equations*, 1930, Luigi Fantappiè, ed.)

Leçons sur la théorie mathématique de la lutte pour la vie, 1931

Les Associations biologiques au point de vue mathématique, 1935 (with Umberto D'Ancona)

Théorie générale des fonctionnelles: Tome 1, Généralités sur les fonctionnelles, Théorie des équations intégrales, 1936 (with Joseph Pérès)

Opérations infinitésimales linéaires: Applications aux équations différentielles et fonctionnelles, 1938 (with Bohuslav Hostinsky)

About Volterra
"Biography of Vito Volterra, 1860-1940." E. T. Whittaker. In *Theory of Functionals and of Integral and Integro-differential Equations*, by Volterra. Translated by M. Long. New York: Dover, 1959.

"The Scientific Work of Vito Volterra." E. S. Allen. *American Mathematics Monthly* 48 (1941): 516-519.

"Vito Volterra and Contemporary Mathematical Biology." A. Borsellino. In *Vito Volterra*

Modeling the Interaction Between Predator and Prey

Volterra developed mathematical models for interactions between members of an ecological community, including the interaction between a predator and its prey.

Pierre Verhulst and Raymond Pearl developed a differential equation, the logistic equation, to explain population growth. Volterra used the logistic equation to explore interactions between species. He modeled competitive interactions and predator-prey interactions. The predator-prey model consisted of two differential equations, one for the growth of the prey population and another for the growth of the predator population.

To generate the equation for prey population growth, Volterra assumed that the population would grow at its maximum rate when the predator was absent and that large populations would grow faster than small ones. The predator would slow the growth of the prey population and would cause population decline when both populations were large.

Volterra generated his equation for predator population growth by assuming that the predator population would decline rapidly in the absence of its prey and that large populations would decline more rapidly than small ones. The presence of prey would allow the predator population to grow, and it should grow more rapidly when both prey and predator populations are large.

The solution of the equations predicts repeated increases and decreases in each population. The prey population increases first, followed by a predator population increase in response to abundant food. The large predator population kills more prey than are born, and the prey population declines. With less to eat, the predator population declines, allowing the prey population to grow. According to Volterra's model, the cycle repeats endlessly.

Volterra's models for competition and predation were independently developed by Alfred Lotka; they are often called the Lotka-Volterra

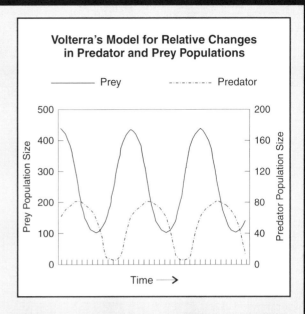

Volterra's Model for Relative Changes in Predator and Prey Populations

models. They do not accurately predict the growth of many natural populations, but they are the foundation for most models of species interaction and for many of the important ideas of ecology.

The predator-prey model produced one of the first successful predictions of mathematical ecology: that an environmental factor that kills predator and prey proportionally will have a more severe impact on the predator, resulting in an increased prey population. Some insecticide applications targeting crop pests confirmed this prediction. The pest's natural predators were more severely affected by the insecticide than the pest. As predicted, an increase of the pest species resulted.

Bibliography

Models in Biology: Mathematics, Statistics, and Computing. D. Brown and P. Rothery. New York: John Wiley & Sons, 1993.

A Primer of Ecology. Nicholas J. Gotelli. Sunderland, Mass.: Sinauer Associates, 1995.

A Primer of Population Biology. Edward O. Wilson and William H. Bossert. Stamford, Conn.: Sinauer Associates, 1971.

Symposium on Mathematical Models in Biology: Lecture Notes in Biomathematics. Vol. 39. New York: Springer-Verlag, 1980.

"Vito Volterra and the Birth of Functional Analysis." G. Fichera. In *Development of Mathematics 1900-1950*, edited by Jean-Paul Pier. Boston: Birkhäuser Verlag, 1994.

(Carl W. Hoagstrom)

John von Neumann

Areas of Achievement: Applied math, mathematical logic, and set theory

Contribution: Von Neumann placed set theory on a solid axiomatic foundation, provided a mathematical framework for game theory, and introduced the basic features of the digital electronic computer.

Dec. 28, 1903	Born in Budapest, Hungary
1925	Receives a chemical engineering degree from the Zurich Institute of Technology
1926	Earns a Ph.D. in mathematics from the University of Budapest and is appointed privatdozent at the University of Berlin
1930	Emigrates to the United States
1933	Named a professor at Princeton's Institute for Advanced Study
1937	Receives the Bochner Prize from the American Mathematical Society
1937	Elected to the National Academy of Sciences
1943	Named to the scientific staff of Los Alamos Scientific Laboratory, New Mexico, to work on the Manhattan Project
1944	Publishes *Theory of Games and Economic Behavior* with Oskar Morgenstern
1955	Appointed to the Atomic Energy Commission by President Dwight D. Eisenhower
1956	Receives the Presidential Medal of Freedom
Feb. 8, 1957	Dies in Washington, D.C.
1958	*The Computer and the Brain* is published posthumously

Early Life

John von Neumann was born in 1903 into a comfortable middle-class family in Budapest, Hungary, the son of Max and Margaret von Neumann. Because his father was a successful banker and his parents valued the world of ideas, John read widely from his family's impressive library in his formative years. Early in life, he displayed precociousness and a photographic memory, which persuaded his parents that he should attend one of Budapest's best high schools, the Lutheran Gymnasium. The school recognized his great talent in mathematics and arranged a special program for him.

Von Neumann's success as a student marked him for university study. Although his talent and interest were strongest in mathematics, his father convinced him that he could not earn a living in Hungary as a mathematician. Therefore, von Neumann enrolled in 1921 at both the University of Budapest to study mathematics and the University of Berlin to major in chemistry. In 1923, he left Berlin to pursue a degree in chemical engineering at Zurich's prestigious Institute of Technology, where he earned his

---

Game Theory

Along with Oskar Morgenstern, von Neumann provided a complete theoretical analysis of the theory of games, which was applied to a wide range of fields from economics to national defense policy.

Game theory, or the theory of strategies, applies mathematical logic to real conflicts. Because these conflicts or games can be performed by humans who do not act rationally at all times, mathematicians sought a precise analysis of this behavior using the tools of their field. A chief problem facing logicians involved accounting for all the choices made in a conflict by all sides, even choices that superficially seem random or irrational.

Building on the pioneering work of Émile Borel, von Neumann turned his attention to game theory and established the principle called the minimax theorem. He stated that in conflicts or games involving only two persons, a logical or rational behavior exists if one person wins and the other loses. He posited that there was an optimal behavior for a player in such a game. Each player, according to this theory, anticipates the opponent's behavior and tries to maximize the reward, recognizing that the opponent will try to do the same.

Another concept from game theory that achieved popular use was the concept of a zero-sum game. This notion assumes that the rewards in a game or conflict are fixed; if someone wins, he or she does so at the expense of someone else. Economists and other social scientists embraced this concept in analyzing public policy decisions or programs in the post-World War II world.

Mathematicians extended the principles of game theory beyond the two-person, fixed winnings concept. As the number of players increases, the analysis requires the use of an n-dimensional matrix—a game with n players is subject to n variables. This theoretical extension led to the use of game theory in economic policy analysis, Cold War defense strategy, and myriad other social or political policies that had zero-sum outcomes.

Placing game theory on a mathematical, and hence rational, foundation strengthened the notions that human behavior is subject to rational analysis and served as a prime example of applied mathematics as an important element in twentieth century science.

Bibliography

Game Theory: A Nontechnical Introduction. Morton D. Davis. New York: Basic Books, 1970.

Prisoner's Dilemma. William Poundstone. New York: Doubleday, 1992.

Theory of Games and Economic Behavior. John von Neumann and Oskar Morgenstern. Princeton, N.J.: Princeton University Press, 1944.

Toward a History of Game Theory. E. Roy Weintraub, ed. Durham, N.C.: Duke University Press, 1992.

"The Use and Misuse of Game Theory." Anatol Rapoport. *Scientific American* 207 (December, 1962): 108-114+.

(Library of Congress)

degree in 1925. A year later, he received a Ph.D. in mathematics from the University of Budapest. The latter degree led to his appointment as a privatdozent (assistant professor) at the University of Berlin; he remained in Germany until 1930.

A Multifaceted Mathematician

During his years of work and study in Europe, von Neumann displayed extraordinary and varied mathematical talents and interests. He established the basic properties of set theory, provided a definition of ordinal numbers, and began his work on producing the mathematical foundations of quantum physics. In these endeavors, he viewed mathematics as the foundation of science and constantly sought the axiomatic or fundamental structure of various aspects of the natural world. This approach mirrored the ancient precepts of the Pythagoreans that mathematics, and especially geometry, held the ultimate means to create models of nature.

Von Neumann's experiences in Hungary and Germany in the decade following World War I soured him on the Europe that he had known since birth. An early but short-lived pro-Communist government followed by an anti-Jewish regime in Hungary in the interwar years, accompanied by the emerging Nazi influence in Germany, finally led von Neumann to emigrate to the United States. In 1930, he received an offer to spend time at Princeton University as a visiting faculty member. A permanent appointment in 1933 to Princeton's newly formed Institute for Advanced Study guaranteed that von Neumann could stay in the United States, which became his new home.

His fertile mind turned to applied mathematics during much of his tenure in Princeton. Von Neumann revived interest and study in numerical analysis, pioneered the mathematical analysis of aerodynamics (especially in the realms of ballistics, shock waves, and turbulence), worked on a mathematical basis for meteorology, and published a fundamental treatise on game theory. Although some academicians and colleagues criticized him for dabbling in too many fields and mastering none, he established an international reputation for success in applied mathematics in the 1930's.

With the outbreak of World War II, the U.S. government sought his counsel for ballistics and ordnance projects; from 1943 to 1955, he served the staff of the Los Alamos Scientific Laboratory. The government valued his talent so highly that he was one of the few members of the Manhattan Project staff allowed to live and work away from that site. His development of an implosion method for detonation was crucial in making nuclear weapons operable.

His war work with ballistics and other projects involving applied mathematics convinced von Neumann that this field needed faster yet accurate computational technology. Mechanical calculating machines in tandem with human operators performing various functions consumed vast amounts of time; this limiting factor denied the timely analysis of certain problems, from ballistics paths to weather forecasting. Von Neumann realized that scientists had to move from mechanical to electronic calculations in order to achieve the speed and variety needed to address these computational-dependent issues.

Von Neumann's intellectual vision and interaction with several other scientists doing pioneering work in electronic calculation allowed him to suggest a computer architecture that became the guideline for the logical design of the digital computers developed in the late 1940's and early 1950's. The theoretical construct that von Neumann articulated became the prototype of digital computers for almost half a century. Concepts such as primary and secondary memory units, an arithmetic unit, a control mechanism with means of input and output, the use of random access memory, stored programs, and magnetic memory storage were hallmarks of von Neumann's early theoretical design. The technology available in the late 1940's was insufficient to reach these goals, however, and von Neumann realized that he could only suggest the kinds of devices or operations needed in an idealized machine.

Computer Architecture

Von Neumann played a leading role in providing the theoretical framework for the electronic digital computer widely used in the latter third of the twentieth century.

Although much work had been done on mechanical and electronic computing machines before World War II, few people provided an overreaching theoretical framework, based on logical processes and numerical analysis, for the design and development of a fully electronic computer. The work of von Neumann and others moved computer science to a new level by articulating the various separate units needed for such a machine. This computer architecture involved primary and secondary memory units, a unit performing arithmetic functions, some means of controlling input and output, random access memory, stored programs that could be accessed readily, and memory storage, such as light-sensitive film, magnetic wire, or magnetic drums.

Among the choices was the format of numbers to be used by the computer. The emerging computer architecture used a binary rather than a decimal format because operations within the electronic computer would be much faster. This approach required converting decimal input numbers to binary form and reconverting them into decimal output, but it allowed for a much more efficient computer operation.

Along with the basic units needed for an electronic computing system, early computer scientists and their mathematician partners addressed the means of instructing a computer to perform certain tasks. Concepts such as the flow diagram and subprograms paralleled the efforts at devising a theoretical system. These logical tools were created by mathematicians versed in formal logic. They saw the advantage of using static code contained within the machine and a dynamic process of accessing information through coding and routines set by the programmer.

Linked to the flow diagram process was one of the most ingenious proposals for computer operations: the use of the stored program. Von Neumann used an analogy linking the human brain with the stored program computer. In particular, he characterized in a theoretical framework the logical operations necessary for each part of a computer using the stored program design. This design became the essential ingredient in the widely used electronic digital computer of the late twentieth century.

Bibliography

The Computer from Pascal to von Neumann. Herman H. Goldstine. Princeton, N.J.: Princeton University Press, 1972.

A History of Scientific Computing. Stephen G. Nash, ed. Reading, Mass.: Addison-Wesley, 1990.

"John von Neumann's Influence on Electronic Digital Computing: 1944-1946." Nancy Stern. *Annals of the History of Computing* 2 (October, 1980): 349-362.

"The Late John von Neumann on Computers and the Brain." Stanislaw M. Ulam. *Scientific American* 198 (June, 1958): 127-130.

"The Scientific Conceptualization of Information: A Survey." William Aspray. *Annals of the History of Computing* 7 (April, 1985): 117-140.

Although several dedicated scientists belong on the list of those who "invented" the digital electronic computer so widely used by the late twentieth century, von Neumann deserves his place as the founder of the basic concepts and the applied mathematics needed to create this new technology. Using his considerable powers of persuasion, he received support from the Institute for Advanced Study to fund a project to create a working electronic computer in 1945. The proposed three-year project took more than six years to produce a viable machine; it never entered the commercial marketplace, but it did pave the way for later successful products.

A Public Mathematician

After World War II, many scientists involved in research and development in the war effort recognized the need for continuing government support for science and technology. Von Neumann, an avid anti-Communist, wholeheartedly served as adviser, consultant, and resource for various government agencies involved in supporting science and in fighting the Cold War. He served on the advisory committee of the U.S. Atomic Energy Commission and became a commissioner of that agency in 1955. For his important service to the government of his adopted country, he received the Presidential Medal of Freedom in 1956. Although he had few reservations about the use of nuclear weapons in the Cold War era, he defended the right of colleagues who publicly opposed nuclear war.

In the summer of 1955, doctors found that von Neumann had bone cancer that had spread throughout his body. This illness did not deter him from continuing his efforts in serving his country and his scientific community, and he worked diligently as a consultant and commissioner. Knowing that his days were limited, he focused his attention on linking the electronic computer to the human brain with an unfinished manuscript, published posthumously in 1958 as *The Computer and the Brain*. As his cancer spread even further, von Neumann weakened and then became totally bedridden. He died in Walter Reed Army Hospital on February 8, 1957.

Bibliography

By von Neumann

Mathematische Grundlagen der Quantenmechanik, 1932 (*Mathematical Foundations of Quantum Mechanics*, 1955)

Theory of Games and Economic Behavior, 1944 (with Oskar Morgenstern)

The Computer and the Brain, 1958

Collected Works, 1961-1963 (6 vols.; A. H. Taub, ed.)

Theory of Self-Producing Automata, 1966 (Arthur W. Burks, ed.)

Papers of John von Neumann on Computing and Computer Theory, 1987 (William Aspray and Arthur W. Burks, eds.)

About von Neumann

John von Neumann. Norman Macrae. New York: Pantheon Books, 1992.

John von Neumann and Norbert Wiener: From Mathematics to the Technologies of Life and Death. Steve J. Heims. Cambridge, Mass.: MIT Press, 1980.

John von Neumann and the Origins of Modern Computing. William Aspray. Cambridge, Mass.: MIT Press, 1990.

The Legacy of John von Neumann. James Glimm, John Impagliazzo, and Isadore Singer, eds. Providence, R.I.: American Mathematical Society, 1990.

(H. J. Eisenman)

John Wallis

Areas of Achievement: Algebra, calculus, and geometry

Contribution: Wallis expressed as algebraic results the principal geometric results of the ancient Greeks. He also made significant contributions to finding areas bounded by plane curves.

Nov. 23, 1616	Born in Ashford at Kent, England
1632-1640	Studies divinity at Emmanuel College in Cambridge
1644	Elected a Fellow at Queens' College, Cambridge University
1649	Appointed to the Savilian Chair of Geometry at Oxford University
1655	Publishes *Tractatus de sectionibus conicus*
1655	Publishes *Arithmetica Infinitorum*
1662	Becomes a founding member of the Royal Society of London
1685	Publishes *A Treatise of Algebra, Both Historical and Practical*, which is published in Latin in 1693
Nov. 8, 1703	Dies in Oxford, England

Early Life

John Wallis was the middle of five children born to John Wallis, the rector of Ashford, and Joanna Chapman. At the age of fourteen, he was sent to Felsted, Essex, to study at the school of Martin Holbeach, a famous teacher of the time. After Felsted, he attended Emmanuel College in Cambridge.

Intent on pursuing an ecclesiastical career, Wallis studied the classics and no mathematics at all. His only training in mathematics, aside from a few days at age fifteen reading his brother's arithmetic book, came in the form of free lessons from William Oughtred.

In view of the times, this is perhaps not surprising. As Wallis explained in his autobiography: "Mathematicks were not, at that time, looked upon as academic learning, but the business of Traders, Merchants, Sea-men, Carpenters, Land-measurers, or the like; or perhaps some Almanack-makers in London." Wallis did not begin serious study of mathematics until in 1649, when he was appointed Savilian Professor of Geometry at Oxford University, a position that he held until his death.

Public Life

Upon completion of his studies at Emmanuel, Wallis was elected to a fellowship at Queens' College, Cambridge University, and took holy orders. He resigned the ministry a few years later when he married.

During the English civil war that began in 1642, Wallis's sympathies lay with the Royalists. He did, however, willingly decode several secret messages for the Parliamentarians—a service that they willingly accepted. With the restoration of the monarchy in 1660, Wallis was appointed one of the chaplains of Charles II.

(Library of Congress)

Wallis's Formulas

Wallis obtained many formulas for areas by comparing ratios.

In the fashion of his time, Wallis viewed plane figures as being made up of infinitely many lines. He quickly abandoned this geometric insight, however, once he was able to express a particular relation algebraically. For example, in the figure on the facing page, the indicated triangles clearly have an area one half the area of the squares containing them.

Comparing the ratio of the sums of the lengths of the vertical line segments in the triangle and square, he obtained

$$\frac{0+1+2+\ldots+n}{n+n+n+\ldots+n} = \frac{(\frac{(n+1)n}{2})}{(n+1)n} = \frac{1}{2}$$

Replacing this square with one that has side of length 1 rather than n, Wallis concluded that the area between the graph of $y = x$ and the x-axis from $x = 0$ to $x = 1$ is ½.

Continuing this line of thinking, Wallis considered the ratios

$$\frac{0^1+1^2+\ldots+n^2}{n^2+n^2+\ldots+n^2}$$

with $n = 1,2,3$ to determine a formula for the area between the graph of $y = x^2$ and the x-axis from $x = 0$ to $x = 1$. He obtained the equations

$$\frac{0^2+1^2}{1^2+1^2} = \frac{1}{3} + \frac{1}{6}$$

$$\frac{0^2+1^2+2^2}{2^2+2^2+2^2} = \frac{1}{3} + \frac{1}{12}$$

$$\frac{0^2+1^2+2^2+3^2}{3^2+3^2+3^2+3^2} = \frac{1}{3} + \frac{1}{18}$$

and then, by analogy, the equation

$$\frac{0^2+1^2+\ldots+n^2}{n^2+n^2+\ldots+n^2} = \frac{1}{3} + \frac{1}{6n}$$

Reasoning that as n gets larger this ratio approaches $1/3$, he concluded that the area between the graph of $y = x^2$ and the x-axis from $x = 0$ to $x = 1$ is $1/3$. Wallis demonstrated similar

formulas for the exponents $m = 3$ and $m = 4$ before claiming that the area between the graph of $y = x^m$ and the x-axis from $x = 0$ to $x = 1$ is $1/(m + 1)$. Wallis further claimed that this result is true for all values of m except for $m = -1$.

Wallis is most famous for a formula obtained in trying to determine the area bounded by the curve "$y = \sqrt{(1 - x^2)}$" and the x-axis from $x = 0$ to $x = 1$. He knew that this area was equal to one-fourth the area of a circle with radius 1, but he wanted to obtain this area by means of infinitesimals in the same manner that he had obtained his other area formulas. Through a complicated series of arguments, Wallis finally arrived at the following formula that now bears his name:

$$\frac{\pi}{2} = \frac{2\cdot2\cdot4\cdot4\cdot6\cdot6\cdot8\cdot8\cdot\ldots}{1\cdot3\cdot3\cdot5\cdot5\cdot7\cdot7\cdot9\cdot\ldots}$$

The formula

$$\frac{2}{\pi} = \left(1-\tfrac{1}{2}\right)\left(1+\tfrac{1}{2}\right)\left(1-\tfrac{1}{4}\right)\left(1+\tfrac{1}{4}\right)\left(1-\tfrac{1}{6}\right)\left(1+\tfrac{1}{6}\right)\cdot\ldots$$

is equivalent to Wallis's formula. Another related formula is

$$\frac{2}{\pi} = 1 + \cfrac{1^2}{2 + \cfrac{3^2}{2 + \cfrac{5^2}{2 + \cfrac{7^2}{2 + \ldots}}}}$$

The latter formula is attributable to Lord Brouncker, the first president of the Royal Society of London. The study of continued fractions arose from this formula, and a proof was given by Leonhard Euler in the next century.

Bibliography

Calculus Gems: Brief Lives and Memorable Mathematicians. George F. Simmons. New York: McGraw-Hill, 1992.

A History of Mathematics: An Introduction. Victor J. Katz. New York: HarperCollins College, 1993.

The Mathematical Work of John Wallis (1616-1703). Joseph Frederick Scott. London: Taylor and Francis, 1938.

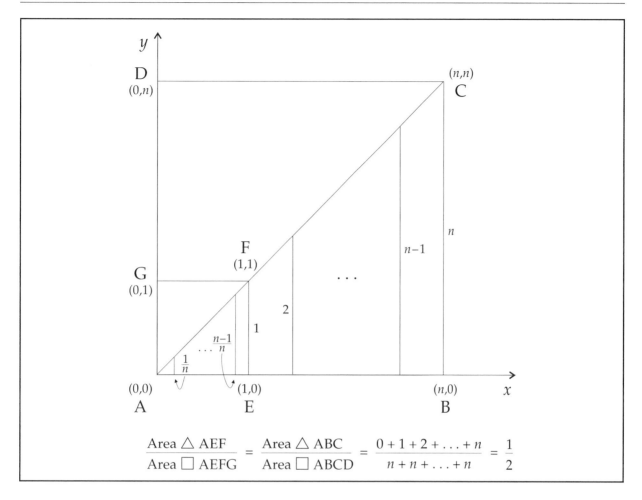

$$\frac{\text{Area } \triangle \text{ AEF}}{\text{Area } \square \text{ AEFG}} = \frac{\text{Area } \triangle \text{ ABC}}{\text{Area } \square \text{ ABCD}} = \frac{0 + 1 + 2 + \ldots + n}{n + n + \ldots + n} = \frac{1}{2}$$

Wallis was a very learned and prolific writer. His articles and books range across all the scientific and mathematical disciplines of his era. In 1662, he became one of the founding members of the Royal Society of London, which still exists today. More than a mathematician and scientist, he was one of the first to devise a system for teaching deaf mutes. Wallis died on November 8, 1703, in Oxford, England.

Mathematical Contributions

Despite having no formal mathematical training, Wallis was the most influential English mathematician of the generation before Sir Isaac Newton. Analytic geometry and infinite analysis were the only two areas of mathematical research at the time, and Wallis made significant contributions to both of them. He was a fundamental part of the transition from the geometric age to the algebraic age in mathematics.

For centuries, most mathematics was expressed geometrically, with a ruler and compass being the principal means of solving problems. Wallis gave the first arithmetic treatment of Euclid's books II and V. In *Tractatus de sectionibus conicus* (1655), he established properties of conic sections using coordinate geometry of the plane—in other words, the familiar second-degree algebraic equations used today. In *A Treatise of Algebra, Both Historical and Practical* (1685), Wallis offered the first systematic use of algebraic formulas for equations of lines and other plane curves as now presented.

Wallis introduced the idea of infinite series systematically in analysis, clearly paving the way for much of Newton's work. In *Arithmetica Infinitorum* (1655), his most-famous work, one sees the results of René Descartes and Bonaventura Cavalieri organized and extended. Wallis essentially replaced the geometric with the algebraic whenever possible. Analytic techniques are applied to Cavalieri's method of indivisibles for finding areas and volumes, with many remarkable results obtained from particular cases. While Pierre de Fermat and others criticized Wallis for his lack of rigor, his results were usually correct and in keeping with the standards of proof for his day.

Wallis was also the first to explain with any completeness the significance of exponents which are zero, negative, or fractional, and he introduced the symbol ∞ for infinity. He obtained a method for finding the arc length of a graph that is equivalent to the present-day method. Wallis is also noted for proving the parallel postulate under the assumption that triangles exist that are similar but not congruent.

Bibliography
By Wallis
Tractatus de sectionibus conicus, 1655

Arithmetica Infinitorum, 1655

A Treatise of Algebra, Both Historical and Practical, 1685 (Latin trans. as *De algebra tractatus: historicus & practicus*, 1693)

About Wallis
"The Autobiography of John Wallis, F.R.S." Christoph J. Scriba. *Notes and Records of the Royal Society of London* 25, no. 1 (June, 1970): 17-46.

A History of Mathematics. Carl B. Boyer and Uta C. Merzbach. Rev. ed. New York: John Wiley & Sons, 1991.

A History of Mathematics: An Introduction. Victor J. Katz. New York: HarperCollins College, 1993.

Mathematics and Its History. John Stillwell. New York: Springer-Verlag, 1989.

(Charles Waiveris)

Karl Weierstrass

Area of Achievement: Calculus
Contribution: Weierstrass developed a firm theoretic foundation for the calculus.

Oct. 31, 1815	Born in Ostenfelde, Bavaria (now Germany)
1834	Begins a unsuccessful tenure as a student at the University of Bonn
1839	Enters the Academy of Münster to prepare to teach high school 1842
1849	Publishes an unnoticed major work on Abelian integrals in a high school program
1854	Discovered by leading mathematicians after publishing an important memoir
1854	Awarded an honorary doctorate by the University of Königsberg
1856	Commences a second career as professor of mathematics at the University of Berlin
1861	Constructs a continuous function having no tangents
1870	Begins a friendship with twenty-year-old mathematician Sofya Kovalevskaya
1891	Burns all correspondence with Kovalevskaya after her early death
Feb. 19, 1897	Dies in Berlin, Germany

(Library of Congress)

Early Life

The eldest son of Wilhelm Weierstrass and Theodora Vonderforst, Karl Theodor Wilhelm Weierstrass (pronounced "VI-ur-shtraws") was born on October 31, 1815. During his youth, Weierstrass regularly read a noted mathematics journal. At fifteen, he worked as an accountant for a prosperous merchant. At the Catholic Gym-nasium at Paderborn, Weierstrass won prizes in German, Latin, Greek, and mathematics.

His father, an autocratic Prussian civil servant, observed his son's talents and decided that young Karl's future lay in accountancy. Success in the accounting profession meant obtaining a civil service position. Hence, Karl would need to study commerce and law at the University of Bonn. Unfortunately, Weierstrass had no interest in these subjects. He wished to study mathematics. Rebelling against his father, Weierstrass spent four years at Bonn perfecting his fencing and drinking skills. He did read one of the great mathematical treatises, Pierre-Simon Laplace's *Traité du mécanique céleste* (1799-1825); that he was able to read this advanced treatment indicates a first-class mathematical mind.

Returning home after four years of college with no degree, Weierstrass found his family distressed. In 1839, he enrolled in the Academy of Münster to obtain a teaching certificate. He was admitted only after promising to amend his ways.

Unrecognized Genius

At the academy, Weierstrass quickly impressed his mathematics professor, Christof Guder-

Rigorous Calculus

Weierstrass developed a firm theoretical foundation for the calculus.

A theory without a firm foundation is a theory waiting to be misapplied. Weierstrass began by showing that the calculus was much more complex than was generally believed, even by experienced mathematicians. In 1861, he constructed a continuous function that does not have any tangents. Previously, it had been assumed that tangents must exist almost everywhere. This example greatly surprised the mathematical community and continues to surprise students even today.

While constructing this unusual function, Weierstrass realized that he needed to understand exactly what irrational numbers such as π or $\sqrt{2}$ are. Trying to explain irrational numbers is a problem that dates back to the ancient Greek mathematician Eudoxus. Weierstrass developed a theory of irrational numbers that explains these numbers in terms of sequences of simpler numbers, the rational numbers. In this way, he constructed all numbers beginning from the firm foundation of the whole numbers.

In order to test the convergence of sequences, Weierstrass developed a powerful test for convergence, now known as the Weierstrass M-test. He also formulated the idea of uniform convergence for functions. It is possible for some parts of a series to converge slowly while others converge quickly. Using uniform convergence, Weierstrass was able to treat all parts as if they were converging at the same rate.

A power series is sometimes called an infinite-degree polynomial. Weierstrass made the idea of an infinite-degree polynomial rigorous and then used his development of the number system, along with the idea of uniform convergence, to show how the development of the calculus can be put on a firm theoretic foundation. He also discovered a result that in now known as the Weierstrass factorization theorem. This theorem states that many power series may be factored into products in a manner similar to that whereby polynomials can be factored.

By the time that Weierstrass began is research, the calculus was more than a century old, but many parts of the theory were not understood properly. Weierstrass began at the bottom and carefully built up an edifice that would withstand the closest scrutiny. He was very careful in avoiding terms that had not been defined and assumptions that had not been stated. The level of rigor that Weierstrass introduced has become the accepted level of rigor for mathematics in general. His place in the firmament of mathematics is assured.

Bibliography

The Higher Calculus: A History of Real and Complex Analysis from Euler to Weierstrass. Umberto Bottazzini. Translated by Warren Van Egmond. New York: Springer-Verlag, 1986.

The Historical Development of the Calculus. Charles Henry Edwards, Jr. New York: Springer-Verlag, 1979.

The History of the Calculus and Its Conceptual Development. Carl B. Boyer. New York: Dover, 1959.

Mathematics for the Nonmathematician. Morris Kline. New York: Dover, 1985.

mann. Weierstrass was one of thirteen students who began Gudermann's course; the second day found only Weierstrass in the audience. Weierstrass was greatly influenced by Gudermann's interest in the theory of elliptic functions and his power series approach to studying functions.

At Weierstrass's insistence, Gudermann gave him an unusually difficult problem to solve in the examination for his teacher's certificate. Weierstrass's solution earned a special certificate indicating his original contribution to mathematics, but Gudermann was unable to include his praise for Weierstrass in the official report. Such praise was considered inappropriate.

From 1842 until 1848, Weierstrass taught at the Pro-Gymnasium Deutsche Krone, a Catholic secondary school. In addition to mathematics and physics, he taught such subjects as German, geography, history, botany, calligraphy, and gymnastics. Weierstrass published a scholarly paper on analytic factorials in the 1842-1843 school program. He also published a paper on Abelian integrals in the 1848-1849 school program of the Royal Catholic Gymnasium, where he taught from 1848 to 1856. Neither of these programs were appropriate outlets for scholarly work, and Weierstrass's genius remained unappreciated until 1854. That year, he published an influential memoir on Abelian functions the well-known *Journal für die reine und angewandte Mathematik,* commonly called *Crelle's Journal.*

Recognition Obtained

During his Gymnasium years, Weierstrass did not have colleagues with whom he could discuss mathematics or access to a research library. Additionally, he was unable to correspond with other mathematicians because of high postage rates. He was a completely unknown, largely self-educated schoolteacher, and the appearance of his brilliant 1854 paper surprised the mathematical community. Its worth was quickly appreciated, and he was hailed as a first-rate mathematician. University mathematicians were surprised that such a talented man had been teaching children instead of the world's best mathematicians.

Weierstrass was awarded an honorary doctorate by the University of Königsberg. A position was obtained for him at the Royal Polytechnic School in 1856, and later that year he was appointed assistant professor of mathematics at the University of Berlin. In 1864, he was made full professor of mathematics, a position he held until his death.

An Influential Teacher

Weierstrass developed a reputation as an excellent teacher. His lectures were not always orderly and well presented, but he was able to attract first-class students, tempting them with interesting problems. One student, Georg Cantor, went on to develop set theory and a mathematical theory of the infinite; the latter controversial theory is now a cornerstone of mathematics.

Weierstrass never married, but he was close to the talented and beautiful Russian mathematician Sofya Kovalevskaya. At twenty, she became a favorite student and confidante. When the University of Berlin refused to admit Kovalevskaya to his lectures because of official prejudice against women, Weierstrass gave her private lessons. He encouraged her career and tried to locate academic positions worthy of her talent. Tragically, Kovalevskaya died at forty-one; in his grief, Weierstrass burned all the letters she had written him.

Weierstrass's influence was through lectures rather than published works. His students spread his results through the mathematical community. These results were later published as part of Weierstrass's collected works. Weierstrass frequented the local taverns, where his students would join him for a drink and a continuation of the day's lecture. He also had the endearing habit of picking up the bill. His many students gathered to celebrate his seventieth and eightieth birthdays. Weierstrass died of pneumonia at eighty-one.

Bibliography

By Weierstrass
"Zur Theorie der Abelschen Functionen," *Journal für die reine und angewandte Mathematik* 47, 1854
"Theorie der Abelschen Functionen," *Journal für die reine und angewandte Mathematik* 52, 1856
Mathematishe Werke, 1894-1927 (7 vols.)

About Weierstrass
High Five: Catholic Mathematicians. Herbert Janson. San Antonio, Tex.: St. Mary's University, 1995.
Men of Mathematics. E. T. Bell. New York: Simon & Schuster, 1937.
"Weierstrass, Karl Theodor Wilhelm." Kurt R. Biermann. In *Dictionary of Scientific Biography,* edited Charles Coulston Gillispie. New York: Charles Scribner's Sons, 1976.

(Jeffrey A. Ehme)

Hermann Weyl

Areas of Achievement: Algebra, applied math, calculus, geometry, mathematical logic, number theory, set theory, and topology

Contribution: Weyl's contributions to geometry influenced the development of point set topology and differential geometry.

Nov. 9, 1885	Born in Elmshorn, near Hamburg, Germany
1908	Receives a Ph.D. from the University of Göttingen
1913	Appointed a professor of mathematics at the Eidgenossische Technische Hochschule (ETH)
1913	Publishes his first book, *Die Idee der Riemannschen Fläche* (*The Concept of a Riemann Surface*, 1955)
1918	Publishes *Raum, Zeit, Materie* (*Space-Time-Matter*, 1922)
1928	Becomes Jones Research Professor of Mathematical Physics at Princeton University
1928	Publishes *Gruppentheorie und Quantenmechanik* (*The Theory of Groups and Quantum Mechanics*, 1931)
1930	Succeeds David Hilbert as chair of mathematics at Göttingen
1933	Leaves Göttingen to accept a post as professor of mathematics at the Institute for Advanced Study in Princeton, New Jersey
1939	Becomes a naturalized U.S. citizen
1951	Retires from teaching in the School of Mathematics of the Institute for Advanced Study
Dec. 8, 1955	Dies in Zurich, Switzerland

Early Life

Hermann Weyl (pronounced "vile") was the son of Ludwig Weyl, a bank clerk, and Anna Dieck Weyl. After graduating in 1904 from the Gymnasium in Altona, he studied at the University of Göttingen, where he received a Ph.D. in 1908. He wrote his doctoral dissertation on integral equations under the supervision of mathematician David Hilbert and was considered the most gifted of Hilbert's students.

Mathematical Work

Weyl was a privatdozent, or unsalaried university lecturer, at Göttingen from 1910 until 1913, when he accepted an appointment as a professor of mathematics at the Eidgenossische Technische Hochschule (ETH) in Zurich, where one of his colleagues was Albert Einstein. Fascinated with Einstein's theory of relativity, Weyl spent several years exploring the mathematics involved; this work resulted in Weyl's 1918 book *Raum, Zeit, Materie* (*Space-Time-Matter*, 1922).

Weyl continued his contribution to the development of mathematical physics with his study of group theory and its connection to quantum mechanics. His book *Gruppentheorie and Quantenmechanik* (1928; *The Theory of Groups and Quantum Mechanics*, 1931) is devoted to his findings in this area.

In *Die Idee der Riemannschen Fläche*, published first in 1913 and rewritten in 1955 as *The Concept of a Riemann Surface*, Weyl combined concepts from geometry, topology, and analysis. This book is considered a classic. Later, Weyl developed an interest in symmetry, studying its properties in snowflakes, crystals, jellyfish, light waves, and mathematical transformations. His findings were published in his 1952 book *Symmetry*, which focused on symmetry and its appearance in science, art, and mathematics.

Because of Weyl's varied interests within mathematics—he was the author of more than 150 articles and books—he was considered a polymath. He believed that mathematics, nature, and philosophy were essentially interrelated. As he said, "The problems of Mathematics are not problems in a vacuum. There pulses in them the life of ideas which realize themselves in concreto through our human endeavours in our historical existence, but forming an indissoluble whole transcending any particular science."

Academic Career

Except for two brief periods, a year of service in the German army and a year as Jones Research Professor of Mathematical Physics at Princeton University in New Jersey, Weyl maintained his teaching position in Zurich until 1930, when he accepted an offer to succeed David Hilbert as chair of mathematics at the University of Göttingen. Within a few years, however, Weyl could no longer tolerate the political climate of Nazi Germany and became one of many European mathematicians to emigrate to the United States.

In 1933, he became one of the first professors

Geometry and the Theory of Relativity

In the early twentieth century, Weyl studied two main subjects: Riemannian geometry and relativity. Although one topic was seemingly mathematical and the other scientific, these two subjects were intimately related—Riemannian geometry was the mathematics used in the study of relativity.

After lecturing on the work of Bernhard Riemann at the University of Göttingen, Weyl developed an interest in Riemannian geometry, a non-Euclidean geometry that enabled mathematicians to deal with spherical surfaces. Taking a mathematical approach similar to that of his mentor, David Hilbert, Weyl sought to apply analytical principles to what had been formerly only approached through intuition. At the time, there was no precise definition of a Riemann surface, although Riemann himself had seen geometry as the study of a set of points with some structure superimposed on it.

Building on this idea, Weyl defined a surface so that the "points" could be mathematical objects of any kind, thereby pioneering the more precise treatment of the Riemann surface. The result of Weyl's work was published in his 1913 book *Die Idee der Riemannschen Fläche*, in which he analyzed the concept of a Riemann surface and developed function theory for closed surfaces. This book was a mathematical classic for more than forty years before it was revised and republished in 1955 as *The Concept of a Riemann Surface*.

Weyl's application of set theory to geometry contributed to the development of point set topology; with his expanded definition of a Riemann surface, he was very close to the notion of a topological space. Topology, sometimes referred to as the mathematical study of continuity, began primarily as a branch of geometry, but it evolved through the twentieth century into a branch of mathematics uniting geometry, algebra, and analysis.

Weyl continued his study of geometry and its connection to Albert Einstein's general theory of relativity. Weyl's book *Raum, Zeit, Materie* (1918; *Space-Time-Matter*, 1922), based on a course that he gave on general relativity, included an explanation of the geometry involved in relativity. As Weyl continued his study, new editions of *Raum, Zeit, Materie* were published, a total of five by 1923. His generalization of Riemannian geometry, a Weylian geometry that he called "purely infinitesimal geometry," formed the basis for his unsuccessful unified field theory of gravitational and electromagnetic forces. Despite this failure, his mathematical contribution to differential geometry was significant.

Bibliography

Hermann Weyl, 1885-1985: Centenary Lectures. Komaravolu Chandrasekharan, ed. New York: Springer-Verlag, 1986.

"Hermann Weyl's Contribution to Geometry, 1917-1923." Erhard Scholz. In *The Intersection of History and Mathematics*, edited by Sasaki Chikara, Sugiura Mitsuo, and Joseph W. Dauben. Boston: Birkhauser Verlag, 1994.

The Mathematical Heritage of Hermann Weyl: Proceedings of Symposia in Pure Mathematics 48. Raymond O'Neil Wells, Jr., ed. Providence, R.I.: American Mathematical Society, 1988.

The Nature and Growth of Modern Mathematics. Edna Ernestine Kramer. Princeton, N.J.: Princeton University Press, 1981, pp. 632-638.

(AP/Wide World Photos)

at the Institute for Advanced Study in Princeton, a private institution dedicated to theoretical research and intellectual inquiry. Weyl remained at the institute, in the company of Einstein and other famous scholars, until his retirement in 1951. Thereafter, he divided his time between Princeton and his home in Zurich, where he died of a heart attack in 1955.

Family and Intellectual Interests
On September 1, 1913, Weyl married Helene Joseph. They had two sons, Fritz Joachim and Michael. After Helene's death, Weyl married Ellen Lohnstein Bär on January 7, 1950.

Even as early as his high school days, when he read the works of the great eighteenth century German intellectual Immanuel Kant, Weyl was interested in philosophy. Near the end of his life, he wrote a short philosophical autobiography reflecting his lifelong study of the discipline, entitled "Erkenntnis und Besinnung" (1954), in which he suggests that intellectual life is divided into two parts: action and reflection upon that action.

Weyl also enjoyed literature and poetry, especially German poetry. He developed his own rich literary style, which became a trademark of his written mathematical work.

Honors and Memberships
Weyl was the recipient of several honorary degrees: a Doctor of Philosophy from the University of Oslo in 1929; a Doctor of Technology from the Hochschule, Stuttgart, in 1929; a Doctor of Science from the University of Pennsylvania in 1940 and from Columbia University in 1954; and a Doctor of Mathematics from ETH, Zurich, in 1945.

He was a member of many organizations, including the American Philosophical Society, the National Academy, the American Academy of Arts and Sciences, the American Mathematical Society, and the Royal Society of London.

Bibliography
By Weyl
Die Idee der Riemannschen Fläche, 1913 (*The Concept of a Riemann Surface*, 1955)
Das Kontinuu: Kritische Untersuchungen über die Grundlagen der Analysis, 1918 (*The Continuum: A Critical Examination of the Foundation of Analysis*, 1987)
Raum, Zeit, Materie, 1918 (*Space-Time-Matter*, 1922)
Über die Hypothesen, welche der Geometrie zu Grunde liegen, by Bernhard Riemann, 1919 (as editor)
Mathematische Analyse des Raumproblems, 1923
Was ist Materie?, 1924
Philosophie der Mathematik und Naturwissenschaft, 1926 (*Philosophy of Mathematics and Natural Science*, 1949)
Gruppentheorie und Quantenmechanik, 1928 (*The Theory of Groups and Quantum Mechanics*, 1932)
Die Stufen des Unendlichen, 1931
The Open World, 1932
Mind and Nature, 1934
The Classical Groups, Their Invariants and Representations, 1939
Algebraic Theory of Numbers, 1940
Meromorphic Functions and Analytic Curves, 1943
Symmetry, 1952
Selecta Hermann Weyl, 1956

Gesammelte Abhandlungen, 1968 (4 vols.; available in German, English, or French)

About Weyl
"Hermann Weyl." F. J. Dyson. *Nature* 177 (1956): 457-458.
"Hermann Weyl." M. H. A. Newman. *Biographical Memoirs of Fellows of the Royal Society of London* 3 (1957): 305-328.
"Hermann Weyl (1885-1955)." In *The Biographical Dictionary of Scientists: Mathematicians*, edited by David Abbott. New York: Peter Bedrick Books, 1985.

(Judith L. Sullivan)

Anna Johnson Pell Wheeler

Areas of Achievement: Algebra, calculus, and set theory

Contribution: Wheeler furthered knowledge of the theory of integral equations and functional analysis.

May 5, 1883	Born in Calliope (now Hawarden), Iowa
1903	Graduated from the University of South Dakota
1904	Receives a scholarship to the University of Iowa for an M.A. degree
1905	Earns a scholarship to Radcliffe College for a second M.A. degree
1906	Wins a fellowship from Wellesley College to study at the University of Göttingen, Germany
1907	Marries Alexander Pell
1909	Earns a Ph.D. magna cum laude from the University of Chicago
1911	Joins Mount Holyoke College as an instructor
1918	Takes an associate professorship at Bryn Mawr College
1920	Her father and husband die
1924	Named chair of the mathematics department at Bryn Mawr
1925	Marries Arthur Leslie Wheeler and becomes a full professor
1927	Delivers a colloquium lecture at the American Mathematical Society
1932	Her second husband dies
1948	Retires from Bryn Mawr
Mar. 26, 1966	Dies in Bryn Mawr, Pennsylvania

(Bryn Mawr College Archives)

Early Life

Two Swedish immigrants, Amelia Friberg and Andrew Gustav Johnson, met and were married in the Dakota Territory, where he began farming. They soon moved to Calliope (now Hawarden), Iowa, where their third child, Anna Johnson, was born on May 5, 1883. Her sister, Esther, was four, and her brother, Elmer, was two. The family moved to Akron, South Dakota, where her father entered the furniture business and later became an undertaker. Anna was enrolled at the Akron public school, which had classes through the eleventh grade.

The University of South Dakota accepted Johnson in 1899 as a subfreshman until completion of the entrance requirements. Nevertheless, she managed to graduate in 1903. While she liked languages, her first love was mathematics, in part because of her professor, Alexander Pell. Pell and his wife, Emma, were well-liked on campus, and both Anna and her sister roomed with them, which fostered his influence on her.

Upon graduation, Johnson received a scholarship to the University of Iowa for a master's degree, where she also taught a mathematics course for freshmen and was received into Sigma Xi. Then came another scholarship and a second master's degree at Radcliffe College in 1905.

Professional Life

Johnson's sterling record brought her Wellesley College's Alice Freeman Palmer Fellowship in 1907. This money would allow her to travel to the University of Göttingen, in Germany, provided that she did not marry during the award period. She went and studied under David Hilbert. He interested her in integral equations, an area that she would later pursue. In July of that year, Anna Johnson became Mrs. Alexander Pell, a marriage to which her parents objected because he was twenty-five years her senior. Pell's wife passed away in 1904, and the professor and his former student had remained close friends.

They were married in Göttingen and then returned to the University of South Dakota, where Alexander Pell was dean of the engineering school. That semester, Anna Johnson Pell taught two courses and returned to Göttingen in the spring to finish her Ph.D. A disagreement with Hilbert caused her to return home without the degree, but she enrolled in the University of Chicago and was graduated magna cum laude in 1910. She was only the second woman to receive a Ph.D. in mathematics at Chicago. Alexander, having resigned over a disagreement with the college's president, had also moved to Chicago, to the Armour Institute of Technology.

With a Ph.D. in hand, Anna's job hunt began. Prejudice was a reality. She was offered one semester of teaching at the University of Chicago because they could not find a man to fill the position. In the spring of 1911, Alexander suffered a stroke, so the Armour Institute hired her for that semester. She badly needed a position, and in 1911 she accepted an instructorship at Mount Holyoke College. She was promoted to associate professor in 1914, which coincided with her publication on non-homogeneous linear equations in infinitely many unknowns. She was able to do some research, but Mount Holyoke had heavy teaching loads and she had to care for her ailing husband.

Therefore, in 1918, she accepted a position as associate professor at Bryn Mawr College, where she would have doctoral students and could become department chair. The noted mathematician Charlotte Angas Scott would soon be retiring. Two tragedies struck in 1920: Anna lost both her father and her husband. She did become mathematics chair in 1924 and full professor a year later.

As an administrator, Pell made the department one of the finest in the nation. She insisted on light teaching loads and time for personal research. She also built an outstanding library collection. In 1925, she married her colleague in classics, Arthur Wheeler, who had just accepted a professorship at Princeton University. Anna Johnson Pell Wheeler accompanied him to New Jersey and commuted part-time to Bryn Mawr. Finally, she could do her research. In 1927, Wheeler received the great honor as the first woman invited to give a colloquium lecture at the American Mathematical Society.

These were happy years, with winters in Princeton and summers in their newly built cottage in the Adirondacks, but they ended quickly. Arthur died suddenly in 1932, and Anna returned to Bryn Mawr. She retired in 1948 and died there in 1966 following a stroke.

Functional Analysis and Integral Equations

As algebra deals with the solution to equations that contain one or more unknowns called variables, functions consist of the relationship between variables. These relationships are often expressed as the lines or curves called graphs.

The concept of a function is important in mathematics because it leads to the calculus. A function is a set of ordered pairs in which the first member of the pair (x,y) will never occur twice in the same set. Suppose that a house is Domain X and the furniture pieces have the value x. The rooms are the Range Y with each room having the value y, so that for whatever x one chooses in Domain X, there is only one y in Range Y. Then x,y are an ordered pair in the set f, a set being any number of pairs. When one assigns a value to x, a corresponding value to y is automatically established in accordance with certain mathematical rules. Being a free choice, x is the independent variable; y, being dependent on x, is the dependent variable. Wheeler used these functions in her study of integral equations. Her particular interest involved quadratic forms with infinitely many variables.

In the calculus, a form of functional analysis is actually applied. Differential calculus has to do with subdividing a curve into smaller and smaller sections. As the size of these sections approaches zero, their sum approaches the curve itself. This technique helps to solve problems involving rates of change.

In integral calculus, the opposite approach is employed. The curve, or function, itself is the unknown sought. It is then possible to determine the areas under a given curve. This analysis led to the mathematics of infinite series and new mathematical applications to scientific problems.

Functional analysis also remains useful in modern science. The use of operators, with their facile conversion from one function into another, has contributed to the understanding of atomic structure and chemical bonding through the quantum mechanical view of the subatomic world. The Fourier series of a function has allowed the construction of powerful instruments, such as the magnetic resonance spectrometers necessary in chemistry and medicine.

Bibliography

Fundamentals of Mathematics. Moses Richardson. 3d ed. Toronto: Macmillan, 1966.

An Introduction to the Foundations and Fundamental Concepts of Mathematics. Howard Whitley Eves and Carroll V. Newsom. Rev. ed. New York: Holt, Rinehart and Winston, 1965.

Mathematical Thought from Ancient to Modern Times. Morris Kline. New York: Oxford University Press, 1972.

Bibliography

By Wheeler

Biorthogonal Systems of Functions, 1910 (Ph.D. thesis, University of Chicago)

"Existence Theorems for Certain Unsymmetric Kernels," *Bulletin of the American Mathematical Society* 16, 1910

"On an Integral Equation with an Adjoined Condition," *Bulletin of the American Mathematical Society* 16, 1910

"Biorthogonal Systems of Functions," *Transactions of the American Mathematical Society* 12, 1911 (thesis, part 1)

"Applications of Biorthogonal Systems of Functions to the Theory of Integral Equations," *Transactions of the American Mathematical Society* 12, 1911 (thesis, part 2)

"Non-homogeneous Linear Equations in Infinitely Many Unknowns," *Annals of Mathematics* 2, no. 16, 1914-1915

"The Modified Remainders Obtained in Finding the Highest Common Factor of Two Polynomials," *Annals of Mathematics* 2d ser. 18, 1916-1917 (with R. L. Gordon)

"A General System of Linear Equations," *Transactions of the American Mathematical Society* 20, 1919

"Linear Equations with Unsymmetric Systems of Coefficients," *Transactions of the American Mathematical Society* 20, 1919

"Linear Equations with Two Parameters," *Transactions of the American Mathematical Society* 23, 1922

"Linear Ordinary Self-adjoint Differential Equations of the Second Order," *American Journal of Mathematics* 49, 1927

"The Theory of Quadratic Forms in Infinitely Many Variables and Applications," *Bulletin of the American Mathematical Society* 33, 1927

"Spectral Theory for a Certain Class of Non-symmetric Completely Continuous Matrices," *American Journal of Mathematics* 57, 1935

About Wheeler

"Anna Johnson Pell Wheeler (1883-1966)." Bettye Case, ed. *Association for Women in Mathematics Newsletter* 12, no. 4 (July/August, 1982).

"Anna Johnson Pell Wheeler (1883-1966)." Louise S. Grinstein and Paul Campbell. In *Women of Mathematics: A Biobibliographic Sourcebook*, edited by Grinstein and Campbell. New York: Greenwood Press, 1987.

Women in the Scientific Search: An American Bio-Bibliography, 1724-1979. Patricia Joan Siegel and Kay Thomas Finley. Metuchen, N.J.: Scarecrow Press, 1985.

(Patricia Joan Siegel)

Alfred North Whitehead

Areas of Achievement: Algebra, applied math, and mathematical logic

Contribution: Whitehead made major contributions to mathematical logic and relativity. His quest for a comprehensive, unified system of knowledge led him ultimately to philosophy.

Feb. 15, 1861	Born in Ramsgate, Isle of Thanet, Kent, England
1884	Elected a Fellow of Trinity College and appointed assistant lecturer in mathematics
1887	Awarded an M.A.
1903	Named senior lecturer
1903	Elected to the Royal Society of London
1905	Receives a Doctor of Science degree
1910	Publishes the first volume of *Principia Mathematica*, with Bertrand Russell
1912	Accepts a position as lecturer in applied mathematics and mechanics at University College, London
1913	Becomes a reader in geometry at University College
1914	Named a professor of applied mathematics at the Imperial College of Science and Technology in Kensington
1924	Joins the philosophy department at Harvard University
1937	Retires and is named emeritus professor of philosophy
1945	Awarded the Order of Merit, Britain's highest academic honor
Dec. 30, 1947	Dies in Cambridge, Massachusetts

Early Life

Alfred North Whitehead was born on February 15, 1861, in the town of Ramsgate on the Isle of Thanet, County of Kent, England. His father was a schoolmaster and clergyman who cared tirelessly for his congregation and was well loved by them. His grandfather was an intellectual who established a successful boys' school at Ramsgate that emphasized mathematics and science. As a child, Whitehead was small and frail. He was not allowed to attend school or to play with the other children. His father tutored him in the classics and mathematics.

In 1875, Whitehead was allowed to attend Sherborne School in Dorsetshire. He excelled in mathematics and was excused from some of the standard courses in order to study mathematics in greater depth. Whitehead played rugby with the same intensity as he did his studies. He became one of the best forwards in the history of Sherborne, eventually becoming captain of games and head of the school.

Early Career

In 1880, Whitehead entered Trinity College at

(AP/Wide World Photos)

Cambridge University in a special honors program in mathematics. Much of his education, however, took place outside the classroom. He engaged in lively discussions about politics, history, philosophy, science, and the arts with his fellow students, sometimes going on through the night. Whitehead described it as "a daily Platonic Dialogue."

Whitehead received his bachelor of arts degree in 1884. His thesis on James Clerk Maxwell's theory of electromagnetism was so impressive that he received a fellowship to Cambridge. He became an assistant lecturer and continued his research. He was eventually named a senior lecturer and was elected to the Royal Society of London. Whitehead's research led to the publication of *A Treatise on Universal Algebra* (1898), which dealt with the algebra of

Proving That "1 + 1 = 2"

From 1910 to 1913, Whitehead and Bertrand Russell published a three-volume text entitled Principia Mathematica, *a monumental work in the area of mathematical logic and the foundations of mathematics. They showed that arithmetic itself can be considered an extension (or a branch) of formal logic.*

In the nineteenth century, a move to "arithmetize" mathematical analysis took place. All the ideas of basic arithmetic were defined exclusively in terms of a few purely logical ideas. Using the symbolism of Giuseppe Peano's ideographic language, Whitehead and Russell demonstrated that all propositions of arithmetic are logical consequences of a small number of axioms. They extended this work with excruciating rigor to conclude that all mathematical analysis is reducible to formal logic.

In order to carry out this rigorous logical analysis, they introduced numerous new definitions and constructed hundreds of demonstrations for preliminary theorems. The books of *Principia Mathematica* are massive—the first and second volumes extending to more than seven hundred pages, with the third almost five hundred pages. The simple, and very fundamental, proof that "1 + 1 = 2" does not appear until well into the second volume.

An example of this technique is one of their earliest proofs. To begin their proofs, Whitehead and Russell first had to list their basic propositions and definitions. Using symbolic logic, for example, negation is symbolized by a tilde (~); alternation is symbolized by a wedge (∨); elementary propositional functions are represented by p, q, r, and s; and assertion is denoted by ⊢, such that "⊢ p" is read as "it must be true that p."

Thus, the notion of implication as a relation between propositions is now defined as:

$$p \supset q. = . \sim p \vee q$$

which is read as "'If p, then q' is the defined equivalent of 'either not p or q.'" For example, "If the prevailing winds continue, then the rainfall will increase" is a version of "either the prevailing winds do not continue or the rainfall will increase."

This process seems like a considerable amount of effort to state something that seems self-evident. It was predicated by another development of the nineteenth century. The development of non-Euclidean geometry demonstrated that postulates were merely assumptions and that it was possible to develop several logically consistent systems on the basis of a set of postulates.

Nothing in mathematics could be taken for granted. Not even the real number system could be considered to be true or obviously self-consistent. It became important to establish the postulates under the real number system in order to maintain the logical consistency of mathematics. This search for a logical foundation for the real number system continues.

Bibliography

Fundamentals of Mathematics. H. Behnke, F. Bachmann, K. Fladt, and W. Süss, eds. Cambridge, Mass.: MIT Press, 1974.

The Prentice Hall Encyclopedia of Mathematics. Beverly Henderson West et al. Englewood Cliffs, N.J.: Prentice Hall, 1982.

The World of Mathematics. James Roy Newman. New York: Simon & Schuster, 1956.

symbolic logic. He received his doctor of science degree in 1905.

During this time, Whitehead met Evelyn Wade on a visit to his parents. The daughter of impoverished Irish gentry, she had black eyes, auburn hair, and a lively personality. Whitehead fell in love with her, and they were married in December, 1891. They had four children: Thomas North, Jesse Marie, Eric Alfred, and an unnamed boy who died at birth. Eric was later killed during World War I. Evelyn's sense of beauty and adventure became a strong influence on Whitehead's philosophy. He said that her example taught him that "beauty, moral and aesthetic, is the aim of existence: and that kindness, and love, and artistic satisfaction are among its modes of attainment."

In 1890, another important person entered Whitehead's life. Bertrand Russell enrolled at Cambridge. Although his entrance examinations were undistinguished, Whitehead recognized Russell's potential. They soon began a collaboration that would last for more than ten years. In 1900, Russell and Whitehead met the mathematician Giuseppe Peano, who had devised a symbolic notation. They recognized the potential of this system and began what would eventually become a three-volume work known as the *Principia Mathematica* (1910-1913), which revolutionized mathematics.

London

In 1910, Whitehead rather mysteriously left his position at Cambridge to move to London. His interests were changing. He was committed to making higher education more accessible to the common person. Until that time, universities had been predominantly for the upper classes. He was also turning his attention increasingly to philosophy.

This was a busy and productive time for Whitehead. He took on a variety of positions, both academic and administrative; was an active member of several education committees, including the chair of the Academic Council; published four books on such wide-ranging areas as mathematics, philosophy, and theoretical physics; and taught applied mathematics and mechanics at University College, London, and at the Imperial College of Science and Technology in Kensington.

Philosophy

In 1924, Whitehead's career took another turn when he was offered a position as professor of philosophy at Harvard University. He was excited about the prospect of teaching philosophy for a change and gladly accepted the position. He taught at Harvard until his retirement in 1937. During this time, he published widely in philosophy, producing four books that are now considered to be classics. Whitehead sought to bridge the gap between mind and nature. "Natural philosophy," he said, "should never ask what is in the mind and what is in nature."

Whitehead was a simple, gentle, and kind man who was well-loved. He was passionately devoted to his family. He was described as an "extraordinarily perfect" teacher who was able to motivate his students to give their best. Whitehead died in Cambridge, Massachusetts, on December 30, 1947. A brilliant thinker, he is today considered to be one of the outstanding philosophers of the twentieth century.

Bibliography
By Whitehead
A Treatise on Universal Algebra, with Applications, 1898
The Axioms of Projective Geometry, 1906
The Axioms of Descriptive Geometry, 1907
Principia Mathematica, 1910-1913 (3 vols.; with Bertrand Russell)
An Introduction to Mathematics, 1911
An Enquiry Concerning the Principles of Natural Knowledge, 1919
The Concept of Nature, 1920
The Principle of Relativity, with Applications to Physical Science, 1922
Science and the Modern World, 1925
Religion in the Making, 1926
Symbolism, Its Meaning and Effect, 1927
The Aims of Education and Other Essays, 1929
The Function of Reason, 1929
Process and Reality: An Essay in Cosmology, 1929
Adventures of Ideas, 1933
Nature and Life, 1934
Modes of Thought, 1938
Essays in Science and Philosophy, 1947
Alfred North Whitehead: An Anthology, 1953

About Whitehead
Alfred North Whitehead: An Anthology. Alfred

North Whitehead. New York: Macmillan, 1953.

Alfred North Whitehead: The Man and His Work. Victor Lowe. 2 vols. Baltimore: The Johns Hopkins University Press, 1985-1990.

The Philosophy of Alfred North Whitehead. Paul Arthur Schilpp, ed. Evanston, Ill.: Northwestern University Press, 1941.

(Linda L. McDonald)

Samuel Stanley Wilks

Areas of Achievement: Probability and statistics

Contribution: Wilks developed improved statistical methods to understand relationships among several variables and how these variables influence one another.

June 17, 1906	Born in Little Elm, Texas
1926	Graduated from North Texas State Teachers College with an A.B. in architecture and begins teaching high school mathematics
1928	Receives an M.A. in mathematics from the University of Texas
1931	Receives a Ph.D. from the University of Iowa
1933	Accepts a position as a mathematics instructor at Princeton University
1936	Appointed to a permanent position at Princeton
1938-1949	Serves as editor of the *Annals of Mathematical Statistics*
1940	Elected president of the Institute of Mathematical Statistics
1941	Works for the National Defense Research Committee and forms the Princeton Statistical Research Group
1947	Awarded the Presidential Certificate of Merit
1950	Elected president of the American Statistical Association
1956	Travels around the world on a lecture tour on statistics
1961	Issues a report on College Board Examinations
Mar. 7, 1964	Dies in Princeton, New Jersey

Early Life

Samuel Stanley Wilks was the son of Chance C. and Bertha May Gammon Wilks. The family owned a farm near Little Elm, Texas. Wilks began his education in a one-room schoolhouse and later attended high school in Denton. During his final year of high school, he skipped study hall in order to attend a mathematics course at nearby North Texas State Teachers College. He continued studies at the college, earning an a degree in architecture in 1926. Wilks, however, believed that his eyesight was too poor for a career in architecture, so he began graduate study in mathematics at the University of Texas.

During his first year in Austin, Wilks taught high school mathematics. The following year, he was named a part-time instructor in mathematics at the University of Texas, and he received an M.A. in mathematics in 1928. He remained as a full-time instructor for another year, until he received a fellowship to attend the University of Iowa. His dissertation, "On the Distributions of Statistics in Samples from a Normal Population of Two Variables with Matched Sampling of One Variable," was completed in 1931 and published the following year. He received a Ph.D. in mathematical statistics from Iowa and married Gena Orr of Denton.

Wilks was unable to obtain permanent employment. He received fellowships from the National Research Council that allowed him to work at Columbia University, University College in London, and Cambridge University. Wilks met and worked with some of the most influential statisticians of the time, and he began to publish a number of important papers on multivariate analysis.

Statistical Work

Eventually, Wilks received an offer to teach mathematics, and later statistics, at Princeton University. He began teaching there in 1933 and remained at Princeton for the rest of his life. Wilks was a founding member of the Institute of Mathematical Statistics in 1933 and became editor of its journal, the *Annals of Mathematical Statistics*, in 1938. He served as editor until 1949 and transformed the journal into the leading publication in the field. When Wilks began teaching courses, few texts covered the field of statistics. He published his lecture notes, and the books soon became classic statistical references for undergraduates, graduate students, and research workers.

His original research transformed the field of multivariate statistical analysis. Statistics was still a young field when Wilks began his research. He developed distributions for a number of multivariate statistics, often using likelihood ratio tests. Wilks found solutions to problems of missing data for cases of several variables describing one observation—situations in which the value of one variable is unknown for certain elements in a sample. Wilks also investigated the notion of tolerance limits, finding that order statistics allowed a researcher to express a level of confidence about the distribution of sample data. His research in mathematical statistics was abstract but was typically based on an actual problem raised by someone needing help with statistical methods.

(Princeton University Libraries)

Wilks Λ Criterion

Wilks discovered new methods to generalize multivariate analysis of variance using likelihood ratio tests.

In the early twentieth century, statisticians developed many new procedures to understand questions involving large numbers of and more complex data. Wilks proposed many criteria for testing multivariate data—observations with several characteristics and measurements. The most recognized was presented in his paper "Certain Generalizations in the Analysis of Variance," published in *Biometrika* in 1932. Other statisticians extended Wilks's findings to further applications. Although Wilks used the simple notation of W, his statistical test became known as Wilks Λ criterion. The Wilks Λ criterion generalizes the analysis of variance F statistic.

Sometimes, researchers need to know how one variable or characteristic is influenced by others. The problem was first introduced for agricultural experiments in order to determine how several factors influence average crop yields, but analysis of variance can be used for a broad range of statistical problems. Researchers seek to find whether differences exist among these averages for the different factors (in the agricultural example, these factors might be soil type, rainfall, fertilizer, and so forth). Wilks attacked this question through the use of a likelihood ratio test, which compared the variance between certain groups (such as conditions of high and low rainfall) with the variance within those groups. The Wilks criteria for multivariate problems are typically powers of ratios of products of determinants of sample covariance matrices.

Wilks's derivations are particularly impressive considering that they were developed at a time before computing. Discovering these statistics and their underlying distributions, as Wilks did, allows researchers to determine whether certain factors or treatments produce an effect on the dependent variable or characteristic. His research also allowed the field of mathematical statistics to advance from simple statistical problems to a more advanced understanding of the relationships among several variables.

Bibliography

An Introduction to Multivariate Statistical Analysis. Theodore Wilbur Anderson. New York: John Wiley & Sons, 1958.

"Memorial to Samuel S. Wilks." Frederick F. Stephan et al. *Journal of the American Statistical Association* 60, no. 312 (December, 1965): 939-966.

"Samuel S. Wilks: Statesman of Statistics." Frederick Mosteller. *American Statistician* 18, no. 2 (April, 1964): 11-17.

"Samuel Stanley Wilks, 1906-1964." T. W. Anderson. *Annals of Mathematical Statistics* 36, no. 1 (February, 1965): 1-27.

Statistical Methods. George Waddel Snedecor and William G. Cochran. 8th ed. Ames: Iowa State University Press, 1989.

"Tests of Significance in Multivariate Statistical Analysis." C. Radhakrishna Rao. *Biometrika* 35 (1948): 58-79.

A Life Devoted to Service

Throughout his early life, Wilks concentrated on pure research in mathematical statistics. As the United States entered World War II, he turned to applied work in statistics and expressed the belief that mathematicians should take on broader responsibilities. In 1941, he started to work on problems of national defense and formed the Princeton Statistical Research Group. Wilks directed many leading statisticians on a number of defense-related problems, including long-range weather forecasting, antisubmarine warfare, explosives sensitivity, and convoy protection. After the war, Wilks was awarded the Presidential Certificate of Merit for his application of statistics to the war effort.

Wilks continued his consulting on defense-related activities and other forms of government service. He also encouraged the use of statistics in the social sciences. He devoted energy to mathematical education at all levels. His passion was to improve statistics training, particularly in Oklahoma and Texas. He also worked with the Educational Testing Service and the College Entrance Examination Board to improve standardized testing. S. S. Wilks was a prominent statistician who contributed in many ways, through research, teaching, and service. He died in his sleep at his home in Princeton in 1964.

Bibliography
By Wilks
Lectures by S. S. Wilks on the Theory of Statistical Inference, 1936-1937, 1937

Mathematical Statistics, 1943; rev. ed., 1962

Elementary Statistical Analysis, 1948

Introductory Engineering Statistics, 1965 (with Irwin Guttman)

S. S. Wilks: Collected Papers, Contributions to Mathematical Statistics, 1967 (T. W. Anderson, ed.)

About Wilks
"Samuel Stanley Wilks." John W. Tukey. *Yearbook 1964, American Philosophical Society* (1965).

"S. S. Wilks." W. G. Cochran. *Review of the International Statistical Institute* 32, nos. 1-2 (June, 1964): 189-191.

"Wilks, Samuel Stanley." Churchill Eisenhart. In *Dictionary of Scientific Biography*, edited by Charles Coulston Gillispie. New York: Charles Scribner's Sons, 1973.

"Wilks, S. S." Frederick Mosteller. In *International Encyclopedia of the Social Sciences*, edited by David L. Sills. Vol. 16. New York: Macmillan, 1968.

(James W. Endersby)

Grace Chisholm Young

Areas of Achievement: Calculus, geometry, and set theory

Contribution: Young worked both independently and collaboratively with her husband, William Henry Young. Her independent work was varied, but the most important achievements concerned derivates of real functions. Jointly with her husband, she contributed greatly to the field of set theory.

Mar. 15, 1868	Born in Haslemere, England
1885	Passes the Cambridge Senior Examination
1889	Enters Girton College
1893	Passes the final examinations (mathematics tripos), scoring the equivalent of a first-class degree
1895	Earns a Ph.D. magna cum laude from the University of Göttingen, the first woman to do so in Germany
1905	With her husband, publishes *The First Book of Geometry*
1906	With her husband, publishes *The Theory of Sets of Points*, the first book on set theory
1915	Receives the Gamble Prize from Girton College for her paper "On Infinite Derivatives"
1925	Publishes "On the Solution of a Pair of Diophantine Equations Connected with the Nuptial Number of Plato"
Mar. 29, 1944	Dies in Croydon, England

Early Life

Grace Chisholm, the youngest of four children, was the daughter of Henry William Chisholm and Anna Louisa Bell. As was the custom with young girls of the upper class, she was educated at home by her mother and a governess. Grace was a very curious and active child who was troubled by fits of screaming and walking in her sleep. Her doctor suggested that all lessons be discontinued, allowing only lessons requested by Grace—mental arithmetic and music.

As a young woman, she was encouraged by her family to work with the poor in London. Grace, however, was much more interested in pursuing her education. Her first desire was to study medicine, but her mother would not allow this. Therefore, she chose to pursue mathematics.

Mathematical Studies

In 1889, Chisholm began her studies at Girton College, part of Cambridge; Girton was the first university-level institution for women in England. It was there that she met a young tutor who would become her husband and collaborator, William Henry Young. She won the Sir Francis Goldschmid Scholarship to attend Girton and obtained the equivalent of a first-class degree after taking the mathematics tripos exams at Cambridge in 1893.

Graduate Education

Since no graduate schools in England admitted women, Chisholm continued her studies at the University of Göttingen, in Germany, where she worked with Felix Klein. Göttingen was one of the leading mathematical centers at the time, and Klein was its leading mathematician.

Chisholm earned a Ph.D. magna cum laude at age twenty-seven, after having secured approval from the Berlin Ministry of Culture to take the doctoral degree. Chisholm was the first woman to receive a doctorate in any field in Germany. Her thesis was entitled "Algebraisch-gruppentheoretische Untersuchungen zur sphärischen Trigonometrie" (the algebraic groups of spherical trigonometry).

Life as a Mathematician and Collaborator

Grace Chisholm and Will Young married in 1896 after she completed her Ph.D. They returned to Göttingen in 1899, staying until 1908. During this period, they were encouraged by Klein to begin the study of set theory and in

1901 began extensive study in this area. They were soon to be among the leaders in this developing field.

Grace Chisholm Young was initially the main researcher of the couple, but she soon recognized her husband's talent as a mathematician. The basic pattern of their collaboration was that Grace worked out much of the detailed arguments of the proofs and saw to the publication of their results. Together, they wrote more than two hundred articles and several books, publishing the first book on set theory, *The Theory of Sets of Points*, in 1906.

At the end of 1908, they moved to Switzer-land, and, in 1914, Grace began doing independent mathematics again. Her work now focused on the foundations of differential calculus. In 1915, she received the Gamble Prize from Girton College for her work, particularly for the results contained in the article "On Infinite Derivates," which appeared in 1916.

Other Interests

In addition to her work in differential calculus, Young also studied geometry, astronomy, philosophy, and medicine. She and her husband published a book on geometry, *The First Book of Geometry*, in 1905. She completed all require-

Differential Calculus

Young classified the behavior of derivates of a measurable function f(x).

Study of the calculus involves analyzing how a function behaves. Of particular interest is the rate of change of a function near a specific point. This is the notion of the derivative of a function f at a point x_0. To arrive at this rate of change, it is necessary to measure the change in the value of the function and divide that by the difference in the x-values over which this change occurs. This is represented by the difference quotient:

$$\frac{[f(x) - f(x_0)]}{[x - x_0]}$$

The derivative of f at x_0 is found by evaluating this difference quotient as x approaches x_0. Another way of saying this is that one finds the limit of the difference quotient as x approaches x_0.

This limiting value, however, may change depending on the direction from which x approaches x_0. It becomes necessary to investigate carefully the behavior of the function on each side of the point x_0. The derivates of a function f at the point x_0 provide for such a close examination. Four derivates are defined for each function: the upper right-hand, lower right-hand, upper left-hand, and lower left-hand derivates.

In 1915, Grace Chisholm Young proved a version of the Denjoy-Saks-Young Theorem for a particular type of function, called a measurable

function. She showed that for almost every real number x, there are only three possibilities for the derivates.

1. They are all equal, in which case the function f is said to have a differential coefficient at x (equal to this common value).

2. The upper derivates on each side are $+\infty$ and the lower derivates on each side are $-\infty$.

3. The upper derivate on one side is $+\infty$, the lower derivate on the other side is $-\infty$, and the two remaining derivates are finite and equal.

The strength of this result lies in the following reasoning: If the last two conditions can be ruled out, then one can conclude that the function f has a differential coefficient almost everywhere. It is often easier to rule out conditions than to prove them directly.

Bibliography

The Fundamental Theorems of the Differential Calculus. William Henry Young. Cambridge, England: Cambridge University Press, 1910. Reprint. New York: Hafner, 1960.

Lectures on the General Theory of Integral Functions. Georges Valiron. Toulouse, France: E. Privat, 1923.

Real Analysis. H. L. Royden. 3d ed. New York: Macmillan, 1988.

ments for a medical degree except the internship; she was unable to leave her home, taking care of their six children, to complete the required residency.

Young also wrote two books for children on the biology of plants and animals: *Bimbo* and *Bimbo and the Frogs*. (Bimbo was the nickname of their first child.)

The World War II Years
In the spring of 1940, Grace left Will in Switzerland while she accompanied their grandchildren to England, intending to return in a few days. The collapse of France came immediately, however, making her return prohibitively dangerous. After two years of separation, during which time Will suffered from depression and senility, he died in July, 1942.

Grace Chisholm Young suffered a heart attack and died on March 29, 1944, at the age of seventy-six, just months before she was to be awarded an honorary degree from Girton College.

Bibliography
By Young
"On the Curve $y = (x^2 + \sin^2\psi)^{-3/2}$, and Its Connection with an Astronomical Problem," *Monthly Notices of the Royal Astronomical Society* 57, 1897

The First Book of Geometry, 1905 (with William Henry Young)

The Theory of Sets of Points, 1906 (with William Henry Young)

"A Note on Derivates and Differential Coefficients," *Acta Mathematica* 37, 1914

"On Infinite Derivates," *Quarterly Journal of Pure and Applied Mathematics* 47, 1916

"On the Derivates of a Function," *Proceedings of the London Mathematical Society* 15, 1916

"A Note on a Theorem of Riemann's," *Messenger of Mathematics* 49, 1919-1920

"On the Partial Derivates of a Function of Many Variables," *Proceedings of the London Mathematical Society* 20, 1922

"On the Solution of a Pair of Simultaneous Diophantine Equations Connected with the Nuptial Number of Plato," *Proceedings of the London Mathematical Society* 23, 1924

"On Functions Possessing Differentials," *Fundamenta Mathematicae* 14, 1929

About Young
"Grace Chisholm Young." Mary Lucy Cartwright. *Journal of the London Mathematical Society* 19, no. 76 (July, 1944): 185-192.

"Grace Chisholm Young." Sylvia M. Wiegand. In *Women of Mathematics: A Biobibliographic Sourcebook*, edited by Louise S. Grinstein and Paul J. Campbell. New York: Greenwood Press, 1987.

"A Mathematical Bibliography for W. H. and G. C. Young." I. Grattan-Guinness. *Historia Mathematica* 2 (February, 1975): 43-58.

"A Mathematical Union: William Henry and Grace Chisholm Young." I. Grattan-Guinness. *Annals of Science* 29, no. 2, pt. 3 (August, 1972): 105-186.

(Deborah A. Lawrence)

Ernst Zermelo

Areas of Achievement: Applied math, calculus, mathematical logic, and set theory
Contribution: Zermelo introduced the first collection of axioms for set theory.

July 27, 1871	Born in Berlin, Germany
1889	Finishes his secondary education at the Luisenstädtisches Gymnasium in Berlin
1894	Receives a Ph.D. from the University of Berlin
1899	Appointed a lecturer at the University of Göttingen
1904	Proves the well-ordering theorem and publishes "Beweis, dass jede Menge wohlgeordnet werden kann" ("Proof That Every Set Can Be Well-Ordered," 1967)
1905	Named an honorary professor at Göttingen
1908	Publishes "Untersuchungen über die Grundlagen der Mengenlehre I" ("Investigations in the Foundations of Set Theory I," 1967)
1910	Accepts a professorship at the University of Zurich
1916	Resigns from his position at Zurich because of poor health
1926	Appointed an honorary professor at the University of Freiburg im Breisgau
1935	Renounces his position at Freiburg to protest the Nazi government
1946	Reinstated at Freiburg
May 21, 1953	Dies in Freiburg im Breisgau, Germany

Early Life

Ernst Friedrich Ferdinand Zermelo (pronounced "TSEHR-mehl-oh") was born in Berlin and spent his early years there. His parents were Ferdinand Rudolf Theodor Zermelo, a college professor, and Maria Augusta Elisabeth Zieger. Ernst was a bright child who succeeded in school, including the Gymnasium (a school designed for university preparation). He passed his final examination in 1889. He attended the University of Berlin, where he studied mathematics, physics, and philosophy. His professors included such great scientists as Ferdinand Frobenius, Lazarus Fuchs, Max Planck, Edmund Russerl, Erhard Schmidt, and H. A. Schwarz.

Zermelo finished his doctoral work in five years. He moved to Göttingen and earned the position of privatdozent (lecturer). There, he made his most significant mathematical contributions.

Applied Mathematics

Although Zermelo is famous for work in abstract mathematics, he was first interested in applied mathematics, particularly the calculus of variations. This continuation of the calculus focuses on finding the "best" curves and surfaces for certain circumstances. Zermelo's first published work in the field was his dissertation, which extended a result of Karl Weierstrass. By 1904, Zermelo was considered an expert on the calculus of variations and collaborated on an article summarizing the progress made in this subject.

Zermelo was also fascinated with physics. He translated into German J. Willard Gibbs's *Elementary Principles in Statistical Mechanics* (1902). Zermelo applied Henri Poincaré's kinetic theory of gases to show that an irreversible process does not exist.

Set Theory

In the nineteenth century, Georg Cantor introduced a new field of mathematics known as set theory. A set can be viewed as a collection of "objects," such as numbers or other sets. If one is not careful, however, contradictions can occur. A famous example is Russell's paradox, named after Bertrand Russell and independently discovered by Zermelo. Consider S to be the set of all sets that are not members of themselves. Such a set cannot exist because S can be neither inside nor outside itself.

Zermelo lectured on set theory at Göttingen and extensively studied the works of Cantor and others. Zermelo made two significant contributions to the field: He proved the well-ordering theorem and established a set of axioms.

The Well-Ordering Theorem

A set can be well-ordered if its elements can be lined up so that every nonempty subset has a "smallest" element with respect to this order. For example, the set of positive integers is well-ordered using the standard ordering of "less than or equal to." The well-ordering theorem states that any set can be well-ordered using some ordering, including the set of real numbers.

This result was proven by Zermelo in 1904 using the axiom of choice. It states that given any collection of sets where any two have nothing in common, one can arbitrarily choose one element from each set. It is accepted that this theorem applies to finite collections, but a

Axiomatization of Set Theory

Zermelo was the first to introduce axioms for set theory.

The term "axiomatization" refers to the establishment of a certain collection of statements that serve as axioms for a subject. From these statements one will then prove other statements about the subject. This is familiar to those who have studied geometry and Euclid's axioms (often called "postulates").

Zermelo's axiomatization began with a collection C of objects which contains all of the possible members of the sets. He then stated his axioms as follows.

1. *Extensionality:* Two sets are the same when they contain the same elements.

2. *Elementary sets:* The following sets exist—the empty set which contains no elements, sets that contain exactly one element from C, and sets that contain exactly two elements from C.

3. *Separation:* Given a set S and what Zermelo called a "definite" property, there is a set consisting of all the elements of S that satisfy the property.

4. *Power set:* Given a set S, there is a set consisting of all the subsets of S. This new set is called the "power set" of S.

5. *Union:* Given a collection of sets, there is a set consisting of all the elements of the sets in the collection. This new set is called the "union" of the collection.

6. *Choice:* Given a collection of sets where any two of them have nothing in common, one can arbitrarily choose one element from each of the sets.

7. *Infinity:* There is a set that consists of the empty set and has the property that if *a* is in the set, then the set containing only *a* is also in the set.

Although some of these statements may appear obviously true, it is still important to state them, for one should always be clear about what assumptions are being made. This helps prevent errors. In the past, some mathematicians have made mistakes, because they used unstated assumptions that were later found to be false.

With some modification this set of axioms has become known as ZFC. The "Z" represents Zermelo, while the "C" denotes the axiom of choice. A needed addition made by Abraham Fraenkel in 1922 accounts for the "F." This system of set theory has been the predominate one up through the end of the twentieth century.

Bibliography

Axiomatic Set Theory. Paul Bernays. 2d ed. Amsterdam: North Holland, 1968.

Elements of Set Theory. Herbert B. Enderton. San Diego: Academic Press, 1977.

Naive Set Theory. Paul R. Halmos. New York: Springer-Verlag, 1974.

"The Origins of Zermelo's Axiomatization of Set Theory." Gregory H. Moore. *Journal of Philosophical Logic* 7, no. 3 (1978).

question arises regarding infinite sets. Many branches of mathematics rely on this axiom.

Zermelo's acceptance of the axiom of choice and the well-ordering theorem began a controversy. Mathematicians known as intuitionists rejected them, believing that for a set to exist, the elements of that set must be described using a finite number of steps. Zermelo gave only an existence proof for the theorem. He did not include a "program" describing how the choices should be made. Also, the well-ordering theorem itself is startling: It seems obvious that the real numbers cannot be well-ordered.

Axioms of Set Theory

Because of the controversy, Zermelo published a second proof of the well-ordering theorem in 1908. He listed the assumptions, or axioms, that he used in the proof, believing that this strategy would clarify his ideas and persuade more mathematicians.

The axioms also eliminated the paradoxes. Zermelo was not concerned about the paradoxes; he considered them to be a limitation on what collections should be regarded as sets. His assumptions allow one to build sets methodically. None of these resulting sets lead to a contradiction.

Later Years

In 1910, Zermelo accepted a position at the university at Zurich. Only six years later, he would resign because of failing health. After years recuperating in the Black Forest, he accepted an honorary position at the University of Freiburg im Breisgau in 1926. In 1935, Zermelo would again resign from a position, this time in protest of the Nazi government, which he found unacceptable. Soon after World War II, Zermelo would be reinstated at Frei-

burg, where he would spend the rest of his life. He died in 1953.

Bibliography

By Zermelo

"Ueber einen Satz der Dynamik und die mechanische Wärmetheorie," *Annalen der Physik und Chemie* 57, 1896

"Beweis, dass jede Menge wohlgeordnet werden kann," *Mathematische Annalen* 59, 1904 ("Proof That Every Set Can Be Well-Ordered" in *From Frege to Gödel: A Source Book in Mathematical Logic, 1879-1931*, 1967, Jean van Heijenoort, ed.)

"Neuer Beweis für die M"glichkeit einer Wohlordnung," *Mathematische Annalen* 65, 1908 ("A New Proof of the Possibility of a Well-Ordering" in *From Frege to Gödel*, 1967)

"Untersuchungen über die Grundlagen der Mengenlehre I," *Mathematische Annalen* 65, 1908 ("Investigations in the Foundations of Set Theory I" in *From Frege to Gödel*, 1967)

About Zermelo

A History of Set Theory. Phillip E. Johnson. Boston: Prindle, Weber & Schmidt, 1972.

"The Mathematical Development of Set Theory from Cantor to Cohen." Akihiro Kanamori. *The Bulletin of Symbolic Logic* 2, no. 1 (March, 1996).

"Zermelo, Ernst Friedrich Ferdinand." B. van Rootselaar. In *Dictionary of Scientific Biography*, edited by Charles Coulston Gillispie. New York: Charles Scribner's Sons, 1976.

Zermelo's Axiom of Choice: Its Origins, Development, and Influence. Gregory H. Moore. New York: Springer-Verlag, 1982.

(*Michael L. O'Leary*)

Glossary

abacus: A device with beads strung along a series of parallel wires that is used to perform arithmetic operations quickly.

acute angle: An angle smaller than a right angle.

addition: The act of finding the sum of two numbers or other mathematical quantities; one of the basic operations of arithmetic.

algebra: The branch of mathematics dealing with equations containing unknown quantities, usually represented by letters.

algorithm: A set of instructions to be followed in order to obtain a desired mathematical result.

angle: The geometric quantity formed when two straight lines meet at a point.

applied mathematics: The application of mathematics to the solution of problems arising in the sciences, engineering, or business.

arc: A portion of a circle.

area: The amount of space bounded by a figure or curve drawn in a plane on a surface.

arithmetic: The branch of mathematics dealing with the elementary operations of addition, subtraction, multiplication, and division applied to numbers.

associative: Being independent of the order in which operations are grouped.

asymptotic: Approaching but never becoming equal to, except perhaps at infinity.

average: The sum of values of a variable divided by the number of instances considered.

axiom: A statement assumed to be true, independent of other statements, as part of the basis for a branch of mathematics.

axis: The horizontal or vertical line on which quantities are marked off on a graph.

bell curve: In statistics, the smooth curve indicating the likely distribution of observed values of a measurable quantity about the mean value.

Bessel function: One of the family of solutions to Bessel's differential equation, related to the sine and cosine function; named for Friedrich Wilhelm Bessel.

bi-: A prefix meaning "two."

binary: Relating to a system in which numbers are expressed by sequences of the digits 1 and 0.

binomial: An expression involving two variables.

Boolean algebra: A set of rules for combining the truth-values of statements in which 1 represents true and 0 represents false; named for George Boole.

calculus: The branch of mathematics dealing with continuous quantities and their rates of change. *See* **derivative**.

cardinal number: The number of members of a set, which can be one of the counting numbers or an infinite quantity. *Compare* **ordinal number**.

Cartesian: The system of coordinates that is set up by two or more perpendicular axes; named for René Descartes.

circle: A smooth curve containing all the points equidistant from a single point.

circumference: The distance around a circle or other smooth curve.

coefficient: The number or symbol that multiplies an unknown quantity in an equation.

combinatorics: The branch of mathematics dealing with alternative ways of arranging objects.

complex number: A number consisting of a real and an imaginary part. *See* **imaginary number**.

computer: A machine, electronic or otherwise, that can manipulate symbols according to programmed instructions.

cone: The figure traced by a line with one point held fixed passing through a closed curve, consisting of two nappes sharing one point in common. *See* **nappe**.

congruent: Of geometric figures, able to be superimposed on each other with all parts coinciding.

constant: A quantity assumed not to change in value.

continuous: Without breaks or sudden changes in value.

convergent: Approaching a constant value or mathematical function.

coordinate: One of several numbers used to identify a point in space.

correlation: A relation between pairs of measured values.

cosine: In a right triangle, the ratio of the side adjacent to an angle to the hypotenuse; abbreviated cos.

cube: Of a shape, a solid bounded by six identical squares; of a number, the result of multiplying a number by itself twice.

cube root: The number whose cube is the number under consideration.

cubic: Relating to a cube; also, relating to the third power.

cubic equation: An equation or expression containing a variable to the third but no higher power.

curve: A set of points connected to each other in space.

deca- or dec-: A prefix meaning "ten."

deci-: A prefix meaning "one-tenth."

decimal place: The position following the decimal point in common numerical notation; used to denote powers of one-tenth.

decimal system: A system of writing numerical values using the numerals $0, \ldots, 9$.

degree: $\frac{1}{360}$th of a circle; also, the highest exponent appearing in an equation.

denominator: The number or algebraic expression written below the dividing line in a fraction.

derivative: The function equal to the rate of change of another function.

di-: A prefix meaning "two."

diagonal: A line that divides a geometric figure into two equal areas.

diameter: A line that divides a circle into two equal areas.

differential: A small change in a variable.

digit: A single symbol used in the representation of a number in decimal, binary, or related systems.

discontinuous: Exhibiting an abrupt change in value.

distribution: A function describing the probability that a measurement will yield a given value.

divergent: Referring to a series that does not approach a finite value as more terms are added together.

dividend: A number that is to be divided by another number.

division: The act of determining the number by which a given number, the divisor, must be multiplied to yield another number, the dividend; one of the basic operations of arithmetic and the inverse of multiplication.

divisor: The number by which a number is to be divided.

domain: The set of values for which a function is defined.

e: The limiting value of $(1 + \frac{1}{n})^n$ as n becomes infinitely large, approximately given as 2.718; also called the Euler number, after Leonhard Euler.

ellipse: The closed curve containing all the points for which the sum of distances from two fixed points, or foci, is a constant.

empty set: The set with no member elements; also called a null set.

equation: A mathematical expression of equality between two quantities.

equi-: A prefix meaning "equal."

equidistant: Being equal distances from a given point.

equilateral: Referring to a geometric figure having sides of equal length.

even: Of a number, being divisible exactly by 2.

exponent: The power to which another number is raised.

exponential: Growing as some power of another quantity.

factor: Any of a group of quantities to be multiplied; also, to express a quantity as the product of factors.

Fibonacci series: A series in which each term is the sum of the two preceding terms; named for Leonardo of Pisa (Leonardo Fibonacci).

field: In algebra, a set with elements that can be combined by addition or multiplication; in applied mathematics, a function of the points in space.

figure: Any geometrical object.

finite: Being smaller than some definite quantity. *Compare* **infinite.**

first principles: An explanation or derivation of a statement from fundamental axioms and postulates.

formula: An equation used to compute a certain quantity.

fractal: A geometric object characterized by a fractional dimension.

fraction: A number expressed as a ratio of two numbers or algebraic quantities.

function: A rule that assigns the values of one variable to another.

functional analysis: The study of the properties of functions in the abstract.

game theory: The mathematical theory of competitions between players, which includes the study of games of chance.

geodesic: A curve that indicates the shortest distance between its member points on a defined surface.

geometry: The study of objects defined in a space.

graph: A diagram used to summarize numerical data or a quantitative relationship.

group: A set, the elements of which can be combined by an operation with some of the properties of multiplication.

height: The vertical dimension of an object.

hexa- or hex-: A prefix meaning "six."

hyperbola: A curve formed by the intersection of a plane with both nappes of a cone. *See* **cone, nappe.**

hypotenuse: The longest side of a right triangle.

identity element: In a group, the element that leaves other elements unchanged when combined with them.

imaginary number: A number that when squared yields a negative number.

indeterminate: Not having a fixed value.

infinite: Larger than any definite quantity.

infinitesimal: Smaller than any definite quantity, but not zero.

infinity: The symbol ∞ used to indicate an infinite quantity.

integer: A whole number.

integral: The solution of a differential equation, or the quantity for which the derivative equals a fixed quantity.

intersection: In geometry, a point at which two lines or curves meet; in set theory, the set of elements belonging to each of two or more sets.

invariant: A quantity that remains unchanged as other quantities change.

inverse: The element that when combined with a given element, yields the identity element; also, an operation that undoes the effect of another operation (for example, multiplication is the inverse of division).

irrational number: A number that cannot be expressed as the ratio of two integers.

isosceles: Having two sides of equal length.

iteration: Each application of an operation that can be repeated.

limit: The value that one variable approaches as another approaches a set value.

line: The set of points that are the minimum distance from two given points.

linear: Depending only on the first power of variable quantities.

logarithm: The power to which a base number (usually 10 or e) must be raised in order to yield a certain number.

logic: The branch of mathematics dealing with the provability of statements.

mathematics: The study of quantity, shape, and dependence using deductive reasoning.

matrix (*pl.* matrices): A rectangular array of numbers or other quantities.

mean: The average of a set of quantities or observations.

measure: A generalized notion of size applicable to sets of infinitely many elements.

Mersenne prime: A prime number that can be expressed in the form $2^n - 1$; named for Marin Mersenne.

Möbius strip: A one-sided surface that can be constructed from a rectangular strip by adding a half twist and pasting the ends together; named for August Ferdinand Möbius.

multiplication: An operation in which two numbers produce the same result as adding one of them to itself the number of times equal to the other; one of the basic operations of arithmetic.

*n***:** A symbol usually used to represent a variable that can take on only integer values.

nappe: One of the two parts of a cone.

natural number: A nonnegative integer (such as 1, 2, 3, . . .).

negative: Less than zero; also, the sign (−) used to indicate subtraction.

notation: A system of symbols used to express mathematical relationships.

null set: The set with no member elements; also called an empty set.

number: A mathematical quantity that can be specified by a single fixed value.

number theory: The study of the property of integers.

numerator: In a fraction, the number or quantity written above the dividing line.

obtuse angle: An angle larger than a right angle.

octa- or oct-: A prefix meaning "eight."

odd: Of a number, not being divisible exactly by 2.

operator: A process, represented by a symbol, that converts one function into another.

ordinal number: The integers used to indicate order (for example, first, second, third, . . .).

parabola: The curve formed by the intersection of a plane with a cone when the plane is parallel to the side of the cone.

paradox: A statement that can be neither true or untrue (for example, the sentence "This sentence is false.")

parallel: Having no points in common even if extended indefinitely.

parameter: A quantity that takes on different values in different situations but does not otherwise vary.

partition: A division of a set into subsets with no members in common.

perfect number: A number equal to the sum of its factors (for example, $6 = 1 + 2 + 3$).

periodic function: A function that takes on the same value whenever its independent variable is increased by a fixed amount called the period of the function.

perpendicular: Forming right angles with.

pi (π): The ratio of the circumference of a circle to its diameter, an irrational number given approximately by 3.14159.

planar: Relating to or lying in a plane.

plane: A surface that contains a straight line through any two of its points.

point: A location in space with no length, width, or breadth; the elementary notion of geometry.

Poisson distribution: The probability of observing n events within a given time period if there is no correlation between the events; named for Siméon-Denis Poisson.

poly-: A prefix meaning "many."

polygon: A figure with three or more sides drawn in a plane.

polynomial: An algebraic expression containing terms with two or more different powers of the same variable.

positive: Greater than zero.

postulate: A statement assumed to be true about a class of mathematical objects.

power: The number of times a number is to be multiplied by itself, indicated by a superscript.

projective geometry: The study of the intersection of higher-dimensional objects with lower-dimensional spaces.

proof: The demonstration that a mathematical statement is true by deducing it from axioms, postulates, and other proven statements.

pure mathematics: The study of mathematical objects without thought of practical application, especially in areas of mathematics for which practical applications have not been discovered.

quadra- or quadr-: A prefix meaning "four."

quadratic: An equation or expression containing a variable to the second but no higher power.

quartic: An equation or expression containing a variable to the fourth but no higher power.

quintic: An equation or expression containing a variable to the fifth but no higher power.

quotient: The result of the division process.

radical: The root sign, used to indicate a square root (or cube root or fourth root, and so on).

radius: The distance from the center of a circle to the circumference.

random: Taking values from set of possible values in a manner not completely predictable. *See* **distribution.**

range: The set of values taken by a function.

ratio: A fraction considered not as a single quantity but as describing the relative size of two quantities.

rational number: A number that can be expressed as the ratio of two integers.

ray: A portion of a straight line beginning or ending at a single point.

real number: A number that has no imaginary part.

reciprocal: The inverse of an element under multiplication.

rectangle: A plane geometric figure having two pairs of parallel sides and four right angles.

rhombus: A plane geometric figure having parallel sides.

right angle: The angle formed by perpendicular lines.

root: A quantity that when multiplied by itself a fixed number of times, yields a certain number; also, the value of a variable in a polynomial for which the polynomial equals zero.

scalar: A quantity that can be specified by a single number (for example, temperature).

secant: The reciprocal of the cosine function; abbreviated sec.

septi- or sept-: A prefix meaning "seven."

sequence: An ordered list of mathematical quantities.

series: An ordered list of quantities being added together.

set: A collection of objects.

set theory: The branch of mathematics dealing with sets and the notion of membership in a set.

sign: The plus (+) or minus (–) sign used to denote a positive or negative quantity.

sine: In a right triangle, the ratio of the side opposite an angle to the hypotenuse; abbreviated sin.

singularity: A point at which the value of a mathematical function is infinite or undefined.

slope: For a line in the x-y plane, the ratio of the change in y to the change in x.

solution: A set of values of a variable or variables that satisfies a mathematical relationship.

sphere: An object bounded by a surface in which all points are at a fixed distance from a center.

square: Of a shape, a plane geometric figure having four equal sides and four right angles; of a number, the result of multiplying a number by itself.

square root: The number whose square is the number under consideration.

standard deviation: The square root of the sum of squares of deviations from the mean divided by 1 less than the total number of observations.

statistics: The branch of mathematics that studies the behavior of distributed quantities. *Compare* **distribution.**

subscript: A number or letter written at the lower-right-hand corner of a symbol to indicate one of its possible values. *Compare* **superscript.**

subtraction: The act of reducing a quantity by another quantity; one of the basic operations of arithmetic.

sum: The result of adding two or more quantities together.

superscript: A number or letter written at the upper-right-hand corner of a symbol to indicate one of its possible values. *Compare* **subscript.**

surface: The boundary of an object.

tangent: In a right triangle, the ratio of the side opposite an angle to that adjacent; also, a straight line that touches but does not intersect a smooth curve; abbreviated tan.

tetra- or tetr-: A prefix meaning "four."

tetrahedron: An object bounded by four planar sides.

theorem: A mathematical statement that can be proved.

topology: The study of the properties of objects that are invariant under stretching.

transcendental number: A number that cannot appear as the root of a polynomial with rational number coefficients.

tri-: A prefix meaning "three."

triangle: The plane geometric figure formed by the intersection of three lines.

trigonometry: The branch of mathematics dealing with the properties of angles.

union: In set theory, the result of forming a set that includes the members of two or more other sets.

value: The number assigned to a variable.

variable: A quantity that may take on a range of values.

variance: The square of the standard deviation.

vector: A mathematical quantity described by an ordered list of numbers, usually associated with a direction in space.

volume: The quantity of space occupied by a solid object.

width: The horizontal dimension of a plane figure.

x-axis: The horizontal axis in a two-dimensional graph or coordinate system.

y-axis: The vertical axis in a two-dimensional graph or coordinate system; also, the axis pointing from back to front in a three-dimensional graph.

***z*-axis:** The vertical axis in a three-dimensional graph or coordinate system.

zero: The symbol 0 representing the result of subtracting any number from itself; used as a placeholder in the decimal and binary systems of notation.

Country List

Each featured mathematician is listed by the primary country or countries where he/she lived and conducted mathematical work, which may not be his/her country of birth or death. In addition, mathematicians who are members of minority groups can be found under **United States** both within the complete listing and grouped by separate headings. The female mathematicians profiled in the encyclopedia are listed both with their respective countries and under the category **Women**.

African Americans. *See under* **United States**

American Indians. *See under* **United States**

Asia Minor. *See* **Greece**

Asian Americans. *See under* **United States**

Australia
Neumann, Hanna

Austria
Bolzano, Bernhard
Gödel, Kurt
Mises, Richard von
Taussky-Todd, Olga

Austro-Hungarian Empire. *See* **Austria; Hungary**

Basra. *See* **Iraq**

Bavaria. *See* **Germany**

Blacks. *See* **African Americans** *under* **United States**

Bohemia. *See* **Austria**

Brandenburg. *See* **Germany**

Brunswick. *See* **Germany**

Canada
Morawetz, Cathleen Synge

China
Chern, Shiing-Shen

Cyrene. *See* **Greece**

Egypt
Hero of Alexandria
Hypatia
Ptolemy

England
Adelard of Bath
Babbage, Charles
Boole, George
Burnside, William
Cartwright, Mary Lucy
Cayley, Arthur
Conway, John Horton
De Morgan, Augustus
Dodgson, Charles Lutwidge
Fisher, Ronald Aylmer
Galton, Sir Francis
Gosset, William Sealy
Green, George
Hardy, G. H.
Harriot, Thomas
Heaviside, Oliver
Lovelace, Augusta Ada
Moivre, Abraham de
Napier, John
Neumann, Hanna
Newton, Sir Isaac
Penrose, Roger
Russell, Bertrand
Scott, Charlotte Angas
Stott, Alicia Boole
Sylvester, James Joseph
Taylor, Brook
Turing, Alan Mathison
Venn, John
Wallis, John
Whitehead, Alfred North
Young, Grace Chisholm

Florence. *See* **Italy**

France
Alembert, Jean Le Rond d'
Borel, Émile
Bourbaki, Nicolas
Carnot, Lazare

Ireland
Boole, George
Gosset, William Sealy
Hamilton, Sir William Rowan
Stott, Alicia Boole

Italy
Agnesi, Maria Gaetana
Bombelli, Rafael
Cardano, Gerolamo
Cavalieri, Bonaventura
Ferrari, Lodovico
Galileo
Lagrange, Joseph-Louis
Leonardo of Pisa (Leonardo Fibonacci)
Peano, Giuseppe
Tartaglia, Niccolò Fontana
Torricelli, Evangelista
Volterra, Vito

Latinos. *See under* **United States**

Mainz. *See* **Germany**

Mecklenburg. *See* **Germany**

Mexican Americans. *See* **Latinos** *under* **United States**

Milan. *See* **Italy**

Native Americans. *See* **American Indians** *under* **United States**

The Netherlands
Brouwer, L. E. J.
Huygens, Christiaan
Stieltjes, Thomas Jan

New Zealand
Sommerville, Duncan MacLaren Young

Norway
Abel, Niels Henrik
Skolem, Thoralf Albert

Papal States. *See* **Italy**

Persia. *See* **Iran**

Poland
Mandelbrot, Benoit B.
Tarski, Alfred
Ulam, Stanislaw

Prussia. *See* **Germany**

Romania. *See* **Hungary**

Russia
Aleksandrov, Pavel Sergeevich
Bari, Nina Karlovna
Chebyshev, Pafnuty Lvovich
Euler, Leonhard
Janovskaja, Sof'ja Aleksandrovna
Kolmogorov, Andrey Nikolayevich
Kovalevskaya, Sofya
Lobachevsky, Nikolay Ivanovich
Oleinik, Olga

Sardinia. *See* **Italy**

Saxony. *See* **Germany**

Scotland
Maclaurin, Colin
Sommerville, Duncan MacLaren Young
Stirling, James

Sicily. *See* **Greece**

South Africa
Cormack, Allan M.

Soviet Union. *See* **Russia; Ukraine; Uzbekistan**

Swabia. *See* **Germany**

Sweden
Fredholm, Erik Ivar

Switzerland
Bernoulli, Daniel
Bernoulli, Jakob I
Bernoulli, Johann I
Cramer, Gabriel
Euler, Leonhard

Syracuse. *See* **Greece**

Syria
Battani, al-

Turkey. *See* **Greece; Syria**

Tuscany. *See* **Italy**

Ukraine
Janovskaja, Sof'ja Aleksandrovna

United States
Backus, John
Birkhoff, George David
Blackwell, David Harold
Chern, Shiing-Shen
Cohen, Paul J.

Cormack, Allan M.
Cox, Gertrude Mary
Erdös, Paul
Feigenbaum, Mitchell Jay
Flügge-Lotz, Irmgard
Gardner, Martin
Gibbs, J. Willard
Gödel, Kurt
Granville, Evelyn Boyd
Hopper, Grace Murray
Lefschetz, Solomon
Mandelbrot, Benoit B.
Mises, Richard von
Morawetz, Cathleen Synge
Noether, Emmy
Pólya, George
Porter-Locklear, Freda
Robinson, Julia Bowman
Scott, Charlotte Angas
Shannon, Claude Elwood
Tapia, Richard A.
Tarski, Alfred
Taussky-Todd, Olga
Taylor, Valerie E.
Ulam, Stanislaw
Von Neumann, John
Weyl, Hermann
Wheeler, Anna Johnson Pell
Whitehead, Alfred North
Wilks, Samuel Stanley

African Americans
Blackwell, David Harold
Granville, Evelyn Boyd
Taylor, Valerie E.

American Indians
Porter-Locklear, Freda

Asian Americans
Chern, Shiing-Shen

Latinos
Tapia, Richard A.

Uzbekistan
Khwarizmi, al-

Venice. *See* **Italy**

Wales
Russell, Bertrand

Women
Agnesi, Maria Gaetana
Bari, Nina Karlovna
Cartwright, Mary Lucy
Châtelet, Marquise du
Cox, Gertrude Mary
Flügge-Lotz, Irmgard
Germain, Sophie
Granville, Evelyn Boyd
Hopper, Grace Murray
Hypatia
Janovskaja, Sof'ja Aleksandrovna
Kovalevskaya, Sofya
Lovelace, Augusta Ada
Morawetz, Cathleen Synge
Neumann, Hanna
Noether, Emmy
Oleinik, Olga
Porter-Locklear, Freda
Robinson, Julia Bowman
Scott, Charlotte Angas
Stott, Alicia Boole
Taussky-Todd, Olga
Taylor, Valerie E.
Wheeler, Anna Johnson Pell
Young, Grace Chisholm

Areas of Achievement

Algebra
Abel, Niels Henrik
Agnesi, Maria Gaetana
Alhazen
Aryabhata the Elder
Bernoulli, Daniel
Bombelli, Rafael
Bourbaki, Nicolas
Brahmagupta
Cardano, Gerolamo (Jerome Cardan)
Cauchy, Augustin-Louis
Cayley, Arthur
Chebyshev, Pafnuty Lvovich
Clairaut, Alexis-Claude
Cramer, Gabriel
Dedekind, Richard
De Morgan, Augustus
Diophantus
Ferrari, Lodovico
Fourier, Joseph
Galois, Évariste
Gauss, Carl Friedrich
Girard, Albert
Hadamard, Jacques-Salomon
Hamilton, Sir William Rowan
Harriot, Thomas
Hermite, Charles
Hilbert, David
Jacobi, Karl Gustav Jacob
Khwarizmi, al-
Klein, Felix
Kolmogorov, Andrey Nikolayevich
Kronecker, Leopold
Lagrange, Joseph-Louis
Laplace, Pierre-Simon
Leonardo of Pisa (Leonardo Fibonacci)
Liouville, Joseph
Maclaurin, Colin
Napier, John
Neumann, Hanna
Noether, Emmy
Oleinik, Olga
Omar Khayyám
Poincaré, Henri
Pythagoras
Ramanujan, Srinivasa Aiyangar
Scott, Charlotte Angas
Shannon, Claude Elwood

Sylvester, James Joseph
Tarski, Alfred
Tartaglia, Niccolò Fontana
Taussky-Todd, Olga
Viète, François
Wallis, John
Weyl, Hermann
Wheeler, Anna Johnson Pell
Whitehead, Alfred North

Applied math
Adelard of Bath
Agnesi, Maria Gaetana
Alembert, Jean Le Rond d'
Alhazen
Archimedes
Babbage, Charles
Backus, John
Bernoulli, Daniel
Bernoulli, Johann I
Bessel, Friedrich Wilhelm
Birkhoff, George David
Burnside, William
Cauchy, Augustin-Louis
Châtelet, Marquise du
Chern, Shiing-Shen
Clairaut, Alexis-Claude
Cohen, Paul J.
Cormack, Allan M.
Dirichlet, Peter Gustav Lejeune
Eratosthenes of Cyrene
Fatou, Pierre
Feigenbaum, Mitchell Jay
Flügge-Lotz, Irmgard
Fourier, Joseph
Fredholm, Erik Ivar
Galileo
Gardner, Martin
Gauss, Carl Friedrich
Germain, Sophie
Gibbs, J. Willard
Girard, Albert
Granville, Evelyn Boyd
Green, George
Hamilton, Sir William Rowan
Harriot, Thomas
Heaviside, Oliver
Hermite, Charles

Hilbert, David
Hopper, Grace Murray
Huygens, Christiaan
Jacobi, Karl Gustav Jacob
Kepler, Johannes
Khwarizmi, al-
Kolmogorov, Andrey Nikolayevich
Kovalevskaya, Sofya
Lagrange, Joseph-Louis
Laplace, Pierre-Simon
Legendre, Adrien-Marie
Leonardo of Pisa (Leonardo Fibonacci)
Mandelbrot, Benoit B.
Maupertuis, Pierre-Louis Moreau de
Minkowski, Hermann
Mises, Richard von
Morawetz, Cathleen Synge
Oleinik, Olga
Penrose, Roger
Poincaré, Henri
Poisson, Siméon-Denis
Pólya, George
Porter-Locklear, Freda
Riesz, Frigyes
Shannon, Claude Elwood
Stirling, James
Tapia, Richard A.
Taylor, Valerie E.
Thales of Miletus
Ulam, Stanislaw
Volterra, Vito
Von Neumann, John
Weyl, Hermann
Whitehead, Alfred North
Zermelo, Ernst

Arithmetic
Alhazen
Aryabhata the Elder
Brahmagupta
Conway, John Horton
Gauss, Carl Friedrich
Khwarizmi, al-
Leonardo of Pisa (Leonardo Fibonacci)
Napier, John
Pythagoras
Thales of Miletus

Calculus
Abel, Niels Henrik
Agnesi, Maria Gaetana
Alembert, Jean Le Rond d'

Archimedes
Babbage, Charles
Bernoulli, Daniel
Bernoulli, Johann I
Bolzano, Bernhard
Borel, Émile
Cartwright, Mary Lucy
Cauchy, Augustin-Louis
Cavalieri, Bonaventura
Châtelet, Marquise du
Clairaut, Alexis-Claude
Cohen, Paul J.
Condorcet, Marquis de
Cormack, Allan M.
Euler, Leonhard
Fatou, Pierre
Fourier, Joseph
Fredholm, Erik Ivar
Gauss, Carl Friedrich
Hadamard, Jacques-Salomon
Heaviside, Oliver
Hermite, Charles
Hilbert, David
Jacobi, Karl Gustav Jacob
Klein, Felix
Kolmogorov, Andrey Nikolayevich
Lagrange, Joseph-Louis
Laplace, Pierre-Simon
Lebesgue, Henri-Léon
Legendre, Adrien-Marie
Leibniz, Gottfried Wilhelm
Liouville, Joseph
Maclaurin, Colin
Newton, Sir Isaac
Peano, Giuseppe
Poincaré, Henri
Poisson, Siméon-Denis
Pólya, George
Riemann, Bernhard
Riesz, Frigyes
Stieltjes, Thomas Jan
Stirling, James
Taylor, Brook
Volterra, Vito
Wallis, John
Weierstrass, Karl
Weyl, Hermann
Wheeler, Anna Johnson Pell
Young, Grace Chisholm
Zermelo, Ernst

Geometry
Adelard of Bath
Agnesi, Maria Gaetana
Alhazen
Apollonius of Perga
Archimedes
Bolyai, János
Brahmagupta
Carnot, Lazare
Cauchy, Augustin-Louis
Cavalieri, Bonaventura
Cayley, Arthur
Chern, Shiing-Shen
Clairaut, Alexis-Claude
Conway, John Horton
Desargues, Girard
Descartes, René
Eratosthenes of Cyrene
Euclid
Eudoxus of Cnidus
Euler, Leonhard
Fatou, Pierre
Fermat, Pierre de
Gauss, Carl Friedrich
Hamilton, Sir William Rowan
Heine, Heinrich Eduard
Hero of Alexandria
Hilbert, David
Huygens, Christiaan
Kepler, Johannes
Klein, Felix
Kolmogorov, Andrey Nikolayevich
Lefschetz, Solomon
Legendre, Adrien-Marie
Lobachevsky, Nikolay Ivanovich
Maclaurin, Colin
Menaechmus
Minkowski, Hermann
Möbius, August Ferdinand
Monge, Gaspard
Oleinik, Olga
Omar Khayyám
Oresme, Nicole
Pascal, Blaise
Plato
Pólya, George
Poncelet, Jean-Victor
Ptolemy
Pythagoras
Riemann, Bernhard
Scott, Charlotte Angas

Sommerville, Duncan McLaren Young
Stirling, James
Stott, Alicia Boole
Taylor, Brook
Thales of Miletus
Torricelli, Evangelista
Wallis, John
Weyl, Hermann
Young, Grace Chisholm

Mathematical logic
Aristotle
Babbage, Charles
Backus, John
Boole, George
Bourbaki, Nicolas
Brouwer, L. E. J.
Cohen, Paul J.
Condorcet, Marquis de
Conway, John Horton
De Morgan, Augustus
Dodgson, Charles Lutwidge
Erdös, Paul
Frege, Gottlob
Gödel, Kurt
Hadamard, Jacques-Salomon
Hilbert, David
Hipparchus
Hopper, Grace Murray
Hypatia
Janovskaja, Sof'ja Aleksandrovna
Kolmogorov, Andrey Nikolayevich
Leibniz, Gottfried Wilhelm
Lovelace, Augusta Ada
Neumann, Hanna
Peano, Giuseppe
Poincaré, Henri
Robinson, Julia Bowman
Russell, Bertrand
Skolem, Thoralf Albert
Tarski, Alfred
Turing, Alan Mathison
Venn, John
Von Neumann, John
Weyl, Hermann
Whitehead, Alfred North
Zermelo, Ernst

Number theory
Archimedes
Cantor, Georg
Cauchy, Augustin-Louis

Chebyshev, Pafnuty Lvovich
Conway, John Horton
Diophantus
Dirichlet, Peter Gustav Lejeune
Erdös, Paul
Euclid
Euler, Leonhard
Fermat, Pierre de
Gauss, Carl Friedrich
Germain, Sophie
Girard, Albert
Gödel, Kurt
Hankel, Hermann
Hardy, G. H.
Hermite, Charles
Hilbert, David
Jacobi, Karl Gustav Jacob
Kronecker, Leopold
Lagrange, Joseph-Louis
Lambert, Johann Heinrich
Legendre, Adrien-Marie
Leonardo of Pisa (Leonardo Fibonacci)
Liouville, Joseph
Mersenne, Marin
Minkowski, Hermann
Pascal, Blaise
Poincaré, Henri
Pólya, George
Pythagoras
Ramanujan, Srinivasa Aiyangar
Riemann, Bernhard
Robinson, Julia Bowman
Skolem, Thoralf Albert
Stieltjes, Thomas Jan
Sylvester, James Joseph
Taussky-Todd, Olga
Weyl, Hermann

Probability

Bernoulli, Daniel
Bernoulli, Jakob I
Bessel, Friedrich Wilhelm
Blackwell, David Harold
Borel, Émile
Burnside, William
Cardano, Gerolamo (Jerome Cardan)
Cauchy, Augustin-Louis
Chebyshev, Pafnuty Lvovich
Condorcet, Marquis de
Fermat, Pierre de
Gauss, Carl Friedrich

Kolmogorov, Andrey Nikolayevich
Laplace, Pierre-Simon
Mises, Richard von
Moivre, Abraham de
Pascal, Blaise
Poisson, Siméon-Denis
Pólya, George
Shannon, Claude Elwood
Ulam, Stanislaw
Venn, John
Wilks, Samuel Stanley

Set theory

Bari, Nina Karlovna
Blackwell, David Harold
Borel, Émile
Bourbaki, Nicolas
Cantor, Georg
Cohen, Paul J.
Dedekind, Richard
Gödel, Kurt
Hankel, Hermann
Kolmogorov, Andrey Nikolayevich
Ulam, Stanislaw
Von Neumann, John
Weyl, Hermann
Wheeler, Anna Johnson Pell
Young, Grace Chisholm
Zermelo, Ernst

Statistics

Babbage, Charles
Bessel, Friedrich Wilhelm
Blackwell, David Harold
Borel, Émile
Chebyshev, Pafnuty Lvovich
Cox, Gertrude Mary
Fisher, Ronald Aylmer
Galton, Sir Francis
Gauss, Carl Friedrich
Gosset, William Sealy
Kolmogorov, Andrey Nikolayevich
Mises, Richard von
Wilks, Samuel Stanley

Topology

Aleksandrov, Pavel Sergeevich
Bourbaki, Nicolas
Brouwer, L. E. J.
Cantor, Georg
Euler, Leonhard
Jordan, Camille

Time Line

Born	Name	Country	Area
c. 624 B.C.E.	Thales of Miletus	Greece	Applied math, arithmetic, geometry
c. 580 B.C.E.	Pythagoras	Greece	Algebra, arithmetic, geometry, number theory
c. 427 B.C.E.	Plato	Greece	Geometry
c. 390 B.C.E.	Eudoxus of Cnidus	Greece	Geometry
384 B.C.E.	Aristotle	Greece	Mathematical logic
c. 375 B.C.E.	Menaechmus	Greece	Geometry
335 B.C.E.	Euclid	Greece	Geometry, number theory
287 B.C.E.	Archimedes	Greece	Applied math, calculus, geometry, number theory
c. 285 B.C.E.	Eratosthenes of Cyrene	Greece	Applied math, geometry
c. 262 B.C.E.	Apollonius of Perga	Greece	Geometry
190 B.C.E.	Hipparchus	Greece	Mathematical logic, trigonometry
fl. 62 C.E. to the late first century	Hero of Alexandria	Egypt/Greece	Geometry
c. 100	Ptolemy	Egypt or Greece	Geometry, topology
fl. 250	Diophantus	Greece	Algebra, number theory
c. 370	Hypatia	Egypt/Greece	Mathematical logic
476	Aryabhata the Elder	India	Algebra, arithmetic, trigonometry
c. 598	Brahmagupta	India	Algebra, arithmetic, geometry
c. 780	al-Khwarizmi	Iraq or Uzbekistan	Algebra, applied math, arithmetic
858	al-Battani	Syria	Trigonometry
965	Alhazen	Iraq	Algebra, applied math, arithmetic, geometry, trigonometry
May, 1044	Omar Khayyám	Iran	Algebra, geometry
c. 1075	Adelard of Bath	England	Applied math, geometry

Born	Name	Country	Area
c. 1170	Leonardo of Pisa (Leonardo Fibonacci)	Italy	Algebra, applied math, arithmetic, number theory
c. 1325	Nicole Oresme	France	Geometry
June 6, 1436	Regiomontanus (Johann Müller)	Germany	Trigonometry
1500	Niccolò Fontana Tartaglia	Italy	Algebra
Sept. 24, 1501	Gerolamo Cardano (Jerome Cardan)	Italy	Algebra, probability
Feb. 2, 1522	Lodovico Ferrari	Italy	Algebra
Jan., 1526	Rafael Bombelli	Italy	Algebra
1540	François Viète	France	Algebra, trigonometry
1550	John Napier	England	Algebra, arithmetic, trigonometry
1560	Thomas Harriot	England	Algebra, applied math, trigonometry
Feb. 15, 1564	Galileo	Italy	Applied math
Dec. 27, 1571	Johannes Kepler	Germany	Applied math, geometry
Sept. 8, 1588	Marin Mersenne	France	Number theory
Mar. 2, 1591	Girard Desargues	France	Geometry
1595	Albert Girard	France	Algebra, applied math, number theory, trigonometry
Mar. 31, 1596	René Descartes	France	Geometry
1598	Bonaventura Cavalieri	Italy	Calculus, geometry
Aug. 17, 1601	Pierre de Fermat	France	Geometry, number theory, probability
Oct. 15, 1608	Evangelista Torricelli	Italy	Geometry
Nov. 23, 1616	John Wallis	England	Algebra, calculus, geometry
June 19, 1623	Blaise Pascal	France	Geometry, number theory, probability
Apr. 14, 1629	Christiaan Huygens	the Netherlands	Applied math, geometry
Dec. 25, 1642	Sir Isaac Newton	England	Calculus
July 1, 1646	Gottfried Wilhelm Leibniz	Germany	Calculus, mathematical logic

Born	Name	Country	Area
Dec. 27, 1654	Jakob I Bernoulli	Switzerland	Probability
May 26, 1667	Abraham de Moivre	France/England	Probability
Aug. 6, 1667	Johann I Bernoulli	Switzerland	Applied math and calculus
Aug. 18, 1685	Brook Taylor	England	Calculus, geometry
1692	James Stirling	Scotland	Applied math, calculus, geometry
Feb., 1698	Colin Maclaurin	Scotland	Algebra, calculus, geometry
Sept. 28, 1698	Pierre-Louis Moreau de Maupertuis	France	Applied math
Feb. 8, 1700	Daniel Bernoulli	Switzerland	Algebra, applied math, calculus, probability
July 31, 1704	Gabriel Cramer	Switzerland	Algebra
Dec. 17, 1706	Marquise du Châtelet	France	Applied math, calculus
Apr. 15, 1707	Leonhard Euler	Switzerland/Russia	Calculus, geometry, number theory, topology
May 7, 1713	Alexis-Claude Clairaut	France	Algebra, applied math, calculus, geometry
Nov. 17, 1717	Jean Le Rond d'Alembert	France	Applied math, calculus
May 16, 1718	Maria Gaetana Agnesi	Italy	Algebra, applied math, calculus, geometry
Aug. 26, 1728	Johann Heinrich Lambert	Germany	Number theory
Jan. 25, 1736	Joseph-Louis Lagrange	France/Italy	Algebra, applied math, calculus, number theory
Sept. 17, 1743	Marquis de Condorcet	France	Calculus, mathematical logic, probability
May 10, 1746	Gaspard Monge	France	Geometry
Mar. 23, 1749	Pierre-Simon Laplace	France	Algebra, applied math, calculus, probability
Sept. 18, 1752	Adrien-Marie Legendre	France	Applied math, calculus, geometry, number theory
May 13, 1753	Lazare Carnot	France	Geometry
Mar. 21, 1768	Joseph Fourier	France	Algebra, applied math, calculus

Born	Name	Country	Area
Apr. 1, 1776	Sophie Germain	France	Applied math, number theory
Apr. 30, 1777	Carl Friedrich Gauss	Germany	Algebra, applied math, arithmetic, calculus, geometry, number theory, probability, statistics
June 21, 1781	Siméon-Denis Poisson	France	Applied math, calculus, probability
Oct. 5, 1781	Bernhard Bolzano	Austria	Calculus
July 22, 1784	Friedrich Wilhelm Bessel	Germany	Applied math, probability, statistics
July 1, 1788	Jean-Victor Poncelet	France	Geometry
Aug. 21, 1789	Augustin-Louis Cauchy	France	Algebra, applied math, calculus, geometry, number theory, probability
Nov. 17, 1790	August Ferdinand Möbius	Germany	Geometry, topology
Dec. 26, 1791	Charles Babbage	England	Applied math, calculus, mathematical logic, statistics
Dec. 1, 1792	Nikolay Ivanovich Lobachevsky	Russia	Geometry
July 14, 1793	George Green	England	Applied math
Aug. 5, 1802	Niels Henrik Abel	Norway	Algebra, calculus
Dec. 15, 1802	János Bolyai	Hungary	Geometry
Dec. 10, 1804	Karl Gustav Jacob Jacobi	Germany	Algebra, applied math, calculus, number theory
Feb. 13, 1805	Peter Gustav Lejeune Dirichlet	Germany	Applied math, number theory
Aug. 3/4, 1805	Sir William Rowan Hamilton	Ireland	Algebra, applied math, geometry
June 27, 1806	Augustus De Morgan	England	Algebra, mathematical logic
Mar. 24, 1809	Joseph Liouville	France	Algebra, calculus, number theory
Oct. 25, 1811	Évariste Galois	France	Algebra
Sept. 3, 1814	James Joseph Sylvester	England	Algebra, number theory

Born	Name	Country	Area
Oct. 31, 1815	Karl Weierstrass	Germany	Calculus
Nov. 2, 1815	George Boole	England/Ireland	Mathematical logic
Dec. 10, 1815	Augusta Ada Lovelace	England	Mathematical logic
Mar. 16, 1821	Heinrich Eduard Heine	Germany	Geometry
May 16, 1821	Pafnuty Lvovich Chebyshev	Russia	Algebra, number theory, probability, statistics
Aug. 16, 1821	Arthur Cayley	England	Algebra, geometry
Feb. 16, 1822	Sir Francis Galton	England	Statistics
Dec. 24, 1822	Charles Hermite	France	Algebra, applied math, calculus, number theory
Dec. 7, 1823	Leopold Kronecker	Germany	Algebra, number theory
Sept. 17, 1826	Bernhard Riemann	Germany	Calculus, geometry, number theory
Oct. 6, 1831	Richard Dedekind	Germany	Algebra, set theory
Jan. 27, 1832	Charles Lutwidge Dodgson	England	Mathematical logic
Aug. 4, 1834	John Venn	England	Mathematical logic, probability
Jan. 5, 1838	Camille Jordan	France	Topology
Feb. 11, 1839	J. Willard Gibbs	United States	Applied math
Feb. 14, 1839	Hermann Hankel	Germany	Number theory, set theory
Mar. 3, 1845	Georg Cantor	Germany	Number theory, set theory, topology
Nov. 8, 1848	Gottlob Frege	Germany	Mathematical logic
Apr. 25, 1849	Felix Klein	Germany	Algebra, calculus, geometry
Jan. 15, 1850	Sofya Kovalevskaya	Russia	Applied math
May 18, 1850	Oliver Heaviside	England	Applied math, calculus
July 2, 1852	William Burnside	England	Applied math, probability
Apr. 29, 1854	Henri Poincaré	France	Algebra, applied math, calculus, mathematical logic, number theory, topology

Born	Name	Country	Area
Dec. 29, 1856	Thomas Jan Stieltjes	the Netherlands/ France	Calculus, number theory
June 8, 1858	Charlotte Angas Scott	England/ United States	Algebra, geometry
Aug. 27, 1858	Giuseppe Peano	Italy	Calculus, mathematical logic
May 3, 1860	Vito Volterra	Italy	Applied math, calculus
June 8, 1860	Alicia Boole Stott	Ireland/ England	Geometry
Feb. 15, 1861	Alfred North Whitehead	England/ United States	Algebra, applied math, mathematical logic
Jan. 23, 1862	David Hilbert	Germany	Algebra, applied math, calculus, geometry, mathematical logic, number theory
June 22, 1864	Hermann Minkowski	Germany	Applied math, geometry, number theory
Dec. 8, 1865	Jacques-Salomon Hadamard	France	Algebra, calculus, mathematical logic
Apr. 7, 1866	Erik Ivar Fredholm	Sweden	Applied math, calculus
Mar. 15, 1868	Grace Chisholm Young	England	Calculus, geometry, set theory
Jan. 7, 1871	Émile Borel	France	Calculus, probability, set theory, statistics
July 27, 1871	Ernst Zermelo	Germany	Applied math, calculus, mathematical logic, set theory
May 18, 1872	Bertrand Russell	England/Wales	Mathematical logic
June 28, 1875	Henri-Léon Lebesgue	France	Calculus
June 13, 1876	William Sealy Gosset	England/Ireland	Statistics
Feb. 7, 1877	G. H. Hardy	England	Number theory
Feb. 28, 1878	Pierre Fatou	France	Applied math, calculus, geometry
Nov. 24, 1879	Duncan McLaren Young Sommerville	Scotland/ New Zealand	Geometry
Jan. 22, 1880	Frigyes Riesz	Hungary	Applied math, calculus, topology

Born	Name	Country	Area
Feb. 27, 1881	L. E. J. Brouwer	the Netherlands	Mathematical logic, topology
Mar. 23, 1882	Emmy Noether	Germany/ United States	Algebra
Apr. 19, 1883	Richard von Mises	Austria/ United States	Applied math, probability, statistics
May 5, 1883	Anna Johnson Pell Wheeler	United States	Algebra, calculus, set theory
Mar. 21, 1884	George David Birkhoff	United States	Applied math
Sept. 3, 1884	Solomon Lefschetz	France/ United States	Geometry, topology
Nov. 9, 1885	Hermann Weyl	Germany/ United States	Algebra, applied math, calculus, geometry, mathematical logic, number theory, set theory, topology
May 23, 1887	Thoralf Albert Skolem	Norway	Mathematical logic, number theory
Dec. 13, 1887	George Pólya	United States	Applied math, calculus, geometry, number theory, probability
Dec. 22, 1887	Srinivasa Aiyangar Ramanujan	India	Algebra, number theory
Feb. 17, 1890	Ronald Aylmer Fisher	England	Statistics
Jan. 31, 1896	Sof'ja Aleksandrovna Janovskaja	Russia/Ukraine	Mathematical logic
May 7, 1896	Pavel Sergeevich Aleksandrov	Russia	Topology
Jan. 13, 1900	Gertrude Mary Cox	United States	Statistics
Dec. 17, 1900	Mary Lucy Cartwright	England	Calculus
Nov. 19, 1901	Nina Karlovna Bari	Russia	Set theory, trigonometry
Jan. 14, 1902	Alfred Tarski	Poland/ United States	Algebra, mathematical logic
Apr. 25, 1903	Andrey Nikolayevich Kolmogorov	Russia	Algebra, applied math, calculus, geometry, mathematical logic, probability, set theory, statistics, topology, trigonometry

Born	Name	Country	Area
July 16, 1903	Irmgard Flügge-Lotz	Germany/ United States	Applied math
Dec. 28, 1903	John von Neumann	Hungary/ United States	Applied math, mathematical logic, set theory
Apr. 28, 1906	Kurt Gödel	Austria/ United States	Mathematical logic, number theory, set theory
June 17, 1906	Samuel Stanley Wilks	United States	Probability, statistics
Aug. 30, 1906	Olga Taussky-Todd	Austria/ United States	Algebra, number theory
Dec. 9, 1906	Grace Murray Hopper	United States	Applied math, mathematical logic
Apr. 13, 1909	Stanislaw Ulam	Poland/ United States	Applied math, probability, set theory, topology
Oct. 26, 1911	Shiing-Shen Chern	China/ United States	Applied math, geometry
June 23, 1912	Alan Mathison Turing	England	Mathematical logic
Mar. 26, 1913	Paul Erdös	Hungary/ United States	Mathematical logic, number theory
Feb. 12, 1914	Hanna Neumann	Germany/ England/ Australia	Algebra, mathematical logic
Oct. 21, 1914	Martin Gardner	United States	Applied math
Apr. 30, 1916	Claude Elwood Shannon	United States	Algebra, applied math, probability
Apr. 24, 1919	David Harold Blackwell	United States	Probability, set theory, statistics
Dec. 8, 1919	Julia Bowman Robinson	United States	Mathematical logic, number theory
May 5, 1923	Cathleen Synge Morawetz	Canada/ United States	Applied math
Feb. 23, 1924	Allan M. Cormack	South Africa/ United States	Applied math, calculus
May 1, 1924	Evelyn Boyd Granville	United States	Applied math
Nov. 20, 1924	Benoit B. Mandelbrot	Poland/ United States	Applied math

Born	Name	Country	Area
Dec. 3, 1924	John Backus	United States	Applied math, mathematical logic
July 2, 1925	Olga Oleinik	Russia	Algebra, applied math, geometry
Aug. 8, 1931	Roger Penrose	England	Applied math
Apr. 2, 1934	Paul J. Cohen	United States	Applied math, calculus, mathematical logic, set theory
1934-1935	Nicolas Bourbaki	France	Algebra, mathematical logic, set theory, topology
Dec. 26, 1937	John Horton Conway	England	Arithmetic, geometry, mathematical logic, number theory
Mar. 25, 1939	Richard A. Tapia	United States	Applied math
Dec. 19, 1944	Mitchell Jay Feigenbaum	United States	Applied math
Oct. 14, 1957	Freda Porter-Locklear	United States	Applied math
May 24, 1963	Valerie E. Taylor	United States	Applied math

BIOGRAPHICAL
ENCYCLOPEDIA
of
MATHEMATICIANS

Index

In the following index, volume numbers appear in **bold face** type and page numbers appear in normal type. The names of mathematicians who are profiled in the encyclopedia are shown in **bold face**.